VIOLENT AMERICA

VIOLENT AMERICA

The Dynamics of Identity Politics
in a Multiracial Society

Ariane Chebel d'Appollonia

CORNELL UNIVERSITY PRESS   ITHACA AND LONDON

Copyright © 2023 by Cornell University

All rights reserved. Except for brief quotations in a review, this book, or parts thereof, must not be reproduced in any form without permission in writing from the publisher. For information, address Cornell University Press, Sage House, 512 East State Street, Ithaca, New York 14850. Visit our website at cornellpress.cornell.edu.

First published 2023 by Cornell University Press

Library of Congress Cataloging-in-Publication Data

Names: Chebel d'Appollonia, Ariane, author.
Title: Violent America : the dynamics of identity politics in a multiracial society / Ariane Chebel d'Appollonia.
Description: Ithaca : Cornell University Press, 2023. | Includes bibliographical references and index.
Identifiers: LCCN 2022017861 (print) | LCCN 2022017862 (ebook) | ISBN 9781501767555 (hardcover) | ISBN 9781501767562 (paperback) | ISBN 9781501767586 (pdf) | ISBN 9781501767579 (epub)
Subjects: LCSH: Violence—United States. | Identity politics—United States. | Ethnic conflict. | United States—Race relations.
Classification: LCC HN90.V5 C483 2023 (print) | LCC HN90.V5 (ebook) | DDC 303.60973—dc23/eng/20220524
LC record available at https://lccn.loc.gov/2022017861
LC ebook record available at https://lccn.loc.gov/2022017862

Contents

Acknowledgments   vii
A Note about Quotations   ix

Introduction   1

Part 1   LESSONS FROM THE PAST   17

  1. Violence as a Proactive Response to Adversity   31
  2. Violence as the Cause of Ethnoracial Identities   44
  3. From Past to Present Ethnoracial Identification Strategy   59
  4. The Dynamics of Contention   72

Part 2   CURRENT TRAJECTORIES OF VIOLENCE IN POST-RACIAL AMERICA   91

  5. Two Tales of One Nation   101
  6. From Identity Politics to Ethnoracial Identity Crisis   120
  7. Centrifugal Dynamics of Ethnoracial Fragmentation   136

Part 3   CURRENT LESSONS FROM AMERICA   155

  8. Is a Violent Society America's Only Possible Future?   157
  9. Is Violent America Europe's Future?   173

Conclusion: Lessons for the Future   194

Notes   205
Index   257

Acknowledgments

This project originated in 2014—when protests and riots were taking place in Ferguson, Missouri, in the aftermath of the fatal shooting of Michael Brown. I completed the manuscript shortly after the January 6, 2021, attacks on the Capitol. These two events, as well as so many other traumatic episodes that took place in the interlude, illustrate the resilience of ethnic and racial violence in America that I attempt to comprehend and explain in this book. In doing so, I had to grapple with the complexity of intergroup relations in America. They have been, and remain, characterized by a peculiar logic of inclusion and exclusion, and by the emergence and consolidation of ethnoracial identities that both employ and respond to violence.

My hope is that this book contributes to a fruitful, forthright, and honest conversation about the virtues of tolerance and the need to promote social solidarity, racial justice, and civic freedom in America—and possibly Europe. It is time to extend the politics of reconciliation to every group and move beyond the polarized racialization and fragmentation that is an increasing hallmark of Western societies.

Over my long journey that culminated in *Violent America*, I have received support from friends and colleagues. I am indebted to the support and assistance of Isabelle Crouzet, Anne and Nicolas Catzaras, Sophie Mahieux, Shawn Kerby, and Cricket Purdy. I am especially grateful to Deborah Morrison-Santana and Miguel Santana for their invaluable support at many crucial moments in the course of this project—bringing me joy, as well as groceries in times of COVID confinement. I owe a great personal debt to Dr. Delia Radovich and the nurses at Saint Barnabas Cancer Center without whom this book would not have been completed.

Comments and criticisms from three anonymous reviewers helped me to improve a prior version of the manuscript, for which I am grateful. I also thank Roger Haydon (for his initial impulse), Mahinder S. Kingra (for his final push), and Bethany Wasik (for her constant assistance throughout the process) at Cornell University Press.

I would like to dedicate this book to my husband, Simon, with love and gratitude for his companionship, friendship, intellectual and moral standards, and merciless criticism.

A Note about Quotations

In this book, the author includes quotations that contain racial slurs to adhere to the historical record; to fully communicate the sentiment conveyed by different historical actors (such as W. E. B. Du Bois); and, most important, to contrast these slurs to different terms employed by the same actors or by other contemporaneous figures.

VIOLENT AMERICA

INTRODUCTION

For many observers, America epitomizes a violent country plagued by racism. That view is substantiated by the historical continuity of both racism and violence since the birth of the republic. "The term *race relations* sounds modern and is in fact of twentieth-century coinage," Roger Daniels argues, "but the fact of race relations, between English and Indians, between English and blacks and, eventually, between all whites and Indians and blacks was a fundamental if largely ignored aspect of colonial life."[1] Commenting on the urban riots of the 1960s, activist Rap Brown succinctly claims that violence was "as American as cherry pie."[2] Historical forms of violence continue to influence patterns of race relations today. In her analysis of the protests in Ferguson and Baltimore, Jennifer Cobbina argues that the killings of Michael Brown in 2014 and Freddie Gray in 2015 were "examples of racial hostility, racial bias, and legalized racial subordination" inherited from the past. She adds that "the issue of racially motivated police killings is not simply a product of individual discriminatory police officers. It is the result of deep historical forces that follow a pattern of social control that is entwined in the very fabric of the United States."[3]

The enduring significance of ethnoracial violence in America raises a fundamental question: How can we explain its resilience over time despite significant institutional and societal changes and America's increasing ethnoracial diversity? In answering this question, I argue that the historic and current use of violence by various ethnoracial groups is not simply a result of socioeconomic competition nor a cognitive statement about ethnoracial difference, but is part of an instrumental "identity strategy," one purposively designed to secure symbolic and material resources. This approach offers a more nuanced appreciation of intergroup relations than the common assumptions included in studies that causally link ethnicity and a disposition for violence. Horowitz, for example, argues that conflicts along ethnic lines are more likely to turn violent than those built on other cleavages.[4] For primordialists like him, antagonism between ethnic groups therefore risks being inevitable because of the inalterable "natural category" character of group members.[5] This kind of essentialist explanation, however, tends to be tautological: racism explains racial prejudice, which, in turn, fuels racial conflicts— motivated by racism. It also obscures other motives that may spur inter- and intragroup violence, which I contend play a key role. These motives can include access to individual material resources (such as work, money, and benefits), nonmaterial resources (authority, recognition, and a sense of empowerment and respect), as well as perceived threats to or opportunities for group interests.

In a multiracial society we need to question our conventional understanding of the dynamics of intergroup relations by analyzing how each group engages in a cycle of reactive identification. Both dominant and minority groups are currently, dynamically, being redefined. So are the relationships among individuals' conceptions of their entitlements, their perception of discrimination, and their own views of their group's status. I therefore eschew a white/black binary approach in favor of a more heterogeneous analysis. Examining the beliefs and attitudes of both white people and various nonwhite people offers a more compelling depiction of the motives and goals of all groups engaged in contentious identity politics in American society.[6]

In doing so, I define and categorize various forms of violence according to two dimensions: the means groups employ and their purposes in using violence. The first dimension can be divided between physical and discursive violence. Physical violence includes mob lynchings and other mass violence that characterized race relations from the colonial period to the second half of the twentieth century, as well as contemporary hate crimes, police brutality, and many aspects of civil unrest. Discursive violence, in contrast, relates to hate speech, antimigrant propaganda, nativist agenda, and other racial discriminatory narratives, religious negative stereotypes, as well as other offensive "speech acts" today labeled as "micro-aggressions." The use of both physical and discursive violence often characterizes relations between ethnoracial groups, as well as relations among ethnoracial subgroups. When it comes to purpose, there are three alternatives. First, violence can be part of a deliberate policy of domination in a zero-sum strategy designed to secure material and symbolic resources to the detriment of other groups. Second, it can be motivated by a reactive defense against predation or prejudice, prompted more by necessity than choice.

Finally, as I argue, the use of both discursive and physical violence can be part of an identity strategy employed by any ethnoracial group in America.

In this book, providing historical and contemporary evidence, I focus on the purposive use of the third option. I do so because it moves beyond the conventional generalities of the first two, about which much has been written. Focusing on how and why violence is used this way is valuable because it addresses the dynamics between actual and perceived adversity in an increasingly diverse American society. My three goals are to provide an alternative way of understanding the complex relationship between racial violence, migrant phobia, white backlash, multiethnic grievances and inter- and intragroup conflicts in contemporary multiracial America; to provide a better understanding of how and why American society has become so violently polarized and fragmented; and ultimately to evaluate the prospects for more harmonious relations in the years ahead and diagnose how that may be achieved.

Core Arguments

When it comes to explaining the causes of violence, many studies emphasize contextual factors as a source of violence or assume that ethnoracial prejudice lies at its source. These studies provide useful insights, but, as I demonstrate, they only partially explain the resilience of ethnoracial violence over time. I, in contrast, reverse the logic of those claims and explore the effects of violence on ethnoracial identification. I contend that violence is a response to adversity, and, as a result, violence and adversity work in tandem. Ethnoracial groups are targeted by violence because of their identity, and their counter-reaction to violence—which sometimes involves its use—provides them with a heightened sense of collective identity. As the result of this dual process, inter- and intragroup relations constantly evolve, as do mutual and self-perceptions, claims, and grievances defined as feelings of dissatisfaction with important aspects of life (such as housing, income, employment, education, health care, safety, and civil rights).

I therefore analyze how and why various ethnoracial groups, white and nonwhite alike, use different forms of violence—rationally if not dispassionately—to achieve goals that relate to their ethnoracial identification. A closer examination of historic violent episodes suggests that the use of violence—either in propagating adversity or as a response to adversity—has been strategically foundational to the emergence of ethnoracial identities in America. American history is replete with examples. Some ethnic groups, for example Irish and Italian migrants, used violence against Blacks as a way of distancing themselves from Blacks to assimilate into mainstream America as "Caucasians."[7] For the Irish, Noel Ignatiev argues, "to enter the white race was a strategy to secure an advantage in a competitive society."[8] Likewise, in California, the "Celts" were "whitened" through the anti-Chinese campaign of the 1870s. Conversely, one way to consolidate a group identity among disparate minorities was to oppose other groups—whites as well as other nonwhite minorities.[9] Opposition engendered a process of a homogenized identity where it was hitherto nonexistent or weak.

My goal is neither to evaluate the degree of legitimacy of various forms of violence nor to reduce victims and transgressors to an equivalent because of their use of violence. It is rather obvious that minorities resort to the use of violence more by necessity than by choice. What was true in the past, as the urban riots of the 1960s illustrated, remains tragically relevant in the 2020s. Eras differ, but issues of poverty, violent crime, police brutality, and racial prejudice persist. Yet we cannot dismiss the fact that American history has proved that "racial groups could be, in varying ways, simultaneously privileged and oppressed, empowered and disempowered, uplifting and subordinating."[10] Nor can we ignore the existence of racial prejudice among minorities. Elements of both the Asian and Hispanic communities express anti-Black prejudice, as Yamamoto notes, based "on vaguely articulated perceptions of African Americans squandering moral capital (accrued as a result of slavery), relying on special privileges detrimental to other racial minorities."[11] Some African Americans react by expressing anti-Asian and anti-Hispanic sentiments, while simultaneously asserting that the increasing number of African and Caribbean immigrants are a source of competition for their distinct mantle. Furthermore, ethnoracial groups can simultaneously engage in intergroup conflicts (as illustrated by the 1992 riot in Los Angeles, the nation's first multiracial riot) while building alliances (as illustrated by the broad multiracial coalition opposing California's anti–affirmative action Proposition 209 in 1996). Interracial communication can reduce competition and animosity by revealing common ground, or it can generate friction by revealing areas of enmity.

Most studies of ethnoracial violence in America have focused on the white/black divide rather than distinct relations between ethnoracial groups for at least two pertinent reasons. The first and most obvious one relates to the uniqueness of the Black experience and its contemporary legacies. As James Jones notes in his comprehensive study of prejudice and racism, "beating slaves, lynching black people, and bombing churches, homes and cars constitute part of the legacy of violence directed against African Americans."[12] The republic was a genuinely racist society from its formation, with a rigid racial stratification buttressed and strengthened by a racist ideology that was used to justify slavery. Racism became the foundation of the American polity as early as 1790 when the Nationality Act limited eligibility for citizenship by naturalization to "free white persons." This act provided the legal basis for white, gendered male identity as a fundamental criterion for membership in the US polity. Racial exclusion was reinforced by the Dred Scott decision of 1857 in which the Supreme Court ruled that freed Blacks could not be citizens of the United States. Anti-Black racism persisted despite, notably, the Fourteenth Amendment of 1868, one of several federal efforts to enforce civic and political equality. The Jim Crow segregation platform illustrated American racism in its starkest form. Racial conflicts have mostly involved white and Black groups, and African Americans were—and are still—more likely to be targeted by racial violence than any other group. There are indeed striking and troubling continuities between past and current patterns of racial oppression, as well as patterns of racial conflict.[13] African Americans comprised around 90 percent of the nearly 5,000 documented lynching victims between 1882 and 1952.[14] Today, the rate of fatal police shootings among African Americans is far higher than for any other ethnoracial group, with a fatality rate 2.8 times greater among Blacks than whites.

The second pertinent factor is that race relations between whites and Blacks have served to frame ethnoracial relations among other groups. Non-Black minorities have historically been defined along a color spectrum, and their level of assimilation has been evaluated in terms of their capacity to cross this biracial boundary. Furthermore, the same institutional and cognitive processes foundational to the discrimination against African Americans have been used to justify discrimination against non-Black minorities. Conversely, non-Black minorities continue to define their respective identities by explicitly distancing themselves from Blackness. They also evaluate their level of assimilation by comparing their socioeconomic achievements to the situation of African Americans.

Consequently, intergroup relations in America are analyzed through the lens of race relations, whether to demonstrate the persistence of the traditional white/black dichotomy or to argue in favor of its declining relevance.[15] Studies of migrant integration are often framed by a similar binary categorization, whether in terms of dominant/minority group interactions or of whites/all nonwhites group relations. As a result, the dominant aspects of migrant phobia and its translation into politics are mostly analyzed from a non-Hispanic, white standpoint. Nonetheless, the Black experience—and current situation—is the benchmark that defines comparability in America.

I acknowledge the centrality of that white/black dichotomy. Yet, given the complexity of intergroup relations in an increasingly multiracial America, I go beyond that persistent template by including a more diverse racial and ethnic palette. Further racial categorizations emerged historically through violence and were in turn invoked to justify violence against immigrant groups. Pointedly, an historical overview of race relations demonstrates that anti-Black prejudice has understandably constituted the major narrative because of the structural and institutional abhorrence of slavery and its aftermath. But it is only one—if a singular and exceptional—form of racial prejudice in America. Other minorities were discriminated against and targeted for violence. These minorities included Asian and Mexican immigrants in the late nineteenth century as well as immigrants from Europe who were not perceived as "white" and therefore suffered from discrimination. This today includes, for example, groups like Muslims who face racial prejudice on the basis of their race, ethnicity, national origin, and religion.

Furthermore, the study of historical and contemporary ethnoracial violence cannot be restricted to only examples of white violence against minorities for two compelling reasons. First, historically, most white immigrants became white by using violence not only against nonwhite groups but also against other whites. Antisemitism, for example, was a major component of the whitening process among Italian Americans. The legacy of the KKK remains vivid today with white supremacists verbally and physically attacking people of color as well as their "white enemies" (primarily Jews, as the 2017 Charlottesville marches demonstrated, as well as white liberals and white anti-fascist activists). Second, what has remained largely ignored, and thus undertheorized, is the contemporary persistence of tensions (often violent) between minority groups. As a result, Michael Omi and Howard Winant note, "policies and politics which are framed in black-white terms miss the ways in which specific initiatives structure the possibilities of conflict or accommodation among different racial minority groups."[16]

My approach clearly runs against the normative assumption that minorities should be regarded as passive objects of politics when it comes to the use of violence. Those few studies that acknowledge its use by minorities often ascribe it to only a primal reactive response to adversity—as angry, unplanned behavior motivated by a frustration fueled by the resilience of racial prejudice and institutional discrimination and violence. Viewed from this perspective, forms of reactive violence are purposeless (as suggested by many criminal stereotypes of African Americans and other minorities). But to tell the story of the historical and contemporary relationship between violence and ethnoracism requires us to take into account the key ingredients of contentious politics by which they all politically participate in the arena of representation and entitlement. More to the point, the assumption that violence initiated by minorities is only an emotional response to the violence they face is misleading. Worse perhaps, such an assumption undermines the legitimacy and value of minority activism. Minority groups are neither passive nor emotionally immature actors who flail out irrationally. Historical and contemporary evidence shows that the distinction between emotional and strategic behavior is irrelevant. Strong emotions fuel protest, but such emotions do not render protestors irrational. They accompany all social action—generating motivations, goals, and strategy.[17]

I therefore argue that all minorities have agency, defined as "the freedom of the acting subject."[18] "Analyzing resistance and agency," Karim Murji and John Solomos argue, "draws attention to the central constituting factor of power in social relations."[19] Victimized minorities can have power, and their behavioral patterns (whether violent or not) are part of a group's conscious, proactive empowerment strategy.[20] From the perspective of the "voluntaristic theory of action," minorities have the cognitive capital and capacity to strategize and act independently of, and in opposition to, structural constraints with the purpose of changing adversarial social structures through their chosen actions. Their freedom may be contingent, their strategies contextual, and their tactics circumstantial. But they nonetheless have the capacity to work within, and indeed to malleably change, those systemic parameters. That is clearly the purpose of, for example, the organizers of the Black Lives Matter (BLM) movement. Their intent is not simply recognition of Black suffering. It is to address systemic racism through purposive action. More broadly, what needs to be addressed are the significant variations in the way ethnoracial groups react to adversity and if, when, and how they are able to redefine those parameters.

Two of these significant variations deserve special attention. First, similar adversarial contexts do not generate similar outcomes. The list of root causes explaining why riots took place in Ferguson after the killing of Michael Brown is easy to document. Yet, many other young African Americans are victims of racial profiling and police brutality in localities where the same conditions exist. These, however, do not lead to peaceful or violent protest. General underlying factors do not explain the variation in community responses across a huge number of cases. Understanding why is imperative for both theoretical and policy reasons.

Second, different minorities facing similar forms of adversity do not react in analogous ways. A broad view of ethnoracial interactions reveals that certain groups (such as Japanese and Chinese Americans) have not had a history of perpetrating violence despite suffering for two centuries as its victims. Furthermore, understandably, media attention has focused on police brutality against African Americans in the last few years. Yet, the Center on Juvenile and Criminal Justice noted that the number of Hispanic victims of police killings is 30 percent above average and at 1.9 times the rate of whites. *The Guardian*'s police killings database documented that 25 percent of the Hispanics killed by police in 2015 were unarmed. The police killing of Antonio Zambrano-Montes in Pasco, Washington in February 2016, for example, drew national attention as a "Latino Ferguson." Yet there was no major local protest, and there still is no comparable

Latino Lives Matter movement across the country despite the increase in casualties. There is no Muslim Lives Matter either despite the precipitous rise in anti-Muslim attacks since 9/11.

Mobilization, as Michael Omi and Howard Winant suggested, may take various forms including "antagonisms and alliance *among* racially defined minority groups, differentiation *within* these groups, and the changing dynamics of white racial identity."[21] Acknowledging those studies framed only in white/black divide terms "miss[es] the ways in which specific initiatives structure the possibilities of conflict or accommodation among different racial minority groups." They analyze this empowerment strategy as a "war of maneuver" . . . "a situation in which subordinate groups seek to preserve and extend a definite territory, to ward off violent assault, and to develop an internal society as an alternative to the repressive social system they confront."[22] Furthermore, as the result of antiracist legislation and multiracial policies, wars of maneuver are complemented by wars of position "as racially defined minorities achieve political gains . . . and are able to make sustained strategic incursions into the mainstream political process."[23]

I believe it is important to evaluate the potential for wars of maneuver and wars of position in America's current "transition to diversity." It is a process that is deeply confrontational to, and rapidly transformative of, America's social fabric. In doing so, I analyze how ethnoracial prejudice remains a source of violence. I also explore the countervailing effects of violence on ethnoracial identification. The predominant forms may have evolved over time, from physical to more discursive violence, but their pattern of usage remains intact.

A Framework for Explaining Three Puzzles

I provide an alternative way of identifying and comparing past and current patterns of ethnoracial violence that attempts to explain three puzzling trends: the diversity of behavioral strategies among groups suffering from racial prejudice; the resilience of inter- and intragroup tensions, despite a greater acceptance of a multiplicity of differences in America today; and the ambivalent coexistence of racial tensions and multiracial coalitions.

In doing so, I combine the main contributions of social movement theory with three distinct yet interrelated perspectives: on reactive identification, identity politics, and contentious politics.[24] In concert, as summarized in figure I.1, they help me explain how both majority and minority ethnoracial groups have used and still use violence, not only in response to adversity but also as a proactive empowerment strategy.

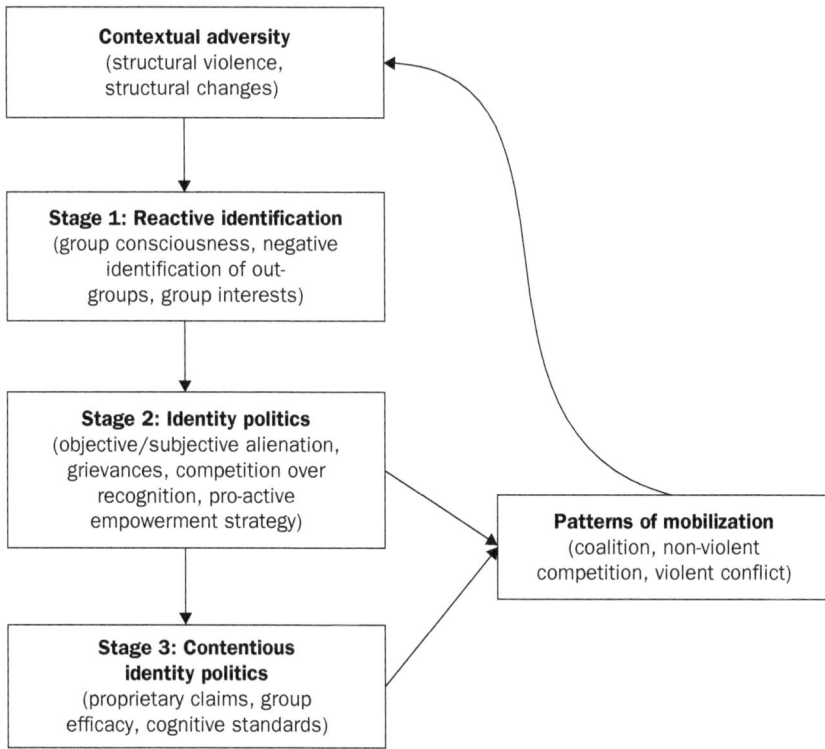

FIGURE I.1. A model of ethnoracial relations

Contextual violence includes forms of adversity targeting ethnoracial groups (such as racism, nativism, and official forms of brutality including segregation laws, racial profiling, and police brutality), as well as structural changes affecting ethnoracial relations. The structural changes that are relevant in this model are those that generate frustration and grievances—either by effectively ignoring the root causes of conflicts (such as resilient socioeconomic inequalities and civic exclusion) or by trying to address these causes but creating new incentives for a zero-sum competition (such as the pendulum effect of conflicts over opportunities provided by affirmative action programs).

Equally important is how the perceptions of contextual adversity generate grievances and how grievances frame identity politics. Differential treatment does not always generate grievances, but, when it does, group-based grievances become politically relevant because aggrieved groups mobilize. Grievance theories, such as relative deprivation and social justice theories, do not focus on mobilization processes even though protest is often analyzed as a behavioral consequence of feelings of injustice.[25] Conversely, social movement approaches do not always address the formation and role of grievances.[26] My goal, therefore, is to combine the findings of grievance theories with resource mobilization theories to evaluate the various ethnoracial patterns of action mobilization. In analyzing the transition from contextual adversity to identity politics based on grievances, it is important to note that the effects of objective material disparities are modified by subjective assessments such as a comparative evaluation of one group's situation with other groups.

Contentious identity politics consists of four components: contentious repertoires, which entails claim-making used by various groups in their struggle for recognition and/or power; rites of violence that employ symbols inherited from the past; relative group positioning vis-à-vis other ethnic groups; and the articulation of cycles of grievances. In tandem, these tools provide the basis for justifying and implementing strategies of violence that transform particular ethnic groups—from membership in the "other" category to integration and inclusion.

Contentious repertoires vary over time as they relate to different historical, political, and socioeconomic structures that, in turn, fuel specific grievances at particular historical junctures. Yet they are not entirely contextual and contingent. Contentious repertoires can also be linked to themes that are culturally inscribed and socially communicated across time and space. The subsequent resilience of these repertoires, as I illustrate, fuels the continuity of violence in America. Furthermore, I consider the policy implications of various forms of mobilization by focusing on their feedback effects on political opportunity structure and integration policies.

What actually matters, I contend, are the dynamics between actual and perceived adversity, a sense of threat, and their effects on each ethnic group's pattern of mobilization. Indeed, rather than exclusively focusing on its members' *objective* status or collective economic welfare, a group's *subjective* view of its status and welfare, and its treatment by others, plays just as important a role in defining its strategy and influencing its behavior. Those perceptions have now commonly become increasingly disconnected from underlying realities as a result of racial and political polarization. Grievances expressed by various ethnoracial groups are therefore legitimate from their perspective, quite independent from any objective metrics.

These types of subjective grievances are today widespread and growing among every ethnoracial group. They are crucial, accounting for a spiraling series of reactive ethnoracial conflicts—generated by the perception of various "others" as posing a threat. Collectively, they engender corrosive and escalating cycles of grievances, demands, and violent acts that increasingly lack definable parameters. They result in a key shift: from "identity politics" to a more aggressive form of "contentious politics" that is very damaging to America's social fabric.

In this book I delineate four main historical periods in identifying and explaining the evolutionary dynamics of contentious identity politics: the emergence of racial identities and their impact on cycles of grievances from the colonial period to the 1960s; the post–civil rights era and the increased complexity of groups' relations from the 1970s to 1990s; the incremental polarization of race relations from the early 2000s to the "Obama effect;" and the culmination of prejudicial racial identities and attitudes during the Trump presidency. I purposively focus more attention on the latter periods in this book to demonstrate their relevance in explaining violence in America today.

Roadmap of My Argument

In the book's first part, I begin by offering a brief historical overview of ethnoracial violence in America. I show that it was initiated by, as well as used against, immigrants and minorities—thereby demonstrating that violence has always been strategically foundational to the emergence of ethnoracial identities. I then critically examine conventional explanations of ethnoracial violence in America that focus on an array of cultural, socioeconomic, and institutional factors including abiding racial prejudice; the widening poverty-wealth gap; a lack of effective socioeconomic reforms; and inequalities in the process of integration as they relate to educational achievements, income, housing, and access to welfare provisions. These explanations provide useful insights, and I acknowledge the importance of these contextual factors. Yet as they are prone to generalizations, these approaches do not address some of the key complexities of the relationship between adversity and violence. They also tend to ignore the role that grievances and emotions play in the emergence of contention.

The book is composed of three parts. Part 1 has four chapters. In chapter 1, I present my theoretical framework by bringing together insights from scholarship on social movements, identity politics, and contentious politics depicted in figure I.1. I focus on the notions of group position and group efficacy. These in tandem frame both the identification process among ethnoracial groups and the forms of their mobilization. I discuss the three stages that structure the dynamical relationship between adversity and patterns of mobilization: how violence generates a reactive identification; how this identification affects the perceptions of other groups by fueling a sense of alienation and grievances; and how the subsequent salience of ethnoracial identities in hostile environments impacts inter- and intragroup relations in varied ways—from multiracial coalitions to violent confrontations.

Chapter 2 addresses the historical emergence of the adversity-identity nexus by focusing on the fluidity and ambiguity of ethnoracial divisions before the

1960s. The overview of this nexus, applied to "whiteness" and "Blackness," illustrates how various forms of violence have been a central component of the formation and organizations of group relations in America. Historical episodes suggest that is not simply imposed on a group; it is also chosen, albeit within contextual constraints. The episodes I describe also demonstrate that violence, albeit disproportionality, has been employed by all groups as circumstances have allowed—to establish domination, to express resistance, or both.

In chapter 3, I examine how the complexity of group relations has increased over time, a product of the ambivalent legacy of the civil rights era. It involved the mobilization of racial conservatives in a white backlash response to what they perceived to be a zero-sum struggle in which African Americans and minorities attempted to secure their rights. But nonwhite groups also engaged in new types of competition (notably over affirmative action programs) and more aggressive forms of the "politics of recognition." As a result, paradoxically, legislative reforms designed to dismantle institutional discrimination and reduce socioeconomic inequalities instead fueled intergroup conflicts.

In part 1's concluding chapter, chapter 4, I explain how the contentious repertoires and rites of violence inherited from the post–civil rights era have fostered new cycles of grievances. Contentious identity politics became widespread during the 1990s with the emergence of activist groups defined by religious, sexual, and gendered identities in the late twentieth century. Protest politics, often still physically violent but also increasingly accusatory and thus discursive, became a defining feature of contemporary America. It was energized by increased competition over material and symbolic resources, and consequently has fueled centrifugal forces that have been detrimental to America's social fabric.

Given this historical context, in part 2 (composed of three chapters), I analyze a series of challenges that America now faces as a result of the emergence of what is widely characterized as a "post-racial" society, albeit one where racism and violence abounds. Progress in racial equality has been slow and remains limited. It was not until 1967 that a Supreme Court decision nullified state laws banning intermarriage. George Fredrickson noted that, as a result of the civil rights revolution, "legalized segregation is as dead today as racial slavery was in 1865."[27] Yet, there is no legislation powerful enough to change unyielding mentalities. Traditional expressions of racial bias have gone "underground" in response to the gains of the civil rights movement of the 1960s and the growing role of government in advancing Black rights.[28] Anti-Black racism has therefore not disappeared but rather has evolved from its original forms into more complex patterns, including symbolic racism, structural racism, and systemic racism.[29] Barack Obama's presidential election in 2008 initiated a controversial debate about the state of race relations among advocates and critics of post-racialism, resulting in a plethora of studies.[30] Yet, here remains little consensus about what defines post-racialism, or prescriptively a consensus regarding what policies it should engender.

In chapter 5, I provide data illustrating the Janus-like nature of America's society in which inter- and intragroup relations occur today. I consider evidence of the positive impact of legislative reforms, the relative improvement of the socioeconomic status of minorities, and the opportunities multiracialism provides in relation to the diversity-tolerance nexus.[31] These developments are driven by four factors that I examine: immigration flows, a growing propensity for intermarriage, the subsequent multiracial baby boom, and the sharp increase in the number of people who identify themselves as "multiracial" (as measured by the US Census since 2000). They raised hopes for greater intercommunal tolerance, dialogue, and acceptance. Yet significant racial and ethnic turbulence persists in America. This includes forms of violence targeting minority groups (such as hate crimes, Islamophobia, anti-Hispanic phobia, and police brutality) as well as violent forms of contentious politics (such as urban riots, civil protests, and political violence) that affect the relationship between ethnoracial groups. I review relevant evidence demonstrating that socioeconomic inequality, racial disparities, and other forms of adversity plague American society—supporting virulent criticism of the "myth of post-racialism."

In chapter 6, I demonstrate that, beyond these contrasting findings, what actually matters is the dynamic interaction between actual and perceived adversity, threats, and patterns of mobilization—from the perspective of every major group engaged in ethnoracial relations. Challenges raised by multiracialism force ethnoracial groups to redefine their position in dealing with a more complex mainstream and, thus, to adjust their integrative strategy. In doing so, all groups express new grievances. Diagnostically, I ultimately identify three key issues that have a negative impact on intergroup relations: first, the diffusion of a culture of fear resulting from the depiction of entire categories of people as innately dangerous;[32] second, a revanchist political syndrome that constitutes a fertile ground for intolerant attitudes and violent behavior; and finally, the banality of physical and discursive violence.

In chapter 7, I therefore identify a spiraling series of reactive ethnoracial conflicts generated by the perception of various "others" as posing a threat. Collectively, they engender today corrosive and escalating cycles of grievances, demands, and violent acts that increasingly lack definable parameters. I provide evidence of this spillover process during the Obama administration when ethnoracial separatism, revanchist policies, and societal fragmentation undermined both defining common goals and generating inclusive politics. I then examine the Trump administration, analyzing the effects of the increasing racialization of every aspect of US politics on intergroup relations.[33] Adversity, however, often generates resistance. In this case it has culminated in the BLM protests, whose objectives are avenues to equal rights, entitlements, and protections—all classic elements of integration and acceptance.

In part 3, building upon the findings in the first and second, I explore the lessons that can be drawn from the current situation. I address two questions: is a multiracial, multiethnic, violent society America's only possible future? And, expanding the scope of my analysis, is a violent America comparably Europe's future?

In addressing these questions, I examine two possible options regarding the future of contentious politics in America in chapter 8. One presages a sustained pattern of future conflicts, entailing more friction and violence. There are strong reasons to anticipate a comparable variance of empowerment strategies by different minority groups, engendering a spiraling dynamic of counterclaims and action. Stubborn socioeconomic inequalities add a further layer of complexity, as illustrated by tensions between social classes within each ethnoracial group. The alternative, more optimistic option entails greater cooperation. There is occasional evidence of the emergence of new forms of interracial coalition building, as illustrated by the Moral Monday movement, which started in North Carolina in 2013 and has since spread to other states. The BLM movement, of course, provides another vivid example of the possibility that ethnoracial groups will use multiracial coalitions to consolidate acceptance in mainstream society.

In addressing the question of Europe, I begin chapter 9 by noting that issues related to ethnoracial relations in European countries are the product of very differing national histories. Yet, there are comparable trends on both sides of the Atlantic. Various forms of racial prejudice are now rampant throughout Europe, as well as xenophobia and other manifestations of anti-immigrant feelings. Furthermore, urban riots motivated by ethnoracial discrimination have become commonplace in several European countries, as well as protests of racial discrimination. Indeed, events on the two continents are often connected. A racial backlash in many European countries in the 1960s was inspired by US conservative assaults against the civil rights movement and subsequent affirmative action initiatives. Enoch Powell's "rivers of blood" speech, for example, echoed the rhetoric of George Wallace, while US publications critical of multiculturalism subsequently inspired both European scholars and policymakers. More recently, former president Trump has been a source of inspiration for some European populist politicians, from Matteo Salvini in Italy to Viktor Orbán in Hungary.

Conversely, the US civil rights struggle framed the mobilization of various ethnoracial groups in Europe during the 1970s, and the mobilization of US minority groups influences similar forms of contentious politics in Western Europe today (such as BLM protests that spread throughout Europe in 2016 and 2020). Contentious repertoires are therefore spreading across Europe, either in response to discrimination or as a factor enhancing violent tensions. Subsequently, contentious identity politics is becoming a transnational phenomenon fueled both by the influence of US groups and by particular political and social contexts in Europe.

In the book's concluding chapter, I provide a critical evaluation of existing policies and suggest reforms designed to assuage ethnoracial relations in America as well as in other Western democracies. My purpose is to diagnose what it would take to make identity-based politics more inclusive and less violent. I contend that it is time to move from antagonism to agonism by promoting democratic contestation based on a positive ethos of engagement and engaging in a more inclusive "politics of difference."

Part 1
LESSONS FROM THE PAST

A brief historical overview of violence in America shows that it has taken many forms, has occurred for varied reasons, has been aimed at a variety of targets, and has taken place in contrasting locations. The intensity of these differing forms of violence has fluctuated over time. Yet, the continuity of violence has fueled the belief that America is a nation of violent par excellence. As Richard Hofstadter, in *Reflections on Violence in the United States*, insightfully argues: "What is impressive to one who begins to learn about American violence is its extraordinary frequency, its sheer commonplaceness in our history, its persistence into very recent and contemporary times, and its rather abrupt contrast with our pretensions to singular national virtue."[1] Hofstadter was referring to the most notable dimensions of violence—the routine use of guns, political assassinations, urban unrest, and domestic terrorism.

At its core, most forms of collective violence relate to racial prejudice and migrant phobia—a disturbing dimension of American exceptionalism. These generally target minorities through nativist and antimigrant propaganda, hate speech, racial killings, religious riots, racial urban riots, and police brutality as well as discriminatory practices implemented, endorsed, or simply accepted by the state. In the following sections, I disaggregate and summarize these various forms of collective violence. My purpose is to address the key questions succinctly articulated by Donald Horowitz: the "who, when, where, how, and what" of violent behavior.[2] In doing so, I critically evaluate the traditional explanations of ethnoracial violence (based on socioeconomic and institutionalist approaches) and offer an alternative way of understanding the complex relationship between migrant phobia, multiethnic grievances, and ethnoracial relations in America.

America's Historical Cycles of Violence
Racial Violence

In terms of the national consciousness, the racial killing of Blacks, extending far back into the eighteenth century, remains the most iconic example of American violence. It dates from the ruthless repression of uprisings (such as in New York in 1712 and 1741) to the mob lynchings and mass violence that characterized race relations from the post-Reconstruction period to the second half of the twentieth century. One of the worst episodes, the Tulsa race massacre, took place in Oklahoma in 1921, when mobs of white residents attacked Black residents and destroyed the "Black Wall Street." According to official estimates, more than 200 Black people were killed and about 10,000 left homeless. Furthermore, more than 3,000 Blacks were lynched between 1882 and 1935 according to official US Census statistics. But even this data minimizes the problem because it excludes both "kangaroo-court" and unreported murders.[3] After World War I, the Ku Klux Klan organized attacks across the South, Southwest, and in the north central states of Indiana, Ohio, and Illinois. These included kidnapping, house burning, tar-and-feather parties, mutilation, and murder.

Racial violence was not confined to the intimidation of Blacks. Others involved attacks against Chinese (such as the "Chinese massacre" of 1871 in Los Angeles), Italians (such as the eleven Italians lynched in New Orleans in 1891), and Mexicans (such as the killing of thousands of Hispanics between 1848 to 1928 in California). These manifestations of violence were not isolated. Rather, they were extreme illustrations of an underlying, broad-based public hostility. Again, neither time nor contrasting racial identities made a difference to this propensity for ethnic violence. A violent confrontation between white US servicemen and Mexican American youths (wearing outfits called zoot suits) occurred in Los Angeles, for example, in the spring of 1943. Although the servicemen instigated the aggression, only the Mexicans were arrested—on the grounds that they were criminal gang members.

Racial Riots

Urban riots today are associated with African American protests. But historically, America's cities have commonly been the primary location for "anti-negro riots." Anti-abolitionist riots, for example, took place in 1834, starting in New York City before sweeping across the country with at least twenty-four major racial conflicts being recorded that year. After the Civil War, radical Reconstruction leaders in several Southern states organized Negro militias (called freedmen) to defend their interests. Southern whites, in turn, created various White Leagues that, in reality, constituted the armed wing of the Democratic Party. The two forces confronting each other in riots was subsequently commonplace in Louisiana, South Carolina, Arkansas, and Mississippi. One notable example was the so-called Battle of Liberty Place in New Orleans in September of 1874, where riots turned into a militarized urban battle. It began as an insurrection of white Democratic supporters, intent on overturning the Republican Reconstruction government. It left more than twenty dead and more than one hundred wounded. Reflective of this trend, 509 whites and 486 freedmen were killed in Texas between 1865 and 1869.

Another wave of interracial riots occurred after World War I. There were at least thirty-three major racial urban riots in the United States between 1919 and 1949. During the "Red Summer" and fall of 1919, major urban riots took place in Elaine (Arkansas), where federal troops were called to "fight against the Black insurrection, and in Chicago where 23 Blacks and 15 Whites were killed, and more than 500 injured."[4] Hundreds of riots took place during World War II, with 242 incidents taking place in forty-seven cities in 1943 alone. That June, for example, thirty-four were killed and more than seven hundred injured in Detroit, while violent incidents occurred in numerous Southern cities (such as New Orleans and Phoenix) as well as at military bases across the country.[5]

Urban interracial violence dramatically increased during the 1960s—as illustrated by riots in Philadelphia in 1964, in Watts in 1965, in Chicago in 1965 and 1966, and in many cities during the "long hot summer" of 1967. Most famously, the assassination of Rev. Dr. Martin Luther King Jr. sparked riots in scores of cities across the country in 1968. In total, more than three hundred riots occurred between 1965 and 1968, resulting in more than two hundred deaths and untold damage to property.

Religious Violence

Violence against white ethnic Catholics has been endemic in America since the early nineteenth century, illustrated by attacks against Irish and German Catholics. Anti-Catholicism became a major social and political force, targeting Irish and German Catholic institutions (such as in Boston in 1834 and Cincinnati in 1853). Leading this "Protestant Crusade," the Know-Nothing Party instigated rioting from Baltimore to Louisville. The 1890s economic depression led to a new wave of anti-Catholicism—orchestrated in the Midwest by the American Protective Association, created by Irish Protestants in 1887. Anti-Catholicism remained popular in the early twentieth century, as illustrated by violent attacks organized by the second Ku Klux Klan against churches in the 1920s, and the murder of priests (notably Father James Coyle in Alabama in 1921). Prejudice against Catholics finally slowly declined in the mid-twentieth century, then faded after the election of John F. Kennedy, the first Catholic to become president.

Other groups were subjected to both religious and racial discrimination—such as Mexicans, Jews, Arab Americans, and Muslim immigrants.[6] In the aftermath of the 1848 US takeover of Mexican territories extending from Texas to California, a number of Catholic dioceses and parishes had to defend themselves from the discriminatory attitudes and actions of native Protestants as well as newly arrived European clergy (whose members despised their Mexican Spanish-speaking coreligionists).[7] Jews were targeted by anti-Semitic violence (as illustrated by Leo Franck's lynching in Atlanta in 1915) and legislation. Some universities (such as Harvard and Cornell) implemented a quota system for Jewish students in 1922. Other universities copied this policy until the 1950s to keep the Jewish student population under 10 percent. In addition, Jews suffered from employment discrimination in various white-collar and professional positions, such as banking, insurance, and public utilities. Immigrants from the Middle East (both Christians who arrived prior to World War I and Muslims, who constituted the majority of those arriving in the second part of the twentieth century) were victims of religious discrimination as well as anti-Arab feelings (even those who were not Arabs).

Institutional Racism and Nativism

Historical forms of institutional racism took varied forms: First, as the legal institution of human enslavement from 1619 to the passage of the Thirteenth Amendment in 1865; Second, the many forms of servitude that lasted until World War II (such as convict leasing and various systems of forced penal labor); Third, the systematic discriminatory practices at the federal level (upheld by the US Supreme Court) that provided the legal basis for the racial segregation and disfranchisement of African Americans;[8] And fourth, the Jim Crow laws—state and local laws enforcing racial segregation in the South. These measures were implemented to lasting effect. Reforms adopted during the New Deal era were inclusive of new immigrants but accentuated racial divisions between Blacks and whites, as illustrated by the exclusion of many nonwhite workers from the Fair Labor Standards Act of 1938 and the housing policies adopted by the Federal Housing Authority (FHA). As a result, "American social policies have reproduced racial hierarchy and the American welfare state has been an instrument more often of social stratification than of social equality."[9] After World War II, the FHA and other lending agencies continued to play a major role in racial and spatial discrimination against African Americans through the process of "redlining" properties in Black neighborhoods. As a result, white people received 98 percent of the FHA's and Veterans Administration's mortgage loans between 1934 and 1964.

Nativism took many forms—from migrant phobia increasingly tainted by eugenics to restrictive immigration policies and discriminatory practices against European and non-European immigrants alike. Major measures included the Chinese Exclusion Act of 1882, a series of laws allowing the deportation of immigrants (defined in 1882 as "likely to become public charges"), and the Immigration Act of 1917 designed to protect what Madison Grant called "the Great Race."[10] Nativists also fraudulently accused immigrants of threatening national or domestic security, thus justifying the use of legal or extralegal means for redress. This was a strategy often employed against white ethnic groups, expanding the targets of violence beyond pigmentation. Nativism was often legitimized by security concerns, exemplified by the notorious Alien and Sedition Acts of 1798. These acts were designed to protect the country from foreign influence by subjecting aliens to governmental surveillance and criminalizing certain forms of political protest. Other comparable initiatives followed, such as the Espionage Act of 1917, the Sedition Act of 1918, and the 1921 law punishing aliens for possessing subversive literature or showing other forms of sympathy for radical organizations. During World War II, the notorious 1940 Alien Registration Act authorized the internment of West Coast residents of Japanese origin—forty thousand born abroad (who remained alien by virtue of the prohibition of their naturalization) and seventy thousand citizens born in the United States.

Although many forms of violence have been a common and continuous feature of American society since the birth of the republic, the key questions (who, when, where, how, and what) related to violence were largely left unaddressed before the mid-twentieth century. Racial and nativist violence, for example, was criticized by some abolitionists and pro-migrant groups. However, racism and nativism were generally accepted, popular among the elites and the emergent working class, and therefore unquestioned. The first major attempt by federal and state authorities to analyze ethnoracial violence focused on urban riots in the aftermath of the "Red Summer." It led to the creation of the Chicago Commission on Race Relations in 1919. Several followed in the 1960s, notably the California Governor's Commission on the Los Angeles riots (the McCone Commission, 1965), the National Advisory Commission on Civil Disorders (the Kerner Commission, 1967), and the National Commission on the Causes and

Prevention of Violence (1968). During the 1960s and 1970s, interethnic conflict became a topical issue for scholars, who framed explanatory models that are still used today.

Conventional Views of Ethnoracial Violence

Conventional studies can be divided into three broad groups. Some analyzed the broader "culture of violence," including America's "gun culture" and the normalization of discursive and physical violence.[11] A second group of studies, based on an institutionalist or political opportunity structures (POS) perspective, focused on contextual explanations for violence (such as systematic forms of political oppression, racist legislation, and socioeconomic inequalities).[12] A third group emphasized individual motivational factors, mostly from the perspective of the perpetuators (such as relative deprivation and an "expectation gap").[13] These various approaches shared one common objective—to understand the recurrence of ethnoracial violence against minorities.[14]

The "Culture of Violence"

For many observers, violence has been a common expression of an exaggerated sense of "Americanism," one deeply enshrined in both a frontier and vigilante tradition. This perspective gained currency in the aftermath of the urban riots that took place across the country in the 1960s.[15] Echoing Richard Hofstadter's diagnosis, John Herbers argues that these riots were "not an aberration of United States history or a sign of the disintegration of American institutions but the usual type of behavior displayed in these country when there is a large division of purpose."[16] "The frontier heritage," Joe B. Frantz notes in a report published by the National Commission on the Causes and Prevention of Violence, "established the idea of the individual's arming himself . . . The prevalence of arms over the fireplace or stacked by the sod-house door endures in the defense which groups like the National Rifle Association membership carry on today against attempts to register arms."[17]

Other observers have diagnosed a proclivity for violence in a US national character fueled by the "American love affair" with violence, illustrated by the cult of the "gangster hero." As a result, "a culture of violence" is deeply rooted in US popular culture. In Henry Giroux's analysis of "America's addiction to violence," he argues:

> Violence runs through American society like an electric current offering instant pleasure from all sources of the culture, whether it be the nightly news and Hollywood fanfare or television series that glorify serial killers. At a policy level, violence drives an arms industry, a militaristic foreign policy, and is increasingly the punishing state's major tool to enforce its hyped-up brand of domestic terrorism, especially against Black youth. The United States is utterly wedded to a neoliberal culture in which cruelty is viewed as virtue, mass incarceration the default welfare program and chief mechanism to "institutionalize obedience."[18]

The assumption that violence is an American tradition remains widespread today both at home and abroad. The casualness of contemporary violence is purportedly fueled by residual elements of America's frontier culture of vigilantism and gun ownership. This is reflected in a plethora of mass shootings, mystifying terror attacks instigated with the intent of generating mass civilian casualties, and a more commonplace resort to arms to settle turf disputes. After the killing of nine people in a historic Black church in Charleston, South Carolina, in June 2015, Senator Harry Reid claimed that "The United States is the only advanced country where this type of mass violence occurs."[19] The US media described the mass shooting in Las Vegas in October 2017—the deadliest one in modern American history with fifty-eight victims—as "the worst kind of American exceptionalism."[20] The mass killings in El Paso, Texas, and Dayton, Ohio—along with a spate of shootings in Chicago—in August 2019 brought renewed attention to deadly gun violence in the United States. These attacks added to a growing list of mass shootings, once again illustrating the routine nature of gun violence in the United States.[21]

Fatalities in mass killings capture the attention of the media, fueling an ongoing controversial political debate. Yet, they account for only a small proportion of national gun violence. The other forms are part of America's social fabric, and the statistics are alarming. So many people die annually from gunfire in the United States that the aggregate death toll between 1968 and 2011 eclipses all fatalities in American wars combined. According to Politifact, there were approximately 1.4 million firearm deaths in that period. This compares with 1.2 million US deaths in every conflict from the War of Independence to the Iraq War. Since 2011, approximately 40,000 people died annually from gunfire. Each violent episode—especially mass shootings—encourages newspapers and other social media to promote the assumption that violence is "the American way of life," both because of the "right to bear arms" and the "attitudes of Americans" traced back to the arrival of the first settlers.[22]

Socioeconomic Approaches

Socioeconomic studies before the 1960s consistently concluded that cycles of ethnoracial violence were mainly explained by a competition for scarce resources. The 1919 Chicago Commission, for example, focused on the effect of the Great Migration—on both the problem of housing shortages for Blacks and the corresponding increasing labor competition between Blacks and whites. Subsequently formalized as competition theory, white-initiated violence prior to the 1960s was explained as the product of grievances fueled by the breakdown of labor market segmentation, increasing the competition for employment and housing. White advantages were threatened by desegregation, leading to high levels of collective violence instigated against minorities. Black-initiated violence, conversely, was supposedly motivated by absolute deprivation resulting from the persistence of racial disparities in income, education, housing, and other economic opportunities.[23] Cities, where high proportions of Blacks had low levels of education or were employed in highly segregated low-paying jobs, were thus more likely to be the venues for racial riots. Competition and deprivation theories remained popular among those social scientists who focused on the racial disparities in terms of economic opportunities.[24]

The violence of the 1960s, however, questioned some components of these theories. Some scholars concurred that America was facing a new form of violence, characterized by a series of what sociologist Allen Grimshaw identified as "modern race riots."[25] This largescale violence (with riots in 125 cities, resulting in forty-six deaths and thirty-five thousand injuries) was puzzling for those who stressed that Blacks were economically better off in the 1960s than ever before. Hugh Davis Graham and Ted Robert Gurr, for example, note the "paradoxical coincidence of black progress and black rage," arguing that "violence cannot be explained on the basis of any objective and measurable criteria such as the number and quality of jobs and the level of employment or income."[26] Other scholars identified some puzzling features—such as similar deprivation levels in cities where riots did and did not take place. Neither a widening gap in income nor occupational prestige could predict the location of riots, their severity, or the participation rates. Furthermore, greater housing and occupational integration was correlated with increases in the rate of racial violence.[27]

A revised version of deprivation theory was thus expanded to incorporate the notion of relative deprivation to explain the paradoxical increase in the volume of racial riots despite reduced disparities.[28] Susan Olzak and Johan Olivier, for example, found that periods of Black protest actually accompanied a decline in racial disparities.[29] Riots therefore took place when the black/white gap in attainment declined, prompting an increase in minority expectations. According to this argument, Daniel Myers explains, "expectations for improved social and economic conditions increase as the disadvantaged group's position improves, thereby leading to heightened frustration if the rising expectations are not met."[30] Grievances were further fueled by a lack of political power, best reflected in the absence of control over local government in minority communities. The "social disorganization thesis" thus emphasized that "poorly integrated individuals are outside the general control of community norms and have less access to traditional mechanisms for addressing social grievances."[31]

Institutionalist Approaches

The assumption that institutional reforms should address the root causes of violence stretched back to the 1919 Chicago Commission on Race Relations. Its report recommended a series of reforms designed to address discrimination in the job market, inadequate housing options, inconsistent law enforcement, and pervasive racial discrimination. In response to the 1935 Harlem riots, Mayor LaGuardia set up a multiracial Commission on Conditions in Harlem, headed by E. Franklin Frazier, an African American sociologist. The commission proposed measures to address socioeconomic discrimination and racial segregation. But the failure to improve those conditions provided the context for further riots in 1943. Mayor LaGuardia then attempted to implement more effective policies, such as pressuring landlords to comply with price controls under the supervision of the Office of Price Administration (which opened an office on 135th Street). More broadly, the explosion of interracial conflicts elsewhere at this time led to the creation of more than one hundred local, state, and national commissions to promote "better race relations." In 1941, President Roosevelt agreed to issue an executive order creating the Committee on Fair Employment Practices (FEPC) in exchange for the cancellation of a March on Washington. The Congress of Racial Equality, created in 1942, promoted nonviolent action intended to end segregation and encouraged students (notably at Howard University) to engage in sit-ins and other forms of peaceful protest. And, in 1943, Executive Order 9346 expanded the coverage of the FEPC to federal agencies until the end of the war.

Yet, the resilience of racial prejudice and discriminatory practices led to the 1960s riots. One continued institutional element was police brutality. The 1968 Kerner Commission's report emphasized key elements of institutional racism—notably the role of police brutality against African Americans in igniting protests that turned violent. There was indeed plentiful evidence that offenses committed by white law-enforcement officials against Blacks triggered outbursts of violence, including the 1964 riots in Harlem, Jersey City, and Philadelphia as well as the

1967 Newark riots triggered by the police arrest and beating of John Smith, an African American taxi driver.

Summarizing the depth of racial prejudice, the Kerner report concluded: "we are a nation of two societies, one black, one white—separate and unequal." Both racial prejudice and police brutality (just one of many aspects of institutional racism) were widespread across the country, fueling what Seymour Spilerman identifies as "disorder-proneness."[32] James Comer, a member of the Commission on the Causes and Prevention of Violence, concluded his analysis of "the dynamics of black and white violence" by asking: "Given the level of social violence toward blacks, the logical question should not be 'why black violence?' but 'why has black-initiated and retaliatory violence been so little and so late'?"[33] Robert Fogelson expressed a similar view: "Until recently the blacks accepted the racist standards of white society . . . This they no longer do . . . Instead, they intend to call attention to their grievances, and are now prepared, even determined, to resort to violence until their grievances are redressed."[34]

Important pieces of legislation were passed and implemented to improve the status of African Americans. The McCarran-Walter Act of 1952 (which ended the exclusion of Asian Americans from citizenship) was in many ways a precedent to the pieces of legislation that followed a decade later. These include the Civil Rights Act of 1964, the 1965 Voting Rights Act, and the 1965 Higher Education Act, along with various affirmative action programs. Parallel measures were intended to facilitate the assimilation of other minorities, such as the Immigration Act of 1965 (which ended a system that largely favored European immigrants).

These reforms, however, activated a new "pendulum effect." They partly dismantled institutional racism but fueled racial violence by increasing competition over material and symbolic resources as well as heightening expectations and grievances among various groups. They increased expectations among Blacks. Yet, the lack of actual improvement of their condition—compared to the situation of proximal whites—fueled grievances, thereby encouraging Blacks to resort to violence. Conversely, minority activism, generated by the slow pace of sociopolitical change, fueled a revival of white nativism. This revival, in turn, increased the level of discontent experienced by Blacks. The result was a new cycle of violence and counterviolence.

Proponents of institutionalist approaches subsequently conceded that the persistence of racial prejudice could be an unexpected product of institutional reforms. Indeed, as Susan Olzak, Suzanne Shanahan, and Elizabeth McEneaney note, "increases in political opportunity for the powerless increase the likelihood of collective action of all types . . . As racial barriers break down, competition and conflict increase. At the same time, advantaged groups fight to retain dominance and isolation from minorities."[35] Analyzing racial riots as a form of social protest,

Craig Jenkins argues that the desegregation of minorities escalated the propensity to riot, especially in settings where segregation had been very high prior to socio-economic and political change.[36] Proponents of resource mobilization theory therefore focused on changes that facilitated collective action, such as economic expansion (rather than deprivation) and decreases in levels of residential segregation (instead of extreme apartheid segregation). This perspective, based on the notion of "critical junctures," showed that "incongruence between the needs and expressed demands of the state and various societal groups is the norm, not the exception... During periods of crisis, politics becomes a struggle over the basic rules of the game."[37] As a result, both federal legislation that reinforced segregation and governmental reforms that dismantled institutional segregation fueled racial violence by increasing competition over symbolic and material resources.

What Can We Learn from the Past?

Analyzing the root causes of ethnoracial violence in terms of these approaches provides useful insights for contemporary events. A reading of the Kerner report about the riots that wracked US cities in the 1960s, for example, provides a better understanding of events in Ferguson, Missouri, in 2014, where the killing of unarmed teenager Michael Brown by officer Darren Wilson prompted local riots. A comparable linkage can be made between the Chicago report of 1919 and one released by the Chicago Police Accountability Task Force after several violent protests in 2016. Violent protests initiated by a white supremacist march on the campus of the University of Virginia in August 2017 sparked a disquieting feeling of déjà vu: torch-bearing white people loudly vocalizing their hate of Jews and African Americans. Counter-protesters, conversely, invoked the legacy of the long fight against racism. What triggered the tragic killing of one antiracist student was a controversy about the removal of monuments associated with the Southern Confederate nation—a major bone of contention in the "culture wars" that have become increasingly widespread in America.[38] The same is true of George Floyd's killing and the Black Lives Matter protests that followed in 2020. America's violent history thus repeats itself. The eras differed, but the issues of poverty, violent crime, police brutality, and systemic racism persist.

Another legacy of the past involved the so-called culture of violence. Both contemporary symbolic and physical forms of violence remain tainted by a mythical reconstruction of the past. The "frontier tradition" has often been invoked by perpetuators of violence to legitimize their behavior—such as white supremacist groups and militias within the so-called Patriot movement who present themselves as the heirs of historical nativist movements. The Minuteman Civil Defense

Corps, for example, justified the armed border controls conducted by its members against migrants illegally crossing US borders by describing them as "inheritors of a civic tradition that has always recognized eternal vigilance as the price of freedom."[39] The Oath Keepers and other antigovernment groups seek "a restoration" of the militia tradition in America to preserve the legacy of patriots who, during the American Revolution, "fought back in justified, righteous self-defense of their natural rights."[40]

Furthermore, the historical overview of violence targeting minorities confirmed that most conflicts were motivated by racial prejudice and that racial prejudice mainly positioned whites as perpetuators and Blacks as victims. From this dichotomous white/black perspective, Michael Omi and Howard Winant argue that "even a cursory glance at American history reveals that the United States has been an extremely 'color-conscious' society. From the very inception of the Republic to the present moment, race has been a profound determinant of one's political rights, one's location in the labor market, and indeed one's sense of identity."[41] Studies of urban riots have reinforced a focus on racial-group relations by analyzing either white-initiated and/or Black-initiated violence.

The white/black perspective was sustained by the continued manifestation of the "pendulum effect." Discrimination and violence have inspired resistance and countermobilization over time. Supporters of Jim Crow policies used violence against Black soldiers during World War II (killing at least fifty-five of them) to "keep them in their place." According to the League for White Supremacy, created in 1942, violence was the only effective means to stop progressive reforms. Each protest of discrimination was seen as a sign of "Negro disloyalty," and many feared that "the more they get, the more they want."[42] Violence erupted in Southern communities where court orders to integrate schools were greeted by white resistance. The 1954 federal ruling in Brown v. Board of Education of Topeka led to violence in Kentucky, Tennessee, and Arkansas. The policy of "massive resistance"—supported by the third KKK—was designed to delay the racial integration of public institutions such as schools.[43] Racial riots in the 1960s were, relatedly, explained as the result of a countermobilization of dissidents, radicals, African Americans, and other minorities expressing their grievances against, and hostility to, middle-class mores and resilient forms of prejudice. This countermobilization, in turn, was perceived by a significant number of white Americans as posing a threat to conservative values and to national security. The white backlash that occurred from the 1960s to the 1990s, was mainly spurred by racial concerns over increased civil rights granted to minorities. The counterreaction culminated with the election of Barack Obama, which, in turn, energized a new cycle of white backlash.

Yet a closer examination of past episodes of violence reveals three major quandaries that are underscored by these conventional approaches. First, the focus on a white/black divide is relevant, but it blurs a more complex historical reality. While the "white privilege" in various forms has been a constant in America, the relationship between these two groups was more complex than often described by studies of racial disorder. When applied by scholars analyzing the 1960s riots, the racial distinctions between Blacks and whites reflected the realities of their time. But it did not reflect the realities of a century earlier. "Whiteness" only became a category, a "self-evident entity," during the civil rights era as a result of the "newly invigorated black-white social dichotomy."[44] It is therefore crucial to avoid employing an anachronous categorization in analyzing historic, and as I will later demonstrate contemporary, episodes of violence.

Second, scholars paid little attention to the situation and behavior of non-Black minorities. They did not include them in their study of racial violence, arguing that attacks instigated by (and on) immigrants had distinct causes. Comparative studies of the histories of ethnic minorities remained scarce and embryonic during the 1960s, although at least twenty "Hispanic riots" took place between 1964 and 1968. There were some impressionistic accounts of non-Black riots during this era but no systematic study of ethnic minority–initiated violence. They subsequently did not provide a clear answer to the important question asked by Robert Fogelson (among the few who examined the behavior of some migrant non-Black groups during the 1960s riots): "If it is true—and I think it is—that many other ethnic minorities have suffered these grievances at one time or another, why only the Blacks resorted to full-scale rioting?"[45]

Third, and critically for this book, most studies of ethnoracial violence tend to assume that minorities are passive objects of politics. For decades, scholars have explored the reasons for this continued violence by focusing on immigrants and minorities only as victims.[46] Black-initiated violence during the 1960s riots was only perceived as a form of impulsive, reactive behavior motivated by frustrations generated by the resilience of institutional racism or a response to poverty. "Racial violence has undergone a fundamental transformation," Graham and Gurr argued, "with the former victims opting for retaliation instead of passively enduring oppression."[47] The "riot ideology"—a controversial notion that emerged in the 1960s and has remained popular since then—illustrates this bias.[48] Graham and Gurr mentioned the "psychological residues of slavery" to explain the "differential inclinations of a people or of groups within a society to resort to violence."[49] August Mier and Elliott Rudwick argued that "retaliatory violence has never been entirely absent from Negro thinking," leading to the emergence of a "militant new Negro"—"an intellectual type who rejected the gradualism and conciliation of his ancestors."[50] Other conservative analysts assumed that stereotypical rioters were Black criminals using violence mainly "for fun and profit."[51]

Students of migrant assimilation in American society also consider nonwhite minorities more as objects than subjects of politics and policies. Alejandro Portes and Ruben G. Rumbaut, for example, argue that "the response of immigrant communities to nativist fears of yesterday and today has been marked more by passive endurance than active opposition."[52] Some scholars did acknowledge activism among minority groups, without explaining how protest sometimes turned violent. Instead, the alleged "violent Black subculture" has been broadened to include other minorities suspected of being prone to violence. Graeme Newman, for example, identified elements of continuity between the violent frontier tradition and the Chicano activism of the 1960s: "Franck and Jesse James had many Southern sympathizers . . . Billy the Kid was idolized by poor Mexican villagers of the South West."[53] Other studies have analyzed conflicts among various minority groups.[54] Competition theorists included the effects of immigration by analyzing ethnic competition in terms similar to racial competition. In doing so, however, they only extended the "racial paradigm" to other nonwhite minority groups.[55]

My point is not to deny that all minority groups were—and still are—victims of violence. However, this is only one aspect of ethnoracial violence in America, masking a broader reality: that all white, Black, and "in-between" groups have resorted to the use of violence, ranging from discursive violence (such as racial stereotyping and nativist agenda) to physical violence as a response to adversity (reactive violence). Furthermore, past episodes of violence often involved groups that were simultaneously the perpetrators and victims of discrimination. As Matthew Frye Jacobson, in his study of "whiteness of a different color," notes, "It is one of the compelling circumstances of American cultural history that an Irish immigrant in 1877 could be despised as Celt in Boston—a threat to the Republic—and yet a solid member of the Order of Caucasians for the Extermination of the Chinaman in San Francisco, gallantly defending U.S. shores from an invasion of 'Mongolians.'"[56]

The story of inclusion and exclusion in America, as well as confrontation and cooperation between and among ethnoracial groups, is more complex than commonly assumed by a binary approach that distinguishes between whites and Blacks, or perpetuators and victims. Furthermore, the use of violence by a minority cannot be assumed to be an expression of anger or a legitimate (but disorganized) form of self-defense. Rather, violent behavior has often been a proactive response to adversity, with meaning and purpose beyond simple reflexive behavior.

1

VIOLENCE AS A PROACTIVE RESPONSE TO ADVERSITY

A reconceptualization of ethnoracial violence requires taking into account the historical complexity of group relations in America. My purpose is to add nuance to the three common assumptions I outlined: the belief that ethnoracial violence is a result of racism exclusively defined as a white/black divide; the widespread tendency to focus on the perpetuators of violence by overestimating the homogeneity of the white category; and the assumption that minorities are mostly passive victims of violence or, when they react, their use of violence is simply an impulsive behavior legitimated by contextual adversity and the resilience of racial prejudice.

These assumptions are partly relevant. They are, however, too simplistic and do not tell a defining part of the history of American violence. What has been largely forgotten in the retelling of American history is that violence, albeit disproportionately, has been used by all ethnoracial groups, white and nonwhite alike. Defining ethnoracial violence as simply acts of violence motivated by racism obscures the motivations of various groups often ignored—but nonetheless engaged—in cycles of violence. Violence against minorities when committed by members of the dominant group can be motivated by both racial and nonracial factors. Violence committed by one minority against another, or indeed members of the dominant group, can be motivated by racism as well as other factors. Although racism therefore remains a key component of group relations, many instances of ethnoracial conflict, discrimination, and exclusion should not be analyzed through the exclusive lens of racism. As Lawrence Blum summarizes in his analysis of the moral quandary of race in America, "not all racial incidents are racist incidents."[1] Conversely, nonexplicit racist beliefs can lead to racialism which, more than often, fuels ethnoracial hatred: "Certain forms of nonconsciousness of race actually support racial inequality."[2]

At least three questions remain unaddressed by traditional studies: How can we explain the diversity of behavioral strategies among groups suffering from similar adversity? Beyond intergroup conflicts, how can we explain the resilience of intragroup conflicts? Why do both interracial conflicts and forms of cooperation take place simultaneously in response to institutional discrimination and socioeconomic inequality?

I believe that the framing of this alternative approach to ethnoracial violence requires a greater attention to proactive responses to adversity—including the use of violence by minorities as an integrative strategy. Any effective understanding of how groups assimilate and effectively integrate requires the study of the interplay between various aspects of adversity—and the choices that minorities make about their preferred forms of mobilization.[3] Indeed, groups engage in distinct forms of self-identification and mobilization. Responses to adversity span a large spectrum, from passivity at one end to violent protest and ruthless lawlessness at the other. Furthermore, understanding the dynamics of ethnoracial relations requires incorporating the impact of violence on racial identification—rather than simply assuming that racial identification fuels violence. As Kathleen Blee notes, "violence can be about *establishing* race rather than being an *effect* of preformed racial categories."[4]

I subsequently present my alternate argument with three components. First, I argue that adversity and prejudice motivate migrants and minorities to define themselves as a group. In doing so, I address what constitutes a core but overlooked dimension of American exceptionalism: the utility of violence. Second, I suggest that the study of adversity as a vector for assimilation should extend beyond majority-minority relations to include inter- and intragroup conflicts among minority groups. Finally, paradoxically, I contend that adversity itself provides opportunity structures for various discriminated groups to mobilize against exclusionary measures, and thus supports their integration—not only despite but also through the active use of violence.

The Utility of Violence

Ascribing utility to violence may itself seem contentious. Yet claiming violence has utility is distinct from justifying its use. My intent, rather, is to examine why and how violence has been used in America by nearly all groups engaged in ethnoracial relations to achieve their goal of integration.

Political scientists and philosophers have attempted to "make sense" of the resilience of violence in the modern era.[5] Donald Horowitz, for example, demonstrates that violence may be instrumentally related to a goal rather than a purely emotional response: "Violence may be a strategy employed to extract benefits from those who control resources, a way of securing influence in the political process for groups without routinized access, a mode of aggressive political participation."[6] "Violence," Hannah Arendt argues, "is distinguished by its instrumental character."[7] John Dodd, when noting that violence was both constitutive of the making of America and endemic to its contemporary fabric, argues that "violence is opportunistic, seizing upon the contingent in order to suspend the normal in favor of the exception."[8] And according to Rene Girard, "violence is frequently called irrational . . . . . . it has its reasons, however, and can marshal some rather convincing ones when the need arises."[9]

In contemplating an instrumental conception of violence, I analyze ethnoracial groups as a distinctive form of social movements. There are significant analogies between ethnoracial groups and comparable social movements that are "involved in conflictual relations with clearly identified opponents," share "a distinct collective identity," and use protest as a major source of pressure.[10] These three factors, according to Mario Diani, differentiate social movements from other forms of collective social or political behavior (such as political parties or unions). The same logic can fruitfully be applied to the study of ethnoracial groups who like other social movement actors:

1. engage in a social conflict to promote "initiatives meant to damage other social actors who are either denying them access to social resources they feel entitled to, or trying to take away from them resources over which they currently exert control"
2. share a collective identity that "defines the boundaries of a movement, which are by consequence inherently unstable"
3. exchange "practical and symbolic resources" in pursuit of the common good because of a shared commitment to a cause[11]

Presenting historical evidence, my purpose is therefore to bridge the gap between studies of social movements that diminish the theoretical significance of the ethnoracial dimensions of collective action, and racial, and immigration studies that often regard racial prejudice as the de facto explanation of intergroup conflict. Borrowing concepts and methods from the social movement literature helps highlight three important points.

First, ethnoracial reactions to adversity cannot be reduced to spontaneous expressions of anger that lead to sporadic and unplanned revolts.[12] Expressions of anger may appear impulsive to some observers but may nevertheless be strategically goal driven from the perspective of those who feel that they have no other option. Both riots and nonviolent demonstrations constitute, according to Doug McAdam, the "only available means by which excluded groups can overcome their traditional powerlessness within institutionalized political channels."[13] Disruptive actions by rioters can focus on short- and long-term goals. The former, for example, may be to express anger and the latter to achieve significant reforms.[14] The two are not mutually exclusive. Most emotions (such as fear, hatred, and resentment) are instrumental, driving people to reach a recognizable goal.[15] Most rational choices include values, preferences, and expectations that make no sense without reference to emotions. Combining rationalist formulations (such as resource mobilization theory) with nonrationalist elements (such as biased perceptions of other groups) may therefore be functional in explaining deliberative strategic decisions by ethnoracial behavior groups.[16]

Second, a cross-disciplinary fertilization between studies of social movements and ethnoracial studies provides a more dynamic understanding of ethnoracial relations in America—notably the varying intensity and forms of conflicts over time. Situations of deprivation do not automatically generate collective mobilizations. Researchers found that cities with less Black poverty experienced more race riots in the 1960s than those cities with higher rates of Black poverty.[17] Furthermore, various groups may adopt different behavioral patterns while facing similar forms of adversity. From a social movement perspective, these variations can be explained by the type and nature of the material and symbolic resources available. Resources explaining the tactical choices made by various groups relate, for example, to the existence of network configurations and social embeddedness. As McAdam notes, the turbulences of the 1960s showed that "while movements often did emerge against a backdrop of rapid change and generalized instability, it was rarely the most disorganized segments of society who were in the forefront of these struggles. On the contrary, analysts of contention began to amass impressive evidence attesting to the catalytic role of established groups of networks."[18] The civil rights movement, for example, was founded on established groups of networks (such as the central institutions of the southern Black community) and was supported by well-organized non-Black activist groups.

Third, defining ethnoracial groups as distinctive purposeful social movements facilitates the identification of the nature and outcomes of protest as well as the nature of intergroup relations—from coalition building to violent clashes. Mobilization can be motivated by competition with potential challengers who are perceived as threatening. It can also promote the emergence of "horizontal solidarity links, within the collective, and vertical links, integrating different collectives."[19] What matters is the purpose of the action (defined based on the social and psychological factors that move people to act collectively) as well as the content of the agenda. For minorities, this agenda may focus on the fight against persistent racial and socioeconomic inequalities. Yet, there are other axes of mobilization, such as class and gender, that form the basis for minority mobilization.[20] Furthermore, minorities mobilize for a variety of causes, contrary to the stereotypical assumptions that, for example, Hispanics are only interested in immigration issues or African Americans only react to racial issues. Adding an extra layer of complexity, collective action participants are not exclusively members of minority groups and/or low-status groups. Advantaged group members also engage in collective forms of action beyond the immediate goals of an ethnoracial group—either to help the disadvantaged or to oppose social changes to maintain their privileges.[21]

Violence as Identity Strategy

I turn now to the three main stages that structure the dynamic relationship between contextual adversity and forms of ethnoracial mobilization (including violent and nonviolent actions): reactive identification, identity politics, and contentious identity politics. The primary purpose is to explain the variety of ethnoracial mobilizations identified in the empirical chapters of this book—including variations in targets of violence, perpetrators of violence, timing of violence, and quality of violence (from urban riots to the so-called microaggressions). The secondary purpose is to identify the actual outcomes of the instrumental use of violence on contextual factors that result from feedback effects.

Reactive Identification

The first stage relates to identity construction as a central component of collective action. It is often regarded as a precondition for collective mobilization, which occurs when actors are able to define themselves vis-à-vis other actors as well as the boundaries of their mutual relationship. The standard assumptions are that a social movement is in place when collective identities develop and that these spurs protest behavior.[22] Studies, however, have questioned these assumptions, arguing that identity is not an immutable characteristic but rather is constructed by collective action. The causal link is therefore not only from identity to collective action but also from collective action to the continuous redefinitions of identity.[23]

Applied to ethnoracial groups, this means that race and ethnicity can be constructed in the course of interracial contact, including as a product of ethnoracial violence.[24] The identification process includes two sequential components.

The first is the formation of group consciousness resulting from being targeted by other groups. External threats intensify group cohesion, as members band together in defensive solidarities—as illustrated by the emergence of "Blackness," or indeed "whiteness." The identification of a "we" leads to the identification of the "other," defined as responsible for the ingroup's condition.[25]

The second component relates to the impact of group consciousness on collective conflictual behavior. A strong identification with a group increases the interest in the well-being of the group and provides incentives to mobilize—along a black/white divide but also, importantly, among ethnoracially defined subgroups. American history, as I document in chapters 2 and 3, is replete with examples of this identity strategy involving conflicts between and among ethnoracial groups. Both a positive identification with the ingroup and a negative identification of outgroups structure intergroup relations as well as intragroup relations. In all cases, identity is not an immutable given. It is, rather, a dimension of individual and group existence that can be constructed and reconstructed, and emphasized or de-emphasized, as the context changes.[26]

Identity Politics

Reactive identification leads to the second stage: identity politics, defined as a reaction to objective discrimination (socioeconomic inequalities, for example) and to subjective discrimination (based on perceptions of threats) quite independent of actual adversity. As a result, grievances expressed by various ethnoracial groups are equally legitimate from their perspective, independent of their objective socioeconomic status. As Jaquelien van Stekelenburg argues, "people live in a perceived world, they respond to the world as they perceive and interpret it."[27] This entails taking into account not only the effects of socioeconomic and institutional factors but also a series of psychological ones—such as feelings of material vulnerability, perceived relative deprivation, and a sense of alienation. As Lawrence Bobo and Vincent Hutchings's seminal study of group threat and competition suggests, this approach requires an analysis of socioeconomic grievances within a larger multiracial context, including "broad beliefs about social stratification and inequality" shared by ethnoracial groups and subgroups.[28] Contributions from political psychology include various approaches that, I believe, should be combined with traditional explanations of conflict such as the prejudice model (hostility based on perceptions and feelings of competitive threat)[29] and the group position model first formulated by Herbert Blumer in the 1950s[30] and later refined by others.[31]

Feelings of alienation subsequently negatively affect intergroup relations by fueling a perverse, if instrumental, competition over a recognition of their collective victimhood. The "belief in having suffered more than the out-group" is partly based on past victimization; it also translates into claims, irrespective of the actual severity of the respective suffering.[32] A minority status, perhaps surprisingly, is not a necessary condition for making such a claim. As Maureen Craig and Jennifer Richardson have demonstrated, members of majority groups can also experience a sense of lack of recognition for their historical victimhood.[33] A sense of relative deprivation results not only from comparison based on objective factors but also from comparison of one's situation measured against a cognitive standard—defined as what one deserves. When one group believes it is receiving less than this standard, discontent turns into grievances.

The main strategic purpose of identity politics is therefore to secure a real or symbolic position within mainstream society through a group's explicit selection of forms of behavior as part of its conscious, proactive empowerment strategy. This selection process relies on material resources available to various groups, such as their political opportunities, existing networks, the size and wealth of the community, and their public image. It also relies on the perception of other groups—compared to the dominant group as well as other minority groups. Variations in the combination of these components configure into different behavioral patterns among groups who objectively suffer from a similar level of discrimination—in terms of socioeconomic status, educational achievements, and civic incorporation. Those victims of structural violence may also, independently, feel subjectively discriminated against. They are therefore more likely to feel resentful and express serious grievances against both the dominant and other minority groups. A high level of resentment, in turn, increases the propensity to use discursive/and or physical violence. Alternatively, people who are objectively discriminated against but do not feel subjectively discriminated against—relative to other minority groups—are less inclined to engage in protest and/or violent expressions of their resentment. The link between objective discrimination and a subjective sense of discrimination is therefore critical in diagnosing the propensity toward violent group action.

Contentious Identity Politics

The third stage involves the shift from identity politics to contentious identity politics, which combines elements of contentious politics and distinctive ethnoracial grievances. The key components of contentious politics explain why and how violence has become a core element of ethnoracial relations in America. These include perceptions of threats that turn into grievances, contentious repertoires (such as claim-making used by various groups in their struggle for power and/or recognition), and rites of violence (such as violent urban protests and the use of symbols inherited from previous episodes of violence).[34] Marches organized by Black activists during the civil rights era, for example, replicated previous demonstrations, such as the parades of the Universal Negro Improvement Association and the Silent Protest Parade of July 28, 1917.[35] Protests of the 1960s inspired other ethnoracial groups (as illustrated by the Chicano movement) and still inspire key forms of activism today, such as Black Lives Matter.

I isolate two relevant elements included in the group position model that link to identity contentious politics. The first relates to the sense of group position, entailing assumptions of "proprietary claims" over specific rights, resources, and privileges. Blumer defined the "sense of proprietary claim" as the "feeling on the part of the dominant group of being entitled to either exclusive or prior rights in many important areas of life."[36] My approach includes proprietary claims expressed by both ethnoracial groups and those defined by religion, class, or gender. The second element relates to cognitive standards that derive from the long-term experiences of the members of ethnoracial groups. Feelings of hostility—and competition—emerge from any group's historically developed judgments about their respective position in the social order. I sum, "an analysis of how the sense of group position is formed should start with a clear recognition that it is an historical product."[37] The analysis should also include the extent to which, and how, a group interprets historic events—including historical amnesia or distortion—to legitimize its current claims about its appropriate relative position in the social order.

It is noteworthy that not all groups engage in a form of collective action. Grievances insufficiently justify protest. Indeed, groups with more resources and opportunities are more likely to mobilize, especially when they believe their actions can affect policies, because a sense of efficacy motivates collective action.[38] That sense of group efficacy, in turn, frames the nature of mobilization. It can stimulate the use of physical or discursive violence when a group perceives that strategy as efficient for its empowerment strategy.[39] Finally, some politicized groups become more radicalized, in terms of claims and/or behavior, leading to the justification of extreme measures (including intergroup violence or illegal direct action) as the only solution to address their grievances.[40]

I analyze these three main stages (reactive identification, identity politics, and mobilization based on contentious identity politics) from an historical perspective in the ensuing chapters. My intent is to provide a better understanding of the genesis and evolution of ethnoracial conflicts in America. Doing so helps to identify elements of continuity to the contemporary era—as illustrated by the 2020 protests of police brutality that echoed the riots of the "hot long summer" of 1968, which were themselves reminiscent of the "Red Summer" riots of 1919. Historic empowerment strategies (including the use of inter- and intragroup violence) influence group relations today, and current emergent groups are inspired by former ones when facing both similar and different challenges.

Key Notions

It is imperative to clarify specific terms I use in this book. In doing so, the main issue is to make sense of the ongoing debates about what is subsumed under terms such as racism, racial prejudice, racialization, and identity politics applied to race relations in a multiracial society.

Racism as a concept has originally involved two core elements. The first one is differentiation, when members of society make distinctions between different groups based on a primordialist conception of individual and group identity. The basis of group characteristics was assumed to rest on a biological conception of race: biological essences are attached to psychological and behavioral characteristics that are presumed to be genetic.[41] The second one is inferiorization, the premise being that the superiority of one's own race justified treating other groups as inferior. Inferiorization was institutionalized in various ways such as slavery, imperialism, and segregation. This type of organicist racism, although widespread among white supremacist and neo-Nazi organizations, is no longer the dominant racist narrative.

Another type, however, subsequently emerged entailing a shift from a biological to a cultural conception of race. "Race as culture" emphasizes group differences in terms of language, habits, religion, and customs. As David Theo Goldberg notes, "primarily at issue in such cultural differentiations are group circumscribed values."[42] This form of identification does not always imply hierarchical judgements of superiority or inferiority as the basis for exclusion, but it always involves an antipathy toward groups who are discriminated against on the grounds of their cultural identity (broadly and vaguely defined). What has been called "new racism" in the 1980s has since fueled nativist propaganda and anti-immigrant policies designed to curb the so-called invasion of America by different peoples threatening its cultural identity.[43] I provide examples in this book of this cultural conception. They are mostly supported by members of the white dominant group but also by other groups whose members justify their antipathy toward others in cultural and religious terms.[44]

In addition, I focus on the extremely troubling effect of this apparent softening of the content of racial beliefs. Categorizations based on culture instead of biology may seem less toxic. Generally, as Lawrence Blum argues, "to attribute characteristics to a group's culture is a way of saying that the characteristics are not inherent."[45] Yet, these characteristics often refer to an implicit reductionist process of cultural differences.[46] This cultural racism produces modes of legitimation that derive from the defense of "cultural identities" by using more refined arguments predicated on privileging difference. The thesis that certain immigrants cannot assimilate illustrates this process, as well as those arguments based on the imperative of preserving the dominant group's identity. Furthermore, some characteristics are viewed as part of "a racial group's 'nature' and hence define its racial fate."[47] Supposedly inherited cultural characteristics, wrongly perceived as more acceptable, remains tainted with the same assumptions as inferiorization although such claims do not explicitly include references to a biological-racial hierarchy. I contend that such assumptions about inherited characteristics play a key role in race relations, as illustrated by the effects of racial stereotypes (such as the Asian minority model or the Black and Hispanic "culture of segregation") on inter- and intragroup conflicts. I demonstrate throughout this book how such unfounded biases generate grievances among various ethnoracial groups and how these grievances fuel cycles of contentious politics.

Prejudice involves, according to Gordon Allport, "an antipathy based upon a faulty and inflexible generalization" that places "the object of prejudice at some disadvantage not merited by his own conduct."[48] Not all antipathy is prejudice, and not all prejudice is racial. Other factors play a role in the negative perception of other groups, such as socioeconomic competition for scarce resources. I provide examples of perceptions of others as posing a threat that do not directly involve racial prejudice. This perspective helps in understanding why minorities can be simultaneously engaged in conflictual relationships and in "rainbow coalitions" against a common threat. However, all antipathy toward a racial group tends to be prejudicial in at least two ways. First, negative perceptions often relate to faulty generalizations, such as immigrants "taking jobs from natives" or being more prone to criminality than natives. Second, the behavioral manifestation of racial prejudice is discrimination based on ascribed characteristics, based on either race or the essentialization of other factors (such as gender, religion, and national origin).

More to the point, racial prejudice results from a group position defined by Herbert Blumer as "the position of group to group" resulting from the degree to which individuals feel their own group is at risk for losing significant resources to other groups.[49] Blumer focused on the sense of group position held by the dominant racial group in its efforts to secure white privilege. The group position perspective has been expanded by race scholars who oppose the color-blind egalitarianism.[50] Whites, they argue, know that their whiteness is privileged but discount it as a now discontinued prerogative of the past. Instead, they focus on the opportunities provided by socioeconomic mobility and its positive effects on race egalitarianism and racial harmony to preserve their material interests while denying their role in the perpetuation of racial inequalities.

Building on these contributions, I add two interrelated aspects of racial prejudice in my analysis. First, feelings of being threatened are widespread among minorities, which explains why I study all the ethnoracial groups involved in the ongoing process of group accommodation and/or hostility. Racial prejudice can be manifested in any racial group. Minorities express racial prejudice toward whites, mostly as the result of racist victimization. Considering this dimension of racial prejudice does not suggest that anti-Black racism and anti-white racism are "morally equivalent."[51] The objective is not to compare the intensity of victimization or the respective degree of legitimacy of any side's grievance. Rather, it is to appreciate the complexity of race relations in an increasingly multiracial society and examine their consequences. This leads to the second aspect that I examine: the targets of racial prejudice expressed by minorities can in fact be other minorities and even—in extreme cases—members of their own group, as I illustrate.

Racialization signifies the extension of racial meaning to social practices, political preferences, and opinions about policies. According to Michael Tesler, it is a process "whereby racial attitudes and race are brought to bear on political preferences." This affects the perceptions of race-targeted policies (such as affirmative action and federal aid to minorities) as well as ostensibly nonracial issues (such as welfare, social security, taxes, and gun control).[52] Racialization has increasingly influenced different political decisions—from political affiliation to voting choices—as well as sociocultural debates such as same-sex marriage and most aspects of "culture wars."[53] This pattern even extended to medical questions, such as the wearing of masks during the COVID-19 pandemic. I provide evidence in the second and third parts of this book about the spillover effect of racialization into mass politics, notably in terms of ideological polarization and societal fragmentation.

Furthermore, I illustrate how racialization affects ethnoracial relations when it involves identity politics by examining four sequential aspects. First, identity politics can be defined as the strategy used by ethnoracial minorities as a response to adversity. This formulation relates to the development of groupness resulting from group categorization and "othering" (the characteristics attributed to an ingroup by outgroup members) as well as self-identification (such as Black Power), which energized the civil rights movement. African Americans have managed their stigma by fighting for their rights on the basis of their collective identity and have—through a painful process—obtained both egalitarian rights (equality before the law with the Voting Rights Act of 1965) and differential rights designed to address socioeconomic inequalities and discrimination (affirmative action program under Title VII of the 1964 Rights Act). During this period, identity politics referred to social protests and political activities rooted in the experience of injustice used to claim greater self-determination, political rights, and social equity.

Second, identity politics can be understood against the background of "pan-ethnicity," when disparate ethnocultural groups (such as Hispanics) coalesce under a common "umbrella identity" to gain visibility, recognition, social justice, political influence, and power. This identity strategy, largely influenced by the legacy of the civil rights era, has helped non-Black minorities gain access to affirmative action programs.[54] The scope of identity politics became broader with the inclusion of various minority groups. These groups asserted a sense of identity based on a shared experience of discrimination. This sense of common identity, in turn, energized their mobilization against discrimination. It also generated tensions with African Americans.

Third, identity politics relates to the struggle of intra groups when they face oppression on the basis of the interconnection between race and other identity factors such as sex and gender. This conception has been central to the emergence of Black feminism (notably the Combahee River Collective), intersectionality, LGBT social movements, and Queer activism. The initial goal of these groups was to overcome marginalization and discrimination. Intersectionality was mainly conceived as a source of social empowerment through an assertion of dignity, a sense of community, and tolerance toward a growing assortment of "different differences."

Fourth, identity politics is also part of the reactive identification strategy increasingly adopted by a multitude of groups (racial and nonracial, left-wing and right-wing). From this perspective, identity politics has become more exclusive, shifting from the fight against oppression to separatist politics based on a sense of entitlement. Some groups have used it as a rallying cry for exclusionary measures that today reinforce harmful structures of race, class, and gender. In the extreme, a minority status is no longer a necessary condition for making identity politics claims, as illustrated by the revival of "white identity" among those who support the current "whitelash."

Consequently, identity politics mostly refers today to various forms of contentious politics by which a group's identity is essentialized for inclusive (more rarely) and exclusive (often) purposes. Interestingly, this trend raises concerns from scholars across the racial spectrum.[55] Building on their contributions, I therefore analyze how contentious identity politics can consolidate ethnoracial coalitions as well as forms of competition between identity-based social movements that favor ethnoracial separatism and possibly sociopolitical fragmentation.

In doing so, I examine varying facets of violence—from the physical to the discursive. Traditional forms of physical violence coexist today with a number of actual or perceived outrages and various breaches of normative expectations.[56] As a result, what is regarded as forms of confrontational behavior has now expanded. It now extends beyond overtly observable behavior to the unilateral subjective perception of a slight by another individual or group (such as microaggressions). This hyperbolic acceptance of a broadened definition of what constitutes violence illustrates a paradoxical aspect of America: it is a uniquely physically violent country among Western democracies—yet one simultaneously becoming more sensitive to nonphysical violence. Complicating matters further, it concurrently nurtures a countervailing reaction to this sensitivity by groups who feel alienated and targeted by antidiscrimination measures. Racism, as well as antiracism and anti-antiracism, subsequently fuel a wide range of grievances that provide the foundation for further conflict. Thus linked, sensitivity to violence and acts of violence continue to wrestle in a corrosive and escalating cycle.

2

VIOLENCE AS THE CAUSE OF ETHNORACIAL IDENTITIES

Historical examples of contentious identity politics predate contemporary ethnoracial group relations based on the white/black divide. Group relations were clearly color coded from the formation of the republic. Yet, they cannot be regarded as static: there is plentiful evidence of the fluidity and complexity of ethnoracial identities since the colonial period.

The emergence of whiteness illustrates this conflictual fluidity. To define white identity "by what it is not: blackness," as Nell Irvin Painter argues in her *History of White People*, was inadequate because whiteness has a "history of multiplicity."[1] David Roediger notes that "evocations of an invasion by non-white 'Slavonic,' 'Latin,' Italian and Jewish races resonate strangely for modern U.S. readers."[2] He adds, "Other labels, such as 'situationally white,' 'not quite white,' 'off-white,' semi-racialized,' and 'conditionally white,' convey the ambiguity and uncertainty of an immigrant racial status that was constantly under review."[3] Matthew Frye Jacobson provided a vivid description of "the racial odysseys" of many groups (including the Irish, Armenians, Italians, Poles, Greeks, Ruthenians, and Finns) who may have come "ashore in the United States as 'free white persons' under the terms of reigning naturalization law; yet those racial credentials were not equivalent to those of Anglo-Saxon 'old stock' . . . All these groups became Caucasians only over time, and all of them found certain challenges to their racial pedigrees along the way."[4]

"Blackness" as a category was mostly constructed by whites through racism, racial policies, and racial violence. As Foner and Fredrickson pointedly suggested, "blacks are the quintessentially racialized Americans. There would be no African American identity had it not been for a history of massive oppression and stigmatization."[5] The evidence is clear: African Americans were subject to far more racial violence than any other group. Records from the mid-nineteenth century to the 1930s showed that the lynching of African Americans exceeded that of new immigrants by 75 to 1.[6] African Americans were required to identify as Blacks, lacking options available to other groups.[7] According to Omi and Winant, the "ethnicity based paradigm," which suggests that race—as a social category—is "but one of a number of determinants of ethnicity," has always denied the "extent to which racial inequality differed from ethnic inequality."[8] However, in addition to the specificity and continuity of racial oppression, it is worth noting that even Blackness has gone through a series of historical vicissitudes (including acts of violence against other minorities).

A historical account of the emergence of ethnoracial identities provides a better understanding of the relative malleability of identity politics in America. It helps clarify the relationship between contextual adversity, reactive identification among ethnoracial groups, mobilization patterns (involving discursive and physical violence between and among groups), and the resulting contentious identity politics based on interrelated cycles of grievances.

Whiteness Defined through Violence

Many aspects of the historical construction of whiteness are well known, predominantly referring to contextual changes, such as the evolution of the demographic composition of the US population and the subsequent reconstitution of racial categorization. The notion of "white entitlement" was applied to the first census in 1790. It was also applied to immigration. The Naturalization Act of 1790, for example, provided that "free white persons of satisfactory character" would be eligible for naturalization after two years of residence in the United States. Blacks were blatantly excluded on racial grounds. Yet, "free" and "satisfactory character" also excluded white immigrants bound in temporary servitude as well as convicts and the indigent. The Naturalization Act of 1870 did deem whites and persons of African descent as eligible for citizenship. This provision, however, proved problematic in practice. It was prejudicially used against African Americans as well as European immigrants whose white identity remained controversial.

Each wave of immigration added further complexity to the racial categorization of groups who, at least until World War II, were "not quite white." Approximately 27.6 million immigrants arrived between 1881 and 1930—mostly from southern and eastern Europe. Although they were defined as white under the law, they were racialized by old-stock Americans who wanted to protect their "sense of propriety claims" over resources, rights, and privileges. As Nancy Foner and George Fredrickson note, "with the arrival in large numbers of immigrants who differed significantly in culture or phenotype from the Americans who were descended from the original (mostly British) colonists, difficult questions arose as to where they might fit in the preexisting racial order."[9]

What was also largely documented was related to consensual, nonviolent forms of integration. Most studies of assimilation focus on traditional patterns of mobilization, such as ethnic lobbies and politics. The main assumption of this work is that European immigrants were able to join the "white mainstream" through the creation of ethnic lobbies, religious organizations, and political participation—as illustrated by the ways in which Irish Americans adapted and changed American politics—notably "urban ethnic politics which they practically invented."[10][11] In addition to democratic incorporation, the other mechanisms of assimilation included acculturation and social mobility, both facilitated by the expansion of higher education from a selective to a mass system.

What remains largely neglected in the retelling of American history is that some "not-yet-white" groups were the victims of violence on behalf of old-stock Americans but were simultaneously perpetrators of racist violence against nonwhite groups to become white, and subsequently assimilate. This violence had numerous dimensions, ranging from discursive to physical violence (such as mobs, riots, lynching, and gang violence). The intensity of these differing forms of violence varied over time. Yet, they played a crucial role in how the racial and ethnic identities of various groups were, and continue to be, formed and transformed.

Violence among "Whites"

Before the mid-nineteenth century, "white persons" were divided between settlers of English birth or descent and the "nonwhite" immigrants—which included Germans and the Irish. The English, classified as superior Saxons, expressed their prejudice against the inferior white races, such as Teutonics, Celts, and Hebrews.

Germans were especially discriminated against in Pennsylvania, where they amounted to one-third of the population by the mid-eighteenth century. Most German immigrants moved to the Midwest after 1850, where they formed the original white settler population—thereby limiting their clashes with "Anglo-Americans." The influx of immigrants from south, central, and eastern Europe, categorized as the new inferior races (such as Iberic, Southern Italian, Eastern European, and Hebrew), benefited Germans who resultingly joined the British and Scandinavians in the great "Gothic family." However, during World War I, German immigrants and German Americans suffered from harassment, internment, and lynchings (such as Robert Prager who was lynched in Illinois in April 1918). The American Defense Society encouraged the public burning of German language books and campaigned to change the names of cities and streets. Even the names of German dishes were anglicized: "liberty cabbage" for sauerkraut, "liberty dog" for Dachshund dog, and "liberty steak" for hamburger.

Ethnic violence targeted Italians in a similar fashion. Approximately fifty Italians were lynched between 1890 and 1920, including one episode in Tallulah, Louisiana, in 1899 where five Italians were murdered. Italians lynched in New Orleans in 1891 were described by newspapers as "colored," illustrating the popular belief that Italians—as "Guineans"—were part African in ancestry. Furthermore, suspicions about ties to anarchist terrorism were focused on Italians during the late nineteenth century. Followers of Luigi Galleani, the guru of anticapitalist anarchism, were blamed for dozens of bombings of police stations, courts, and other public places. Suspicion, and discrimination, increased after the Wall Street bombings of 1920, which resulted in thirty-eight deaths and 140 injuries. Thousands of Italians were arrested and five hundred deported, although their culpability was never proven.

Anti-Semitism among Anglo Saxons was widespread. Born into a Jewish American family and a graduate of Cornell University, Leo Frank was famously lynched by a white mob in Atlanta in 1915. Photographs of the lynching were sold as postcards in local stores, and newspapers declared him to be "inconclusively white."[12] An immigration quota imposed in 1924 severely affected Jewish Poles. Restrictionism remained firmly entrenched from 1932 until World War II during a period when anti-Semitism peaked in America. Jews were targeted by the KKK and other extremist organizations that perceived them either as representative of evils of capitalism or, conversely, as Bolshevik agents.

Furthermore, some members of other "probationary white" groups, such as Italians, expressed strong anti-Semitic feelings while they themselves suffered from racial discrimination. Italian Americans and Jewish Americans were two of the largest immigrant minorities in America during the interwar period. Most Italian Americans distanced themselves from the anti-Jewish policies adopted by Mussolini in the mid-1920s. According to Stefano Luconi, however, anti-Semitism in the "Little Italies" could be explained by "competition on the job market and for cheap housing in immigrant slums."[13] Yet other factors suggested the importance of crude racial and religious prejudice, as illustrated by the anti-Semitic campaign launched by the New York City–based *Il Grido della Stirpe* newspaper. Other Italian American outlets, such as *La Tribuna Italiana d'America* reprinted the virulent anti-Semitic speeches of Charles E. Coughlin—a Catholic priest of Irish descent whose weekly radio program and newspaper, *Social*

Justice, enjoyed a broad audience in the late 1930s. These anti-Semitic feelings in the Italian American community widely persisted during the war and, indeed, in the early postwar period, as illustrated by attacks against Jews committed by Italian American students in Chicago in 1943.

Securing Whiteness through Violence against Nonwhites

To become "Caucasian" from the 1930s onward entailed not simply looking "white," but, as Jacobson argues, it required being sanctioned as *"conclusively, certifiably, scientifically* white."[14] One way to achieve this objective was through the use of violence by immigrants against nonwhite groups. Geographical location often mattered, as illustrated by variations in the scapegoating mechanism. Italians were not considered white on the East Coast where their main goal was to mark their separation from Blacks. But, as the largest foreign-born group in California, Italians had long been white in San Francisco, where the racial "inferiors" were the Chinese, Japanese, and Mexicans. Some, such as prominent congressman Anthony Caminetti, were active members of the anti-Japanese movement prior to World War I.

In the urban Northeast, hostility toward African Americans became an essential component of an Italian integration strategy. In her study of Italian American and African American encounters in New Jersey's cities, for example, Nancy Carnevale notes: "Going back into the twentieth century, it is not difficult to find incidents of racial violence by Italian Americans. Although other white Catholics participated in such violence, Italian Americans have long been considered the vanguard of white racism."[15] Their hostility toward African Americans was often fueled by competition over employment and housing, which continued for several decades. Even during the civil rights era, "any existing racism on the part of Italian Americans tended to intensify through particular experiences with blacks—public housing, neighborhood desegregation—that Italian Americans perceived as threatening their interests."[16] Yet, before Italians became Caucasians in the postwar era, this hostility was also part of "the construction of white racial identities through anti-Black violence."[17] This latter point was epitomized by the exacerbation of the antipathies between Italian Americans and African Americans in the aftermath of Italy's 1935 invasion of Ethiopia.[18] Events thousands of miles away, involving the descendants of very few African Americans, provided the pretext for hostility. This axis of conflict transcended the war. After World War II, Italian Americans organized violent protests of school desegregation and busing in northern cities such as Boston. This anti-Black violence persisted long after the 1960s, as illustrated by the killing of Yusef Hawkins, a Black male, in Brooklyn in

1989 by Italian American youths who wrongly believed he was dating a local girl, themes explored in Spike Lee's celebrated movie *Do the Right Thing*.

The Irish immigrants were frequently referred to in the early nineteenth century as "n——turned inside out," and "the negroes, for their part, were sometimes called 'smoked Irish.'"[19] Willing to cooperate with other whites on a racial basis, Irish communities increasingly rejected incursions of African Americans into their neighborhoods to enhance and consolidate their relatively new "whiteness." Urban competition with African Americans sometimes turned violent, as illustrated by a rampage through the Black district of Philadelphia in 1834. By the 1850s, the New York waterfront had become an "Irish preserve" where Irish longshoremen battled Black workers. In 1862, a largely Irish mob in Brooklyn attacked the Black employees of a tobacco factory. The factory was allowed to reopen only after Irish workers obtained the guarantee that no Blacks would be hired. Like their Italian counterparts, Irish anti-Black hostility was a way, according to Ignatiev, "to enter the white race . . . a strategy to secure an advantage in a competitive society."[20] As a result, many Irish opposed abolitionism, supporting the proslavery stance of Southern Democrats. After World War I, Irish Americans used anti-Black sentiments to forge an alliance with other whites (such as Greeks and Austrians) in opposition to new immigrants. During the Chicago race riots of 1919, for example, members of an Irish gang dressed in blackface and burned down homes in a neighborhood populated by Polish and Lithuanian immigrants. They hoped that the eastern Europeans would believe that Blacks attacked them and use retaliatory violence against Blacks, in solidarity, as a way to consolidate the whitening solidarity of all Europeans.

Irish Americans often expressed the same hostility toward Asians and Mexicans in California. The Order of Caucasians, created in Sacramento in 1876, attracted Irish workers who wanted to expel the Chinese from America. Anti-Asian sentiment helped the Irish become white as well as successful political leaders, as illustrated by James D. Phelan. The son of an Irish immigrant, Phelan was the mayor of San Francisco from 1897 to 1902, before later representing California as a senator between 1915 and 1921. Between holding the two offices, he established himself as the leader of the Anti-Asian movement—fighting for the "holy cause" of Japanese exclusion and pushing through California's discriminatory Alien Land Law of 1913. He remained active in the anti-Asian movement after World War I, collaborating with the Japanese Exclusion League of California and supporting the anti-Asian Immigration Act of 1924.

German Americans also distanced themselves from African Americans to secure their whiteness. Previously some German immigrants, especially among the Forty-Eighters, had supported the Abolitionist movement until the late 1860s, assisting the former bondsmen in their battle for equality. Hermann Raster, a notable Forty-Eighter for example, published antislavery pamphlets and helped Lincoln secure the electoral support of German Americans. Yet, solidarity with the Black antislavery movement rapidly declined among German immigrant communities after 1870. In his study of German immigrants in America, Mischa Honeck notes that "Contrary to many of their older kinsmen, the next generation of arrivals from German lands had no personal recollections of emancipation . . . Pressure to succumb to the white American majority was further magnified by the influx of new immigrant groups—Italians, Eastern Europeans, Russian Jews." As a result, "to avoid identification with these 'other whites,' German Americans learnt to despise the country's Black population."[21] Violent confrontations ensued, illustrated by anti-Black riots initiated by Germans in Rochester in 1872. Anti-German sentiment, which peaked during World War I, provided incentives for Germans to identify themselves as white ethnics—thus distancing themselves further from African Americans, who arrived in many neighborhoods during the Great Migration. Furthermore, anti-Black sentiment was reactivated during the interwar period, especially among supporters of neo-Nazi organizations.

Jews proved the exception among European immigrants to this trend toward rejecting African Americans. Jews themselves lived in a racial limbo right up until the 1950s. They were formerly characterized as "marginally white" and only progressively, incrementally defined as white relative to Blackness. This "middleman minority status"[22] began in the mid-nineteenth century, when Jews and Blacks shared key elements—from physical proximity in the northern cities (where Jews from eastern Europe settled during the Great Migration) to a similar experience as the victims of racial persecution, notably in the south. Jewish newspapers drew parallels between Blacks and Jews living in ghettos as well as between violence against Blacks in the United States and the pogroms endured by European Jews. Jewish organizations—such as the American Jewish Committee and the American Jewish Congress—were actively involved in campaigns against anti-Black racial prejudice. In the early twentieth century, they contributed to the funding of the NAACP and supported racially mixed labor organizations. These Black Jewish political affinities were based on a shared rejection of the discriminatory dominance of Anglo-whiteness as well as a greater degree of cultural accommodation. Jewish producers in the entertainment industry, for example, often included Black culture in music, films, and plays.

Cooperation between Jewish and African American organizations peaked during the civil rights movement—the so-called golden age of Jewish and African American collaboration. The two leaders of the Leadership Conference on Civil Rights were Walter White, an African American, and Arnold Aronson, an American Jew. "My people were brought to America in chains," Martin Luther King Jr.

told the Jewish Congress, "Your people were driven here to escape the chains fashioned for them in Europe. Our unity is born of our common struggle for centuries."[23] Jewish leaders, such as Abraham Joshua Heschel, joined Martin Luther King Jr. during the marches from Selma to Montgomery. During the "Freedom Summer" of 1964, two Jewish activists (Andrew Goodman and Michael Schwerner) and one Black activist (James Chaney) were murdered together by the KKK outside Philadelphia, Mississippi. Their deaths, symbolically so important, marked the culmination of the rapprochement between American Jews and Black civil rights activists.

Yet, problems nonetheless existed. One source of tension was the claim of Black American Jews that they were the authentic descendants of the ancient Israelites. Furthermore, while some more radical Jewish activists remained involved in the civil rights movement, most Jews began to question the violent tactics used by the Black Power Movement. The 1960s sit-ins and riots heightened tensions between Jews and African Americans. From the Jewish perspective, "pickets, civil disobedience, and nationalist rhetoric seemed particularly dangerous;" furthermore, "Skeptical Jewish leaders backed off from earlier alliances. Many of their constituents, now in suburbs, felt less concerned with urban strife."[24] Dozens of episodes reflected these tensions between the late 1960s and the 1990s, as illustrated by the struggle over control of schools in Brooklyn and legal fights about affirmative action programs.

The Jewish community's pathway to becoming white was therefore the result of a largely nonviolent process. It originated in the post-Holocaust rejection of the concept of a "Jewish race" and concluded with their self-assignation of having an ethnocultural identity. Nonetheless, despite rejecting the strategic violence common to other European groups, they distinguished themselves from African Americans. According to anthropologist Karen Brodkin, for example, "Jewish whiteness became American whiteness" after World War II when Jewish intellectuals "contrasted themselves with a mythic blackness."[25] Jews, the historian Eric Goldstein argues, "hoped they could assuage the doubts of the dominant society by affirming their place as unqualified whites. Central to this effort was demonstrating a clear social distinction between themselves and America's principal racial outsiders, African Americans."[26] Furthermore, Jews for a while became a "model minority," despite persistent anti-Semitism among both whites and Blacks, when successive immigrant communities (mainly Asians and Hispanics) became the "new foreigners." Reciprocally, however, American Jews had to pay "the price of whiteness" when anti-Semitism became a core component of a more generalized antiwhite sentiment among nonwhite minorities.[27]

Complicated Blackness

"Before the Civil Rights revolution of the 1960s," Painter notes, "American history was largely the story of white people."[28] The capacity for Black people to mobilize against oppression remained limited. However, they did not remain passive. One response to violence was civil protest (sometimes violent) in combating the "racial state," dating back to the republic's founding.[29] At least twenty-five insurrections took place before the American Revolution. Antilynching campaigns were launched during Reconstruction, and a series of riots followed that stretched from the interwar period to after World War II. Another response was nonviolent initiatives. These included boycotts and "Self-Help" campaigns during the 1930s and 1940s—as illustrated by the "Don't Buy Where You Can't Work" campaign in Harlem in 1942. Martin Luther King Jr. and other leaders of the Montgomery Improvement Association, inspired by Mahatma Gandhi's nonviolent movement for independence in India, led nonviolent initiatives such as the Montgomery bus boycott and other desegregation initiatives in the South. In 1961, activists from the Student Nonviolent Coordinating Committee (SNCC) tested the parameters of desegregation on interstate transportation as "Freedom Riders." Two years later, the Southern Christian Leadership Conference (SCLC) launched a series of protest marches, starting with the Birmingham campaign and culminating with the March on Washington under the leadership of Martin Luther King Jr. Then, in March 1965, the SCLC and Martin Luther King Jr. organized two marches from Selma to Montgomery.

Blackness as a Reactive Identity

The quest for an identity fueled these various forms of mobilization. Enduring the effects of categorization imposed by whites, African Americans fought to turn them into a positive sense of "peoplehood."[30] Efforts to forge a group consciousness dated back to the colonial period, when African Americans had to affirm their own sense of group identity in reaction to a negative conception of Blackness constructed by whites. During their enslavement, Painter argues, "African Americans created value systems that critiqued and countered those of mainstream American society."[31] From a white perspective, slave insurrections were "conspiracies" organized by "bad" Blacks. Insurrectionists, in contrast, were regarded by Blacks as heroes who gave new meaning to the word "bad." "In black vernacular," Painter notes, "'bad' designated a person of strength and bravery, a good person."[32]

Efforts to reinforce a positive image of Blackness persisted over time, illustrated by the growth of Black newspapers and magazines (up to two hundred by

1908). They fought negative stereotypes, as well as celebrating the Black cultural flowering during the Harlem Renaissance in the 1920s whose major theme was Black pride, symbolized by the "New Negro." The collection of essays edited by Alain Locke in 1925 illustrated the "rebirth and renewal" of Black Americans through "self-expression"—a pride in Blackness as a counterreaction to racial discrimination.[33] Black writers and artists sought to challenge negative stereotypes by promoting a vibrant Black identity, as well as the contribution of African Americans to the process of American modernity. Du Bois, in the name of "race unity," called for the creation of "race organizations: Negro colleges, Negro newspapers, Negro business organizations, a Negro school of literature and art . . . Not only is all this necessary for positive advance, but it is also absolutely imperative for negative defense."[34]

Securing Blackness through Prejudice

Another related way to homogenize group identity among Blacks was to oppose other ethnoracial groups—whites, broadly defined, but also white subgroups as well as nonwhite minorities (such as Asians and Hispanics). Like "conditionally whites" discriminating against nonwhites to secure their whiteness, African Americans manifested antipathy and hostility toward other ethnoracial groups. "In the original meaning of 'racism' the assumption was that it was something that white people felt, believed, and practiced toward people of color," Lawrence Blum notes in addressing the vexed question "Can blacks be racists?"[35] Historical and contemporary evidence suggests that the use of the vocabulary of racism is not confined to whites: Blacks, Asians, Hispanics, and other minority groups have expressed—and still express—racial prejudice toward whites, other groups of color, and members of their own group. When Blacks manifest racial antipathy against whites, it is generally a form of what Blum defined as "reactive racism"—"racist attitudes developed as a result of racist victimization." But Blum importantly adds that "not all racism on the part of persons of color is reactive racism."[36] Hostility against nonwhites is often compensatory for actual or perceived racism toward Blacks. It is worth noting the role of historical legacy in the resilience of racial contempt. This legacy operates by way of the identity of the target group "insofar as that identity is bound up with the memory of oppression"—regardless of its veracity.[37]

The complexity of the relationship between African Americans and Jews provides a relevant example of this process. Black negative perceptions of Jews dated back to the colonial period, fueled by the issue of slavery. A nominal number of Jews were engaged in international trade, and thus in the triangular flows of slavery, sugar, and rum.[38] A few Jews owned or traded slaves in the South—a fact recalled in the 1960s by Black organizations—while the overwhelming proportion of northern Jews opposed slavery. Interactions between Jewish immigrants and Blacks increased in the north during the Great Migration, when they lived together in the same neighborhoods. In some places, however, there were tensions between Jewish shop owners and Black customers, as well as between Jewish landlords and Black tenants. Martin Luther King Jr., evoking these tensions, wrote: "The Negro ends up paying a color tax, and this has happened in instances where Negroes actually confronted Jews as the landlord or the storekeeper."[39] Scholars of race relations questioned the use of Black culture by Jewish producers and artists, as illustrated by the controversial role played by Al Jolson in *The Jazz Singer*. Jewish actors who portrayed Blacks were retrospectively perceived as being exploitative. Historian Jeffrey Melnick, for example, argues that "While both Jews and African-Americans contributed to the rhetoric of musical affinity, the fruits of this labor belonged exclusively to the former."[40] Other scholars and Black activists were even more vehement, accusing Jewish producers of racism to preserve control of the film industry.[41]

As I noted, African Americans and Jews cooperated closely over civil rights in the mid-twentieth century. Yet economic tensions between Blacks and Jews also crystalized during the same period, mostly due to increasing socioeconomic inequalities. In short, "while relatively few blacks and Jews interacted politically (outside of the Left), far more encountered each other in economic venues. In virtually every case, Jews had the upper hand . . . they were able to benefit from the American system and to succeed more quickly than African Americans."[42] In some cities, Jews owned a large majority of the stores in many Black neighborhoods while an increasing number of them resided in suburban neighborhoods. Like African Americans and other minorities, Jews were excluded from new suburban developments and rental properties under restrictive covenants during the interwar period. Yet despite housing discrimination, Jews subsequently avoided the urban ghettoization that African Americans faced. Jews may not have fully benefited from the "smooth residential dispersal" of "white ethnics." But African Americans, in most places, endured "persistent seclusion."[43]

Furthermore, some radical Black activists distrusted whites, including white liberals who supported the civil rights movement—among whom Jews were overrepresented. Black anti-Semitism became visible, as illustrated by the claims against Jews in speeches made by some leaders of the Nation of Islam (NOI) such as Elijah Muhammad, Khalid Abdul Muhammad, and Louis Farrakhan. According to the NOI's publications, Jews significantly benefited from a repressive Jim Crow system by exploiting Black workers and spreading "white working-class racism" in the labor unions. NOI also claimed, contrary to all historical evidence, that "Jews were found collaborating with and even financing such racial terrorists as the Ku Klux Klan . . . When lynching and massacres occurred in America, Jewish leaders often praised them, and some in the Jewish press cheered them on."[44]

Black Jewish relations finally turned violent in the Afro-Caribbean and Orthodox Jewish neighborhoods of Brooklyn's Crown Heights in 1991. After the accidental death of a Black child, Black youths attacked Jewish passersby and stabbed one Jewish child to death. For many, this event marked a turning point in the history of Black and Jewish relations. It appeared that few shared issues remained, even for those still committed to Black-Jewish collaboration. The Black community struggled with problems of poverty, racism, crime, and poor education, while Jews became increasingly concerned with issues surrounding Israeli security, Jewish "continuity," and church state separation.[45] Meanwhile, anti-Semitism grew among Black faculty and students on college campuses. Africana Studies programs competed with Jewish Studies programs for college curricula funding. African American historians of slavery collected data on Jewish participation in the slave trade. Leonard Jeffries, a professor at the City College of New York (where he organized the Black Studies department in 1972), for example, denounced the "Jewish conspiracy against African people" and apportioned the blame for everything—from the slave trade to the allegedly anti-Black content of Hollywood movies—to "rich Jews."[46]

Opposition to non-Black groups encouraged the homogenization of Blackness. Yet, there were centrifugal forces that counteracted the popular ideal of Black unity—such as socioeconomic cleavages and political or religious affiliations. These were enhanced by the arrival of Black immigrants—primarily from Africa, Latin America, and the Caribbean—who added another layer of complexity regarding the contours of Blackness. This foreign-born Black population represented less than 1 percent of the US Black population in 1960. But the Hart-Cellar Act of 1965 facilitated the number of Black immigrants multiplying by nearly sevenfold by 1980. Perceived as African Americans by non-Blacks, they defined themselves differently by focusing on their distinct ethnic identity/nationality. In her study on racial positioning in US higher education, Chrystal A. George Mwangi notes that "because of racial discrimination, some black immigrants actively work against being perceived as African Americans . . . social distancing can include the use of cultural objects (e.g., national flags, accents) to highlight an ethnic/foreign identity that can protect them from racial stereotypes and prejudice that are projected towards African Americans. Another form of social distancing includes avoiding relationships with African Americans."[47] Some African Americans, in turn, perceived Black immigrants as latecomers who align with whites and benefit from opportunities that African Americans fought for, without having a concern about continuing Black subordination.

Together as Different "Others"

While white groups were becoming accepted as white at different speeds, Asian and Hispanic groups remained "in-between peoples" for a long time after World War II. The uncertainty of their racial status (neither Black nor conclusively white) was the product of efforts by whites to consolidate their own recognition as fully white. Asian and Hispanic immigrants shared with African Americans a history of violent persecution—as illustrated by the lynching of Chinese workers in the Rock Spring, Wyoming, massacre in 1885 and multiple episodes of mob violence that killed thousands of Hispanics between 1848 and 1928. Indeed, Hispanics were so frequently the targets of lynch mobs, in southwestern states as well as in states far from the border (such as Wyoming and Nebraska), that they ranked second to African Americans in the scale and scope of these crimes.[48]

Like African Americans, both Asian and Hispanic immigrants faced a formidable system of racial oppression and economic exploitation. Institutionalizing anti-Asian prejudice, various discriminatory measures were passed and implemented such as the Page Act of 1875, the Naturalization Act of 1870 (which extended citizenship rights to African Americans but barred the Chinese from naturalization, even when born in the United States), and the Chinese Exclusion Act of 1882. Furthermore, two Supreme Court rulings sharply curtailed the opportunity of all Asian immigrants to be naturalized in a process comparable to white citizens: The *Ozawa* case of 1922 declared that a Japanese immigrant was not white and therefore ineligible for naturalization; the *Thind* case denied whiteness to an Asian Indian the following year.[49] Asian immigrants also endured de jure and de facto segregation. In California, for example, a school law passed in 1860 segregated specific minorities—including children of Black, Chinese, and Indian descent. It was not until 1947 that the official segregation of Chinese Americans was repealed,[50] and only in 1952 were all Asians granted the ability to naturalize and thus vote.

Legal immigration from Mexico dramatically increased in the 1920s (from 220,000 in 1920 to 639,000 in 1930). So did illegal immigration. This rapid rise in Mexican immigration fueled nativist concerns about the purity of the "US stock." Restrictive immigration initiatives such as the Deportation Act of 1929 were adopted in response. More than four hundred thousand Mexicans were expelled during the Depression—including US-born children. Hispanics were also barred entry to Anglo establishments and segregated into deprived urban barrios. They had to wait for the 1954 Supreme Court ruling in Hernandez v. Texas to benefit from equal protection under the Fourteenth Amendment of the US Constitution. Furthermore, Hispanics faced de facto school segregation: no law explicitly barred their access to schools, but students were assigned to inferior "Mexican schools" based on their name and complexion.

Not surprisingly, these similarities in the treatment of African Americans and other racialized minorities led to comparable acts of resistance—such as public protest, the creation of mutual defense organizations, and the formation of civil rights associations. Resistance to racial prejudice and economic exploitation sometimes resulted in interracial cooperation, as illustrated by the "Black-brown" alliance forged during the Chicago Freedom Movement (which was led by King) as well as the collaboration between the SCLC and the Mexican United Farm Workers in the Poor People's Movement.[51] The rapprochement between the Young Chicanos for Community Action (YCCA) in Los Angeles and the leaders of the Black Power Movement in 1967 is another example. The YCCA evolved into the Brown Berets, linking Chicanos to Black civil rights activism. Similarly, the Asian American movement drew from the Black Power Movement an "understanding of the United States as a fundamentally oppressive nation and a conviction that the U.S. functioned as an empire on the world stage."[52] Some Black activists, mostly from the Black Panther Party, supported Asians in their struggle for racial justice. In addition, Asian American radicals expressed interracial affinity with Hispanics in numerous ways, as illustrated by the support provided to the Mexican union farm workers strikes (1965–1970) and to the Chicano Moratorium—the latter a massive antiwar protest held in Los Angeles in August 1970.

Yet, despite these examples, the relationship between Hispanics and African Americans was mostly characterized by conflict and competition. Segments of the Hispanic population expressed anti-Black prejudice to consolidate their "not Anglo but white nevertheless" identity. Black people from Latin America were segregated from white Hispanics and became part of Black communities in the United States.[53] Racial prejudice was multifaceted: African descendants from the Caribbean had to perform Black roles in American movies and TV shows, as illustrated by the famous Afro–Puerto Rican actor Juano Hernandez. In contrast, Hispanics who could pass as "honorary whites"—such as Cuban actor Ricky Ricardo in *I Love Lucy* (1951)—enjoyed popularity in all-white shows. Opposition to Blackness increasingly defined Hispanic identity both during and in the aftermath of the civil rights movement. Although the Chicano Movement was partly influenced by the Black Power Movement, Chicano activists, "operated in the ambiguous space between those rights guaranteed to Mexican Americans as nominal 'whites' and the policies used by Anglos to limit equality."[54]

The result was a new Chicano identity politics, forged in opposition to the Caucasian racial identity but also increasingly distant from Black activism. In turn, proponents of Black essentialism excluded Afro-Hispanics from their conception of African Americanism. Other forms of intergroup tension included a series of conflicts between African Americans and Mexican Americans in major Texas cities, as well as between African Americans, Cubans, and Haitians in Miami. These conflicts were tangibly politically expressed: In California, for example, about 47 percent of African Americans voted in favor of Proposition 187 in 1994—a law restricting state assistance to illegal immigrants—although the NAACP condemned the measure.

Meanwhile, the main challenge of the American Asian Movement was to create the identity of "Asian American" as a multiethnic category—despite the extreme diversity of Asian Americans in terms of national origins, educational achievements, residential segregation, and socioeconomic status.[55] Asian Americans distanced themselves from other minorities, especially African Americans. Asian immigrants often imported anti-Black sentiments from their countries of origin where years of colonialism and "colorism" fueled systemic prejudice against "darkskin" people. To many Asian Americans, nativist "whiteness" has often become equated with success alongside other elements intrinsic to that paradigm. One of those, historically speaking, has been anti-Blackness.[56]

Reciprocally, anti-Asian sentiments increased among African Americans—especially in California, as illustrated by conflicts between African Americans and Koreans. According to Sumi Cho, many African Americans "characterized Korean merchants in Los Angeles as rude in their provision of service to, and as exploitative in their business practices toward, African American customers."[57] In illustrating these negative sentiments, Cho quoted the lyrics of a popular song (entitled "Black Korea") by the rap artist Ice Cube: "Pay respect to the black fist, or we'll burn your store right down to a crisp." Conflicts between Korean immigrant merchants and Black communities became commonplace in many major US cities, as illustrated by the Flatbush boycott of 1990 in central Brooklyn.

The historical overview of the emergence of ethnoracial identities illustrates how various groups have engaged in a process of "reactive identification"—the first stage of the dynamic model I presented in the previous chapter. Group consciousness has emerged as a result of external threats (leading to defensive solidarities), and all groups have attempted to secure their position in the mainstream by opposing other groups perceived as posing a threat to their status. Both a positive identification with the ingroup and a negative identification of outgroups frame ethnoracial identity politics, the second stage of mobilization based on feelings of alienation, actual and symbolic competition, and cycles of grievances. How ethnoracial groups have defined and used identity politics explains the resilience of conflicts as well as variations in the intensity and nature of violence—a claim I address in the next chapter.

3

FROM PAST TO PRESENT ETHNORACIAL IDENTIFICATION STRATEGY

The historical overview of group identification illustrates that the racialization process has been so ingrained in American society that all forms of identity politics relate to violent inter- and intragroup relations. However, violence (physical and discursive) was not only the result of antagonisms fueled by essentialist ethnoracial differences. It was also an essential source of the emergence of these identities. As I described, conflicts among various groups were fueled by a fluid color divide. This led to violence, either as a source of adversity (such as nativism and racial legislation) or as a response to adversity (from nonviolent protest to riots). More to the point, the use of violence was a core element in the emergence and consolidation of a reactive identity among all ethnoracial groups that, in turn, framed their respective mobilization to achieve actual and symbolic gains within mainstream society.

In that sense, contentious identity politics can be seen as part of American society's "deep structure," by which I mean a set of intergroup dynamics through which most assimilation strategies have been constructed. If so, this begs a key question: What was the impact of previous ethnoracial conflicts on cycles of grievances that developed in the 1980s and 1990s? I provide evidence that these cycles were fueled by three factors: the competitive tensions that spread in reaction to the relative achievements of the post–civil rights era, the evolution of America's overall demographic composition, and the legacy of past contentious repertoires and rites of violence. Greater racial and ethnic diversity complicated established patterns of identification, further exacerbating conflicts over the (re)distribution of resources. Contrary to the expectations of some political activists and scholars, the multiracial movement of the 1990s and multicultural policies did not help resolve conflict; rather, it fueled interracial grievances and distrust among communities.

The Legacy of the Whitening Strategy

The move from "in-between-ness" to whiteness during the interwar period was consolidated by the shift of "old" European immigrants into a broadening white category—as a result of intermarriage, urban cohabitation in "ethnic neighborhoods," school attendance, and participation in political and cultural associations. European immigrants and their children suffered from discrimination in various fields such as housing and employment. By and large, however, they benefited from New Deal federal programs (notably the Federal Housing Authority and the Public Works Administration). The consequence, as Roediger notes, was that in the aftermath of World War II, "the ghetto had unequivocally become black, and eastern and southern Europeans far more securely a part of the master race."[1]

Benefiting from their reclassification as "conclusively white," these white subgroups were able to simultaneously emphasize their commonalities and cultivate their specific ethnic consciousness. The most violent aspects of their painful integration were expurgated from a historic retelling. Instead, it was represented as the "assimilation model," the ideal path other minorities should follow to be part of the success story of Americanization. As US historian Oscar Handlin suggested in 1951, the "epic story of Great Migrations... made the American people... Immigrants were American history."[2] Episodes of conflict were filtered through a collective historical amnesia that gave rise to enduring myths such as the harmonious "melting pot" into which all groups were able to meld while preserving some unique elements of their identities. The ethnic revival that started in the 1960s, illustrated by increasingly popular "hyphenated" identities, was not perceived as posing a threat to American mainstream culture. That process was, rather, analyzed as the result of new symbolic identities consonant with assimilation, while the ideal of American creed was simultaneously stressed. This trend was part of the "American character" defined by Rupert Wilkinson—the dual attraction of Americans to individualism and community.[3] In a similar fashion, Mary C. Waters argues that "symbolic ethnicity fulfills this particular American need to be 'from somewhere.' Having an ethnic identity is something that makes you both special and simultaneously part of a community. It is something that comes to you involuntarily through heredity, and at the same time it is a personal choice."[4] According to Nathan Glazer and Daniel Patrick Moynihan, somewhat ambivalently, "Americans become more American and less ethnic all the time. But, in the course of participating in this process, they may also simultaneously become more ethnic."[5]

Ethnic identification was supposedly the expression of voluntary, rather than prescribed, affiliation based on descent, subsequently offering multiple options. The Irish, for example, effectively assimilated by revitalizing their symbolic ethnicity based on ancestry (as Irish Americans) and cultural characteristics (as illustrated by Saint Patrick's Day becoming part of American mainstream culture). These assumptions were both appealing and reassuring at a time that American society was facing dramatic socioeconomic and demographic changes. It was comforting to believe that the descendants of immigrant groups would face diminished pressures to assimilate compared with those of earlier generations, that the diversification of diversity would not lead to separatism, and that the changes that affected the social meaning of race would benefit African Americans. Studies of migrant assimilation argue that multiracialism was key to resolving racial tensions by generating new opportunities to build interracial alliances and promoting mutual tolerance through a smooth assimilation of all ethnoracial groups.[6] As ethnic boundaries became more porous, ethnic heritage and racial ascription were, according to Jennifer Lee and Frank Bean, "no longer barriers to mobility in America's opportunity structure."[7] David Hollinger announced the emergence of a "post-ethnic America" characterized by "the trans-ethnic solidarity of the American civic nation."[8] Peter Salins comparably argues that "conflicts between immigrants and natives and between blacks and whites could be resolved peacefully because America's first principles could not, in the end, be denied."[9]

Such views of American society omitted two less sanguine consequences of the whitening process. First, some descendants of those white immigrants who fought to benefit from "white privilege" could now both participate in various forms of white backlash—to consolidate their group position—and yet simultaneously dismiss the notion of "white privilege" by evoking their historical ostracization as "little races" and part of the underclass. This complicated legacy is today illustrated by a fierce resentment some poor whites have—the so-called "white trash"—against minorities as well as privileged whites embodied by the "one percent." As Mary Waters notes in her analysis of the emergence of white ethnics, "the fact that there are no longer any *legal* constraints on choice of ancestry does not mean these choices are completely *free* of social control."[10] One of the many complexities of the assimilation of European immigrants is that they felt increasingly threatened by newly arriving immigrants while successfully joining the dominant majority. They also gradually subscribed to the mistaken belief that African Americans were better treated by the affirmative action programs implemented during the civil rights era while they suffered.[11] As Eric Lott argues, attitudes toward Blackness have been increasingly shaped by "white self-examination and insecurity, rather by the realities of African-American life. Indeed, contemporary white perceptions of blacks probably tell us more about the dangers of being 'white' in this era than about strongly held beliefs regarding black inferiority."[12]

Second, European immigrants came to share the racial grievances initially forged by established whites. Racial prejudice became a core feature of American society as some whites considered it an inherent part of the Americanization process. Nativist concerns were exacerbated by the increasing diversification of many aspects of American society, including the ethnoracial composition of workplaces, schools, neighborhoods, and political institutions. This trend was fueled by the speed and breadth of changes in migration patterns. By ending the quota system, the 1965 Hart-Cellar Immigration Act had a strong impact on migration flows, as Asians and Hispanics increasingly migrated to the United States. The foreign-born population doubled from 9.7 million in 1960 to 19.8 million in 1990. Conversely, the proportion of the total foreign born who had arrived from European countries declined from 85 percent in 1900 to 60 percent in 1960, and to 22 percent by 1990. Furthermore, the nonwhite ethnic minority population grew seven times as fast as the non-Hispanic white majority population during the 1980s. By 1990, the non-Hispanic white population represented 75.6 percent of the total population—compared to 85.6 percent in 1960.

A strong nativism movement resurged in the 1990s. It has often been associated with a "white backlash" to the so-called "browning of America."[13] Yet, it only partially mirrored historical episodes of antimigrant phobia. Many restrictionists espoused racist views of immigrants and—by extension—of all minorities. This trend was accentuated by US Census Bureau estimates forecasting the disappearance of a white majority by the middle of the century as a result of demographic changes and the subsequent sharp increase in people identifying themselves as "multiracial" (as measured by the US census since 2000 by people who marked "one or more races" on the form). A Census Bureau Report finding showed that the population reporting multiple races (nine million) grew by 32 percent between 2000 and 2010, while those who reported a single race only grew by 9.2 percent. More than half of the nation's children were expected to be part of a minority race or ethnic group by 2020. Nonwhites are forecasted to no longer comprise more than 50 percent of the population by 2044, compared with 62.1 percent in 2014. The minority population is projected to rise to 56 percent of the total by 2060, compared with 38 percent in 2014. According to Richard Alba, "the anxieties about the end of white majority status have fueled a conservative backlash against the growing diversity of the country. Numerous sites on the web offer advice and counsel on how whites can handle their imminent minority status."[14]

Yet not all restrictionist positions were based on racial assumptions. Other factors played a key role, such as the belief that immigrants were posing a threat to economic prosperity by taking jobs from natives, reducing their wages, and consuming more social benefits than they contributed by paying taxes.[15] This assumption was shared by scholars, politicians, and segments of the US population (mostly among poor and/or uneducated whites).[16] In 1993, about two-thirds of Americans agreed that "immigrants today are a burden on our country because they take our jobs, housing and health care," while only one-third agreed with the contrasting statement that "immigrants today strengthen our country because of their hard work and talents." The belief that immigrants are a burden to America increased among whites with less than a high school degree.[17] That view was also shared by low-skilled and/or less educated African Americans and Hispanics who therefore expressed support for reduced immigration levels and said they believed that unauthorized immigrants were hurting the economy.[18]

The Legacy of Black Identification

The civil rights movement added a new dimension to the Black identity. Black people, Painter notes, "began to be seen as truly American people."[19] She adds: "People who had earlier been known as 'American Negroes,' or, simply, 'the Negro,' became 'black' and 'Afro-Americans.'"[20] This integration was the culmination of a long process. "We are Americans," W. E. B. Du Bois argued in 1897, "not only by birth and by citizenship, but by our political ideals, our language, our religion . . . We are those people whose subtle sense of song has given America its only American music, its only American fairy tales, its only touch of pathos and humor amid its mad money-getting plutocracy."[21] During the 1950s, Du Bois, Paul Robeson, and other activists promoted the American values of liberty and free speech, despite the McCarthy-led House Un-American Activities Committee; and, in the late 1960s, Martin Luther King Jr. aligned his opposition to the Vietnam War by reinterpreting the American Creed to include socioeconomic equity, social justice, and antiracism.

African Americans had to pay a high price for their inclusion in the "American people." Despite racial violence and segregated armed forces, most of them supported the national effort during World War I and, as Painter characterizes it, they "hoped that military service would improve the situation of the race as a whole."[22] Many again enrolled to fight in World War II although the US Army remained segregated, limiting Black soldiers to labor brigades and providing them with inferior conditions. More than 2.5 million African American men registered for the draft, and African American women volunteered in large numbers. When combined with Black women enlisted into Women's Army Corps, more than one million African Americans served in the Army. However, it was not until 1948 that President Harry S. Truman issued an executive order to desegregate the military, although it took the Korean War before the Army fully integrated. Vietnam was the first American war in which African Americans were thoroughly integrated into all armed forces. The statistics were revealing: they were more likely to be drafted and more likely to be killed. Of all enlisted men who died in Vietnam, African Americans made up 14.1 percent of that total (while they made up only 11 percent of America's young male population).[23]

Black identity increasingly included elements of what Juan Battle defined as "invested patriotism"—"the African American faith that generations of toil, racial struggle, and societal contributions might one day secure a full shareholder status in a clearly deferred American dream of racial equality."[24] This was partly accomplished by the Civil Rights Act of 1964 and the Voting Rights Act of 1965. Furthermore, the cultural awareness of the contributions of African Americans led to the official recognition of celebrations and holidays of particular interest to African Americans (such as Juneteenth in 1966, Black History Month in 1976, and Martin Luther King Day in 1986). Meanwhile, African Americans revitalized American popular music through gospel, jazz, rhythm'n'blues, and rock'n'roll.

Having confirmed their own sense of American-ness, African Americans increasingly shared beliefs and attitudes related to their African heritage within the community. This cultural nationalism, however, differed significantly from the ethnic revival among whites, whose hyphenated identities were mostly based on self-identification. By contrast, African Americans were obliged to identify as "Blacks." Studies of racial formation subsequently criticized this "ethnicity-based paradigm"—one predicated on the European immigrant experience as a model of assimilation, which therefore excluded many identified as racial minorities. According to Michael Omi and Howard Winant, "the framework of European (white) ethnicity could not appreciate the extent to which racial inequality differed from ethnic inequality."[25]

The emphasis on African roots was thus part of a reactive identification, a response to stigmatization that would serve as a source of pride and liberation from oppression. This process was illustrated by the campaign organized by Rev. Jesse L. Jackson, the longtime civil rights leader. He popularized the term "African-American" in an effort to highlight the cultural heritage of those with ancestral ties to Africa: "We built the country through the African slave trade. African-Americans acknowledge that. Any term that emphasizes the color and not the heritage separates us from our heritage."[26]

Some Black leaders criticized a moderate cultural integrative strategy and promoted a more radical identity, one based on the notions of pan-Africanism, Black nationalism, and internal colonialism. The Black Nationalist Nation of Islam (NOI), for example, "considered white people to be 'devils' from whom nothing good could ever come."[27] Black Muslims, such as Malcolm X, promoted the creation of a distinct Black nation within the American nation rather than seeking institutional integration.[28] Debates, and sometimes violent tensions, persisted between integrationists and nationalists in the 1970s. After the moderate demands of the civil rights movement were met in 1964–65, the radicalization of the Black Movement led to the emergence of the Black Power Movement—defined by Stokely Carmichael and Charles V. Hamilton as "self-defense as well as self-definition." They argued: "throughout this country, vast segments of the black communities are beginning to recognize the need to assert their own definitions, to reclaim their history, their culture. As a result, "the goal of black people must not be to assimilate into middle class America."[29] It was, rather, to create separate organizations without paying attention to white views and thus achieve "full participation in the decision-making processes affecting the lives of black people, and recognition of the virtues in themselves as black people."[30]

With the disintegration of the Black Panther Party and other organizations related to the Black Power Movement, these separatist ideals declined in popularity by the late 1970s. The movement morphed into Black caucuses and professional organizations designed to promote political incorporation and social mobility. The integrationist expectations were further, incrementally fulfilled by the Equal Opportunity Act of 1972 and other affirmative action programs. Hopes raised by civil rights legislation and socioeconomic reforms, however, were indeed short-lived. Structural changes to the economy (such as deindustrialization) and recessions (in 1982 and 1991) dramatically affected African Americans. In addition to resilient prejudice, socioeconomic inequalities generated a heightened sense of insecurity that, in turn, initiated another cycle of grievances and tensions with white and other nonwhite ethnoracial groups alike.

Furthermore, controversies about the contours and nature of Blackness continued throughout the 1980s and 1990s. Like whites, African Americans had to face significant demographic changes resulting from immigration flows. Before 1965, Black people of foreign birth residing in the United States were nearly invisible. According to the 1960 census, their percentage of the population was less than 1 percent. But after 1965, men and women of African descent entered the United States in ever-increasing numbers. During the 1990s, more than nine hundred thousand Black immigrants came from the Caribbean, another four hundred thousand came from Africa, and still others came from Europe and the Pacific rim. By the beginning of the twenty-first century, more people had arrived from Africa to live in the United States than during the centuries of the slave trade. In 2000, nearly one in ten Black Americans was an immigrant or the child of an immigrant. These changes, Ira Berlin argues, had a profound impact on Black identity: "The new arrivals frequently struggled over the very appellation "African-American," either shunning it—declaring themselves, for instance, Jamaican-Americans or Nigerian-Americans—or denying native black Americans' claim to it on the ground that most of them had never been to Africa. At the same time, some old-time black residents refuse to recognize the new arrivals as true African-Americans."[31]

The Legacy of "In-Between-ness": Asians and Hispanics

Meanwhile, other immigrant groups increased in size and influence. By 1990, 2.9 percent of Americans were Asians (increasing from 0.5 percent in 1960), and 9 percent were Hispanic (up from 3.2 percent in 1960). Some scholars emphasized the similarities between African Americans and other minorities. Sociologist William Petersen, for example, in a 1966 piece in the *New York Times Magazine* entitled "Success Story, Japanese-American Style," notes that "Like the Negroes, the Japanese have been the object of color prejudice. Like the Jews, they have been feared and hated as hyper efficient competitors."[32] Gregg Lee Carter, in his analysis of Hispanic rioting during the civil rights era, comparably draws empathetic parallels, arguing that "Mexican Americans, Puerto Ricans, and blacks had much in common . . . They all suffered from prejudice, discrimination, and segregation, and were consequently disproportionately poor. They were sent to poor schools and were poorly educated. They felt abused by the police and were ignored by those with political power. In short, they were being denied the American dream."[33]

Like other ethnoracial groups who had fought for their recognition, Hispanics and Asians had to engage in a reactive identification process. A sense of interracial solidarity did exist; yet their respective group consciousness was mostly consolidated through a process of "racial triangulation."[34] It involved: self-identification as a group (despite the heterogeneity of both Hispanic and Asians subgroups), conflicted identification related to whiteness, and conflictual distancing from Blackness.

After 1965, Asian American groups became increasingly internally fragmented along ethnic or national origin lines and socioeconomic achievements. Eric Liu, in his 1998 book *The Accidental Asian*, for example, criticizes the myth of an Asian American community with uniform interests. "Unlike blacks," he writes, "Asians do not have a cultural idiom that arose from centuries of thinking of themselves as a race; unlike Jews, Asians haven't a unifying spiritual and historical legacy; unlike Latinos, another recently invented community, Asians don't have a linguistic basis for their continued apartness."[35] Heterogeneous Asian communities, therefore, had to continuously manage an "in-between position."[36] The answer to Gary Okihiro's question—"Is yellow black or white?"—was "neither" in terms of racial identification.[37] However, poor Asians stood in a horizontal (and often conflictual) relationship with disadvantaged African Americans while being perceived as "virtually white" in terms of their socioeconomic status.[38]

Dealing with this in-between status (both at the margins and mainstream), Asians continued to distance themselves from African Americans while, like Blacks, being targets of racial prejudice. As I discussed earlier, anti-Asian activities can be traced back to the middle of the nineteenth century and included some violent episodes.[39] By the early 1970s, Asian Americans were finally granted the rights long extended to other citizens. Yet, anti-Asian feelings also resurfaced and led to racial incidents—from racial name-calling to physical assaults and, on several occasions, murders (as illustrated by the killing in 1982 of Vincent Chin who was beaten to death in Detroit by two white men who mistook him for Japanese). These incidents intensified a sense of reactive solidarity among Asian subgroups who banded together in defensive pan-Asian organizations (such as the American Citizens for Justice, originally created to seek justice for Chin's death).[40]

These pan-Asian organizations differed from the prior organizations created during the civil rights era in two ways. First, while the Asian American movement was predicated on the Black Power and antiwar movements, pan-ethnic activities moved toward the mainstream to fit the needs of post-1965 Asian immigrants—especially those highly skilled middle-class professionals with little contact or shared experience with African Americans.[41] Among the US-born Asian American population, anti-Blackness was mostly generated by the assumption that whiteness was equated with success. A 2000 National Health Survey showed that among those who self-identified as both Asian and white, close to half of the respondents marked white as their "main race."[42]

Second, Asian American identity increasingly related to the dominant popular perception of Asians (broadly defined) as being able to overcome modes of oppression through group agency, faith in capitalism, and patriotic allegiance. Such a perception led to the "model minoritization" of Asian Americans.[43] According to Giselle Chow, "the development of this model minority myth was a useful counterpoint amid the growing social unrest in the 1960s in the wake of the Watts riots and from the emergent Black Power Movement. Here was a racial group that could seemingly do it all, without complaint and without government aid."[44] As a result, Asians were perceived as a racial bridge between whites, on the one hand, and Blacks and Hispanics on the other. They subsequently became both idealized US citizens in popular, mostly white, imaginary and yet simultaneously marginalized minorities. Some Asian Americanists rejected this model minority myth, arguing that it exaggerated both Asian American prosperity and ethnic homogeneity.[45] However, Claire Jean Kim and Taeku Lee note that "to the extent that Asian Americans themselves buy into this myth and evince feelings of superiority toward blacks, the racial hierarchy becomes that much more entrenched."[46] Their acceptance of this myth, in turn, aroused Black (and Hispanic to some extent) resentment toward Asian Americans.

Mexican Americans led in dealing with both assimilation and racialization. They were the largest Hispanic group, the second largest non-European ethnoracial group, and one of the earliest immigrant groups (the first cohort even being part of the original population resident in territories that were incorporated into the United States). They were also among the most organized groups, resulting from a long history of activism. During the civil rights era, the Chicano movement allowed Mexican Americans to distance themselves from both whiteness and Blackness by promoting their own status as brown people. This paved the way for the inclusion of the nonracial "Hispanic category" in the 1970 census. Some Mexican Americans nonetheless continued to claim a white racial status that they equated with a successful integration.

In the post-1965 era, Mexicans' emblematic status and large presence were challenged by newly arrived immigrants from Latin American nations.[47] These immigrants increased the heterogeneity of the so-called Hispanics, a pan-ethnic identity they were reluctant to embrace as their main identity. The changing demographic and ethnic makeup of the Hispanic population sparked new divisions among them, in addition to assorted factors such as education, residential segregation, legal status, political affiliation, and—obviously—racial identification. Some Hispanics continued to identify as whites—mostly light skinned, middle-class, and/or married to non-Hispanic whites.[48] The adoption of whiteness served as a protection against anti-immigrant sentiment and legislation, such as Proposition 187 in California, which provided a strong incentive to "adopt a national identity that reflects one of whiteness and less Mexican ethnic group membership."[49] Newly arrived immigrants perpetuated prejudicial attitudes toward African Americans, bringing a negative perceptions of Blacks with them from their host societies. According to the 1999 *Lilly Survey of American Attitudes and Friendships*, Hispanics were more likely to reject African Americans as neighbors than they were to reject members of other ethnoracial groups. They also identified African Americans as their least desirable marriage partners.[50]

Others embraced a "brown" or multiracial identity. The 2000 US Census showed that Hispanics were almost evenly divided between those who identified as white and those who picked "some other race." A minority of Afro-origin immigrants from the Spanish-speaking Caribbean had almost no choice but to identify as Black, even when they resisted this imposed identification. As a result, they had to deal with anti-Black prejudice expressed by both Hispanic and non-Hispanic whites, while African Americans called their very Blackness into question.[51]

Conflicted and Conflictual Identitarian Strategies

The overview of the evolution of reactive identification among various ethnoracial groups during the post–civil rights era demonstrates the historic, situational, and relational contingencies that reshaped the identification process within the context of shifting racial boundaries. Minorities had no choice in being targeted by racial prejudice. They had more leverage in selecting what kind of reactive identification would best protect their respective ingroup against external threats. As I illustrated, minority groups formerly had to adopt the dominant group's categorization of them to turn prejudice into a positive group consciousness and to gain access to symbolic and material resources. Some of them continued to realign themselves with the dominant group as a way of benefiting from the tangible rewards of whiteness. Individuals with the appropriate social and economic credentials indeed better controlled their ethnoracial identification. The result was, according to Yvette Alex in her study of multiracial politics, that they were more likely to be perceived by members of other minority groups "as representatives of the very power structures and institutions by which they were once seen as victimized."[52] They were also perceived by white Americans, especially descendants of "inconclusive whites," as posing a threat to their "wages of whiteness." In her analysis of various surveys, Jennifer Hochschild pertinently summarizes the state of ethnoracial separation in American society by the late 1990s: "Blacks feel most in common with Latinos, who feel least in common with them. Latinos feel most in common with whites, who feel little in common with them. Asian Americans feel most in common with whites, who feel least in common with them. Each group is chasing another which is running from it."[53]

The situation was further complicated by the politicization of identitarian strategies. The linear model of party identification commonly assumed that Hispanics and Asian Americans fell between whites (the group most likely to support Republicans) and African Americans (that most likely to identify as Democrats). Surveys and studies conducted in the 1990s showed a more complex situation.[54] For example, political differences between Mexicans, Puerto Ricans, and Cubans were too great to lend themselves to a characterization of a united Hispanic electorate. The share of Hispanic voters in the GOP remained small, about 3 percent in 1992. In specific locales, however, Hispanic conservatives emerged as a political force—mostly in Texas and Florida, where the GOP enjoyed strong support among Cuban and Venezuelan Americans. In 2003, 64 percent of Cubans nationally identified with the GOP, only 22 percent favoring the Democratic Party. In 2004, George W. Bush won 78 percent of the Cuban vote in Florida, compared with 56 percent of the state's overall Hispanic voters, enough to tip the national election in his favor. Hispanic organizations became increasingly divided along both ethnic/national lines and in party identification patterns. The Republican members of the Congressional Hispanic Caucus, for example, withdrew from the caucus in the late 1990s in protest over its support for improved relations with Cuba—and in 2002 formed a caucus for Hispanic Republicans to counter the Democratic dominance over Hispanic representation. This initiative subsequently led to the creation of the Congressional Hispanic Conference in 2003—one among many other conservative Hispanic associations (such as the Somos Republicans and the Cafe Con Leche Republicans).

Comparably, some Asian subgroups—such as the Vietnamese and, by some accounts, Koreans—were more likely to identify as Republicans, while Asian American organizations internally debated critical issues.[55] This increased diversification of pan-ethnic categories led to more diverse political orientations. In 1992, George H. W. Bush received 55 percent of the Asian American vote—drawn mostly from a combination of a new generation of anti-communist Asian refugees and Filipino Americans. But during the 1990s, Asian American electoral support shifted from majority support for the GOP to increased support for the Democratic Party. Explaining why conservative Asian Americans like him were not "strange and new political animals," Anthony Wang listed several reasons for opposing liberals in 1997. He notes: "our disagreement with traditional civil rights ideology and emerging critical race theory results from a different reaction to and understanding of the events affecting the Asian American community, the greater minority community, and society at large . . . Distinguishing ourselves from Asian American progressives, we choose to critically question the future path of our increasingly complex and multiracial America from a fundamentally different set of beliefs."[56]

Affirmative action was one of the issues dividing Black conservatives (mostly Republicans) from the majority of African Americans who tended to support the Democratic Party. In 1992, 17 percent of Democratic voters were Black, and only a small minority (2 percent) of Republican voters were Black.[57] Yet, Black conservatives—such as Supreme Court Justice Clarence Thomas, economist Thomas Sowell, and Congressman Alan Keyes—emerged after Ronald Reagan's election and gained prominence in the early 1990s during the George H. W. Bush administration. The two administrations of President George W. Bush included high-ranking Black Cabinet officials, notably two secretaries of state (Colin L. Powell and Condoleezza Rice). Black conservatism voiced opposition to affirmative action and abortion, as well as support for limited government (even those elements designed to redress discrimination), privatizing social security, and the death penalty.[58]

In addition to the political fragmentation of minorities, ethnoracial resentment undermined class-based coalitions intended to resist conservative legislation. Racial divisions, Roediger argues, hurt efforts to create minority labor alliances designed to defeat antiunion policies.[59] Other scholars concurred that, as a result, a racialized politics of resentment had undermined policies that helped the least affluent. Less prosperous whites, for example, were "diverted from pursuing their economic interests by their desire to maintain their position above African Americans."[60] A class-based divide also began to affect minorities, notably African Americans, in fragmented ways. According to Dominic Capeci Jr., for example, the civil rights movement "enhanced black political power, which assisted the black middle class but inadvertently isolated lower working-class blacks further. They became increasingly insecure with the introduction of drugs, gangs, and violence in their neighborhoods, and continued white hostility beyond them."[61] A "new Black middle class"—as opposed to the "old" one that emerged during a period of economic prosperity after World War II—benefited from the civil rights era. Affirmative action programs expanded the ranks of Black students on white campuses and thus affected the class structure of Black America. Middle class workers moved increasingly into white-collar occupations, especially in the public sector. The remarkable gains in Black income resulted, according to William Wilson, in a wider gap between "two nations" within Black America—the Black haves and have-nots. While those making $100,00 or more nearly quadrupled between 1970 and 2014 (up to 13 percent of the Black workforce), the portion of Black workers with incomes below $15,000 declined by only four percentage points (to 22 percent). Consequently, those doing poorly felt increasingly alienated from those doing well (among both members of the white and Black middle class), while wealthier and better-educated African Americans continued to face pronounced disparities in relation to the white middle class counterparts.

The overview of the evolution of identity-based strategies among ethnoracial groups illustrates the complexity of inter- and intragroup relations during the 1980s and 1990s. What needs to be addressed is how these strategies affected patterns of mobilization (from violent to nonviolent interactions) through contentious identity politics. This I do in the next chapter.

4

THE DYNAMICS OF CONTENTION

Racial prejudice and social distance both grew over time—as illustrated by the multiplication of interracial conflicts between 1965 and 1993. Suzanne Shanahan and Susan Olzak identify, for example, at least 597 racial and ethnic collective actions—defined as the "public expression of racially- or ethnically-based grievances against a given ethnic or racial target"—during this period.[1] Significant episodes of violence included four riots in Miami during the 1980s involving African Americans and Cuban newcomers. Extensive rioting took place in Los Angeles in April 1992, following the acquittal of the four policemen who had viciously beaten Rodney King. These riots resulted in fifty-two deaths, reputedly 2,380 injuries, more than $750 million in property damage, and sixteen thousand arrests. Hispanics and whites joined Blacks in demolishing Korean, Hispanic, and Chinese businesses. In fact, more Hispanics (51 percent) than Blacks (36 percent) rioted, while Koreans and Hispanics represented the majority of targeted store owners. Other forms of ethnoracial violence in the 1990s included the increase of hate crimes against African Americans and other minorities, leading to the adoption of the Hate Crimes Prevention Act in 1999,[2] the multiplication of anti-immigrant incidents, intragroup conflicts among various ethnoracial groups, and the increase in violent activism by both leftist and rightist organizations.

The Los Angeles riots magnified the explosive combination of socioeconomic issues (such as very high unemployment and reduced government assistance), ethnic diversity, and increased competition over existing resources.[3] Olzak, for example, suggests that conflict was inevitable among Hispanics, Asian Americans, and African Americans because they were forced to compete for jobs and economic opportunities in urban settings with stuttering economies.[4] As I previously documented, relations between African Americans and Asians, for example, were often historically conflictual. Resentment by Blacks toward non-Black-owned businesses was not novel—as illustrated by the Jewish-owned businesses destroyed in Black urban neighborhoods during the 1960s riots. And the Rodney King verdict was only one of many examples of the white oppression of Blacks. More generally, blatant discrimination in the job market, repressive labor policies and practices, and income inequalities were unabated—all of these factors fueling tensions along a race/class divide.[5]

These riots, however, were not simply the product of material conditions. They also illustrated, as did other episodes of violence, the continued cycles of grievance inherited from the past, coupled with unprecedented contentious repertoires. The historical legacy dimension involved numerous similarities between the pre—and post–civil rights eras. I address these similarities according to the three main components of contentious identity politics: the effect of group position, the spillover process of identity politics, and the multiplication of contentious repertoires.

The Effect of Group Position

Perceptions of groups as competitive threats were shaped by a sense of group position consisting of two related elements. The first was the belief that access to important social resources was a zero-sum process—in which one group's betterment necessarily implied making another worse off. The second related to the effect of increased multiracialism on inter- and intragroup perceptions. In tandem, these two elements generated a higher level of competition and contention. They also had a negative impact on race relations. Lawrence Bobo, among many observers, offers a gloomy diagnosis: "Throughout the 1990s, assessments of racial and ethnic relations in the United States suggested that we have become increasingly racially polarized."[6]

At the same time that immigration increased ethnoracial diversity, the rates of racial/ethnic intermarriage also increased. Cross-group marriages among whites, Hispanics, Asians, Native Americans, and African Americans soared from 150,000 in 1960 to 1.6 million in 1990, and to 3.1 million in 2000. Marriage between Black and white Americans steadily increased after the Loving v. Commonwealth of Virginia Supreme Court ruling—which overturned antimiscegenation laws. By the late 1990s, 10.2 percent of married Blacks had white spouses, compared to less than two percent in 1970. Intermarriage rates between both whites and Asians and whites and Hispanics were even higher, reaching more than 30 percent by the late 1990s.[7] Almost two million children had parents of different races in 1990, compared to less than five hundred thousand in 1960. Such increases in intermarriage resulted in a growing multiracial population. That visibility grew when the 2000 census changed, allowing Americans to mark "one or more race" as a way of identifying themselves. This change in the census was the result of the mobilization of a multiracial movement, which included, for example, the Association of Multiethnic Americans (AMEA) and A Place for Us (APFU).[8]

Only 6.8 million Americans (or 2.4 percent to the total population) identified themselves as multiracial in 2000, with 93 percent reporting two races and 6 percent three races. Yet, the evolution of America's overall demographic composition raised new concerns within each group regarding their respective position relative to mainstream America because new questions surfaced concerning the status of ethnoracial groups in an increasingly diverse society.[9] These concerns were widespread among white supporters of the conservative movement of the 1980s.[10] This movement rallied whites who believed they were unfairly treated by affirmative action programs and felt threatened as members of a declining dominant group. They concurred that immigrants, mostly Hispanics, were threatening natives' economic and material interests—regardless of the actual impact of immigration.[11] New restrictive immigration policies were implemented, confirming the effects of negative perceptions of minorities as posing a threat on conservative legislation.[12] Antimigrant legislation gave credence to the ideological agenda of antimigrant groups, such as the various movements created by John Tanton including the Federation for American Immigration Reform (FAIR), the Center for Immigration Studies (CIS), and US English.[13] This agenda was supported by violent vigilantes patrolling along the United States-Mexico border, such as the Minuteman volunteers who legitimized their use of paramilitary violence by claiming their filiation of ideas with the civilian colonists during the American Revolutionary War.[14]

In addition, affirmative action programs were accused by some portion of the white population of unfairly discriminating against nonminority groups—a belief fueled by the color-blind assumption that racial discrimination was a thing of the past and that everyone working hard had an equal chance to become successful.[15] In 1995, roughly three in five whites reported that African Americans were as well or better off than whites with regard to employment, access to health care, and education; and more than two in five said the same with regard to income and housing. By contrast, only 14 to 30 percent of Blacks agreed that they were as well off as whites, depending on the particular socioeconomic arena in question.[16] Redistributive race-conscious programs were therefore widely favored by African

Americans but opposed by a majority of whites.[17] A Gallup survey conducted in 1997 showed that only 22 percent of whites believed that the government should increase affirmative action programs while 37 percent wanted these programs to be reduced; by contrast, 53 percent of Black respondents wanted these programs to be expanded, and only 12 percent wanted fewer programs.[18]

More to the point, the zero-sum competition extended beyond the traditional white/minority divide. All minority groups felt they were threatened with the loss of significant resources to other minority groups—leading to fierce competition over affirmative action programs. Studies that included Hispanics and Asians showed that their attitudes toward affirmative action were fragmented due to controversial questions about entitlement to social resources, status, and privilege. They did show greater support among minorities for affirmative action than whites. Nonnegligible portions, however, expressed concerns. When asked about their policy preferences for congressional action in 1995, for example, 38 percent of whites preferred "to limit affirmative action." But 30 percent of Hispanics, 27 percent of Asians, and 25 percent of Blacks provided the same answer.[19] In 1996, 60 percent of whites voted in favor of Proposition 209 to abolish the public use of affirmative action by state institutions in the areas of public employment, public contracting, and public education. Yet so did 45 percent of Asian Americans and 30 percent of Hispanics.[20]

The belief that immigrants (broadly defined) were posing a threat to the economic prosperity of the country, as well to national identity, transcended ethnoracial boundaries. Proposition 187, for example, won widespread approval across a range of ethnic groups—including 67 percent of whites and 50 percent of both Asian Americans and African Americans, while only 23 percent of Hispanics voted in favor.[21] Furthermore, minority groups feared that, in addition to facing racial discrimination, they would be negatively affected by the evolution of census data because it might make them more visible. As Charles Hirschman et al. argue, census data "show the potential size of a political constituency. In interethnic politics, increases in population numbers can be used to make a case for increased governmental attention, changes in electoral districts, and the allocation of resources."[22] Decreases in a community's population numbers therefore raised countervailing concerns. Civil rights activists increasingly perceived the multiracial movement as a threat. According to Kim Williams, they "feared that a multiracial category would dilute the count of minority populations. Their shared position was that a multiracial identifier would undercut existing civil rights safeguards."[23]

The ideal of a multiracial solidarity based on a future "race-lessness," an idea promoted by the AMEA, was contested by supporters of "blackness" such as Kweisi Mfume, president of the NAACP. He declared: "With some figures showing 70 percent of African Americans fitting into a multiracial category, will we be able to identify black voters in terms of fair representation?"[24] As Jennifer Lee and Frank Bean note, others Black advocacy groups "feared that many blacks would become 'racial defectors' who would exit out of the black category by choosing to identify with another race if given the opportunity."[25] Non-Black minority organizations expressed similar concerns, including the National Council of La Raza, the Mexican American Legal Defense Fund, and the National Council of American Indians.

The Spillover Process of Identity Politics

Concerns about "demographic balkanization," combined with the spiraling effect of color-coded resentment fueled by the widespread belief of policy unfairness, led to the radicalization of identity politics in America. Feelings of a competitive threat were reinforced by religious, cultural, and political divisions. Group relations were increasingly affected by multifaceted prejudice and intense political fragmentation. All these trends took place in an extremely polarized atmosphere—very similar to the current state of American society.

African American efforts to achieve civil rights and recognition became the model process for numerous other activist minority groups. It encouraged them to further consolidate their identity strategy to maximize their opportunities and influence in shaping social institutions.[26] This process constituted a double-edged sword. On the one hand, the proactive use of ethnoracial identity, initially designed to combat the effect of racialization, in turn reified a new series of ethnoracial claims as soon as it became clear that structural barriers were challenging the myth of equal opportunity. Originally based on ancestry and culture, the ethnic identity of non-Black minorities was increasingly perceived as intrinsic, "essential or indelible and made hierarchical."[27] In other words, as George Fredrickson argues, culture did "the work of race" by adding additional ways to classify groups.[28] Conversely, on the other hand, intergroup relations increasingly involved efforts by members of each to maintain their cultural dominance over the space in which they resided. As Kathleen Kemp notes, "Should a group perceive that their dominance is threatened by the residential movement of other groups, spatial conflict is likely to occur and enter the political arena."[29]

The 1990 Flatbush boycott in central Brooklyn, for example, has been commonly depicted as representative of the tensions between Korean merchants and Black customers. It is worth noting, however, that most of the activists engaged in the boycott were immigrants from the Caribbean who wanted to affirm their particular Afro-Caribbean identity in relation to other Black subgroups. "Proud of Our Haitian Heritage" was therefore the motto of Haitian religious and civic leaders who benefited from the support of community organizers and Muslims from the UMMA group. The claims by Afro-Caribbeans persisted, as illustrated by the creation in 2017 of the Little Caribbean cultural district—an area bounded by Flatbush, Church, and Nostrand Avenues—as well as recent attempts to create a "Little Haiti" as a subdistrict. These efforts, tellingly, were and remain opposed by other Caribbean locals.[30]

Other minority groups also engaged in identity politics in their fight for recognition. The result of this spillover process was the diversification of identities beyond traditional racial categories—including sexual and gendered identities alongside religious, ethnic, and racial lines. As Yale professor Amy Chua notes in her study of tribal affiliations and rivalries, "in reaction to a growing awareness that 'colorblindness' was being used by conservatives to oppose policies intended to redress racial inequalities, a new movement began to unfold on the left in the 1980s and 1990s—a movement emphasizing group consciousness, group identity, and group claims."[31] According to Todd Gitlin, the initial core values of these movements were "an assertion of dignity, a remedy for exclusion and denigration and a demand by the voiceless for representation."[32]

A new generation of feminists—labeled the "third wave" by the writer and activist Rebecca Walker—emerged during the 1990s.[33] They focused less on civil rights issues and more on identity claims than previous generations, emphasizing the contribution of poststructuralist interpretations of gender and sexuality. One key goal was "consciousness-raising" based on the rejection of essentialist and heteronormative assumptions about identity, as well as the recognition of multiple and overlapping forms of oppression. The concept of intersectionality became its defining feature. Coined by the law professor Kimberlé Crenshaw, it asserted that people often had to face multiple sources of oppression—such as race, gender, class, sexual orientation, religion, and other identity markers. By understanding a wide range of differences (including an individual's sexual orientation, age, class, disability, and more), intersectionality aimed at the inclusion of specific groups who had previously felt excluded from previous feminist activism—such as women of color, and transwomen.[34] That claim has become a defining feature of contemporary America.

Liberal activists shared a similar conception of identity politics to that ingrained in the original civil rights movement. Feminists and LGBTQ groups, for example, were engaged in widespread political activism, including lobbying, street marches, and protests. During the Washington March for Lesbian, Gay and Bi Equal Rights and Liberation in 1993, between eight hundred thousand

and one million people gathered at the National Mall demanding civil rights bills against discrimination and pushing for increased AIDS research funding and reproductive rights.

Organized protests by the left energized conservative revanchist responses—as illustrated by the "Make America Great Again" motto that was used by Ronald Reagan during the 1980 presidential campaign before being popularized by Donald Trump in his campaign. Revanchism was "a visceral reaction against the liberalism of the post-1960s period and an all-out attack on the social policy structure that emanated from the New Deal and the immediate postwar era."[35] Revanchist policies ranged from police hyper-activism (as illustrated by the "zero tolerance" campaign promoted by Rudolph Giuliani, then mayor of New York) to the infringement of civil liberties and civic rights that minorities had painstakingly gained during the previous three decades.

Revanchism was also fueled by the fears raised by many of the cultural changes that occurred since the 1970s, when the Christian Right initiated protests (some violent) against the secularization of society, changing sexual and cultural mores, and the legalization of abortion (after the passage of Roe v. Wade in 1974). The 1980s and 1990s saw the growth of political activism by evangelicals and conservatives. Antiabortion activists, for example, increased the blockading of abortion clinics in addition to issuing threats and carrying out bombings. A new wave of feminism energized antifeminist movements, expressed as material as well as symbolic concerns.[36] Seeing feminist identity claims as a threat to their values and status, antifeminist groups not only rejected abortion and the Equal Rights Amendment (ERA) but also opposed the denial of innate gender differences. Other groups claimed that men were oppressed and discriminated against in an abusively feminized society.[37] The most radical component of the men's rights movement advocated a more patriarchal society based on "male supremacy"—as illustrated by the mythopoetic men's movement.[38] According to Alastair Bonnett, this movement represented "an attempt to reaffirm and reinstate male power, and undermined the gains that have been made by feminism" by employing claims which "once served anti-sexism" but are "employed to celebrate and affirm gender essentialism."[39]

Revanchism led to the promotion of the traditional assimilation, including pressure for the use of English in all public schools and the acceptance of "core patriotic values."[40] As Rogers Brubaker argues, the "return of assimilation" involved "a shift from an overwhelming focus on persistent differences... to a broader focus that encompasses emerging commonalities as well." Normatively, it involved "a shift from the automatic valorization of cultural differences to a renewed concern with civic integration."[41] This shift was supported by conservative politicians as well as scholars who strongly opposed philosophies of difference such as Samuel Huntington and Alan Bloom. For Huntington, multicultural practices had the effect of delaying migrant and minority integration, and threatened national unity.[42] For Bloom, the modern liberal philosophy was plagued by relativism and a rather sterile critical deconstructionism—resulting in the spiritual impoverishment of students.[43] These were significant salvos in the "culture wars" that became increasingly popular in political and academic arenas.

This revanchist trend has had dramatic effects on ethnoracial relations—from racial disparities in law enforcement and the worsening of race relations to physical violence against minorities and immigrants. The 1990s white backlash combined elements inherited from previous waves (such as socioeconomic grievances, racial prejudice, and moral panic) with new concerns about identity politics. David Savran notes that the 1990s ushered in the "ascendency of a new and powerful figure in US culture: the white male as victim."[44] Charles Gallagher reaches a similar conclusion in his study of white college students: "Many whites see themselves as victims of the multicultural, pc, feminist onslaught."[45] Central to this construction of whiteness as someone victimized were fears of white subjugation and marginalization, as well as feelings that the nation was "falling apart."

The Multiplication of Contentious Repertoires

Meanwhile, propriety claims to certain rights, resources, statuses, and privileges bolstered the fragmentation of ethnoracial minority groups.[46] In the late 1990s, for example, feminism became increasingly fractured by the development of subgroups that made it more difficult to simultaneously further their collective interests. The spiraling effect of ethnoracial identity politics resulted, according to Nancy Ehrenreich, in the "infinite regress problem: the tendency of all identity groups to split into ever smaller subgroups, until there seems to be no hope of any coherent category other than the individual."[47] These subgroups distinguished, for example, between white feminist, Black feminist, and Black/white feminist lesbian organizations.[48] Hispanic feminists split into Chicana lesbians and the Mujerismo movement. They often lacked a shared perception of the challenges raised by oppression in a multiracial society.[49] Hundreds of thousands of women converged in October 1997 Philadelphia for the Million Women March—a rally that inspired the Women's March that took place in January 2016 after the inauguration of President Trump. Yet, despite calls for unity, the themes of the Philadelphia rally mostly focused on the issues faced by Black women, as well as the need for Black women to set aside their differences to achieve common goals.

The Million Man March organized in October 1995 by Louis Farrakhan, the controversial leader of the Black Muslims, provided another illustration of internal fragmentation. The march mobilized the Black community against the white Republican majority in Washington who supported cuts in social programs. Marchers were there to "prove Black unity" and featured an extensive array of speakers—such as Jesse Jackson (president of the National Rainbow Coalition), Donald Payne (chairman of the Congressional Black Caucus), and civil rights figurehead Rosa Parks. Yet, this event more illustrated the fragmentation and crisis of the Black community than its unity. The call to march was aimed at Black men, to the exclusion of Black women and whites in general, raising accusations of both sexism and racism. Some African American leaders decided to skip the event because of Farrakhan's leading role. Paradoxically, according to Marianne Debouzy, "the march brought to light the absence of black leadership . . . The black silent majority failed to exit from its silence while white leaders showed themselves to be incapable of taking meaningful measures in favor of the poor."[50]

Even the fight for reparations for slavery has divided African Americans, some feeling threatened by incoming Black immigrants since the first legislative attempt was made to create a Commission to Study Reparation Proposals for African Americans in 1989.[51] Kevin Brown, a legal scholar, suggested renaming African Americans as "ascendants" in order to establish a clear distinction from other Blacks living in the United States. Ascendants, he argued, should refer only to people who "experienced America's racially discriminatory history their entire lives or were born from parents who were generally black at the time that affirmative action was adopted."[52] Brown's purpose was to secure privileges: "special rights and consideration" for ascendants in terms of admissions and scholarship programs in higher educational institutions. This goal was supported by other scholars, as well as small groups of activists, in their defense of the "Black face of affirmative action."[53] According to Antonio Moore, leader of the American Descendants of Slavery (ADOS), authentic Blackness should be defined by historical lineage instead of skin color. Calling Black immigrants and their children "African Americans" he argued, "erases the history of most black people in this country, whose ancestors were American slaves and who have suffered for generations as a result." Only descendants of slaves, therefore, should receive reparations for slavery as well as special considerations for affirmative action programs.[54]

Furthermore, increasingly aggressive forms of the "politics of recognition" bred politicized collective identities that, in turn, shifted identity politics from a dynamic of inclusion to one of division. Some men's rights groups, for example, turned "male supremacy" into "white male supremacy" by using historical aggressive visions of manhood, such as the idealization of military training and armed combat.[55] What all groups shared in common was an interest in affirming tribal identity—leading to various symbolic ceremonies and processes of ritual initiation. Some processes involved Asian Indian rituals—which raised objections from liberals (condemning the movement's "cultural appropriation") and from white right-wing radicals (condemning the subversion of whiteness).[56] These groups expanded their audience by joining the alt-right, a far-right movement based on an ideology of white nationalism, anti-Semitism, nativism, and antifeminism. The broad movement's self-professed goal was the creation of a white state and the destruction of "leftism"—"an ideology of death." Richard B. Spencer, a leader in the movement, described the movement as "identity politics for white people."[57]

Patterns of Mobilization

What remains to be addressed at that stage is how various groups usually engaged in different forms of contentious politics, why they engaged either in multiracial alliances or in inter- and intraracial conflicts, and why some used more violent behavior than others. We have learned from the historical perspective of contentious identity politics that, in addition to competition for material and symbolic resources, what really mattered was the perception by each group of other groups. That perception then turned grievances into contentious politics. Past tensions between groups were memorialized into twin narratives of blame and threat, perpetuating spirals of hostility over time. In their study of Hispanics based on the 1992 Los Angeles County Social Survey, for example, Lawrence Bobo and Vincent Hutchings found that underlying prejudices and existing animosities contributed to the Latino perception that African Americans were posing an economic threat.[58] By contrast, the relative success of previous forms of contentious politics inspired various groups to engage in identity politics—mimicking the civil rights activism of the 1960s—and occasionally in collaborative protest tactics. By the end of the 1990s, America had become a "social movement society," David Meyer and Sidney Tarrow argue, as the "result of the institutionalization of protest as a political tactic."[59]

Behavior, however, varied. Grievances were sometimes an insufficient reason to mobilize, and some groups mobilized more than others. Some groups protested more than others and some more violently. Differences in behavior were explained by two sets of factors. The first were structural reasons such as resources, opportunities to mobilize, or social embeddedness. The second set comprised emotional reasons, such as the extent to which they believed that the group was being treated unfairly and the degree of group efficacy. Together, confronted by racial prejudice, they combined in varied ways to generate differing forms of behavior, ranging from violent confrontations to nonviolent contentious politics and a few examples of ethnoracial coalitions.

Violent Confrontations

Compared to the 1960s, large-scale interethnic conflicts remained rare. Tensions, however, remained pervasive and commonplace while ethnoracial relations were increasingly plagued by prejudice. Apart from urban riots, interethnic violence took many forms (such as gang membership, white supremacism, and race-based violent criminality) in an increasingly polarized political context. Political leaders deliberately used widespread resentment to gain votes. This process was popularized during the Nixon presidency and termed "the Southern Strategy." Nixon, according to Doug McAdam and Karina Kloos in their study of racial politics and social movements, aligned himself with racial conservatives on many controversial issues (such as school integration and voting rights) to tap Wallace's supporters and be re-elected.[60] Kevin Philipps, Nixon's special counsel, claimed, for example, to be a specialist in "the whole secret of politics—knowing who hates who."[61] Many conservatives followed Nixon's example and gained votes by covertly stressing the role of race. It was expanded during the "Reagan Revolution," Reagan rebranding the GOP by deepening the connection between Republicans, whiteness, and Christianity.[62] This color-coded strategy sought, according to McAdam and Kloos, to depict the GOP as "the party of the law-abiding, tax-paying, 'silent (mostly white) majority' and demonize the Democrats as the party of liberals and the undeserving (disproportionately minority) poor whose dependence on social programs was taking money out of the pockets of hard-working, overtaxed (white) Americans."[63]

Some groups turned contentious politics into extreme forms of political polarization—as illustrated by violent controversies about the so-called historical "Confederate heritage." As civil rights activism increased in the 1960s, some white southerners became firmly attached to the Confederate flag, statues that largely dated from the Jim Crow regime, and monuments mostly built from the 1920s to the early 1940s.[64] Long before 2015, when local authorities began to remove statues after the killing of Black churchgoers in Charleston, the contentious Confederate symbology fueled a violent and unrepentant white supremacist ideology used by various extremist movements during the 1980s and 1990s consisting of traditional southerner supremacists as well as neo-Nazis, racist skinheads, white supremacist religious sects, and white supremacist prison gangs. It is noteworthy that white supremacists killed more people during this period than any other type of domestic extremism, in addition to several terrorist plots and attacks.[65]

The resilience of ethnoracial tensions continued to characterize the banality of violence in American society, notably the increasing number of hate crimes and gang violence. One Californian observer noted, for example, that "violent conflict in the prisons has been replicated in communities as some Latinos gangs have marked random black people living in the same neighborhood for death."[66] Gang homicides remained a serious problem in most US cities during the 1990s—especially in Los Angeles and Chicago where gang-related homicides in 1994 made up a substantial percentage of total homicides (44 and 32 percent respectively).[67] Structural conditions—including unemployment and poverty—explained both the likelihood of gang membership and homicides among members of minority groups who were both victims and perpetuators of street-level violence.[68]

Equally important was the relationship between gang affiliation and the use of violence as an identity strategy. This relationship dated back to the white street gangs that first emerged in the 1820s in New York City and multiplied in other cities after each wave of massive immigration. Italian, Polish, and other European immigrants monopolized gang activities until the early twentieth century, when they were joined by Hispanics, Asians, and African Americans in the eastern and Midwest region. Mexican gangs appeared in California as early as the 1890s, while black gangs developed there much later, starting in the 1970s, as a result of the "great migration."[69] What all these gangs shared was the willingness to strengthen a common sense of groupness based on oppositional street cultures that cultivated a self-image based on violence. That conception itself then reinforced learned patterns of violence. The purpose was twofold: to reaffirm a group or subgroup's ethnoracial identity, leading to interracial gang violence, and to control a particular territory that was mostly delineated by segregated drug markets. Acts of violence were actually rites of passage—not only for newly arrived immigrants but also among members of the second and third generation.[70]

City-level violence peaked in the mid-1990s in a climate of rising intolerance and growing acceptance of racial prejudice. From 1992 to 1996, for example, the number of hate crimes reported against African Americans increased by 52 percent. Of all the hate crimes reported in 1996, approximately 61 percent were motivated by racial prejudice. Of these, African Americans were the victims in 66 percent of the cases reported to the police (compared to 15 percent for whites).[71] Crimes against other minorities were—and are still—underreported. Yet violent incidents multiplied, often as mass casualties such as the killing of Asian children in a California elementary school in 1989. Most analysts concurred that scapegoating and stereotyping attitudes were encouraged by the poisoned social and political climate of the 1980s and 1990s—a period characterized by a backlash against affirmative action, the funding of social programs, bilingual education, and immigration. Torres noted that "the attitude in the United States today gives rise to the belief that bigotry is no longer politically incorrect, and is once again finding a degree of respectability,"[72] and Edward Dunbar argued that hate crime laws, as well as anti-discrimination policies, were "promulgated to assuage special interest advocacy groups, thus creating a climate of identity politics and, in turn, producing more strident and frequent complaints from social out-group members."[73]

More to the point, this climate was conducive to violent acts that repeated rites of violence inherited from the past such as the burning of 73 Black churches between 1995 and 1999. These were legitimized by perpetuators in terms reminiscent of the "culture of hate" dating back to the Manifest Destiny of the colonial period. Analyzing the similarities between historical and modern hate crimes, Carolyn Petrosino notes that "American culture, both past and present, includes similar beliefs and values. Systematic bigotry and discrimination, or the 'culture of hate,' continuously reaffirmed the identity of unworthy members of society, thus instigating and ensuring their victimization."[74] She adds that the growing incorporation of extremist views in mainstream political platforms encouraged supremacist, survivalist, and separatist groups—leading to the blurring of the line between hate crime and domestic terrorism.

Nonviolent Contentious Politics

Many forms of contentious politics in the post–civil rights era did not involve the use of physical violence. Among equally frustrated groups, some did not have the inclination or the opportunity to engage in violent protest or forms of illegal activity. Newly arrived immigrants, as well as undocumented immigrants, were more likely to avoid violent protest or illicit activity than US-born citizens and naturalized immigrants. Minorities, African Americans in particular, did not benefit from the legal protection—and sometimes immunity—granted to white violent activists and hate crime perpetuators who shared a sense of impunity. Even the ability to resort to discursive violent was color-coded. Ethnoracial groups, as previously discussed, did express racial prejudice. However, it paled in comparison to "First Amendment purists who argued for their constitutional rights to espouse their vitriol in public and even construed cross-burnings as protected speech."[75]

Groups and subgroups therefore chose legal activity as the most effective way to fight for their rights and gain access to material and symbolic resources. Successful examples of a peaceful politics of recognition, based on historical race-related discrimination, included the Civil Liberties Act of 1988 that granted reparations to Japanese Americans wrongfully interned during World War II and the Apology Resolution of 1993 acknowledging the maltreatment of Native Hawaiians. Concerns raised by affirmative action programs motivated various organizations, some composed of African American conservatives. The American Civil Rights Institute (ACRI), cofounded in 1996 by Ward Connerly and Thomas L. "Dusty" Rhodes, two African Americans, for example, supported anti-affirmative initiatives. They both opposed gender and racial preferences, and in 2000 the ACRI proposed a constitutional amendment, the "Racial Privacy Initiative," designed to ban state and local government from collecting racial data. Conservative Asian Americans similarly claimed to be disadvantaged by racially based group preferences and affirmative action. Their grievances resulted in several reverse discrimination cases, such as Ho v. San Francisco Unified School District (1997) in which they challenged the use of racial quotas limiting the enrollment of Chinese Americans. This case was widely supported by those opposed to affirmative action—including the organizers of Proposition 209, and California governor Pete Wilson. Furthermore, as the law professor Caitlin Liu noted at the time, "the *Ho* case has also carved deep divisions within the Asian American Community and strained relations with other minority groups (including the NAACP, Hispanics, Native Americans, and Southeast Asians) who gained from San Francisco's desegregation plan."[76]

The choice to exclusively pursue a legal course of action was not immune from racial or ethnic considerations. Among Asians, this choice was motivated by, and fueled in turn, the "minority model" stereotype. Among California's large Asian community, for example, only a small minority participated in the protests organized by Hispanic leaders, although some were themselves affected by anti-immigration measures. Afro-Asian collaboration during the civil rights era was confined to a few organizations and faded in the 1980s. Asian Americans distanced themselves from Black activism; in turn, the influence of Mao and "Bandung humanism" on Black activists proved short lived.[77]

Ethnoracial Coalitions

As previously discussed, the height of successful ethnoracial coalitions occurred in the 1960s with the civil rights movement, when Blacks, whites, and Hispanics formed political alliances in the pursuit of social justice, civil rights, and economic equality. During the 1980s and 1990s, some multiracial alliances were formed locally, as illustrated by collaboration between African American and Mexican American activists during antipoverty campaigns in California.[78] Another example was the multiracial coalition of Asian Americans, Mexicans Americans, and some African American residents in Oakland—leading to the 2000 mayoral victory of Jerry Brown, a candidate with no racial agenda.[79] In New York City, the Coalition Against Anti-Asian Violence built a multiracial grassroots alliance after the killing of Chin, dedicated to fighting racially motivated violence and police brutality.[80] Most studies of ethnoracial coalitions concurred that neither racial solidarity nor class played a major role. As David Roediger succinctly suggested: "Common misery did not produce interracial unity in a simple way."[81]

Ethnoracial coalitions were more likely to happen under specific circumstances: when groups resisted a narrow race-based politics; were able to share a common perception of inter-minority relations; and could set aside short-term, group-specific considerations to jointly address fundamental social and political issues.[82] Collective mobilization benefited all groups when these conditions were fulfilled. For example, such alliances led to the election of many Black mayors in large cities, who increased minority hiring and funding for minority businesses, even when the Black electorate was small.[83] As Jason Rivera et al. note, these coalitions succeeded when they attempted "to decrease competition between ethnic groups within the coalition so that more benefits for the total racial-political coalition can be gained."[84] Other contributory elements to their collective success were their ability to share common interests and develop trust over time as well as inherent respect for all members of the coalition. By contrast, coalitions based on special interests, seeking narrowly defined goals, and espousing individualistic ideologies did not last long, often being used by some group members to acquire individual benefits.

Collective action along ethnoracial lines in the pursuit of ethnically specific concerns was further hampered when members of ethnoracial groups lacked a sense of shared purpose and/or distanced themselves from other groups. Being targeted by discriminatory discourse and policies did create a sense of commonality within the group, but this also impaired collaboration for two reasons. First, the perception of "linked fate" varied from one group to another, undermining a strong linkage between African Americans and Hispanics. As Michael Jones Correra notes, "for discrimination to lead to joint mobilization, it must not only be similarly experienced, but also similarly interpreted."[85] For African Americans, "linked fate" related to the legacy of slavery and the resilience of racism in American society. For Hispanics, it referred to their "immigration experience" rather than their "discrimination experience"—especially among members of the first generation. Relations between Mexican Americans and Mexican immigrants were also tenuous, which made achieving any consensus regarding the immigration debate more difficult.[86] Coalitions between African Americans and Hispanics also broke down over immigration issues because African Americans tend to harbor anti-immigrant sentiments and thus oppose liberalizing legislation.

Second, the perception of "linked fate" was weakened by other factors such as class-based cleavages, religion, country of origin, and racial identity. Hispanics, for example, overwhelmingly supported the instrumental construction of a pan-ethnic "Hispanic community" for political purposes. Yet, their primary identification remained based on their countries of origin rather than group commonality. A Hispanic common identity was further fragmented by socioeconomic disparities between subgroups, in addition to different levels of acculturation. Mexican Americans and Puerto Ricans shared common historical experiences—the memory of the colonization of their ancestors, and arrived on the lowest rung of the working class. Cubans, in contrast, came to the United States as affluent political refugees and became economically more successful. Yet, paradoxically, the 1992 Latino National Political Survey (LNPS) reported that Mexican Americans felt closer to Anglos than to Puerto Ricans. Puerto Ricans likewise felt closer to Anglos than those of Mexican or Cuban ancestry and ranked African Americans equally to those of Mexican ancestry in terms of closeness.[87] As a result, the resurgence of Hispanic protest movements in the 1990s under the leadership of former Chicano activists mostly involved Hispanics of Mexican origin and remained geographically limited to California in response to antimigrant ballot measures such as Propositions 187 and 209.

There was also a comparable degree of internal heterogeneity among Asian communities along national, ethnic, and religious lines. This led to friction between Koreans, Chinese, and Filipinos.[88] Most Japanese Americans were of the third and fourth generations and were socioeconomically and culturally well integrated into mainstream American society. Other communities were still primarily composed of first- and second-generation members, with varying degrees of wealth. Not surprisingly, their sense of commonality remained weak, although Asian groups shared the frustration of being treated as "racialized outsiders" by non-Asian ethnoracial groups.[89] Another example of fissures between subgroups involved the lack of commonality between Black Muslims and immigrant Arab Muslims. Those immigrants, while benefiting from being labeled white according to the US racial classification, nonetheless faced the negativity associated with Islam. Yet, their religious identification did not strengthen the relationship with Black Muslims who suffered from dual discrimination (religious and racial) and who in turn distanced themselves from white Muslims. In a similar fashion, anti-Black prejudice among segments of the South Asian population undermined Muslim solidarity. In the 1980s and early 1990s, Arab Americans and new Muslim immigrants focused on US foreign policy issues affecting the Islamic world, principally the Israeli-Palestinian conflict, US sanctions against Iraq, and conflicts in Afghanistan and Chechnya. African American Muslims, in contrast, tended to focus on domestic issues and to support the Democratic Party. Formulating a united political platform between the two groups was not easy, as illustrated by the recurrent tensions between African American organizations and immigrant Muslim organizations, such as those that bedeviled the Islamic Society of North America (ISNA).

By the end of the 1990s, the sociopolitical and cultural climate had increasingly polarized as the result of the multiplication of both leftist and rightist revanchist policies. Despite the 1992 election of the Democrat Bill Clinton as president, conservatism remained strong, as illustrated by the "tidal wave" of congressional Republican gains in 1994 under the banner of Newt Gingrich's Contract with America. The combination of ethnoracial minority claims, political protests, civil disorder, street crimes, and fears generated by a global sense of social insecurity laid the foundation for the political demand for "law and order."[90] Attacks on liberal social programs, increasing socioeconomic inequalities, racially motivated "wars on culture," and widespread gerrymandering provided ethnoracial minorities with strong incentives to mobilize. However, in practice, the radicalization of contentious politics often precluded ethnoracial coalitions forming, which, in turn, undermined the fight for decent working conditions, employment opportunities, and civil rights.

Interestingly, the intensification of identity politics at this time raised concerns among liberals. They began criticizing the negative effect of centrifugal forces on American democracy. Indeed, Wendy Brown argued that identity politics was creating "ressentiment"—a "corrosive resentfulness on the part of those political actors motivated by or engaging in identity politics."[91] This logic of ressentiment, which she powerfully described as the "moralizing revenge of the powerless," promoted a sense of victimhood and a consequential obsessive demand for recognition. Other leftist critics claimed that identity politics posed a threat to democratic politics by promoting a politics of "dispersion and separateness" of distinct and embattled groupings. Reflecting on this period, "what began in the late 1960s as an assertion for dignity by various groups," Todd Gitlin noted in 1993, has resulted in the balkanization of America, which prevents us from "imagining a common enterprise." The "academic left," in particular, he asserted, "has lost interest in the commonalities that undergird its obsession with difference."[92] Jean Bethke Elshtain emphasized the potentially damaging implications of ressentiment on societal cohesion: "To the extent that citizens begin to retribalize into ethnic or other 'fixed-identity' groups, democracy falters. Any possibilities for human dialogue, for democratic communication and commonality, vanishes."[93]

What elements of this depiction are relevant for America today? And what will be their long-term effects on ethno-racial relations? I will examine these issues next.

Part 2
CURRENT TRAJECTORIES OF VIOLENCE IN POST-RACIAL AMERICA

Three major events in the last two decades have had significant consequences for ethnoracial relations in America. The first was the terrorist attacks of September 11, 2001. Some of the consequences of these attacks were the securitization of immigration policies, an upsurge of migrant phobia, and a virulent nativist campaign. The second was the election of Barack Obama as president in 2008. This event initiated a controversial debate about the state of race relations among advocates and critics of post-racialism. It also raised unprecedented expectations for racial progress among minorities as well as concerns among opponents to multiracialism. The third was the election of Donald Trump in 2016, which signaled the strength of extremist nativism and led to the culmination of the conservative revanchist policies that first emerged in the late 1990s.

From the "War on Terror" to Attacks on Minorities

The perception of immigrants (broadly defined) as posing a threat, as well as the militarization of border controls, predated 9/11—as ably illustrated by the broad application of the "war" metaphor to many policy areas.[1] The "war on terror" adjoined previous other initiatives such as the "war on poverty," the "war on drugs," and the "war on crime." The "war on crime," for example, was expanded by the Violent Crime Control and Law Enforcement Act of 1994. Likewise, the criminalization of migrants by the Anti-Terrorism and Effective Death Penalty

Act of 1996 coincided with the adoption the same year of the Personal Responsibility and Work Opportunity Reconciliation Act of 1996. This law, according to Loïc Wacquant, replaced the right to "welfare" with the obligation of "workfare," symbolizing the convergence of the "war on crime" with the criminalization of poverty in addition to the anti-immigrant initiatives of the 1990s.[2]

The gradual convergence between immigration and counterterrorist policies—based on the assumption that immigrants were potential terrorists—culminated after 9/11 as illustrated by security-driven immigration measures. The Immigration and Nationality Act, adopted within a week after 9/11, allowed the INS to detain any alien for forty-eight hours without charge and to extend detention for an additional period in the event of an "emergency or other extraordinary circumstances." It initiated a series of reforms toward the implementation of harsher immigration restrictions, all supposedly designed to strengthen security (such as the USA Patriot Act of 2001 and the Real ID Act of 2005). Policymakers consolidated the terrorism-immigration nexus in two ways. First, they justified a zero-tolerance approach to immigration offenses and tougher border controls by the claim that foreigners were more liable than citizens to commit terrorist attacks. Second, they broadened the "others" category—those outside the mainstream society who were considered to pose a threat. It henceforth included foreigners, immigrants, and suspicious ethnic and/or religious minorities—despite strong evidence that the linkage between immigration, border controls, and internal security was more complex than commonly anticipated by the Bush administration.[3] Further security-driven measures increased the surveillance powers of federal law enforcement authorities, such as the power to conduct "sneak and peek searches" (section 213 of the USA Patriot Act of 2001) and the collection of private communications of Americans (the Protect America Act of 2007). Federal officials and local authorities ramped up the surveillance of mosques by using techniques similar to those introduced in the late 1960s to repress student protesters and Black Power activists, notably the NYPD Muslim Surveillance Program launched in 2003. This program singled out religious and community leaders, organizations, businesses, and individuals by using video surveillance, police informants, and the collection of information in intelligence databases.

Negative sentiments against Muslims and those who look like Muslims (including Sikhs and non-Muslim Middle Easterners) spiked as part of a wave that then extended to immigrants more broadly. Both legal and illegal immigrants were affected by the government's war on terror. The 2001 Patriot Act, for example, restricted the civil rights of noncitizens. Illegal immigrants were denied access to an increasing number of social rights and economic benefits. Furthermore, the US government authorized unprecedented secret proceedings as well as the use of secret evidence to detain and deport immigrants. The Secure Fence

Act (HR 6061), signed by President Bush in October 2006, militarized America's borders (particularly its southern one). It doubled funding for border security, deployed thousands of National Guard members to assist the Border Patrol and allowed further use of military technology to achieve "war-style objectives." Yet the restrictive measures applied after 9/11 did not significantly reduce the flow of illegal immigrants. Nearly 4.3 million (37 percent) of the estimated number of illegal immigrants living in the country in 2008 had entered the United States between 2000 and 2007.

Still, the major outcome of the securitization of immigration was the resurgence of nativist propaganda, based on concerns about societal fragmentation allegedly associated with ethnic minority separatism in general, and a failure to integrate on the part of Muslims and Hispanics in particular. In Tom Tancredo's book, entitled *In Mortal Danger: The Battle for America's Borders and Security* (2006), the then Republican member of the House of Representatives synthesized common arguments made by nativists, using language reminiscent of Pat Buchanan's pamphlets about Mexicans nearly two decades earlier. All categories of "others" were depicted as posing a threat to economic prosperity, cultural identity, and national security. While the war on terror targeted immigrants and religious minorities, critics of multiracialism intensified their attacks on nonwhites as "outsiders and intruders bent on oppressing whites."[4] During the Bush administration, nativist organizations (such as FAIR and the Center for Immigration Studies) joined forces with racially conservative groups who used the judicial and political systems to achieve their political objectives under the guise of national security. Examples of this use of lawfare included a wave of legislative attempts to reform the immigration system in 2006–2007 and a series of legal cases in which the US Supreme Court struck down some aspects of affirmative action in higher education (such as both Grutter v. Bollinger and Gratz v. Bollinger in 2003).

The Ambivalence of Post-Racialism

The election of Barack Obama as president of the United States in 2008 raised two related questions over the increasing ethnoracial diversity in America: Does post-racialism presage the solving of ethnoracial tensions and thus imply that intergroup conflicts will abate? Or does post-racialism, by contrast, downplay the resilience of racial prejudice and obscure the socioeconomic differences between and among ethnoracial groups? These questions echoed the debates of the 1990s over multiracialism.[5] Yet, the election of Obama was an historic event, portrayed as the culmination of the civil rights movement and amplifying both hopes and concerns about multiracialism. Jabari Asim, editor in chief of *The Crisis* (the main NAACP publication), attributed the victory of Barack Obama to "the alignment of irreversible cultural trends, substantial political developments, and unstoppable market forces."[6] For Thomas L. Friedman, columnist at the *New York Times*, Obama's election finally signaled an end to the Civil War. Thus, he suggested, "Let every child and every citizen and every new immigrant know that from this day forward everything really *is* possible in America."[7]

Some commentators viewed Obama's election as illustrative of America's move toward post-racialism. Wilbur Rich, for example, argues that Obama's ascendancy was part of a "deWASPing" process through which nonwhite elites "not only transcend the racial stereotypes but now rival their white counterparts in terms of education, incomes and relative influence."[8] David Hollinger argues that the "historic event of the election of a black president of the United States made it easier to contemplate a possible future that might be called post-ethnic or post-racial." In this "possible future," he adds, "ethnoracial categories central to identity politics would be more matters of choice than ascription (. . .) mobilization by ethnoracial groups would be more a strategic option than a presumed destiny attendant upon mere membership in a group."[9] According to the most optimistic commentators, this process transformed America into a "more open society," with positive effects on race relations and the democratic inclusion of all minorities. This optimistic narrative focused on the positive impact of legislative reforms, the relative improvement of the socioeconomic status of minorities, and the opportunities provided by the emergence of a multi-ethnoracial society. Reflecting this perspective, Richard Alba and Victor Nee argue that "because of the subsequent extension of civil rights to nonwhites, the monitoring and enforcement of formal rules that once worked to effect exclusion from the mainstream now contribute to lowering the barriers to entry from immigrant minorities and the new second generation."[10] They add that "the changes could lead ultimately to a broad decline in the significance of racial/ethnic boundaries, and this could finally soften the hitherto hard-and-fast character of the black-white divide."[11] Other studies similarly focused on the positive impact of multiracialism on ethnoracial categorization and intergroup relations.[12]

Other commentators, like Eduardo Bonilla-Silva, strongly opposed this optimism and argued instead that the "Obama-hope-liquor" was corrupted by new racial practices, apparently nonracial but largely institutionalized.[13] He suggested that this "new racism" is fueled by a "color-blind" ideology, abstract liberalism, and cultural prejudice (such as the "culture of poverty" thesis). From this perspective, the growing number of multiracial Americans does not mean that the color line is fading. America's racial stratification is indeed changing, but the result is not a post-racial society. Rather, it is characterized by a shift from the traditional bi-racial to a tri-racial system composed of whites, "honorary whites," and a nonwhite "collective black" group. In this system, color gradations remain the main criteria of within-group differentiation and "will become more salient factors of stratification."[14] According to critical race scholar Alana Lentin, "undoubtedly, much of what comes under post-racialism is racism under another guise."[15] Post-racialism, she argues, refers "to the ways in which, by bypassing or denying race as an adequate means of making sense of discrimination, we risk ignoring how allied concepts such as culture and diversity have been incorporated into the denial of the significance of race."[16] Culturalism, based on the essentialization of cultural differences, should subsequently be understood as the continuation of racialization—as illustrated by discrimination on the grounds of cultural/religious differences as well as the implicit racism involved in "culture wars." As Thomas Sugrue demonstrates in *Not Even Past: Barack Obama and the Burden of Race*, a prospective post-racial era does not guarantee a color-blind future.[17] Nor does it presage various groups coexisting in greater harmony.

These conflicting approaches illustrate a lack of consensus about what post-racialism is, or prescriptively should be, despite a plethora of studies.[18] As David Hollinger summarizes, "the gap between what is being refuted and what is being affirmed is a discursive Grand Canyon."[19] Post-racialism has subsequently fueled grievances among all ethnoracial groups based on conflicting perceptions of what a post-racial society should look like. For progressives, American society remains much too racialized (mostly in terms of racial prejudice and socioeconomic inequalities)—a belief that leads them to resentment and frustration. For conservatives, America has become too diverse as the result of a "browning process"—a trend that threatens their group position in an increasingly complex racial status hierarchy. Hopes to move beyond age-old racial divisions rapidly receded. Among Obama's supporters, the dream of a post-racial America ended with a series of painful wake-up calls—such as the dramatic effect of the 2008 economic crisis, the killing of Trayvon Martin in 2013 (followed by the killings of Michael Brown, Eric Garner, and Freddie Gray), and the continuation of antimigrant policies (which led some Hispanic organizations to name Obama "Deporter in chief"). Among Obama's opponents, racial and ethnocentric attitudes were stronger predictors of their votes in 2008 and 2012, their rejection of social policies (such as "Obamacare"), and their perceptions of ethnoracial relations. Racially motivated polarization involved the birther movement (with Donald Trump as spokesperson), the Tea Party Movement (spreading the rumor that Obama was a secret Muslim), libertarian interest groups, Fox News commentators, and congressional leaders who coalesced around absolute legislative obstructionism.

The racial divides that were already salient to American politics before 2008 subsequently became even larger during Obama's presidency. As summarized by Michael Tesler, "Barack Obama's presidency further racialized American politics, despite his administration's best effort to neutralize the political impact of race."[20] This trend paved the way for the 2016 election of Donald Trump who did his best to appeal to prejudicial racial identities and attitudes.

The Trump Effect

Donald Trump made racial issues central to his presidential campaign. His supporters were worried about their status and identity as white Americans, a concern that allowed him to build a broad electoral coalition. Michael Tesler and John Sides, in their analysis of the ANES findings, argue that "both white racial identity and beliefs that whites are treated unfairly are powerful predictors of support for Donald Trump in the Republican primaries."[21] Data from the American National Election Studies showed that "being white" was very or extremely important for 47 percent of Trump's supporters—compared with 31 percent among supporters of other Republican candidates.[22] Trump's rhetoric during the 2016 presidential campaign also combined nativist arguments (such as advocating that priority should be given to native workers over immigrants for employment and social benefits) with xenophobic fear tactics—conflating the notions of "terrorist" (against Muslims) and "criminal" (against Hispanics). Trump voters strongly subscribed to this rhetoric. A public opinion poll conducted by the Pew Research Center in November 2016 found that 79 percent of Trump voters believed that illegal immigration was a "very big" problem in the country, while only 20 percent of Clinton voters expressed such a belief.

Since 2016, this "racial anxiety" has framed perceptions of immigrants and minorities. Trump's election was symptomatic of a broader American identity crisis. Christopher Parker and Matt Barreto, for example, showed that what actually motivated Tea Party supporters was not simply one-dimensional racism but rather the fear that the country was changing for the worse, as it slipped away from the "real America: a heterosexual, Christian, middle-class, (mostly) male, white country."[23] In their study of Trump's election, John Sides and his colleagues show that "issues like immigration, racial discrimination, and the integration of Muslims boil down to competing visions of American identity and inclusiveness."[24] Diana Mutz reaches a similar conclusion in her study of "status shock" among high-status groups (whites, Christians, and men): "both growing domestic racial diversity and globalization contributed to a sense that white Americans are under siege by these engines of changes."[25]

Racially charged comments were conducive to violence. Soon after the election of Trump, the number of hate groups nearly tripled (from thirty-four in 2015 to

101 in 2016). According to the Southern Poverty Law Center (SPLC), it was an effect of Trump's rhetoric that "electrified the radical right"—especially white nationalist and anti-Muslim groups. The SPLC recorded at least 1,097 racial incidents during the first thirty-four days following the election.[26] The FBI data showed that hate crimes rose the day after Trump was elected. Violence persisted over time. In 2018, the number of violent hate crimes was the highest in sixteen years. The number of offenses rose 12 percent from 2017 to 2018.[27] Anti-Semitic incidents surged more than one-third in 2016 and jumped nearly 60 percent in 2017.[28] The number of anti-Semitic incidents increased again in 2018 (including the attack against a synagogue in Pittsburgh killing eleven people) and reached a peaked in 2019 (up to 2,107).[29] Racial violence targeted Hispanics and other minorities as well. According to the FBI, the number of victims of Hispanic hate crimes rose by 21 percent in 2018. Anti-Black crimes increased by 16 percent. Anti-transgender remained an epidemic, with at least twenty-nine murdered, while all crimes motivated by sexual and gender orientation increased by 5 percent.[30]

However, as proved by the historical examples I provided in the first part of this book, adversity provides opportunities for ethnoracial groups to mobilize. The KKK-style rally in Charlottesville in 2017, leading to the killing of a young woman by a white nationalist, was followed by large demonstrations and protests targeting Trump and his agenda. There were also significant Democratic gains in the elections held in 2017 and 2018. Other racially motivated initiatives (such as the Muslim ban and threats against Dreamers) incentivized minorities to mobilize. During the summer of 2020, about 20 million people in more than 550 places across the country participated in demonstrations over the death of George Floyd and others—turning Black Lives Matter into the largest protest movement in American history. All forms of activism have been more intense since 2016—from street protests to social media and from nonviolent resistance to urban unrest.

How Can We Analyze Ethnoracial Violence in America Today?

In the coming sections, I examine the Janus-like nature of America's society in which inter- and intragroup relations occur. I consider evidence of the positive impact of legislative reforms, the relative improvement of the socioeconomic status of minorities, and the opportunities post-racialism provides related to the diversity-tolerance nexus. From this perspective, American society is becoming more amenable to various forms of diversity, raising hopes for a shift toward greater intercommunal tolerance, dialogue, and acceptance. But I also review the relevant empirical studies supporting the diversity-intolerance nexus, with data showing that socioeconomic inequality, racial disparities, and other forms of adversity plague American society.

In the context of these conflicting realities, I analyze the controversial debates raised by the concept of post-racialism by specifically including both objective socioeconomic variations related to the diversification of American society and the subjective combination of expectations and fears raised by this diversification. Data about America's demography vividly demonstrates that transition. Its increasing racial and ethnic diversity results from four factors: immigration flows, a growing propensity for intermarriage, the subsequent multiracial baby boom, and the sharp increase in the number of people who identify themselves as "multiracial" (as measured by the US Census since 2000). As a consequence, no single ethnoracial group will comprise a majority of the population in the decades ahead. This trend is already evident. America will become a plural society by the early 2020s: more than half of the nation's children are expected to be part of a minority race or ethnic group. The Black/white paradigm of assimilation is being indisputably dismantled by these new demographic realities.

Through the ethnoracial lens, it appears that both dominant and minority groups are currently being redefined, as well as their perceptions of their relationship to a sense of entitlement, perceived discrimination, and group standing. Today, concerns raised by new demographic realities challenge the traditional racial paradigm of assimilation. The ambivalent nature of post-racialism incites all ethnoracial groups and subgroups to engage in a spiral of expectations, claims, frustration, and competition for the allocation of material and symbolic resources. I believe that it is important to explore the mobilizing effects of several types of threats produced by changing economic conditions, demographic shifts, and political competition. All these changes, as Tilly demonstrates, inspire reactive mobilization in response to the real or perceived loss of power or resources.[31] Reactive social movements subsequently involve attempts by a group to reassert claims to political/economic resources that they have lost or perceive they have lost. As a result, groups tend to mobilize when they perceive either increased or decreased levels of opportunity because their feelings are partly disconnected from reality.

In the ensuing chapters, I subsequently apply all the components of contentious politics I have identified to the study of current forms of inter- and intragroup relations. I pay particular attention to the role played by perceptions in constructing conflict in order to provide a better understanding of physical and symbolic violence from the perspective of both dominant groups *and* their challengers. In doing so, I systematically focus on three main aspects of contentious identity politics that have framed inter- and intragroup relations since the 1990s:

grievances fueled by both objective and subjective discrimination, relative deprivation based on perceived group competition, and cycles of contention sustained by the belief that the "others" (broadly defined) pose a threat.

Furthermore, "the same conditions that create favorable conditions for collective action by one movement may present an increased threat for another."[32] This trend, I demonstrate, explains the institutionalization and routinization of protest politics in America, a product of the current spread of social movements and the movement-countermovement dynamics. Not all forms of protest activity involve the use of symbolic or physical violence. However, as I discuss, there is little reason to believe that inter- and intragroup relations are going to improve anytime soon.

5
TWO TALES OF ONE NATION

The continuing debate over post-racialism is fueled by opposing empirical evidence. Some findings sustain the argument that the diversification of ethnoracial diversity facilitates the integration of nonwhite minorities and immigrants, who have thus benefited from the loosening of previously constraining ethnoracial boundaries. There is also strong evidence that African Americans have specifically achieved significant socioeconomic progress. Perceptions of both immigrants and racial minorities tend to improve in the post-racial stage as various forms of intergroup contact increase. From an optimistic perspective, America is becoming a more appeased, if not peaceful, multiracial society in which various groups coexist in increased harmony. Yet, America is simultaneously experiencing significant forms of turbulence, mostly fueled by the persistence of racial prejudice, socioeconomic inequalities, and resilient negative attitudes toward some categories of immigrants and religious minorities. Forms of adversity that ethnoracial groups today face include discursive violence (such as hate speech, supremacist propaganda, and a nativist antimigrant narrative), discriminatory legislation (such as antimigrant laws, racial profiling, and limitation of civil rights), and physical violence (such as police brutality).

Diversity and Tolerance

Over the last two decades, American society has become more open, more diverse—and more tolerant toward various forms of diversity. Americans' perception of immigrants, for example, has improved. In 1996, 63 percent of Americans said that immigrants were a burden, and only 31 percent said they had a positive impact. In 2015, these figures had substantially altered: 45 percent said that immigrants were "making American society better," and 51 percent said immigrants "strengthen the country because of their hard work and talents." A residual 41 percent considered them more of a burden, "taking our jobs, housing, and health care."[1] Still, overwhelming majorities today believe that immigrants are hardworking (87 percent) and have strong family values (82 percent). As a result, the percentage of Americans wanting to increase immigration levels increased fivefold, from 5 percent in 1997 to 25 percent in 2013.[2] A 2019 Pew Research Center study indicated a continuation of this positive trend. The United States ranked sixth among eighteen countries according to its citizens' views on immigrants. As the study results showed, 59 percent of Americans expressed the view that immigrants make the country stronger because of their work and talents, whereas only 38 percent said they believe that immigrants take jobs and social benefits. The United States also ranked second regarding citizens' views on immigrants and crime. Seventy-seven percent expressed the view that immigrants in America are no more to blame for crime than other groups. Moreover, 54 percent of Americans said they believe that immigrants want to adopt America's customs and way of life as opposed to 37 percent who said the opposite.[3]

Furthermore, there is evidence that a growing number of Americans endorse an inclusive definition of American identity. Only a minority of Americans, when asked to define the main components of American identity, support a narrow ethnocultural definition of "Americanism"—where "being Christian" (19.3 percent), having "European ancestry" (7 percent), or "being white" (3.8 percent) is "very important." By contrast, overwhelming majorities emphasize the importance of "respecting American political institutions and laws" (80.9 percent), "respecting other people's cultural differences" (80.1 percent), and "seeing people of all backgrounds as American" (73.1 percent).[4]

The data suggests that the scope of tolerance has expanded and now includes most religious and ethnoracial groups, as well as other minorities. Americans have a favorable opinion of African Americans (89 percent), Hispanics (82 percent), Catholics (83 percent), and Jews (84 percent). Support for same-sex marriage grew from 35 percent in 2001 to 55 percent in 2015—and up to 60 percent among Catholics and white Protestants.[5] In 2019, four years after the landmark 5-4 Supreme Court decision in Obergefell v. Hodges, 61 percent of Americans favored the legalization of same-sex marriage while 31 percent opposed. Accordingly, while a partisan gap persists, the percentage of Democrats who favor same-sex marriage had increased by 32 percent—from 43 percent to 75 percent between 2004 and 2019. But the percentage of Republicans who favor same-sex marriage increased by

25 percent, albeit from 19 percent in 2004 to 44 percent in 2019.[6] Furthermore, disapproval of interracial relationships has significantly declined. In 1968, more than 70 percent of Americans disapproved of marriage between whites and Blacks—compared with less than 13 percent in 2013.[7] While the percentage of Americans who regarded interracial marriage as a "good thing" increased and as a "bad thing" correspondingly decreased between 2010 to 2017, most remained indifferent; 52 percent did not believe that the increased number of interracial marriages makes much of a difference.[8]

A majority of Americans have consistently supported affirmative action programs for women and minorities. An *NBC News/Wall Street Journal* poll conducted in 2009, for example, found that 63 percent of respondents felt that these programs were still required, in contrast to only 28 percent who favored their termination.[9] In 2011, 60 percent of the public supported affirmative action programs designed to increase the number of Black and minority students on college campuses. Three years later, that support increased to 63 percent. By 2017, 71 percent held that view. When divided by race, 83 percent of Hispanics, 82 percent of Blacks, and 66 percent of whites said that these kinds of programs were good. In terms of political affiliation, 84 percent of Democrats favored such programs, although 52 percent of Republicans did so as well.[10]

Diversity and Intergroup Relations

A greater acceptance of "different differences" seems to have been fueled by recent shifts in the population's racial and ethnic composition. The Census Bureau estimates that the United States will become a "majority-minority" nation by 2044. By then, more than half of all Americans are projected to be members of a minority group (any group other than non-Hispanic white). These shifts are part of the so-called "third demographic transition" which has increased the numbers of Americans who belong to minority groups. A Pew Research Center study found that the "multiracial experience" reinforces tolerance toward ethnoracial diversity. People who report themselves as being of multiple races tend to hold pro-immigrant attitudes. About 59 percent of multiracial Americans, for example, feel that their racial heritage has made them more open to other cultures. Fifty-five percent believe they are more understanding of people of different racial backgrounds.[11] Furthermore, respondents with cross-racial friendships report lower levels of prejudice, as do those living in more racially and ethnically integrated neighborhoods.[12]

Diversity seems to have some positive social consequences, notably for race relations and other forms of intergroup contact. Projected changes in the ethnoracial composition of American society should therefore accentuate positive social cohesion as well as peaceful patterns of integration. Like other scholars analyzing the "multiracial experience" among Blacks, whites, and new immigrant groups, Jennifer Lee and Frank Bean argue that the rapid growth of nonwhite groups will not increase ethnoracial tensions. Focusing on intermarriage (a yardstick for assimilation) and the subsequent growing numbers of mixed-raced children, they argue that diversity itself contributes to more favorable attitudes toward members of other groups. Furthermore, they added, shifts in the racial and ethnic composition of the population have increased the numbers of minority ingroup members who hold more pro-immigrant attitudes, which in turn will generate boundary-breaking behaviors and experiences.[13]

Some evidence supports their optimism. A poll conducted in 2011 by the Public Religion Research Institute (PRRI), showed that young Americans are far more comfortable with—and sympathetic to—ethnic, racial, and religious diversity than older Americans. Yet, even Americans uneasy with diversity accept it in important ways as a norm. Americans who are part of the millennial generation (ages 18–29) were twice as likely as seniors (ages 65 and older) to have daily interactions with African Americans (51 percent versus 25 percent, respectively) and Hispanics (44 percent versus 17 percent, respectively). In addition, 54 percent of respondents regarded Muslims as an important part of the US community, and 60 percent felt that "too many Americans think that all Muslims are terrorists."[14]

A study conducted in 2019 by the Pew Research Center supported the findings of the PRRI. It showed that younger Americans favor today a growing racial and ethnic diversity in the United States. Overall, most Americans said it makes the country a better place to live. About 58 percent of Americans said that an increasing number of people of different races and ethnicities makes the United States a better place to live, whereas only 9 percent said it makes it a worse place to live. Questions by age cohort are also revealing. Fifty-eight percent of Americans aged 18–29 said that a diverse America is a better place compared to 7 percent who disagreed. Interestingly, 51 percent of Americans aged over 65 also concurred, while 15 percent disagreed.[15] Furthermore, while racial tensions persist, 79 percent of college graduates claimed to have only experienced discrimination from "time to time" in comparison to 20 percent who experienced discrimination "regularly." Furthermore, 83 percent of Blacks experienced discrimination from time to time as opposed to 17 percent regularly.[16]

The Changing Black Experience

From the end of World War II until the civil rights movement, African Americans gained an economic foothold. A Black middle class, comparable to its white counterpart, began to emerge as African Americans secured coveted white-collar occupations and became more educated.[17] A racial gap persisted, especially in terms of "net worth" (calculated by taking all assets such as real estate and stocks in addition to earnings, and subtracting liabilities). Yet, the median net worth for African Americans increased over time. It almost doubled between 1984 and 2005 (from $6,679 to $12,124).[18]

According to the US Census and the Bureau of Labor Statistics, by 2009 there were 117 million households in America. The median household income for all households then was $49,777, compared to $32,584 for Black householders. About 47 percent of all householders were middle class (classified as incomes between $35,000 and $100,000). According to this metric, 38.4 percent of the 14.7 million Black householders in America were middle class. Furthermore, 8.1 percent were upper middle class (between $100,000 and $200,000), and 1.2 percent reached the upper class ($200,000 and over). The situation therefore consistently improved. Terrible areas of poverty persisted in the African American community. But, when adjusted for inflation, the percentage of African Americans making at least $75,000 more than doubled between 1970 and 2014 (from 11 to 26 percent). Furthermore, the unemployment rate among Black Americans by June 2018 was 5.9 percent, the lowest on record. That was only 2.4 percent higher than the white unemployment rate, compared with the 12 percent differential in 1985).

African Americans have achieved significant progress in some cities. In Atlanta, for example, about 46.9 percent of the metro area's Black population owned their own homes in 2013, well above the 38 percent major metro average for African Americans nationally. In the greater Washington, DC area, the median Black household income in 2013 was $64,896 (compared to $34,598 for the average Black median household income, and about $65,000 for whites). A new residential trend has emerged: a "Black outmigration," with middle-class African Americans moving into suburban neighborhoods that better reflect their economic status. Among the 40 percent of African Americans who now live in the suburbs, some live in neighborhoods with high median incomes, high household value, low crime, and great public schools—such as "Black Beverly Hills" (California), DeSoto (Texas), and Hillcrest (New York).

African Americans have also achieved more educationally. Black enrollment in colleges and universities has increased dramatically over the past two decades. By 2014, Black students accounted for 16 percent of enrollments at institutions that primarily grant associate degrees. There were 3.9 million Black college students in 2015, an increase of roughly 2 million in 18 years. Approximately 22 percent of Blacks 25 years and older held at least a bachelor's degree (compared with 11 percent in 1988). It is notable, however, that Black students represented only 6 percent of students at top-tier universities, a statistic that has remained largely the same for twenty years. Furthermore, foreign-born Black adults are more likely than native adults to hold a bachelor's degree or higher, by a ratio difference of 10 percent.[19]

There is still clear evidence of racial and ethnic disparities in healthcare. Data from the US Department of Health and Human Services shows that Blacks are still at a major health disadvantage compared with whites. Yet Blacks have gained, both in absolute and relative terms, in life expectancy. The life expectancy gap between Blacks and whites was seven years in 1990; by 2014 it had shrunk to 3.4 years—with life expectancy at 75.6 years for Blacks and 79 years for whites. Infant mortality among Blacks has declined by more than 20 percent since the late 1990s, double the decline for whites. The death rate from cancer among Blacks fell by 29 percent between 1995 and 2013, compared with 20 percent for whites, substantially driven by the decline in deaths from lung cancer. It is noteworthy that Blacks have had lower smoking rates than whites over the past 15 years. The suicide rate for Black men also fell between 1999 and 2014—the only group to decline. According to the US Department of Health and Human Services, Medicare and Medicaid have made screening and new treatments more accessible to Blacks.[20] Furthermore, the rate of deaths by homicide decreased by 40 percent for Blacks between 1995 and 2013, compared with a 28 percent drop for whites.[21]

The Migrant Optimism

Data suggests that migrant integration is steadily proceeding in the United States. Various studies using several socioeconomic measures illustrate that today's immigrants show a remarkable ability to integrate. According to Tomás Jiménez, a sociologist at Stanford University, they learn English faster than the large previous waves of immigrants. Among immigrants who arrived in the 2000s, approximately 20 percent already speak English well, and 27 percent very well.[22] This trend is also true among Hispanic immigrants, with 34 percent speaking English proficiently—although only 5 percent spoke only English at home in 2013.[23] In 2017, there were 27.4 million foreign-born persons in the US labor force—comprising 17 percent of the total. Their unemployment rate was then only 4.1 percent (compared with 4.4 percent among native-born workers). Foreign-born workers are more likely to be employed than native-born workers in numerous sectors, such as services.[24] Most immigrants say they quickly became comfortable in the United States. A large majority of immigrants have a positive attitude toward the United States: 87 percent are happy living in the country, and 76 percent believe that it is a unique country that stands for something special in the world.[25]

Socioeconomic integration by the children of immigrants generally dramatically increases across successive generations. Studies of social mobility, however, find divergent outcomes with Hispanics having a lower social capital than other minority groups.[26] Nevertheless, the socioeconomic advancement among successive generations is quite broad, a product of civil rights legislation and formal antidiscrimination mechanisms that have lowered the barriers to mainstream entry for non-Blacks. According to Richard Alba, "one momentous change involves the rapidly growing presence of Americans from recent waves of immigration at the top of the U.S. workforce, in domains that were previously monopolized by native whites."[27] In a study conducted with Guillermo Yriza Barbosa, he focused on the upper quartile of all workers who work in the most lucrative occupations (as defined by annual earnings). The expanding groups in these upper ranks were Asians (both foreign and native-born), US-born Hispanics, and African Americans. Meanwhile, the share represented by whites had dipped from 85 percent before 2000 to below 70 percent in 2015.[28]

There is strong evidence that immigrants and their children are integrating in the United States reasonably well. The proportion of immigrants speaking only English or speaking English very well, for example, increased to more than 80 percent in the second generation of all ethnoracial groups.[29] Among US-born Hispanics—who represent today more than 65 percent of Hispanics—89 percent spoke English proficiently in 2013.[30] Twenty-nine percent of adult immigrants did not hold a high school diploma in 2015, but native- and foreign-born adults hold bachelor's degrees at similar rates (32 percent and 30 percent, respectively). And a much higher percentage of foreign-born adults gained graduate degrees (24 percent and 31 percent, respectively). Second-generation adults are doing better (up to 36 percent) than their parents in terms of gaining college degrees and better than the overall population (31 percent). At the opposite of the educational spectrum, only 10 percent of second-generation members have less than a high school diploma (compared with 12 percent of the overall population). They also do better than first-generation members in terms of median household income ($58,000 versus $46,000) and homeownership (64 percent versus 51 percent). They are less likely to be impoverished (10 percent versus 28 percent) and less likely to live in segregated neighborhoods. A large majority of them identify as "typical Americans" (up to 61 percent among Hispanic Americans and Asian Americans—compared with 33 percent and 30 percent, respectively, among first-generation immigrants). Furthermore, 52 percent of second-generation Hispanics and 64 percent of second-generation Asians believe their group gets along well with other ethnoracial groups.[31]

Overall, naturalized immigrants lag behind the native-born population in terms of their rates of participation in the electoral process (61 percent versus 72 percent in 2008). However, they are very active in other forms of political participation, such as hometown association (HTA) membership and civic engagement in religious and nonreligious organizations.[32] Hispanics, for example, actively participate in nonvoting forms of politics, such as attending public meetings in the community where they live (26 percent), contacting elected officials (22 percent), and volunteering their time to religious organizations (42 percent).[33] Multiple associations promote civic engagement, such as Movimiento Hispano which was created in 2012 in partnership with the Hispanic Federation, the Labor Council for Latin American Advancement (LCLAA), and the League of United Latin American Citizens (LULAC). Other organizations focus on civil rights in multiracial America, such as the Association of Multiethnic Americans (AMEA), Project Race, and A Place for Us (APFU). Their main goals are to promote multiracialism by pushing the Census Bureau to modify its racial categorization, fighting discrimination, and encouraging ethnoracial relationships.

Diversity and Intolerance

Based on this reading of the diversity-tolerance nexus, it is believable that the "dream of a post-racial America" is becoming reality.[34] However, there is also strong evidence supporting a more pessimistic appreciation of the actual and perceived effects of post-racialism. Daunting socioeconomic and discriminatory practices remain as obstacles to minority integration. Racial disparities in law enforcement have remained widespread, casting doubt on the expected benefits of dismantling the racist legislative framework during the civil rights era. Indeed, the diversification of diversity has not dramatically improved race relations, and antimigrant feelings continue to be widely shared. These trends, together, demonstrate the limitations of the socioeconomic and institutional reforms that have been implemented since the 1960s.

Migrant Phobia and Race Relations

Migrant phobia remains widespread. Although 50 percent of Americans said that newcomers strengthen American society in 2016, 34 percent contended that they represent a threat to American customs and values. Negative attitudes were higher among Republicans (53 percent), white evangelical Protestants (53 percent), and white Americans (40 percent) while 67 percent of Hispanics and 56 percent of African Americans said immigrants have a positive influence in American society.[35] Even more disturbingly, ethnoracial and religious minorities are increasingly victims of violence. According to the FBI, there were 6,100 reported incidents of hate crimes in 2016, up from 5,800 the year before. Anti-Semitism was the leading cause, motivating 55 percent of these episodes, followed by anti-Muslim sentiment

(25 percent).³⁶ The Southern Poverty Law Center (SPLC) found that the number of hate groups (mostly white supremacist and anti-immigrant groups) rose to 954 in 2017—from 917 the year before. Black nationalist groups (representing 20 percent of all hate groups) also expanded, from 193 to 233, in reaction to rising white supremacy.³⁷

Most religious and ethnic groups are relatively favorably viewed in polling. Yet, some groups are less positively perceived than others, as illustrated by the situation of American Muslims. In 2017, 25 percent of US adults said they believe that Muslims are "anti-American," 35 percent suspected that Muslims support extremism, and 50 percent affirmed that Islam is not a part of "mainstream American society."³⁸ There are however significant differences in attitudes about Muslims among political, religious, and demographic groups. According to the PRRI, 58 percent of Americans hold a favorable view of Muslims—compared to 83 percent having a favorable view of Catholics, 84 percent of Jews, and 67 percent of Mormons. Among those surveyed in 2016, roughly two-thirds of Democrats (65 percent), millennials (68 percent), religiously unaffiliated Americans (68 percent), and non-Christian religiously affiliated (69 percent) reported a favorable view of American Muslims. In contrast, less than half of Republicans (47 percent), Americans who identified with the Tea Party movement (44 percent), seniors (46 percent), and white evangelicals (44 percent) polled had a favorable view. Furthermore, 63 percent of Republicans and 66 percent of those who identified with the Tea Party said they believe that the values of Islam are at odds with American values. A majority of Democrats (55 percent) and political independents (53 percent) disagree.³⁹ Political partisanship also affected the perception of discrimination against Muslims. In 2019, Democrats were more likely than Republicans to say that Muslims face at least some discrimination in the United States (92 percent versus 69 percent, respectively). Democrats also were more likely than Republicans to say that Jews face discrimination (70 percent versus 55 percent). Conversely, Republicans were much more likely than Democrats to say that evangelicals face discrimination (70 percent versus 32 percent).⁴⁰

Other statistics cast a shadow on the notion of improved race relations in America. In 2015, 39 percent of Americans said that relations between Blacks and whites had worsened since the election of Obama (compared with 15 percent who believed that these relations had improved).⁴¹ Overall, positive perceptions have sharply declined—from 68 percent in 2008 who believed that relations between Blacks and whites were "very good" or "somewhat good" to 47 percent by 2015. Negative perceptions, by contrast, increased from 30 percent in 2008 to 53 percent.⁴² According to a poll conducted by the *New York Times* and *CBS News* in 2015, public perceptions of race relations in America grew substantially more negative in the aftermath of the death that April of Freddie Gray while in police custody in Baltimore. Comparably, about 61 percent of respondents said that race relations were generally bad in the country—up from 44 percent after the fatal police shooting of Michael Brown in August 2014 and the unrest that then followed in Ferguson, Missouri. About 68 percent of African Americans had a negative perception of race relations—the highest level of discontent was recorded during the Obama presidency—close to the numbers recorded in the aftermath of the Los Angeles riots in 1992. Furthermore, 44 percent of all respondents then believed that race relations would worsen. Both Blacks (41 percent) and whites (46 percent) were negative about the future of ethnoracial diversity in America.

Pessimism about the evolution of race relations increased after the presidential election of Donald Trump in 2016. About 42 percent of Americans worried in 2017 "a great deal" about race relations in America (more than doubling from 2014), and 61 percent believed that racism against Blacks was widespread (including a large racial split with 82 percent of Blacks versus 56 percent of whites). Furthermore, 65 percent of nonwhites were more concerned about discrimination and violence against minorities under Trump, while only 43 percent of whites agreed. Various opinion poll surveys showed that minorities believed that they were increasingly discriminated against. Conversely, a growing number of Americans believed that discrimination against whites is as big a problem as discrimination against Blacks and other minorities—up to 57 percent among whites and 66 percent among white working-class Americans.[43] Two years into Donald Trump's presidency, 53 percent of those surveyed said race relations were getting worse, and 56 percent of Americans said that Trump specifically had made race relations worse.

Socioeconomic Discrimination

Racial socioeconomic discrimination is extensively documented in terms of educational achievement, housing, access to health care, income, education, and job opportunities. A multitude of reports and studies provide evidence that African Americans and Hispanics are, on average, lagging behind white Americans.[44] Overall, as I have demonstrated, minorities have made significant progress. But that progress has often been insufficient to catch up with their non-Hispanic white counterparts. Furthermore, this progress has been always fragile as illustrated by the impact of the 2008 crisis, with minorities suffering much more than whites in times of economic and fiscal crisis. As a result of the COVID-19 recession, the Black-white economic divide went back to what it was in 1968.[45]

Data from the US Census Bureau, as illustrated in Table 5.1, shows the relative improvement of the socioeconomic situation of minorities—notably in terms of median family income over three decades. Yet, each socioeconomic indicator

TABLE 5.1 Relative improvement of the socioeconomic situation of minorities

	1980	1990	2000	2010
Poverty	- Black: 32,5%	- Black: 31,9%	- Black: 22,5%	- Black: 27,4%
	- Hispanic: 25,7%	- Hispanic: 28,1%	- Hispanic: 21,5%	- Hispanic: 26,5%
	- White: 10,2%	- White: 10,7%	- White: 9,5%	- White 13%
	- Asian —	- Asian 15,3%	- Asian: 9,9%	- Asian: 12,3%
Income (median family)	- Black: $10,764	- Black: $18,676	- Black: $26,667	- Black: $32,126
	- Hispanic: $13,651	- Hispanic: $22,330	- Hispanic: $33,168	- Hispanic: $37,631
	- White: $18,684	- White: $31,231	- White: $43,916	- White: $51,709
	- Asian —	- Asian: $38,450	- Asian: $55,757	- Asian: $64,259

Source: United States Census Bureau.

demonstrates a resilient gap between whites and minorities. By then, Asians had come closest to whites and performed better than any other minority group. But African Americans consistently had the worst outcomes by 2010—with a higher percentage of Blacks in poverty compared to whites, Latinos, and Asians. Blacks also had the lowest annual incomes. Blacks had the highest unemployment rate in 2010 at 16 percent, compared with 9 percent for whites, 8 percent for Asians, and 13 percent for Hispanics. Furthermore, the income gap between Blacks and Latinos increased over time (from a gap of $2,887 in 1980 to $5,507 in 2010).

As a result of the 2008 financial crisis, poverty rates increased among all ethnoracial groups. Yet, Blacks were more affected than other groups.[46] Unemployment rates also significantly declined in the decade that followed: down to 3.9 percent for adult men and 3.6 percent for adult women by January 2018. Yet, racial disparities remained significant. Unemployment rates for adult white men and women were 3.4 percent and 3 percent. Hispanic men and women had unemployment rates of 4.3 percent and 4.6 percent, respectively. But Black men and women had an employment rate of 7.5 percent and 6.6 percent, respectively.[47] Furthermore, median income disparities persisted, with Blacks earning on average 50 percent less than Asians, 40 percent less than whites, and 18 percent less than Hispanics. Black median net worth significantly declined due to the 2008 recession, from $12,124 in 2005 to $5,677 in 2009—lower than it was in 1984. White median net worth also declined, but only from $134,992 to $113,149—a startling difference.[48]

A decade after the recession, data from the Census Bureau showed that Asians were at the very top, with an average household income of $87,194. Whites were second with an average household income of $70,642. Hispanics (all races) and Hispanics (any races) were in third ($63,179) and fourth ($51,450) places, respectively. Blacks were in the last place with an average household income of $41,361.[49]

In terms of the Black-white wealth gap, no progress has been made since the 1960s. A study published by the Federal Reserve Bank of Minneapolis showed that it would need to combine the net worth of 11.5 Black households to match the net worth of a single typical white US household.[50]

Another study by the Institute for Policy Studies found that it would take 228 years for the average Black family, and 84 years for the average Hispanic family, to amass the same level of wealth as the average white family. By 2043—the year in which it is projected that people of color will make up a majority of the US population—the wealth divide between white families and Hispanic and Black families was forecast to double (from about $500,000 to over $1 million).[51] Not surprisingly, the American upper middle class has remained overwhelmingly white. The proportion of Blacks and Hispanics in their forties in the upper middle class has not increased in recent decades. Hispanics make up approximately 17 percent of the overall population aged forty to fifty but just 9 percent of the upper middle class. For Blacks, the numbers are 12 percent and 7 percent, respectively. The only minority that contravenes this trend is Asians, who make up 7 percent of the overall population but 11 percent of the upper middle class.[52]

These disparities are explained by a combination of factors, such as educational achievement and hiring discrimination. In 2000, the percentage of the white population aged twenty-five and over with a college degree was 23 percent. Asians performed better, at 35 percent. Blacks performed better than Latinos, 12 and 5 percent, A. By 2015, all groups had made progress over time (as I discussed in the last section), but the persistent variation among groups remained significant. More than half of all Asians had a bachelor's degree or higher compared with 36 percent of whites, 22 percent of Blacks, and 15 percent of Hispanics. The gap between whites and Blacks slightly increased (from 11 to 14 percentage points) as did the gap between whites and Asians (from 17 to 18 percentage points).[53] Racial gaps in elementary and secondary education raised serious concerns. Studies conducted to commemorate the fiftieth anniversary of the 1966 Coleman Report on "Equality of Educational Opportunity" showed that the gap between white and Black students has barely narrowed over the last five decades. The Coleman Report, for example, found that the average Black student in twelfth grade placed in the thirteenth percentile of the score distribution in both math and reading—meaning that 87 percent of white students scored ahead of their average Black counterparts.[54] In 2013, according to data from the National Assessment for Educational progress, the average twelfth-grade Black student placed only in the 19th percentile in math and in the 22nd percentile in reading.[55] Furthermore, Black and Hispanic students had higher dropout rates than white students in both private and public high schools.[56]

High levels of education are associated with a greater likelihood of employment and higher income for all ethnoracial groups. Globally, there have been improvements over the years among minorities. Yet, the composition of the US labor force, measured by educational attainment, varies by race and ethnicity. In 2016, 60 percent of Asians and 43 percent of whites participating in the labor force had obtained at least a bachelor's degree. By comparison, 28 percent of Blacks and 20 percent of Hispanics had at least a bachelor's degree. Conversely, 26 percent of Hispanics participating in the labor force had less than a high school diploma, compared with only 7 percent of Blacks, 6 percent of Asians, and 4 percent of whites.[57]

There is no reason to expect major improvements soon. For example, the legacy of the landmark decision in Brown v. Board of Education is under threat. According to the Government Accountability Office, the proportion of public schools segregated by race and class—where more than 75 percent of children receive free or reduced-price lunch, and where more than 75 percent are Black or Hispanic—rocketed from 9 to 16 percent of schools between 2001 and 2014. The number of more intensively segregated schools (where more than 90 percent of low-income and minority students attend) more than doubled over that period. As a result, minority students who are concentrated in high-poverty schools do not have the same access to educational opportunities as students in other schools.[58] Regionally, this issue is more extreme in the South where more than 50 percent of Black students attended the most segregated schools in 2014, compared to 25 percent in 1972.[59]

Educational inequalities have a significant impact on job occupations. Service industries, several hit by the COVID-19 recession, employ disproportionate numbers of minority workers with low levels of qualification. Unemployment rates skyrocketed during this recession, especially among low-income workers and Black self-employed workers. There is strong evidence of the dramatic effects of blatant discrimination against some minorities. According to a study published about discrimination in the job market by the *Harvard Business Review*, white applicants received, on average, 36 percent more callbacks than Black applicants and 24 percent more callbacks than Hispanic applicants with identical résumés between 1990 and 2017.[60] With respect to housing, residency is heavily divided by ethnoracial status. The average white resident lives in a neighborhood that is 79 percent white—compared with 46 percent for Blacks and 45 percent for Hispanics. Only a small minority of people who identify themselves as multiracial live in fairly diverse neighborhoods. There has been a modest reduction in racial residential segregation, as suburbs opened to Blacks in the 1980s. For example, sixty-one of the one hundred largest metro areas (mostly

Sun Belt cities) registered declines in Black-white segregation between 2000 and 2010. Yet, there were still twelve metro areas where segregation had increased—primarily Detroit, Chicago, Cleveland, and New York.

Simultaneously, residential segregation by social class has continued to rise. Poor families thus face racial prejudice and significant obstacles in finding and maintaining affordable housing. Matthew Desmond, in a study conducted for the Institute for Research on Poverty, found that the percentage of renter households paying at least half of their income toward housing costs rose from 21 to 30 percent between 1991 and 2013—due to a combination of rising housing costs, falling incomes among the poor, and a shortfall of federal housing assistance. Desmond adds, "African American and Hispanic families, the majority of whom rent their housing, were disproportionately affected by this trend. In 2013, 23 percent of black renting families and 25 percent of Hispanic renting families spent at least half of their income on housing."[61]

Racial Disparities in Law Enforcement

Racial profiling worsened after a Supreme Court ruling in 1996 that police officers could use traffic stops to investigate suspicious individuals, "even if the offense they were investigating did not have anything to do with the offense for which the individual was stopped" (Whren v. United States, 517 U.S. 806). Data from the Bureau of Justice Statistics showed, for example, that Hispanic drivers were most likely to receive a ticket and Blacks were most likely (and twice as likely as whites) to be arrested during a traffic stop.[62] Furthermore, Black drivers in 2011 were twice as likely to experience the threat or use of violent force at the hands of police officers than both white and Hispanic drivers. In 2019, 84 percent of Black adults claimed that, in dealing with police, Blacks are generally treated less fairly than whites. Blacks were also about five times as likely as whites to say they had been unfairly stopped by police because of their race or ethnicity (44 percent versus 9 percent), a view felt especially strongly among Black men (59 percent).[63]

Critics of police reforms—often political conservatives and police unions—typically argue that the reason more Black men and women are arrested, shot, and killed by police is that African Americans commit more violent crime.[64] However, the relationship between violent crime and police brutality is more complicated than commonly assumed. There is evidence that a disproportionate number of crimes are committed by Black Americans, partly because of higher levels of criminality in disadvantaged neighborhoods, predominantly Black neighborhoods. As noted by Wesley Lowery in his analysis of data collected by the *Washington Post* in 2015, "when factoring in threat level, black Americans who are fatally shot by police are no more likely to be posing an imminent lethal threat to the officers at the moment they are killed than white Americans fatally shot by police."[65] Other studies have shown that African Americans were more often targeted for use of police force than white Americans, even when adjusting for whether the person was a violent criminal.[66] For example, about 13 percent of all Black people killed by the police in 2015 were unarmed, compared with 7 percent of all white people.[67] Furthermore, police brutality is taking place in a context of impunity: the excessive use of force by police officers persists because overwhelming barriers to accountability, such as the rule of "qualified immunity," make it possible to escape punishment or criminal prosecution. The Minneapolis contract allowed Derek Chauvin, who held his knee to George Floyd's neck for nearly nine minutes, to keep his job for almost two decades despite eighteen reports of abuse. Chauvin's conviction in April 2020 has so far been the exception in the long history of police abuse. Over the past fifteen years, only 110 police officers have been charged with felony homicide in the United States, and only five have been convicted of murder.[68]

Discrimination by law enforcement officials has increased further since 9/11 toward citizens and immigrants of Middle Eastern and South Asian descent, as well as those perceived to be Arab or Muslim. A 2003 Department of Justice guidance outlawed the use of race or ethnicity by federal law enforcement as an element of suspicion. Yet, as noted by Amnesty International USA, "it contains a blanket exception for national and border security, does not cover profiling based on religion, and is neither legally binding nor applicable to state and local law enforcement."[69]

Racial disparities are omnipresent in the criminal justice system. The United States has the highest incarceration rate in the world, and the majority of inmates are members of ethnoracial minorities. According to the Sentencing Project, "racial minorities are more likely than white Americans to be arrested; once arrested, they are more likely to be convicted; and once convicted, they are more likely to face stiff sentences. African-American males are six times more likely to be incarcerated than white males and 2.5 times more likely than Hispanic males."[70] In 2017, Blacks were the highest subpopulation imprisoned at federal detention centers (33 percent) although they represented only 13 percent of the population. Hispanics represented 23 percent of the federal prison population (and 16 percent of the total population). Whites, representing an overwhelming 64 percent of the population, accounted for only 30 percent of the US federal prison population in 2017.[71] As Marc Mauer, executive director of the Sentencing Project, noted a decade ago, "if current trends continue, 1 of every 3 African American males born today can expect to go to prison in his lifetime, as can 1 of every 6 Latino males, compared to 1 in 17 white males."[72]

Racial disparities in sentencing for drug offenses are significant. As a result, "minorities and immigrants are subsequently more likely than whites to be searched, arrested, detained, prosecuted, given harsher sentences, and face death penalty."[73] According to the Office of National Drug Control Policy, African Americans represent only 14 percent of all illegal drug users. However, they constitute 36 percent of drug arrests, 53 percent of drug convictions, and 63 percent of all drug offenders committed to state prisons. By contrast, whites make up 69 percent of drug users, but only 25.8 percent of defendants. African Americans are prosecuted and incarcerated for drug offenses at a much higher rate than white Americans. Nationally, African Americans are incarcerated at 8.2 times the incarceration rate of whites.[74] One of the most dramatic long-term consequences of the mass incarceration of low-level offenders is that millions of minority citizens are often disenfranchised for life by state laws regarding certain classes of offenders.

Law enforcement officials also disproportionately target Blacks and other minorities for gang-related activities. Contrary to the assumption that minorities are predisposed to higher involvement in crime, whites make up the largest proportionate group of adolescent gang members. A study from the Justice Policy Institute showed that, although law enforcement sources reported that over 90 percent of gang members were nonwhite, whites in fact accounted for 40 percent of adolescent gang members. African American and Latino communities, however, bear the cost of failed gang enforcement initiatives. Young men of color are disproportionately identified as gang members and targeted for surveillance, arrest, and incarceration. In contrast, whites—who make up a significant share of gang members—rarely show up in accounts of gang enforcement efforts. For example, "the Los Angeles district attorney's office found that close to half of black males between the ages of 21 and 24 had been entered in the county's gang database even though no one could credibly argue that all of these young men were current gang members."[75]

Once racial minorities enter the criminal justice system, they confront more hurdles and racial bias at every stage of litigation. Black and Hispanic defendants, for example, "are often more likely than white defendants to rely on an indigent defense system of overworked, underpaid attorneys—therefore increasing their chances of being convicted."[76] Once minority defendants are convicted, they are likely to be sentenced more harshly than white defendants convicted for similar crimes. Racial disparities are particularly pronounced in cases involving the death penalty. African Americans are considerably more likely than whites to be victims of violent crime. However, defendants convicted of the homicide of a white victim are substantially more likely to face the death penalty than those convicted of killing nonwhite victims. According to Mauer, "persons who kill whites are about four times as likely to receive a death sentence as those who kill African Americans."[77] A 2016 study on capital punishment in Louisiana, for example, showed that a Black man is thirty times more likely to be sentenced to death for killing a white woman as for killing a Black man. Regardless of the offender's race, death sentences are six times as likely—and executions fourteen times as likely—when the victim is white rather than Black. The study emphasized that "the single most shocking element of Louisiana's experience with the death penalty is that no white individual has been executed for killing a black since 1752."[78]

Civic Exclusion

The enforcement of civil rights remains an important instrument in a context characterized by persistent racism and socioeconomic discrimination. The legacy of the civil rights movement is threatened by the weak criminal liability of police officers, the role of predisposed local grand juries "seemingly shielding these officers from criminal prosecution," and the multiplication of obstacles to the pursuit of civil rights litigation under 42 U.S.C. Section 1983 (the federal statute providing a civil cause of action in federal courts for constitutional rights violations).[79]

The protection of voting rights remains fragile, despite the Voting Rights Act (VRA) of 1965 and other measures designed to secure the enfranchisement of different groups. A 2016 study from the Sentencing Project found that an estimated 2.5 percent of the US voting-age population is denied the right to vote because of a felony conviction after completion of sentences. Felony disenfranchisement, targeting mostly minority and poor communities, increased from 1.17 million people in 1976 to 5.9 million in 2010, and 6.1 million in 2016. African Americans are more than four times more likely to lose their voting rights than the rest of the population.[80] Gerrymandering, the practice of rearranging the boundaries of electoral districts, preponderantly reduces the impact of racial minority voters—as well as many barriers to the ballot box (such as the ID Law and restrictive election laws). According to the American Bar Association, more than 180 restrictive voting bills were introduced in forty-one states in 2012, affecting more than five million eligible voters. "Today, mechanisms reminiscent of the Jim Crow measures," notes Denise Lieberman (a former senior attorney in the Voter Protection Program), "make it more difficult, if not impossible, for millions of voters to cast a ballot—disproportionately African Americans and Latinos, young voters, low-wage earners, people with disabilities, and senior citizens."[81] The US Supreme Court ruling Shelby County v. Holder (2013) made Section 5 of the VRA inoperable and therefore opened the door to racial discrimination at every step of the electoral process. Further disenfranchisement tactics were adopted ahead of the 2016 election, with fourteen states adopting measures to restrict votes (including mass poll closures). This arguably contributed significantly to a decline in minority voter participation—for example, 16 percent of African American voters in North Carolina.[82] In 2021, eighteen states in America enacted thirty laws restricting voting access. These laws, targeting minorities, made mail voting and early voting more difficult, imposed harsher voter ID requirements, and made faulty voter purges more likely.[83]

Minorities subsequently remain underrepresented in the US political system. The white share of eligible voters declined (from 75.2 percent in 2004 to 68.9 percent in 2016). Yet, the profile of voters tends to be whiter because turnout rates among minorities remain lower. Mexicans, for example, have the lowest rates of naturalization (36 percent) compared with other immigrants from Central and Latin America (49 percent) and all other immigrants (72 percent).[84] Among eligible voters, the share of Hispanic voters increased from 13.2 million in 2000 to 27.3 million in 2016 due to demographic changes. Yet, their proportion of the electorate has remained below their percentage of the total population (12 percent of eligible voters and 16.3 percent of the population in 2016). Furthermore, only 48 percent of registered Hispanic voters actually voted in 2012—compared to 67 percent of Blacks and 64 percent of whites. The Hispanic voter turnout rate declined slightly in 2016 (47.6 percent), while the rate among whites increased (from 64.1 percent in 2012 to 65.3 percent in 2016). The Black voter turnout rate declined in 2016 in a presidential election for the first time in twenty years, falling to 59.6 percent (compared with 66.6 percent in 2012). That, arguably, decided the election.

Furthermore, minorities are underrepresented in electoral positions. Only six members of the 114th Congress, for example, were foreign born. This number represented 1 percent of the total number of both senators and representatives, while the foreign-born population constituted about 13 percent of the total population. The number of Hispanics in Congress has remained lower than their percentage of the US population. Although the numbers of Hispanics nearly tripled between 1980 and 2010, their representation did not change proportionately. In 1981, there were nine Hispanic Americans in Congress—one representative for every 1.6 million Hispanics. In 2011, this ratio remained unchanged with thirty-one Hispanic Americans in Congress. There was greater representation of African Americans in the House in 2015 (with forty-four members), but only two senators and one governor were Black. African Americans have made gains in political leadership. In 1965, for example, there were no Blacks in the Senate, nor were there any Black governors. Only six members of the House were Blacks. By contrast, in 2019, fifty-two House members were Blacks (12 percent of members—consistent with the share of Blacks in the US population overall for the first time in history). Yet, there has been little change in other elected positions (with only three Black senators and no Black governors).[85]

These starkly contrasting findings about American society are generating hopes as well as fears among all ethnoracial citizens. Post-racialism may be a fact in terms of growing minority populations, representation, and economic mobility. But it simultaneously fuels grievances based on conflicting perceptions of what a post-racial society should look like, contributing at least to one dimension of the polarization characteristic of American politics today. In the next chapter, I examine how these grievances today generate a centrifugal dynamic of societal fragmentation.

6
FROM IDENTITY POLITICS TO ETHNORACIAL IDENTITY CRISIS

The objective data presented in the last chapter supports both the optimistic and pessimistic diagnostics of the current—and future—patterns of assimilation. American society is becoming more amenable to various forms of diversity—which raises hopes for greater intercommunal tolerance. Yet, significant ethnoracial inequalities nonetheless persist in America, as well as racial prejudice and resilient negative attitudes toward some categories of immigrants and religious minorities. Reflecting on the Obama administration, Robert Gooding-Williams and Charles Mills purportedly summarize these conflicting findings, noting "it was the most postracial of times, it was the least postracial of times."[1]

What is the impact of these quite distinct, often ambivalent contextual changes on ethnoracial relations? Does greater access to American mainstream society adequately sustain a progressive inclusion of minorities and subsequently assuage ethnoracial conflicts? When addressing these questions, I focus on the challenges that all ethnoracial groups face by analyzing what it means—from their standpoint—to live in a multiracial society. This requires combining the effects of actual changes with the perceptions of these changes among various groups. These perceptions are sometimes disconnected from reality, as illustrated by the significant discrepancy between actual and perceived discrimination. Members of a dominant group, who are less discriminated against than minorities are, can feel subjectively excluded. Alternatively, minorities who are objectively discriminated against do not always feel subjectively excluded, or at least do not have a negative attitude toward their host society.[2]

There is a complex relationship between expressions of prejudice and perceptions of both actual and perceived discrimination, and between perceived discrimination and responding attitudes toward society as a whole. A sense of alienation reinforces group consciousness, which, in turn, increases either solidarity among groups or the radicalization of contentious repertoires.

The options are so numerous that we need to closely examine the various ways diversity now affects both majority and minority groups' identity-based strategies in their efforts to join a dynamically changing mainstream society. As Richard Alba and Jan Willem Duyvendak argue in their study of assimilation in super-diverse times, the fact that "very few people seem to be *indifferent to difference*" can lead to either conviviality or, conversely, greater boundary intensification.[3] Studies of super-diversity, a concept introduced by Steven Vertovec in 2007 to characterize the "multicultural condition of the twenty-first century," are not directly concerned with issues of ethnoracial violence.[4] Yet they provide useful insights about how different groups perceive diversity, how the changing mainstream both provides new opportunities and fuels grievances, and how mainstream groups now feel threatened—quite independently of their objective situation.

The Identity Challenges of Diversity

One of the common conceptions about American society is that the ethnoracial landscape has been radically transformed by the impact of multiracialism and the consequential acceptance of different differences. However, the actual significance of these changes remains unclear. Scholars are often dealing with conflicting assessments. For example, Richard Alba and Victor Nee argue that multiculturalism has prepared "the way for a redefinition of the nature of the American social majority, one that accepts a majority that is racially diverse."[5] From this perspective, multiracialism is key in providing new opportunities to build interracial alliances and promote tolerance by smoothly assimilating all ethnoracial groups. Consequently, the boundaries between Blacks and other groups (including whites) are likely to blur further as a result of "black social mobility into core institutional structures and organizations."[6]

On the other hand, Alba and Nee contend that there is still "a racial and ethnic stratification system, and placement within it matters for the life chances of individuals."[7] Other studies of immigration disparage the alleged benefits of multiracialism on migrants' assimilation. Joe Feagin and José Cobas, for example, demonstrate that Hispanics continue to suffer from racism and institutional violence, contrary to the optimistic assertions about an emerging post-racial society.

They argue that Hispanics cannot follow the same trajectory of assimilation as white ethnic groups because they remain racialized as a culturally and biologically inferior "mongrelized" group.[8]

Both the pessimistic and optimistic assessments suffer from limitations. The assumption that the fluidity of ethnoracial identities generated by multiracialism makes racial boundaries less rigid—a core argument of the optimistic scenario—is actually misleading. Increasing complex identities have fueled concerns, indeed fears, about what groupness can achieve in terms of symbolic recognition and access to resources—a process illustrated by the multiplication of grievances among all ethnoracial groups when multiracialism started to emerge in the 1990s. When identities shift, or the borders between two groups become blurred, ethnoracial groups tend to consolidate their ingroup position through the strengthening of their opposition to what they regard as threatening outgroups.

Furthermore, changes generally regarded as positive (such as antidiscrimination policies, the lowering of socioeconomic obstacles, and political achievements) are nevertheless perceived as negative by some groups and subgroups. This activates the pendulum effect, as seen in the post–civil rights era. The election of Barack Obama, for example, elicited negative reactions from across the racial spectrum. For some, like Wornie Reed and Bertin Louis Jr., his election provided "proof positive that racism does not exist and, by extension, that blacks have 'no more excuses' with regard to their collective condition in the United States." They claim that this belief was shared by "the *Afristocracy*—upper-middle-class blacks and the black elite . . . who rain fire and brimstone upon poor blacks for their deviance and pathology, and for their lack of couth and culture."[9] For others, President Obama represented a post-racial leadership model that was perceived as a threat by those Americans who were part of the white backlash that gained influence during his presidency, and played a key role in the election of Trump.

That there is still a Black/white divide is beyond question. Yet, the belief that it frames all aspects of ethnoracial relations risks simplistic judgments. Many other factors help structure the relationship between groups and subgroups, as well as inter- and intra-ethnoracial conflicts. It is therefore not surprising that key components of the contentious identity politics of the 1990s continue to influence patterns of ethnoracial mobilization. Furthermore, as increasing cultural and socioeconomic diversity of ethnoracial groups leads to greater pluralistic assimilation, levels of both tolerance and intolerance vary significantly across societal spheres. Whites, for example, can support affirmative action programs while being reluctant to share their neighborhoods with nonwhites. Hispanics and nonwhites can live in segregated neighborhoods while being integrated in the labor market or live in integrated neighborhoods while expressing racial prejudice toward other groups. And, as previously mentioned, ethnoracial groups can simultaneously be perpetuators and victims of physical or discursive violence.

Before the multiracial transformation of American society, the main objective for minorities was to enter a mainstream society still dominated by the white native majority. Today, Alba and Duyvendak argue, "the mainstream majority is no longer visible, or at least no longer seems dominant."[10] Furthermore, as a result of the spillover process of identity politics that emerged in the 1980s, tensions have increased about the creedal principles of American identity and the values that should cement a political community. Reflective of white and nonwhite conservatives, 57 percent of Republicans and Republican-leaning independents in 2019 said they believe that America is losing its identity because of immigration and multiracialism. Diversity, they contend, is threatening American customs and values.[11] Only 39 percent of them said that they believe ethnoracial diversity is a "good thing" (compared to 71 percent of Democrats), and 21 percent said that ethnoracial diversity has a negative impact on American culture (compared to 5 percent of Democrats).[12] Such beliefs are the basis for violent opposition to the "balkanization" of America, fueling culture wars reminiscent of Pat Buchanan's popularized "struggle for the soul of America" in the 1990s. According to one critic, affirmative action and ethnic politics "supposedly designed to bring people into the system, have the effect of turning people against each other ... The tribes won't disappear."[13] Echoing this denunciation of "tribalism of conviction," other conservatives such as Charles Krauthammer railed against "leftists identity politics" that "balkanizes society, creates state-chosen favored groups and fosters communal strife."[14]

Some white and nonwhite liberals share concerns about the declining cohesiveness of American society, but for very different reasons. Mark Lila, for example, echoed critics of identity politics. In a best-selling 2017 pamphlet he argues that "identity politics on the left was at first about large classes of people—African-Americans, women—seeking to redress major historical wrongs by mobilizing and then working through our political institutions to secure their rights." However, "by the 1980s it had given way to a pseudo-politics of self-regard and increasingly narrow and exclusionary self-definition that is now cultivated in our colleges and universities ... Every advance of liberal identity consciousness has marked a retreat of liberal political consciousness ... The very concept of *we* seemed suspect"[15] Amy Chua reaches a complementary conclusion, arguing that identity politics has fueled political tribalism among minorities, as well as being directed against minorities on behalf of right-wing tribal groups.[16]

Against this background, the outcome of the 2016 presidential election depended less on policies than on partisan identity battles grounded in racial issues. The campaign, Sides argues, "reinforced and exacerbated those cleavages as it focused on issues related to race, immigration, and religion. The result was an epic battle not just for the White House but about what America is and should be."[17] All ethnoracial groups were involved in this battle, leading to a redefinition of the content and purpose of their respective identity politics.

The Crisis of White Identity

For members of the shrinking white majority, diversity can make them more aware of their distinctiveness. Evidence of concerns about demographic and cultural shifts are not new, illustrated by the findings I have already provided. These concerns have been shared by three distinct white subgroups since the 1990s.

For the first group, white identity has become more important as a result of what Tomas Jiménez called "relational assimilation," by which whites adjust to varied aspects of multiracialism such as mixed marriages and integrated neighborhoods.[18] For these whites, white identity is not defined by racial animus. As Ashley Jardina demonstrated in her study of white identity politics, "whites who identify with their racial group are not simply reducible to bigots."[19] Rather, they identify with their group without feeling prejudice toward ethnoracial minorities, and they support diversity policies.

The second group comprises those who express a high level of "white consciousness" based on the feeling that many policies are unfair to whites. This white consciousness, Jardina argues, can be motivated by racial prejudice. But it can also be the product of nonracial factors for one main purpose: to claim the right of whites to share a sense of commonality and solidarity with their racial groups—like other groups do—without systematic feelings of prejudice toward ethnoracial minorities.

The third group is made up of whites who express a very high level of racial resentment. They mostly fall on the right side of the political spectrum. They perceive all aspects of American society through the lens of racism and migrant phobia and—predictably—support a white supremacy agenda. These are the people most likely to participate in marches such as those that captivated the nation's attention in Charlottesville.

Many studies confirm that these groups coexist today—with tensions along political, socioeconomic, and cultural lines. Yet, major changes in the last decade have had a significant impact on both intrawhite and interracial relations. One relates to a pervasive white anxiety among some whites. Surveys since 2010 suggest that white people are increasingly likely to say that they are losing status and feel threatened by minorities—especially among Republicans. These GOP voters resent what they perceive as antiwhite discrimination (up to 60 percent, compared to 24 percent of Democrats).[20] In 2019, albeit before the staggering growth of the BLM movement, only 19 percent of them agreed that Blacks faced a lot of discrimination (compared to 69 percent of Democrats).[21] A survey conducted by PRRI among white working-class Trump voters showed that fears about immigrants and cultural displacement (such as the feeling of "being strangers in their own land") were among the more powerful factors motivating them. About 68 percent of respondents said, "the U.S. is in danger of losing its culture and identity," and 62 percent said that immigrants threaten American culture.[22] Some whites push the argument further by claiming victimhood. In 2016, for example, 64 percent of Trump voters said that "average Americans" have gotten "less than they deserve."[23] Some resent that there is no "white history" month or other opportunities to openly identify with and celebrate their race.[24]

A second crucial change is the shift from white anxiety to racial animosity and the subsequent radicalization, shifting former members of the second group into the third one. This move has been explained by some observers as the consequence of worsening economic inequality coupled with rapidly changing ethnoracial demography. Lawrence Bobo, for example, emphasizes that "more and more Americans are experiencing a serious economic vulnerability" that—combined with concerns about their ethnoracial status—"opens the door to a powerfully resonant blend of antiminority populism."[25] In her historical review of the white working class, Nancy Isenberg offers a similar perspective on the challenges that poor whites have to face, emphasizing that "marginalized as a class, white trash have always been near the center of major debates over the character of the American identity."[26]

Evidence suggests that economic anxiety, fueled by actual or perceived class-based alienation, plays a role in the fear and hostility of outgroups. Trump portrayed himself as the savior of the poor white working class. Among his supporters, 63 percent said that the lack of job opportunities for working-class Americans was a "very big" national problem. Most were white, more likely to work in blue-collar occupations, and less likely to have a college degree than those who supported Clinton. Yet, when compared to the general population, they had higher-than-average incomes, were 60 percent more likely to be self-employed, and tended to live in communities without manufacturing jobs and with high levels of racial homogeneity.[27]

Contrary to popular belief, Trump was thus elected by a large swath of voters with relatively high incomes who shared nothing in common with the working class except a strong sense of economic insecurity.[28] More pointedly, numerous studies found that hardened racial attitudes have increasingly structured public opinion about immigration, as well as perceptions about economic conditions. Notably, data from the Cooperative Campaign Analysis Project (generated between 2008 and 2012) demonstrated that economic anxiety was not causing racism; in fact, racial resentment was driving economic anxiety.[29] In their 2016 American National Election Study, for example, Michael Tesler and John Sides argue that both white racial identity and beliefs that whites suffer from discrimination were powerful predictors of support for Trump.[30]

Trump's election showed that "the backlash against diversity could be a winning issue."[31] Identity politics has intensified since then, with growing divisions along political partisanship and ethnoracial lines. The gap between supporters and opponents of Trump has increased among whites, disputing what it means to be American. This ideological battle increasingly overlaps party and racial attitudes, sometimes turning into violent confrontation (as illustrated by the confrontation in Charlottesville in 2017). Trump's election incentivized white liberal advocacy on behalf of racial and ethnic minorities. White Democrats, for example, are far more likely today than white Republicans to support the statement that the "country hasn't gone far enough when it comes to giving black people equal rights with whites" (64 and 15 percent, respectively). Most white Democrats (70 percent) believe that racial discrimination impairs Blacks' ability to succeed, and 75 percent also point to less access to good schools. In contrast, fewer than a third of white Republicans agree that these issues are major obstacles for Blacks. Furthermore, a 2019 Pew survey reported that 86 percent of white Democrats (even more than the 79 percent of Black Democrats) believe that Trump has worsened race relations, compared to only 20 percent of white Republicans.[32]

The New Contours of Black Identity

Black voters, overwhelmingly Democrats, share many concerns and expectations with white Democrats. However, the 2016 election proved more traumatic for them: not only did Democrats lose—mostly because of their inability to mobilize the full multiracial coalition that had twice elected Obama—but they lost against a presidential candidate who ran on an overtly racialized agenda. Subsequently, recurrent racial hostility from the Trump administration was added to resilient socioeconomic inequalities, civic exclusion, and police brutality. Not surprisingly, debates about Black identity now combine two sets of issues: the first related to discouragement (encapsulated by the notion of "Black fatigue") and the second to the demand for racial justice and dignity (two of the core elements of BLM's agenda).

African American disappointment has increased in recent years. At the end of Obama's second term, opinion polls showed that Black respondents remained divided about his handling of race relations. A nominal majority (51 percent) of Black Americans believed he made progress toward improving race relations, 34 percent said he tried but failed, and only small minorities said that he made these relations worse or did not address this issue at all (5 and 9 percent, respectively).[33] However, three years after Trump's election, 73 percent said that he had made race relations worse. In addition, 78 percent believed that not enough has been done to give Black people equal rights with whites, 87 percent believed that Blacks are treated less fairly than whites by the criminal justice system, and 63 percent believed that Blacks are treated less fairly than whites by the police.[34]

African Americans have preponderantly reacted to objective and perceived adversity by reactivating a strong sense of racial identification. The overwhelming majority of Black Americans today view their racial identity as a core part of their overall identity. Surveys show that Black respondents are more likely than other ethnoracial groups to view their race as central to their identity. About 52 percent of non-Hispanic Black Americans said in 2020 that being Black was "extremely important" to how they thought about themselves (compared to 5 percent among whites, 31 percent among Hispanics, and 27 percent among Asians). Another 22 percent said it was "very important" (compared to 10 percent, 28 percent, and 29 percent among whites, Hispanics, and Asians, respectively).[35] This Black identity has been heightened by multiple episodes of police brutality leading to a series of killings in 2019 and 2020, and the resulting debate over the status of Black people in the United States.

It is noteworthy, however, that this reactive racial identification only partially homogenizes the American Black community. President Obama has crystalized its ambivalence, being too Black for some Americans, and too white or "brown" for others. Princeton University professor Cornel West, for example, challenged Obama's Blackness in 2011 by describing him as a "white man with black skin." At the converse end of the political spectrum, Ben Carson attacked Obama during his 2016 presidential campaign by echoing this sentiment in declaring that Obama was not African American but an "African raised white."[36] Sociologists Wendy Moore, Joyce Bell, and Joe Feagin concurred that the election of Obama reinforced the "white racial frame" among those who believed he was a representative of a dominant white ideology that functions to secure the reproduction of white privilege.[37] Kamala Harris, of Indian and Jamaican ancestry who identifies as Black, was the target of comparable attacks during her presidential campaign, and later when she was nominated as Joe Biden's running mate. For some, she illustrates the "basic truth that Black America is a multitude." For others, like radio host Mark Levin, she "is not an African American, she is Indian and Jamaican. Her ancestry does not go back to American slavery."[38]

There is, nonetheless, an overwhelming consensus among Black Americans that America is a country plagued by racism, which fuels frustration against the actual or symbolic power associated with the broad notion of "white privilege." New forms of racist regimes have replaced the de jure racism of the Jim Crow era. Some call this regime "symbolic racism," defined by John McConahay as "a new form of antiblack feelings, attitudes, and behaviors perceived to be emerging among relatively affluent, suburban segments of the American white population." Like D. O. Sears and other proponents of this trend, McConahay argue: "It is not the racism of the red-neck bigots of old who spewed forth hatred, doctrines of racial inferiority, and support for de jure segregation." It is instead "the racism of those who are both sociologically and psychologically 'the gentle people of prejudice.'"[39] Other scholars prefer to use "color-blind racism" to characterize the resilience of racial inequalities and prejudice, despite progressive policies and widespread multiculturalism. Eduardo Bonilla-Silva and David Dietrich, in their critics of "Obamerica," note that "color-blind racism is in many ways central to Obama's stance on race, his post-racial politics, and his own persona. Accordingly, the blessing of having a black president may become a curse as he can legitimate whites' color-blind views."[40] The notion of "systemic racism" has become more popular in recent years. It is sometimes characterized as being the main *cause* of institutional racism, the source of inequalities rooted in the systemwide operation of a society that excludes members of particular groups—despite antidiscrimination policies and anti-racist legislation. Elsewhere, it is supposedly the *result* of institutional racism and/or characterizes the main effects of both conscious and unconscious racist beliefs and practices—both at the individual and collective levels. Cause and symptom are therefore heavily debated.

Yet what these approaches share is the critical evaluation of white majority power as expressed in societal (economic, political, and educational) institutions as well as in social and cultural settings (such as to dominant norms, values, and other forms of social capital). For proponents of the "White Privilege Analysis" (WPA), it is insufficient for whites to admit that Blacks suffer from discrimination and resilient inequalities. Whites have to acknowledge their personal complicity in racial injustice, based on the fact that whiteness provides them with morally unacceptable privileges—especially when "a white person benefits from the injustice to the persons of color."[41] From this perspective, whites have to become aware of their own implicit privileges (independently from their socioeconomic status) in addition to being able to identify forms of recurrent racial discrimination targeting Black communities. Efforts to achieve these goals led to the multiplication of diversity training programs as well as the mushrooming of the "prejudice reduction literature."[42]

Furthermore, this WPA perspective has encouraged a new generation of grassroots movements to combine the legacy of previous movements (such as the Student Nonviolent Coordinating Committee and other components of the civil rights movement) with the more recent forms of identity politics inherited from the 1980s and 1990s. Today's most influential group is the BLM movement that originated in reaction to George Zimmerman's 2013 acquittal for the death of Trayvon Martin. BLM gained momentum during the riots that took place in Ferguson in 2014 after the killing of Michael Brown and morphed into a national widespread organization after the killing of George Floyd in Minneapolis in 2020.[43] Building on strategies used by the 1960s civil rights movement, BLM engages in nonviolent direct action to highlight police killings and promote basic equality and respect for African Americans.[44]

Yet, BLM critically differs from prior movements because of the importance it stresses on intersectionality in the BLM original platform.[45] The movement was created by three women—Alicia Garza, Patrisse Cullors, and Opal Tometi—who, by opposing the male-dominated hierarchical style of leadership, intended to give a special voice to the needs of Black women, Black queers, and Black transgendered.[46] According to Garza,

> Black Lives Matter is a unique contribution that goes beyond extrajudicial killings of Black people by police and vigilantes. It goes beyond the narrow nationalism that can be prevalent within some Black communities . . . keeping straight cis Black men in the front of the movement while our sisters, queer and trans and disabled folk take up roles in the background or not at all . . . It centers those that have been marginalized within Black liberation movements.[47]

This novel approach has contributed to the success of BLM within some Black and non-Black communities, as illustrated by the multiplication of BLM chapters across the country (and abroad) as well as the emergence of similar movements with deep ties to Black queer and transgender groups in their fight against injustice.[48]

However, BLM has been criticized because of its intersectional identity politics, as well as for being disorganized and sometimes aggressive—as illustrated by a series of violent incidents either involving some of its members or occurring during BLM's protests. For Barbara Reynolds, a former civil rights activist, "activists in the 1960s confronted white mobs and police with dignity and decorum . . . But at protests today, it is difficult to distinguish legitimate activists from the mob actors who burn and loot."[49] Other critics have focused on the issue of how representative BLM is and subsequently questioned its legitimacy to speak for all Black people. As queer activist Mary Hooks noted in Atlanta, "the expectation is that it would be comprised of all Black people. That was not always the case."[50] Barbara Ransby, a historian and the author of *Making All Black Lives Matter*, emphasizes the growing disconnect between BLM's initial agenda and expectations of the "people on the street" who have so many different expectations (from racial and economic justice to fair treatment for women, immigrants, and incarcerated minorities, as well as police reform and voting rights). According to Ransby, "in the spirit of Black literary genius James Baldwin, they are 'demanding the impossible,' or the seemingly impossible."[51]

The Invisibility of Hispanics and Asian Americans

Referring to the invisibility of Hispanic and Asian minorities may seem paradoxical, given their growing demographic and sociopolitical presence. The Asian population, for example, grew by 72 percent between 2000 and 2015 (from 11.9 million to 20.4 million), the fastest of any major ethnoracial group. Asians are projected to become the largest immigrant group in America in 2055, surpassing Hispanics, when they will represent 38 percent of all US immigrants. Asian Americans are also the fastest-growing segment of eligible voters out of the major ethnoracial groups. Between 2000 and 2020, the number of Asian American eligible voters grew by 139 percent. By 2018, more than 11 million were able to vote, constituting nearly 5 percent of the nation's eligible voters. The Hispanic population increased by 60 percent between 2000 and 2019 (from 50.7 million to 60.6 million), making up 18 percent of the US population. The Hispanic electorate grew by 121 percent between 2000 and 2020. A record 29 million Hispanics were eligible to vote in 2018 (12.8 percent of all eligible voters in the United States). In several states with competitive races for US Senate and governor, they made up a notable share of eligible voters including Texas (30 percent), Arizona (23 percent), and Florida (20 percent).

Despite these trends, both Hispanics and Asian Americans have to deal with issues related to their relative invisibility that results from their respective identity crises. Each relates to the problematic dilemma of racial identification that they face, with tensions between an ambivalent pan-ethnic identity and a flight to whiteness. As during the 1990s, Hispanics and Asians remain considered as "in-between" groups. Demographics changes, as well as new sociopolitical controversies, have made their positions more difficult to manage. Complexities abound, including a Hispanic self-redefinition as whiteness. How does this work? The US Census Bureau, for example, estimates that non-Hispanic whites will no longer be the majority of the population in 2042. Yet, this projection is flawed because it ignores the effects of intermarriage and, more importantly, the variations in ethnoracial identification among minorities. About 85 percent of third-generation Hispanics are the offspring of mixed marriages. Nearly half of all Hispanics remain unwilling to identify with a single standard race (including 42.6 percent who identify as "some other race"). Among those who select a single category as their racial identity, there is a strong preference for whiteness (up to 53 percent in 2010). As a result, whites (multiracial whites as opposed to non-Hispanic whites) are actually projected to increase their majority (up to 70 percent in 2050).

The effect of this trend is twofold. First, it makes Hispanics more invisible in the US Census data. In their study of US-born Mexican Americans, Richard Alba and Tariqui Islam addressed the "ethnic-identity mystery" raised by this "disappearance" of Hispanics defining themselves as white. They listed a series of reasons, such as the effect of mixed ancestry, socio-economic factors (those having a higher income being more likely to identity as white), and a desire to distance themselves from recently immigrated Mexicans. As Alba and Islam speculated, "an additional push in this direction may stem from the high rate of undocumented status among the immigrants and the hostility expressed towards them by many Anglos."[52]

Second, the very the nature and content of the Hispanic identity is therefore becoming more complex. About 89 percent of US adults with Hispanic ancestry self-identified as Hispanic in 2017 although only about 59 percent of Hispanics said in 2019 that being Hispanic is very important to their overall identity.[53] The gap between the pan-ethnic identification and the emotional sense of groupness can be explained by instrumental factors. The pan-ethnic categorization, for example, provides "opportunities for advancement that have been generated by affirmative action and diversity policies ... The nature of the political system, which favors larger groups over smaller ones, points in the same direction."[54] Hispanic identity, however, fades across generations (from 97 percent among immigrants to 50 percent among members of the fourth or later generation) while attraction to whiteness increases.[55]

Whether self-identification as white translates into social identification by others as white is another matter. A 2015 study indicated, for example, that only 6 percent of Hispanics who said they were white also believed they were perceived as white by others.[56] The discrepancy between self-identification and perception by others is accentuated by actual and perceived discrimination. The Hispanic preference for whiteness parallels a flight from Blackness, with only 2.5 percent of Hispanics self-identifying as Black. Yet, Hispanics are aware of the effect of skin color when they report experiences with discrimination. Approximately 58 percent of all Hispanic adults reported in 2019 that they had been treated unfairly because of their race or ethnicity. Hispanics with darker skin tone were more likely to experience discrimination (64 percent) than those with lighter skin tone (50 percent).[57]

Hispanics, for some observers, embody an "unstable constellation of ethnoracial realities." They inhabit the "in-between space" crossing racial, cultural, and gender identities—and "sometimes fall into the cracks."[58] To add another layer of complexity, Hispanics are increasingly frustrated by another dimension of their invisibility: They barely figure in America's ongoing conversation about racism while simultaneously being targeted for discrimination and other forms of institutional prejudice. As Angelo Falcon, the president of the National Institute for Latino Policy, notes, "no matter how much people talk about multicultural things and how diverse they are, it seems to revert to black and white . . . How the hell do you break through that black-white way of looking at policy issues?"[59] Part of the problem relates to the lack of data. The Department of Justice's reporting system of people killed by the police, for example, is broken down by race but not by ethnicity. Victims of police brutality are therefore either classified as white or Black. In addition to this statistical invisibility, police brutality against Hispanics does not receive the same level of national attention as similar incidents involving African Americans.[60] As the journalist Haya El Nasser noted after the killing of Manuel Angel Diaz, an unarmed 25-year-old Hispanic, in Anaheim (California) in 2012, "That starkly different response to police shootings of minorities raised a question: Don't brown lives matter, too?"[61]

There are, of course, significant differences between Hispanics and Asian Americans. Asian Americans have become an increasingly diverse group since the 1990s. They now trace their roots to more than twenty countries in East, Southeast, and South Asia—each with unique cultures, languages, and histories. Roughly half of these groups more than doubled in size between 2000 and 2015, and no single country-of-origin group dominates the Asian population (in contrast to Mexicans within the Hispanic population). While the majority of Hispanics today are native born, 59 percent of the Asian population was born in another country (up to 73 percent among adults). Asians represent only 13 percent of the 11 million undocumented immigrants (compared to Mexicans who constitute 47 percent). Finally, the Asian population is doing well on measures of economic well-being compared with the US population and, despite significant variations among Asian subgroups, is doing extremely well compared to other minorities.[62]

However, like their Hispanic counterparts, Asian Americans are facing issues related to their relative invisibility. It is one of the main consequences of their complicated position within the US racial categorization. When asked to fit into the Census's categories, of the 17.3 million people who reported themselves as Asian in 2010, 85 percent identified as solely Asian. Yet, only about 56 percent of Asians believed that being Asian is very important to their overall identity. Predictably, the Asian population's growing heterogeneity since the 1990s has not increased an emotional attachment to pan-ethnic groupness. The Asian identity thus remains a distinctive "third position," somewhere between Black and white, a position that today raises two series of issues.

First, Asian Americans continue to face racial prejudice but, like Hispanics, remain largely excluded from the conversation about "systemic racism" in America. Resentment has therefore increased, especially among young members of the second and third generation. In a 2016 op-ed titled "As an Asian American, I Am Invisible in This Country," David Yi summarizes the feelings of his generation. Addressing the problem of anti-Asian discourse during the presidential campaign, he complains about the lack of any reaction among political leaders or in public opinion. This resulted, he argues, from the assumption that anti-Asian prejudice was not perceived as racism. He adds: "it is clear I am invisible. Like my people, I have no voice. I have no grounds to stand on. No foundation in politics, no cultural icon like Jay Z, no place in American history."[63]

Second, the attraction of whiteness remains strong—but it does not secure all its privileges. The number of Asian Americans who identified themselves as both Asian and white grew by 87 percent between 2000 and 2010. Among the 2.6 million people who reported themselves as Asian in combination with one or more additional races, 61 percent identified as Asian and white (compared to 5 percent for Asian and Black).[64] In terms of their status, many affluent Asian Americans are often described as "virtually white," although they are mostly perceived as "honorary whites" or worse, "forever foreigners." While suffering from prejudice, they have limited options to protest because of the ambivalence produced by the "model minority" stereotype. On the one hand, Asians are represented as overachievers who, by doing better than other minorities, enjoy all the benefits of integration. This perception, as Qin Zhang notes, serves to "silence the charges of racial inequality, discredit the demands for social justice, and delegitimize the protests of racial discrimination."[65] One the other hand, they are targeted by some whites who resent their success and who react by reactivating the foreigner stereotype, denigrating Asian Americans as less American than other ethnoracial groups.

Asian American political representation remains limited, despite some elected leaders and the efforts of the Congressional Asian Pacific American Caucus (CAPAC). Asians make up a small slice of the electorate, although their influence is growing in some states, such as Nevada where Asians, Alaskans, and Pacific Islanders represent 11 percent of the population. Yet, the heterogeneity among various groups translates into the lack of a monolithic vote. As Tony Choi, the leader of the social media group Sons and Brothers, explains, "there are a lot of Korean Americans who don't identify with Indian or Bangladeshi Americans... With Asians, you have Protestants, Catholics, Muslims. We are not as cohesive or monolithic as people think we are."[66] Asian Americans expressed mixed feelings when Kamala Harris was announced as the vice president pick for Joe Biden. For some, she was not Asian enough and/or too Black. For others, mostly South Asians, her nomination made them "feel seen," but they complained that the media focused on her Black identity. As *Washington Post* reporter Seung Min Kim tweeted, "Kamala Harris is also the first Asian American vice-presidential nominee in history—which a lot of new organizations seem to be forgetting."[67]

The invisibility of Asian Americans is further fueled by socioeconomic criteria. The model minority stereotype does not address the situation of those poor Asians who also do not fit into the categories of "white trash" or disadvantaged Blacks. For example, eight out of the 19 main Asian groups have poverty rates higher than the US average (which was 15 percent in 2018), such as Hmong (28.3 percent) and Burmese (35 percent). Four groups have household incomes below the median household income for all Americans ($53,600)—including Bangladeshi ($49,8000) and Nepalese ($43,500). The class polarization that exists among various Asian groups tends to be detrimental to their ethnic solidarity. Income inequality in the United States is rising most rapidly among Asian Americans—spanning from $100,000 for Indian Americans to $36,000 for Burmese Americans. A weak ethnic solidarity among Asians combines with a weak class solidarity with other ethnoracial groups. In addition, Asian Americans have frequently been excluded from affirmative action and other social service programs designed to assist disadvantaged minority groups. They fall through the cracks in data representation, making it difficult to evaluate their needs. A study of the death toll from COVID-19, for example, demonstrated that Asian Americans were "invisible in data and in the public health response." According to some estimates, they were disproportionately hurt by the pandemic—as were Hispanics and African Americans—but not part of the debate about health racial disparities because US health systems do not collect accurate disaggregated data on Asian ethnicity.[68]

The peak of the tragic paradox of this invisibility was anti-Asian prejudice fueled by Trump's rhetoric about the "Chinese flu." It reactivated discursive and physical violence against Asian Americans and Asian immigrants, who were both targeted as a "visible threat" while the extent of anti-Asian hate crimes remained underplayed.[69] Andrew Yang, a candidate for the 2020 presidential elections, suggested that Asian Americans react to anti-Asian violence by embracing their "American-ness in ways we never have before" in order to ease tensions.[70] He consequently faced a backlash from Asian American communities, whose members opposed the idea that they had to display their American-ness when facing discrimination. Set to play Shang Chi, the first Asian American superhero in the Marvel industry, Simu Liu argues that "@Andrew Yang basically just told us to suck up, eat a cheeseburger and buy an American flag . . . It frames the onus on us, somehow, we have to prove we are worthy of belonging. We do belong, the burden should not be on us."[71]

Needing to face diversity in various settings (such as in the workplace, schools, and urban neighborhoods) generates concerns among all ethnoracial groups about their status. It also simultaneously translates into more tolerance, more intolerance, or a combination of both. This raises a critical question: How can we explain these variations? This contemporary ethnoracial milieu displays complex, contradictory patterns, which I analyze in the next chapter by focusing on the sociopolitical effect of centrifugal forces that contribute to the fragmentation of American society. Similarities with previous periods are easily identifiable. Yet, there are significant novel characteristics, and uncertainties, that deserve attention: the polarization of intergroup relations and the spillover of racialization into politics and other spheres of American society. Together, as explained in the coming chapters, these characteristics explain the resilience of ethnoracial violence in America today.

7
CENTRIFUGAL DYNAMICS OF ETHNORACIAL FRAGMENTATION

The last two decades have been characterized by a high level of protest politics. Liberals contested the controversial aspects of the security-driven policies adopted in the aftermath of 9/11 by the Bush administration. They emphasized these measures' nefarious antidemocratic infringement on civil liberties and violations of human rights. Many participated in protests against the war in Iraq organized by antiwar activists. In March 2003, for example, fifty thousand people attended the largest rally in Boston since the end of the Vietnam War. Liberals were among the four million who attended the immigrant rights protests in more than 150 cities in opposition to H.R. 4437's criminalization of unauthorized status between February and May 2006. More broadly, the growing attractiveness of contentious politics and protest tactics actually fueled the engagement of social movements in various battles—from the fight against socioeconomic inequalities to civil disobedience. This political tactic was sometimes characterized by a leftist revanchism that attacked elites, the establishment, and the "one percent," well illustrated by the Occupy Wall Street Movement (OWS) that began in New York City in 2011.

At the other end of the ideological spectrum, the election of Barack Obama energized the Tea Party, an arch-conservative partisan movement fueled by a sense of grievance among white people in response to the perceived decline of their sociopolitical dominance. The movement, whose name referenced the Boston Tea Party of 1773, sponsored multiple protests such as the "Porkulus Protest" in Seattle on Presidents Day, and the "Nationwide Chicago Tea Party" protest (coordinated with protests in forty cities) in 2009. Trump supporters subsequently organized countless rallies between 2015 and 2020. It generated counter-demonstrations—including a long list of anti-Trump protests across the country in November 2016, the countless Women's Marches of January 2017, and the 2019 protests against Trump's declaration of a "national emergency" to build a border wall.

Civil protests can be a healthy sign of democratic vitality. Yet, they become grounds for serious concerns when they are fueled by racial prejudice—and turn violent. The list of civil unrest sparked by police brutality includes the Cincinnati riots in 2001 (after the shooting of the unarmed African American 19-year-old Timothy Thomas); the Flatbush riots of 2013 (prompted by the shooting of 16-year-old Kimani); the Ferguson, St. Louis, and Oakland riots of 2014 (in the aftermath of the shootings of Michael Brown and Eric Garner); the Baltimore riots of 2015 (following the death of Freddie Gray); the Charlotte riots (after Keith Lamont Scott's shooting); the Saint Louis riots of 2017 (after the killing of Anthony Lamar); and the George Floyd riots of 2020 across the nation.

Violence resulted from the confrontation between white nationalists and left-wing counter-protesters in other instances—such as the Sacramento riots of 2016 and the 2017 Unite the Right rally in Charlottesville (during which Heather Heyer was murdered). In 2020, violent protests opposed Trump supporters and BLM activists, notably in New York City, in Louisville (Kentucky) after the police shooting of Breonna Taylor, in Portland (Oregon) where one supporter of Patriot Prayer was killed, and in Kenosha (Wisconsin) where Kyle Rittenhouse, a Trump supporter, killed two BLM protestors.

Not surprisingly, by 2019, large majorities of Americans said they believed that political debates were becoming more toxic (85 percent) and that heated rhetoric leads to violence (78 percent).[1] This trend was exacerbated by Trump's unsubstantiated claims of fraud in the aftermath of the 2020 presidential elections. There are growing concerns about how race, class, and political partisanship are dividing Americans.[2] None of these divisive factors are new, but combining them has magnified their effects over time. Furthermore, this hostility between groups has been mostly fueled by negative emotions (such as anxiety, resentment, anger, and rage) resulting from the ethnoracial identity crisis I previously analyzed. All groups are involved in a centrifugal dynamic that makes violence (both physical and discursive) more commonplace and coalitions more difficult to achieve.

Polarization and Racialization of Contentious Repertoires

Political polarization predated the Trump administration. Opinion poll surveys showed that partisan differences on political values widened during George W. Bush's two terms (from 11 to 16 percentage points between 2000 and 2008).

Indeed, the values gap between Republicans and Democrats became greater than those measured by gender, age, race, or class. More Republicans then described themselves as conservatives (from 60 to 68 percent) while a growing number of Democrats identified as liberals (28 to 34 percent). Democrats became more secular, more positive in their views of immigrants, and more supportive of affirmative action programs. By contrast, only 17 percent of Republicans in 2007 supported equal opportunity policies. About 60 percent of Republicans also believed that newcomers threatened traditional customs and values, compared with just 39 percent of Democrats.[3]

That trend toward polarization increased dramatically after 2008. In their analysis of the convergence between social movements and racial politics, McAdam and Kloos reflectively note that the United States was "certainly no stranger to convulsive political and intense partisan animus." They list compelling examples of polarization, such as the passions aroused by the Vietnam War, the sustained drama of the Watergate period, and the political violence generated by the Clinton impeachment proceedings. Yet, they argued in 2014 that, "when it comes to party polarization, all these examples pale in comparison to the acrimony, bitterness, and willful sabotage of policymaking that has characterized Obama's time in office."[4] Political partisanship extended beyond the normal contested areas, such as the scope and role of government in economic and social policies, to climate change and even formerly bipartisan areas such as foreign policy.[5] Even less salient issues were subject to intense polarization, such as flu vaccinations.[6] Polarization fueled, and was fueled by, high levels of distrust and discontent among Americans—with higher levels among Republicans, especially white conservatives and evangelical voters who were members of the Tea Party movement.[7]

More pointedly, partisan rancor became closely linked with racial resentment, ethno-nationalism, and racial prejudice. This trend played a major role in attracting Trump voters in 2016. Not only was party identification more polarized than before Obama's election, but it was strongly related to racial prejudice, authoritarianism, and intolerance.[8] As a result, an increasing number of dimensions of American politics became racialized. Polarization and racialization "made politics 'feel' angrier," John Sides and his colleagues argue, "because debates about ethnic, racial, and national identities engender strong emotions . . . The upshot is a more divisive and explosive politics."[9] Other studies confirmed that racial resentment and anger had created a perfect storm of conditions, allowing Trump to exploit racially motivated divisions within the electorate and leading to his election.[10] Furthermore, Trump effectively reinforced the rise of negative partisanship—"voting based on hostility toward the opposing party and its leaders." This negative partisanship was, again, strongly linked to racial re-sentiment, with a dramatic increase in support for Republicans among the most racially resentful fraction of white working-class voters. In Alan Abramowitz and Jennifer McCoy's analysis of data from the American National Election Study (ANES), they found that those working-class whites scoring high on racial resentment voted 62 percent for Bush in 2000 and 87 percent for Trump in 2016. In contrast, among those who were the least racially resentful, support for Republicans fell—from 48 percent in 2000 to 24 percent in 2016.[11]

Political and racial polarization have affected political partisanship as well as the perceptions of various public policies. Analyzing the "spill-over of racialization," Michael Tesler demonstrated that, for example, anti-Black attitudes became a significant predictor of opposition to health care reform. He found that "health care positions were significantly more racialized when attributed to President Obama than they were when these same proposals were framed as President Clinton's 1993 reform efforts."[12] The same dynamic applied to debates over immigration reform, with a growing impact of ethnocentric attitudes on the perception of immigrants.

Yet, beyond these generalizations, various ethnoracial groups have responded to polarization in differing ways, with important consequences for intergroup relations.

The Racial Polarization of White Repertoires

In the last two decades, an increasing white ingroup identity and solidarity has enhanced a sense of groupness. It has generated increasingly opposite behaviors: ingroup favoritism without racial animus toward other groups and outgroup hostility fueled by white anxiety and racial resentment. The conflict between these two attitudes has been part of American politics for decades. However, there is evidence that the gap between white subgroups has become bigger than ever.

Trump's election emboldened those whites who were already highly prejudiced, and who hated white liberals almost as much as nonwhite minorities. In turn, his behavior translated into changing voting patterns that represented a continuation of the realignment that began during the Obama presidency. According to Matthew Yglesias's analysis of the "Great Awokening," "as Obama pushed racially conservative whites out of the Democratic Party, the remaining Democrats become more racially liberal." Indeed, "for all the attention paid to the politics of the far right in the Trump era, the biggest shift in American politics is happening somewhere else entirely. In the past five years, white liberals have moved so far to the left on questions of race and racism that they are now, on these issues, to the left of even typical black voters."[13]

About 74 percent of Biden voters in 2020 believed "it is a lot more difficult to be a black person in America than it is to be a white person;" and 84 percent agreed that "the growing number of newcomers strengthens American society." Conversely, only 9 percent and 32 percent of Trump voters respectively shared those beliefs.[14] Seventy-nine percent of Republicans and Fox News's audience said they believed that the killings of African Americans by police were isolated incidents (compared to 17 percent of Democrats), and only 17 percent said that racial inequality was a major issue (compared to 68 percent of Democrats).[15] Against this background, the data shows that the average levels of anti-Black and anti-Hispanic prejudice expressed by white Americans actually dropped between 2016 and 2018.[16] Liberal whites became even more enthusiastic about diversity than other groups. In 2018, 87 percent of white liberals said they believed that ethnoracial diversity makes the United States a better place to live (compared to 54 percent of Black respondents, 46 percent of Hispanics, and 42 percent of nonliberal whites).[17]

Perceptions of minorities intersect with class, education, and gender divides. As a result, while the polarization of American society and politics has made racial identification more salient, whites have become increasingly divided into various "tribes" engaged in bitter and often violent confrontations. Whites are fragmented, for example, into progressive activists, traditional liberals, moderates, traditional conservatives, and devoted conservatives.[18] Their perceptions of African Americans and other ethnoracial groups differ widely, as well as their conception of America's mainstream society and views on specific governmental policies, religion, and social justice.

White subgroups resort to violence in this polarized environment—not only against minorities but also against each other. This includes virulent rhetoric against political opponents and violent confrontations between Trump supporters and anti-Trump activists. Contrary to the widespread misconception that minorities pose the greatest violent threat to whites, evidence suggests that "white people should be more afraid of other whites than they are of people of color." Mile Males, researcher at the Center on Juvenile and Criminal Justice in San Francisco, provides data from the CDC showing that "rate of homicides, gun killings and illicit-drug fatalities are highest in counties where nine in 10 residents are white and where President Trump won in the 2016 election." Correspondingly, the white Americans "who are safest from such deaths are those who live in racially diverse areas such as Los Angeles, New York and Chicago, where two-thirds of residents are nonwhite, where millions of immigrants live, and where voters favored Hillary Clinton in 2016."[19] Other studies confirm that, statistically, whites typically commit more crimes against whites than against minorities because they tend to live in segregated neighborhoods.[20]

Political polarization and other socioeconomic and cultural divides today explain significant variations among white repertoires of violence. The "gun culture" remains largely part of the white identity and is increasingly affected by the polarization of identity politics. About 36 percent of white people report that they are gun owners, compared to 24 percent of Blacks and 15 percent of Hispanics. Republicans are more than twice as likely as Democrats to have a gun (41 and 16 percent, respectively), and nearly three times as likely as Democrats to say that owning a gun is very important to their overall identity (31 and 12 percent, respectively). Nearly 76 percent of Republicans also believe it is important to protect gun rights, compared to 22 percent of Democrats.[21]

For some whites—those motivated by an intense and old-fashioned racial prejudice—the use of violence is a legitimate self-defense reaction against the threats posed by minorities to their racial status. This category includes white supremacists who use violence against minorities and against other whites who oppose their views and/or are not "truly" white according to their narrow conception of American identity. White supremacists share a culture of violence that fuels various acts of violence ranging from property offenses to bomb-making. In their study of white supremacist violence, Steven Windisch and his colleagues found that 76 percent of the white supremacists they interviewed had a history of delinquent activity, and 69 percent had an arrest record. Furthermore, they targeted whites as much as minorities, mostly homeless people, homosexuals, and "hippy kids" whom they consider "bad for America."[22] White supremacists justify attacks against extremely vulnerable people by a sense of superiority—an expression of their identity crisis—leading to a violent expression of their masculinity and physical prowess.[23]

Other whites define themselves in terms of class—the poor white working class—to separate themselves from nonwhite workers as well as privileged whites. A portion can express racial resentment, such as the 25 percent of whites who opposed interracial dating yet voted for Obama in 2008 before voting for Trump in 2016.[24] The core element of their contentious repertoire relates to their feeling of being perceived as beneficiaries of white privilege to which, in reality, they have no access. Contemporary discussions of white privilege therefore "ignite hostility in these marginal whites." Hostility turns into rage when their complaints are dismissed because their plight purportedly pales in comparison to that of low-income minorities.[25] White anger translates into attacks against the establishment, the federal government, banks and financial institutions, and political and intellectual elites. These grievances constitute the main components of the rightist populism illustrated by the Tea Party and by Trump's rhetoric, notwithstanding the gap between populist propaganda and the actual outcomes of policies that have not actually improved the economic or social conditions of poor whites.

White anger also inspires a leftist form of populism, especially among liberals who blame Democrats for focusing on identity politics to the detriment of class-based economics. Explaining why anger has become "as American as apple pie," David Phoenix argues: "There is a clear through line from the colonists of the Occupy Wall Street protesters, from the Tea Party activists to the so-called Bernie Bros to the throngs of people gathered at Trump rallies, shouting 'make America great again.'"[26] However, attitudes toward minorities are radically opposite in these groups that often use violence against one another.

Antiracist liberals try to navigate their way between white race consciousness, a sense of guilt leading them to support policies that reduce racial inequality, and the frustration they feel from having to justify themselves when they are suspected of not being a trustful ally in the fight against racism. Their repertoire includes the legacy of historical alliance with racial minorities. There were many examples of multiracial and ethnic coalitions of liberal activists that long predated the civil rights movement of the 1960s. It is noteworthy, for example, that the national leadership of the National Association for the Advancement of Colored People (NAACP) was all white—with the notable exception of W. E. B. Du Bois—when it was created in 1909. The labor movement forged ties between white and minority workers, and in Los Angeles multiracial groups formed civil rights, labor, and neighborhood coalitions from the 1930s to the early 1950s.[27] This civil rights activism increased minority representation in the city and shaped historic Supreme Court decisions—such as Brown v. Board of Education and Shelley v. Kraemer (which upheld that courts could not enforce restrictive covenants to preclude Black membership or housing). Civil rights initiatives were supported by white liberals, especially Jews who viewed anti-Semitism and racism as comparable and organically related.

Support for BLM constitutes the more recent and visible engagement of white liberals in favor of racial justice. BLM protests peaked on June 6, 2020, when half a million people demonstrated in nearly 550 places across the country over the death of Floyd the previous month. Polls indicated that a total of 20 to 26 million participated in demonstrations in the summer of 2020. The population was exclusively white in dozens of towns that held protests. Nearly 95 percent of counties that had a protest were majority white, and nearly three-quarters of those counties were more than 75 percent white. In June 2020, 92 percent of white liberals supported BLM (compared to 37 percent of white Republicans).[28]

The Racial Polarization of Minority Repertoires

Anger, frustration, and racial fatigue are widespread among minorities, with a significant impact on their intergroup relations and propensity to resort to protest. Migrant minorities faced intensified verbal and physical attacks, and anti-migrant initiatives by the Trump administration—such as threats against the Deferred Action for Childhood Arrival program (DACA), the Muslim travel ban,[29] and the separation of immigrant parents and children at the US border.

Half of Hispanics express serious concerns about the worsening of their situation since 2016. A majority (55 percent) worry that they, a family member, or close friend could be deported; and about 54 percent believe it has become more difficult in recent years to be Hispanic in the United States.[30] Hispanics also worry about discrimination as well as police brutality. According to the few available estimates, Hispanics were killed at the second highest rate in the United States (23 per million residents) behind African Americans (31 per million) between 2015 and 2020.[31] The trauma of recent mass killings is vivid: numerous Hispanics were killed during a nightclub attack in Orlando (Florida) in 2016, and the attack at a Walmart store in El Paso (Texas) in 2009 was the deadliest anti-Hispanic attack in modern American history (killing 20 people and wounding 27).

Furthermore, most Hispanics express concerns about the economic effects of the COVID-19 pandemic as well as their health situation. The majority of workplace outbreaks took place in sectors where Hispanics comprise the majority of workers, such as construction, manufacturing, meat processing, and the wholesale trade. They are also overrepresented in front-line occupations with more risk of COVID-19 exposure—in addition to the systemic social inequalities that affected their health even before the pandemic.

Asian Americans express similar concerns. Anti-Asian assaults and hate crimes rose as Coronavirus spread. Statements by Trump referring to COVID-19 as "the Chinese flu," "Wuhan flu," or "Kung Flu" exacerbated the scapegoating of Asian Americans.[32] As a result, 40 percent of them reported negative experiences because of their race, such as being subjects to slurs or being subject to suspicion even when wearing a mask in public. Up to 26 percent feared someone might threaten or physically attack them.[33] Furthermore, despite their relatively higher socioeconomic achievements than other minorities, Asians have been hard hit by the pandemic. A study from the Federal Reserve Bank of Chicago showed that the unemployment rate for Asian Americans was 8.9 percent in November of 2020. This is better than the respective Black and Hispanic unemployment rates of 12.1 percent and 10.3 percent, but worse than the white unemployment rate of 7 percent. However, there was a huge disparity among

Asian Americans. When controlling for the same level of education, those with no college education were hit harder than other minority groups. Among Asian males with no college degree, for example, the employment rate fell by 31 percent (from 77 percent in January to 46 percent in June) while the decline for Blacks and Hispanics was 10 and 12 percent respectively (from 58 to 48 percent among Blacks, and from 80 to 68 percent among Hispanics).[34]

American Muslims have faced recurrent hostility and acts of violence since 9/11, and not surprisingly perceived a lot of discrimination against their religious group. Anti-Muslim rhetoric and policies during the Trump administration reinforced their fears of being targeted as well as their concerns about not being accepted into mainstream society. In 2017, 75 percent agreed that there was a lot of anti-Muslim discrimination in the United States; 68 percent said that Trump worried them, and 50 percent believed that being a Muslim made their life more difficult.[35] After peaking at 93 cases in 2001 in the aftermath of 9/11, the number of assaults against Muslims declined until 2015, rising again in 2016 when the FBI reported a record 127 victims of aggravated assaults. By 2020, there were more than 40 anti-Muslim hate groups across the country, many having close ties with elected officials at both the state and local level.[36] Anti-Muslim violence also took the form of police brutality, especially against African American Muslims— illustrated by the killing of Yassin Mohamed near Atlanta in May 2020.

Against this background, how ethnoracial minorities mobilize results from the combined effects of political and racial polarization. As stated before, minorities are not only passive victims of racialization; they are active agents in their own rights, and their contentious repertoires include elements of reactive political and racial polarization.

Hispanics, for example, have responded by increasing their political mobilization. Major Hispanic organizations (such as the League of United Latin American Citizens, La Raza, and the Mexican American Defense and Educational Fund) have very actively organized voter registration campaigns to improve their political lobbying. Hispanic voters now make up increasingly larger shares of the electorate, notably in battleground states such as Florida and Arizona. With 32 percent of eligible voters, Hispanics constituted the second largest group of American voters in 2020 and the largest group of nonwhite voters. Political polarization among Hispanics had become more intense by 2020. About 66 percent of Hispanic voters supported Joe Biden (comparable to their support for Hillary Clinton in 2016) but 32 percent supported Trump (compared to 28 percent in 2016).

Political divisions among Hispanics are not new. A majority of Hispanics have traditionally supported the Democratic party. Yet, 37 percent of them voted for Ronald Reagan in 1982, 40 percent favored George W. Bush in 2004, and 42 percent backed Republican nominee John McCain in 2008. More pointedly, the divide between Hispanic Democrats and Hispanic Republicans is widening, not only in terms of political affiliation but also along social values and perceptions of other ethnoracial groups. Both support for and opposition to Trump has been energized by cultural and religious antagonisms. Hispanic Republicans, especially Evangelicals and other prolife groups, supported Trump in exchange of the nomination of three conservative US Supreme Court judges.[37] They also agreed with many aspects of the restrictive immigration measures implemented by the Trump administration. Indeed, 86 percent said that their main goal was to improve border security, 81 percent supported further measures designed to reduce illegal crossings along the US-Mexican borders, and 63 percent favored the deportation of illegal immigrants. By contrast, Hispanic Democrats opposed most aspects of the Trump agenda, including his attacks on ethnoracial and gender minorities. Their main policy goal was to establish a path for unauthorized immigrants to legally stay in the country (89 percent), followed by admitting refugees (85 percent). Only 21 percent of Democrats support deportation measures.[38] Like non-Hispanic whites, Hispanics are therefore divided into subgroups defined along political, cultural, and religious identities.

Hispanics are not only more intensely engaged in US politics; they also have the incentive, resources, and opportunities to react to discrimination in general, and to police abuse in particular. Most Hispanic protests have been organized in response to issues related to immigration policies. Union leaders, for example, launched the Immigrant Workers Freedom Rides (IWFR) in 2003 in support of civil rights, legalization, and family reunification for immigrant workers. In 2004, the United States Conference of Catholic Bishops promoted the "Justice for Immigrants Campaign" in support of comprehensive immigration reform. NotOneMoreDeportation originated in 2013 as a project of the National Day Laborer Organizing Network (NDLON) and transitioned in 2015 to a campaign involving civil society actors designed to challenge unfair deportations. Young Hispanic activists have channeled their energy into the DREAMers movement that resulted in the DREAM Act (Development, Relief, and Education for Alien Minors). They actively supported the Day Without Immigrants in February 2017, triggered by President Trump's plans to build a new border wall and to potentially deport millions of illegal immigrants. Shops and restaurants closed in solidarity with immigrant workers in major cities, with a march taking place in Washington, DC.

Some protests were also initiated by the police killing of Hispanics. Examples include the protest in Anaheim after the killing of Manuel Angel Diaz and Joel Acevedo in 2012, in Albuquerque in 2015 after the death of Christopher Torres, and in Los Angeles in 2016 after the death of Jesse Romero. Yet these violent encounters with police seldom garnered national attention. Indeed, newer organizations such as Mi Familia Vota and the Latino Victory Project have organized demonstrations targeting immigrant rights and civic rights, but not necessarily the killings of Hispanics by the police. The killing in February 2020 of Antonio Valenzuela in Las Cruses (New Mexico) only three months before Floyd's death did not lead to global protests, fueling resentment among Hispanics about their relative "invisibility."

Nonetheless, support for BLM among Hispanics reached a peak in June 2020 (up to 77 percent), and although this support declined after the summer (down to 66 percent), a vast majority of Hispanics share the goals of the movement—especially the pursuit of racial equality.[39] Young activists joined the BLM protests carrying "Tu lucha es mi lucha" signs. Yet, there is no "Brown Lives Matter" movement. Analysts and activists offered a few explanations: The fear of undocumented immigrants in confronting the police, the fact that police killings may involve Hispanic police officers (as illustrated by the death of Valenzuela in a city where Hispanics represent 60 percent of the population), and the need to prioritize other concerns. "You have to pick and choose your battle," professor of criminal justice Gregory Brown explained. He added: "They have a lot of agendas and the issue of police brutality is on the back agenda."[40]

The racialization of contention repertoires among minorities may, however, generate other reasons why Hispanics do not prioritize police brutality—despite desperately claiming that "Brown lives matter too." "It is a recurring complaint among Latino leaders," the president of the National Institute for Latino Policy Angelo Falcon argues. He adds: "No matter how much people talk about how multicultural things are, it seems to revert to black and white . . . How the hell do you break through that black-white way of looking at policy issues?"[41] The assumption shared by many Hispanics—that they do not fit in the national conversation about racial discrimination—is linked to three issues.

First, their pan-ethnic collective identification remains weak—and it is even weaker today as the result of political polarization. This precludes the emergence of a large "Hispanic/Latino Lives Matter" movement. There is no "Brown Lives Matter" movement because the term "brown" is often used to describe people from multiple continents and cultures, including people of Middle Eastern and South Asian descent who have very little in common with Hispanics.

Second, there is the history of anti-Black racism among Hispanics to contend with, as well as prejudice against Afro-Latinos who today comprise 25 percent of Hispanics. The majority of both Blacks and Hispanics have favorable views of each other (77 and 79 percent, respectively). Yet only 57 percent of Hispanics believe that the two groups get along well, compared to 70 percent of Blacks. Hispanics are also more likely than Blacks to believe that intergroup relations are strained (30 versus 18 percent).[42] In June 2020, in a Miami Herald op-ed, more than forty organizations expressed support for the BLM movement and acknowledged the Hispanic community's failure to combat racism: "We have failed to grapple with anti-blackness that exists in our community... We must ask ourselves how our own actions contribute to racism and colorism in this country."[43]

Third, any sense of a "linked fate" between African Americans and Afro-Latinos remains weak as the result of the complexity of identity and race among Hispanics. When asked about their race, only 18 percent of Afro-Latinos identify their race as Black—compared to 39 percent who identify as white or white in combination with another race, and 24 percent who identify as Hispanic.[44]

Like Hispanics, Asian Americans do not have similar repertoires of contention and therefore do not always cohere in pursuit of shared interests. What unites them is the feeling of being racialized as "permanent aliens." Yet, they are politically divided, and their response to the discrimination they face is not immune from their racialized perception of other groups. The political division among Asian Americans has remained consistent. Sixty-five percent voted for Hillary Clinton and 27 percent for Donald Trump in 2016. In 2020, 63 percent of Asian Americans voted for Joe Biden and 31 percent for Trump). Ethnicities demonstrate varying voting behaviors. Indian Americans, for example, tend to vote for Democrats while Vietnamese Americans are more likely to vote for Republicans (up to 48 percent in 2020).[45] Asian Americans favor progressive positions on many issues, such as immigration policy, health care, and gun control. Yet, some express more conservative values when debates relate to family, religion, and law and order. Vietnamese Americans and Filipino Americans, who tend to identify more as Catholic, are more socially conservative and more likely to support the Republican party than other groups, despite the Trump administration's anti-Asian rhetoric.[46]

In June 2020, a majority of Asian Americans (75 percent) supported the BLM movement. Younger Asians were especially enthused, as were activists who, in reference to the legacy of previous Asian-Black solidarity, believed that BLM protests should also be a pivotal moment for all Asian communities in the fight against racial prejudice. Their goals, as listed in various social media, consisted of dismantling the "model minority myth" by returning to the Asian-Black solidarity of the 1960s; rejecting the temptation to assimilate into whiteness; buying from Black-owned businesses; learning the history of a feminist, Black-Asian alliance; calling out microaggressions; and joining other minorities in dismantling white supremacy.[47]

However, support for BLM among Asian Americans began declining during the summer of 2020 (down to 69 percent in September), mostly as the result of the violence involved during some protests—and especially among first-generation members. Terry Nguyen, in her study of the perception of BLM among Asian communities, found that some immigrants—especially those from

Vietnam—"who might not understand the nuances of racism in America felt threatened by the social unrest and looting in cities. A few even became counter protesters at local Black Lives Matter rallies."[48] Other older Asian generations shared similar concerns, in addition to a reluctance to characterize the fight for social justice in racial terms.

The intersection of race, class, and national origin has become more salient as the result of a polarization among immigrant minorities. It has crystalized a dividing line among religious minorities, illustrated by the divide between Black Muslims and non-Black immigrant Muslims. About 20 percent of Muslims in the United States today are Black Americans. They are outnumbered by immigrant Muslims who declare themselves as white (30 percent), Asian (21 percent), other/mixed (19 percent), and Hispanics (6 percent).

These two groups have very different histories. Black Muslims share with other African Americans the infamous legacy of slavery in addition to being discriminated against because of their religious beliefs.[49] Black Muslims played a key role in the civil rights movement—from the Nation of Islam to Malcolm X who converted to Sunni Islam in 1964 after leaving the Nation of Islam.[50] Immigrant Muslims, by contrast, constitute a very heterogenous group united by their "migrant experience" and the shared assumption that they know more about Islam because they arrived from Muslim-majority countries. In turn, most African American Muslims argue that group solidarity (asabiya) must be given priority because of the umma or the universal Muslim community. They also do not accept the customs of immigrant Muslims and dislike being guided by these "new Americans." Furthermore, while a vast majority of non-Black Muslims have successfully integrated into America's socioeconomic mainstream, Black Muslims remain the target of discrimination and socioeconomic exclusion. Immigrant Muslims are collectively better off than US-born Muslims by several measures used to measure their financial wellbeing and educational achievements, such as a household income of more than $100,000 (23 percent versus 15 percent) and having a college degree (26 percent versus 16 percent).[51]

All Muslims have, however, expressed a very high level of perceived discrimination after 9/11—as a result of widespread Islamophobia and anti-Muslim policies enacted in the guise of fighting terrorism. But Black Muslims are more likely to feel discriminated against on the basis of their race and religion. In 2017, 61 percent of Black Muslims reported that it was becoming more difficult to live in the United States because of religious intolerance (compared with 51 percent of immigrant Muslims), and 92 percent said there was a lot of discrimination against Muslims in the United States (compared with 50 percent of immigrant Muslims).[52] In 2019, the same figure, 92 percent of Black Muslims, believed there was a lot of discrimination against Black people—compared with 66 percent of non-Black Muslims.[53]

BLM protests provided an opportunity for mobilizing around a common agenda. Muslim scholars point out significant commonalities between racism and Islamophobia. These included the enduring legacy of racialized oppression and the double consciousness of being American and Black—one that expands to a triple consciousness with the addition of being Muslim to proclaim that "Black Muslim Lives Matter."[54] In the summer of 2020, a large coalition of Muslim civil rights and faith groups representing both African Americans and immigrant Muslims declared their support for BLM's agenda. In a joint statement, they declare that "black people are often marginalized within the broader Muslim community. And when they fall victim to police violence, non-black Muslims are often too silent, which leads to complicity."[55]

However, there is evidence of an anti-Black sentiment among non-Black Muslims "Does the Muslim American Community have a problem with intra-Muslim racism?" asks Maha Elgenaidi, executive director of the Islamic Networks Group (ING). Answering her own question, she asserts that "It's hard for a community that feels under siege from Islamophobia to admit that it has a problem with racism and bigotry within its ranks; it's hard, but necessary."[56] Another Muslim leader, Imam Abu Laith Luqman Ahmad, echoes this sentiment: "As America battles its own racial problem, Muslim America has its own festering racial problem between Black American Muslims and converts, and the larger Muslim immigrant community . . . Racism in Muslim America is the proverbial elephant in the room."[57] Existing research on intra-Muslim racism is limited. However, a study from the Institute for Social Policy and Understanding (ISPU) in 2020 found that 33 percent of Black Muslims believed that a fellow believer discriminated against them because of their race.[58] A report from MuslimARC confirmed that African American Muslims face intra-Muslim racism from other Muslim communities, specifically South Asians and Arabs.[59]

Adding another layer of complexity to racial polarization, there is also the issue of anti-Muslim prejudice among African Americans. Tea Party Republican Herman Cain, when running for the presidency in 2012, for example, proposed creating a loyalty test for any Muslim before allowing him/her to serve in the administration. Ben Carson, before joining the Trump administration, declared that Islam was inconsistent with the US Constitution. Their position can be explained by the rise of anti-Muslim sentiment among Republicans. For example, 60 percent of GOP voters favored the Muslim ban across the country (up to 78 percent in Alabama and Arkansas).[60] More to the point, these two prominent African American Republicans illustrate the legacy of an anti-Muslim brand of Afrocentrism that became popular during the 1970s and 1980s. Then, some Black intellectuals, such as Chancellor Williams, depicted Islam as a foreign religion to America. They further contended that Muslim attitudes toward race and slavery rendered Islam complicit in the oppression of Black people.[61] From their perspective, Black cultural nationalism should criticize the anti-Black dimension of Muslim societies and mobilize against the popularity of Islam among African Americans. According to Molefi Kete Asante, progenitor of the Afrocentricity paradigm, the "indoctrination by an Arabic faith" has contributed to the demise of the Black Movement.[62] In more recent years, this conception of Afrocentrism has morphed into the Hotep subculture, which defines Egyptian history as the core element of Black identity. Some Afrocentrists highlight a relationship between ancient Egypt and modern Black Americans to instill a sense of pride as well as more controversial negative attitudes toward various minorities (from religious minorities to LGBTQ) and an opposition to interracial marriage.[63]

So, to Whom Do Black Lives Actually Matter?

Do frustration and anger provide a solid ground on which to base coalitions in the search for the common good? The interaction between centripetal and centrifugal forces between and within different minority groups in America is, somewhat ironically perhaps, well-illustrated by the BLM movement itself. It generates incentives for an unprecedented large mass mobilization and, conversely, the conditions for a further fragmentation of intergroup solidarity.

What began as a post on Facebook and then a hashtag on other social media a few years ago has now become the largest social movement in US history. The BLM movement first emerged in reaction to George Zimmerman's 2013 acquittal for the death of Trayvon Martin. It was created by three women—Alicia Garza, Patrisse Cullors, and Opal Tometi—who, in opposition to the male-dominated hierarchical style of leadership, intended to give special attention to the needs of Black women, Black queers, and Black transgendered.[64] According to Garza, "Black Lives Matter is a unique contribution that goes beyond extrajudicial killings of Black people by police and vigilantes. It centers those that have been marginalized within Black liberation movements."[65]

Since its creation, BLM has sought to address a broad range of issues, such as a lack of economic justice and community control, and an inadequate protection of civil rights and liberties, as well as demanding a more effective fight against persistent racial prejudice and racial practices. The movement gained momentum during the riots that took place in Ferguson in 2014 after the killing of Michael Brown and morphed into a large protest movement after the killing of Eric Garner, Michael Brown, and numerous others. BLM protests peaked on June 6, 2020, when half-a-million people demonstrated over the death of George Floyd in nearly 550 places across the country. By late 2020, BLM encompassed over thirty chapters in the United States and abroad, including a dozen Black-led organizations, as well as affiliated non-Black groups. Support for BLM increased by nearly as much as it had over the previous two years in the weeks after the death of Floyd, with more than half of American voters (52 percent) supporting the movement in early June compared to the 28 percent who opposed it.[66]

BLM protests helped reframe American politics in 2020. Issues of racial violence, discrimination, and violation of basic rights were at the forefront of the 2020 presidential debate. In a notable change of attitude, by the summer of 2020 Americans were now more likely to say that the protests will help (53 percent) rather than hurt (34 percent) bringing about racial justice and equality.[67] According to a Washington Post-Schar School Poll conducted in June 2020, 69 percent of Americans believed the death of Floyd reflects a "broader problem in the way black people are treated by police" (up from 43 percent in 2014, after Brown's death).[68] City councils in many cities pledged to dismantle or reform their police department. New laws banned chokeholds. Measured in terms of levels of support and number of protesters, by the end of 2020 BLM had already achieved more than all the civil rights marches in the 1960s. Yet a nagging question remains whether this means that these protests are setting into motion a sustained and widespread social, political change.

There are certainly significant variations in the perceptions of BLM, symptomatic of the current intense political and racial polarization. Not surprisingly, support for BLM remained high among Blacks (87 percent in September 2020, similar to the share who supported the movement in June). Declining support for BLM among other ethnoracial groups was in part of the result of recurrent tensions between Black and non-Black communities. Disagreements quickly emerged about the BLM's main objectives. Beyond the overwhelming condemnation of police brutality, various ethnoracial groups disagree—for example—about police reform and reparations, while elements express resistance to efforts to integrate public schools and neighborhoods.

BLM actually encapsulates the main grievances of African Americans. In addition to the anger fueled by police brutality and persistent socioeconomic inequalities, they express concerns about racist attacks linked to the pandemic. By July 2020, 45 percent of them noticed an increase of racial slurs since the outbreak, and 27 percent feared being threatened or physically attacked.[69] Hard hit by the COVID-19 (with a death rate 2.1x higher than whites), they also faced declining employment—notably among those without a college degree (down from 58 to 48 percent between January and July 2020).[70]

Some Black activists, however, criticize BLM. Carol Swain, Conservative African American law professor, proclaimed that BLM was "a very destructive force in America."[71] Other Black scholars, such as economist Glen Loury contend that BLM was" off the wrong foot with tactics that alienate needed allies." He supports a more inclusive approach, "a comprehensive political strategy that, in collaboration with other strands of activism in this country, can lead toward the enactment of the structural changes necessary for undermining the subordination of black people and enhancing the quality of black lives." In summary, he concludes, "while race remains important in America, the core problem here ought not to be defined as a racial justice problem. It is a social justice problem" affecting "the lives of all Americans."[72]

Another fissure relates to groups supporting their own specific agenda alongside that of BLM. The Black trans community, for example, with more than 130 transgender or gender non-conforming people killed between 2013 and 2018, focuses on the increasing anti-trans violence in America. Some activists have expressed their frustration with the weak support their cause gets in Black communities. "We must affirm that Black Trans Lives Matter," argued Alphonso David, president of the Human Rights Campaign (HRC), after the killing of Riah Milton and Dominique "Rem'mie" Fells in June 2020.[73] During Pride Month, an estimated fifteen thousand people demonstrated in Brooklyn to demand justice for victims of anti-Black and anti-trans violence. All the various groups involved in the protest invoked the initial intersectional inspiration of BLM—with a special attention paid to the needs of Black queers, transgendered, undocumented, and incarcerated. Most activists thus lamented that violence against Black men garners more national media attention, fearing that "cisgender privilege has taken precedent over gay and transgender people." Jonovia Chase, coleader of the House Lives Matter, added: "We are a prime target because of our Blackness, and our intersectionality of being trans adds an extra target on our backs."[74]

Friction persists between African Americans and white liberal supporters of BLM, the former expressing the view that "sympathetic white people" are no help because "good deeds will not dismantle systemic oppression."[75] According to Elwood Watson, the relationship between Black Americans and white Liberals remains complex. While admitting that "an acute minority" of white liberals have dedicated their time and energy to issues that have directly impacted Black people, he adds that the "rhetoric for racial justice and equality that flowed from the mouths of White liberals is just that: rhetorical exercises in self-congratulations." From his perspective, white liberals embrace progressive attitudes when it is politically expedient to do so. Otherwise, "they sell out their non-White colleagues in a heartbeat."[76] Interestingly, and paradoxically, attacks against "sympathetic white people" increase as white support for BLM increases, not decreases.

The popularity of BLM, notwithstanding the tensions among its supporters, has provided new incentives to its opponents who have organized their countermobilization. Blue Lives Matter, for example, was created in 2014 after the killing of two police officers in Brooklyn. Presenting BLM as an anti-police movement, Blue Lives Matter intends to protect law enforcement personnel against "illegitimate complaints, frivolous law suits, and physical threats" as well as "to honor and recognize the actions of law enforcement" in order to "strengthen the public support of an understandably naive society."[77] Its members claim that there is today a "war on cops," that they are discriminated against, and that killing a police officer should be considered a hate crime. During their demonstrations, they rally around the Blue Lives Matter flag, which replaces the red of the traditional American flag with Black bands and a thin blue line representing their professional pride. There are concerns, however, that Blue Lives Matter has some racist connotations—notably as its flag was spotted alongside Confederate flags during the 2017 violent protests in Charlottesville.[78] Supporters dismiss these concerns by arguing that Blue Lives Matter is not anti-Black (pointing out the increasing number of Black police officers in many departments), but rather a reaction against "anti-law enforcement sentiment." According to Andrew Jacob, president of Thin Blue Line USA, "the flag has no association with racism, hatred, bigotry. It's a flag to show support for law enforcement—no politics involved."[79] Yet, the flag was politicized by taking a prominent place at Trump rallies in 2020.

Many commentators, in their analysis of the current state of American society, draw parallels between the current moment and the 1960s, "a decade that saw sharp peaks and valleys in white support for the civil rights movement."[80] Some emphasize the similarities between the strong mobilization in favor of BLM, quickly followed by a declining support, with the backlash to the civil rights movement that took place in the second half of the decade in the wake of Martin Luther King Jr.'s assassination in 1968 and the riots erupting in several cities across the country. As the history professor David Krugler notes, 76 percent of Americans were in favor of civil rights legislation in 1965; yet, in 1968, "people see chaos, they see a breakdown of civil order and they make an association between that the civil rights movements and Black power."[81] In his analysis of the literature on BLM, Alvin B. Tillery Jr. found that there is a consensus about the style and nature of this social movement: BLM activists intentionally reject the "respectability politics" model that animated the African American Civil Rights movement of the 1960s; and they "see intrinsic value in the disruptive repertoires of contention that they utilize to draw attention to their causes."[82] While this strategy explains the success of BLM, critics suggest that BLM would be even more successful if it emulated movements inspired by the "minority-rights revolution" of the 1960s.

Other commentators focus on the resilience of forms of violence over time, noting that recent acts of aggressive activism and political violence echo those of the late 1960s. During the 2020 presidential campaign, Trump supporters armed with military-style rifles in Texas confronted left-leaning activists, with demonstrators on both sides exchanging punches or beating one another with sticks and flagpoles from Kalamazoo, Michigan, to Chicago and Portland, Oregon. Violence was intensified by the incendiary rhetoric of the Trump administration against "Antifa" and BLM protesters—a rhetoric reminiscent of the "law and order" posture of Richard Nixon in his 1968 presidential campaign.[83]

Does history actually repeat itself, again? I address this question in the coming chapters by evaluating the likelihood of violent contentious politics in America.

Part 3
CURRENT LESSONS FROM AMERICA

America remains a country plagued by ethnoracial division, ideological polarization, and subsequent various forms of violence. The racialized political violence that increased during the Trump administration reached a crescendo beginning in August 2020 when a supporter of "Back the Blue" killed two people in Kenosha, Wisconsin. Then in September, a pro-Trump demonstration turned violent in Washington, DC, when white nationalist groups (including the Proud Boys) roamed the streets. Finally, in January 2021, five people were killed when pro-Trump insurrectionists clashed with police and security forces before breaking into the US Capitol as Congress met to certify electoral college votes for president-elect Joe Biden, ransacking offices, vandalizing the House and Senate chambers. The attack represented the apotheosis of the racialization of politics, shocking most Americans who perceived the attack as an assault against US democracy.

Efforts to end institutional racism have failed. Longstanding fault lines over socioeconomic inequalities, gender roles, and sexual norms have deepened—a product of profound changes in a fracturing social landscape.[1] As a result, the centripetal melting pot metaphor has been replaced by a centrifugal one in which tensions have become endemic—paradoxically as a product of various groups seeking to have their claims recognized and rights accepted. This has led to a society with fewer points of commonality. "Just about every policy issue has become a wedge issue," the political journalist Michael Grunwald argues, "not only traditional us-against-them social litmus tests like abortion, guns, feminism, and affirmative action . . . all domestic issues normally associated with wonky panels at Washington think tanks have been repackaged into cultural-resentment fodder."[2] Blue and Red America have split into warring tribes living in separate realities: urban and rural, CNN and Fox News. Americans' opinions have become more racially polarized: their evaluation of the 2020 electoral results; their perception of climate change; their attitude toward the coronavirus pandemic and wearing a mask; and even their cultural preferences about TV shows, music, and Starbucks non-Christmas-specific holiday cups.

Other observers express similar concerns about polarization and violence in America. "We are sort of at the stage of polarization where there are more and more people who are seeking confrontation, where they are not simply satisfied with disagreeing with the other side or yelling at the other side, but they want to confront," said Mark Pitcavage, a historian and senior research fellow at the Anti-Defamation League's Center on Extremism. "We are not just a polarized society—we are increasingly a confrontational society now."[3] According to Thomas Carothers of the Carnegie Endowment for International Peace, "no respite from polarization is in sight." Rather, "the serious dangers that polarization presents to our democracy—including growing citizen alienation from political gridlock, and the ever-rising potential for aggravated and even violent conflict between citizens on opposing sides—will probably grow."[4]

Many characterized this as a precursor of America's future. But to what extent will such a pessimistic diagnostic apply in the next decade? America, I contend, is at a crossroads.

8

IS A VIOLENT SOCIETY AMERICA'S ONLY POSSIBLE FUTURE?

There are grounds for optimism. Some aspects of the current social and political fragmentation of American society may be surprisingly temporary. Certainly, we may expect a decrease of aggressive activism or, minimally, an attenuation of political unrest. Partisan identification will remain polarized, but the most incendiary effects of racialized politics are likely to dampen. White supremacist groups, notably, lost their foundational institutional support with Donald Trump's departure from the White House and the suppression of his Twitter account. Much of their leadership structure will be decapitated if Trump is found guilty of insurrection and sedition. They may have fewer opportunities to engage in quasi-paramilitary operations without the benefit of the endorsement of political leaders and the leniency of law enforcement authorities now observed by a racially sensitive Democratic federal government.

Furthermore, some of the most controversial issues that have been politically racialized are becoming less divisive. Racial considerations, for example, were one of the many factors that shaped public opinion about the Affordable Care Act (ACA) and other health care reforms during the Obama and Trump presidencies. However, support for ACA has continued to increase (from 42 percent in 2010 to 55 percent in 2020) as well as support for Medicare for All—up to 69 percent of Americans during the winter peak of the coronavirus crisis. Indeed, a product of the pandemic has been a more widespread belief that the ACA should be incrementally expanded rather than abandoned.[1]

More generally, the proportion of white Americans supportive of anti-Black and anti-Hispanic prejudice actually declined during the course of the Trump presidency. Trump's rhetoric generated a boomerang effect that has increased the salience of antiracist norms as Trump's not so subtly closeted racial claims were decoded by the public. After Trump criticized NFL players for kneeling during the playing of the national anthem, for example, more white Americans supported them and better understood the symbolic significance of protesting social injustice. Likewise, Trump's attacks against Muslims increased their positive perception by the general public, while his attitude toward women elevated gender discrimination and sexual harassment to the list of top social issues in America.[2]

Yet, more pessimistically, other processes of fragmentation may persist over time. The patterned evolution of contentious repertoires I have identified offers strong reasons to believe that racial polarization will continue framing ethnoracial relations and fueling violence even after Trump's departure. Grievances, as I have demonstrated, are more and more disconnected from reality. What matters is the perception of the "others" as posing a threat, independent of objective socioeconomic data. In the ensuing sections, I identify the current features of ethnoracial relations that are more likely to leave a lasting imprint on American society. They include the emotional components of contentious identity politics, such as anger and frustration, that are likely to persist over time and continue to be key factors shaping patterns of mobilization.

Over time, these trends lead to two possible options. The first entails more friction resulting from the spiraling dynamics of backlash effects. Racism, as well as antiracism and anti-antiracism, fuel a wide range of grievances that will provide the foundation for further conflict as long as ethnoracial categorizations remain the most static and salient aspect defining what it means to be "American." A second, alternative, option involves greater cooperation based on new forms of interracial coalition building—based on both racial and nonracial commonalities.

The Potential Long-Term Effect of Ethnoracial Divides

Minority groups do not have similar priorities, and this current feature may translate into more divergent contentious repertoires in the coming years. Polling in the run up to the 2020 election illustrated that trend. When surveyed, for example, the top issues for Hispanic voters in 2020 were the economy (80 percent), health care (76 percent), and the coronavirus outbreak (72 percent). Racial inequality was important for 66 percent (comparable to their concern about Supreme Court appointments), while immigration was important to 59 percent (one point below climate change).[3] This ranking of concerns shows that, contrary to the assumption that Hispanics are predominantly concerned about immigration issues, they actually mirror the general population. Furthermore, immigration policy divides Hispanic subgroups. Overall, 83 percent of Hispanics support the legalization of most unauthorized immigrants—89 percent among Democrats and 71 percent among Republicans. Hispanic democrats are significantly more likely to oppose expanding the border wall than are Hispanic Republicans (87 percent versus 46 percent).[4] Some subgroups, notably Hispanics of Mexican origin, are more tolerant toward illegal immigration than those of other origins—except in Texas where the majority of Mexican Americans held restrictive positions on immigration.[5]

African Americans share some priorities with Hispanics, such as more affordable housing and higher paying jobs (which 68 percent support), and health care (67 percent). Not surprisingly, they tend to be more concerned by racial equity, reforming the criminal justice system, and eliminating barriers to vote.[6] In November 2020, about 80 percent of Black voters supported reducing the number of people in jails and prisons, as well as accountability for brutality and broader police reforms.[7] But only 47 percent of African Americans said they believe that illegal immigrants should be allowed to stay in the country—far less than Hispanics but more than whites (33 percent). Yet, conversely, despite being more supportive of undocumented immigrants, African Americans are still more likely to feel that immigrants take jobs away from American citizens than whites (by 34 to 25 percent). A sense of competition remains widespread, especially in areas where the Hispanic population has grown rapidly in the last three decades.

Socioeconomic Differentiation

Increasing socioeconomic inequalities add another layer of fragmentation, as illustrated by tensions between social classes within each ethnoracial group. The wealth gap between America's richest and poorer families more than doubled between 1986 and 2016, with the richest five percent of families holding 248 times as much wealth at the median net worth. The United States has the highest level of income inequality among the G7 countries. Income disparities are so pronounced that America's top 10 percent now average more than nine times as much income as the bottom 90 percent. Americans in the top 1 percent average over 39 times more income than the bottom 90 percent.

The income gap *between* ethnoracial groups has persisted over time. In 2019, the median white worker made 28 percent more than the typical Black worker, and more than 35 percent more than the median Hispanic worker.[8] The income gap within ethnoracial groups has also persisted, with a significant gap between social classes. The Black middle class, for example, included 61.2 percent of African Americans in 2018. Yet, there has been a simultaneous rise in the impoverishment of the Black working class—leading to a larger split between low-income Black workers and the Black middle class.[9] This split, limited in the 1980s and overtly significant today, has increasingly undermined the "linked fate" that has historically united African Americans of different classes.[10] "Black Bourgeois" face the contradiction of being economically privileged while being racially vulnerable—which simultaneously complicates their relationship with both the Black working class and the white middle class.[11] The problem of inequality is thus not bifurcated between a Black and white divide. It also extends to inequality between rich and poor whites, between "Black haves and have-nots," and reflects the broader distrust between impoverished communities and the elites.

Facing inequality rarely motivates white and nonwhite groups to unite in protest against social injustice. Indeed, racial disparities may worsen. Cornell University sociologist Daniel T. Lichter suggests that if the demographic profile of poverty remains constant, over 70 percent of America's poor will be from minority groups by 2050. As a result, a shrinking population of older whites will be more likely to support more conservative positions on many issues—including limited access to public services for nonwhite groups.[12] Meanwhile, poor whites—as well as formerly middle-class whites who fell into poverty during the Great Recession and/or the coronavirus pandemic—are ill-equipped to handle the economic struggles that African Americans have been facing for many decades. This has led to an increasing number of "deaths of despair" through opioid addiction, alcohol or drug overdose, and suicide that has particularly hit middle-aged white people without a college education. Life expectancy has declined since 2018 among all ethnoracial groups; yet findings on rising white mortality rates came as a shock—at least for whites not aware that they were facing health issues commonly associated with minorities.

Poor whites who support a conservative or Trumpist ideology face a painful dilemma. They can either support political leaders who claim that poor people should blame themselves for their economic misfortunes (the conservatives) or admit that—as Carol Graham puts it—the poor, whites and nonwhites, "have been screwed over by crony capitalism and a rigged game" (the Trumpists). Analyzing the effect of "decades of poor-bashing" from right-wing media and fundamentalist Pentecostals, Graham suggests that one of the reasons for rising despair among poor whites relates to the so-called "prosperity gospel" which "teaches that the rich are blessed with affluence because of their moral superiority and that the poor are poor because of their immoral, sinful ways."[13] By contrast, paradoxically, African Americans who suffer even more poverty than poor whites are almost three times as likely to be higher on an optimistic scale than poor whites.

Indeed, the most disadvantaged of them, those earning less than the official US poverty line ($24,000), are even more optimistic than rich Black people.[14]

Poor whites and African Americans continue to live in very different physical and spiritual worlds. One distinct attribute is that other minorities show higher levels of resilience than their white counterparts. Like African Americans, for example, Hispanics are much less likely than whites to express pessimism, report depression, or commit suicide. This may be due to several factors: resilience built up as a result of generations of hardship or informal safety nets such as extended Hispanic families or Black churches (notably African Methodist Episcopal churches that often deliver material and spiritual support to their communities). It may also relate to feelings of relative incremental, tangible, material, generational gains despite ongoing poverty. In 2019, poverty rates for African Americans and Hispanics were 18.8 percent and 15.7 percent respectively—compared to 30 percent and 28 percent in 1990. These groups remain over-represented in terms of poverty as a percentage of the overall population. Yet, median household income has increased 14.1 percent for Black households and 24.3 percent for Hispanic households since 2008.[15]

There is no reason to assume, however, that African Americans and Hispanics are satisfied with their situation. They show resilience despite their concerns about their financial and health situation, and their relative optimism is tempered by a distinct sense of resignation. Optimism and resignation may superficially appear antinomic emotions, but their combination actually explains key variations in mobilization patterns. For example, while a large majority of white liberals support Black Lives Matter, mobilizations initiated by whites remain largely white as illustrated by the Occupy Wall Street movement. Launched in 2011 in New York City's Wall Street financial district, this protest movement against economic inequality spread across the United States while African Americans were much more affected by the Great Recession than whites. A few prominent African Americans—such as Cornel West, Representative John Lewis, and Kanye West—made appearances at Occupy protests. "Occupy the Hood," a short-life offshoot, tried to get more African Americans involved. Yet, nationwide, Black people made up less than two percent of the Occupy movement at its height. For journalism professor Stacy Patton, this lack of participation sent a message to the white Occupiers: "Blacks are not seeing anything new for themselves in the movement. Why should they ally with whites who are just experiencing the hardships that blacks have known for generations? Perhaps white Americans are now paying the psychic price for not answering the basic questions that blacks have long raised about income inequality." A sense of resignation accentuated this resentment: "We told you so! Nothing will change. We've been here already. It's hopeless."[16]

Other commentators expressed similar arguments, notably when activists tried to resurrect the Occupy movement in 2019–2020. Leaders of the Debt Collective, for example, connect Occupy to Senator Bernie Sanders's 2016 and 2020 presidential campaigns (notably the student debt cancellation and free public college issues).[17] Yet, this agenda is perceived as being "too white" because of the obvious impossibility for African Americans to focus on economic justice without fighting for racial justice. Another related reason is the "anger gap" that may have lasting effects. As Davin Phoenix notes, "black people are certainly no strangers to insurgent protest strategies" before and after the civil rights movement. However, he adds, Black anger does not translate into the same set of political actions as white anger because of "the risks associated with being *angry* while *black*: whereas expressions of grievance from white Americans are typically viewed as legitimate, such expressions from black people are often view through lenses of suspicion and derision."[18]

The Issue of Distrust

More to the point, there is an issue of continued distrust that will affect ethnoracial relations for the foreseeable future. The enthusiasm expressed by white liberals during the Black Lives Matter protests during the summer of 2020 has been criticized by some activists and analysts who argued that white people, despite their genuine concerns for racial justice, are motivated by their sense of shame: benefiting from unfair privileges as a product of their racial identity rather than their achievements being based on their actual merits.[19] Other criticisms are inspired by "black fatigue" which, according to Mary-Frances Winters, is fueled by the myriad dire consequences of "living while Black": "It is exhausting to have to constantly explain this to white people, even—and especially—well-meaning white people, who fall prey to white fragility and too often are unwittingly complicit in upholding the very systems they say they have dismantled."[20]

From the perspective of Critical Whiteness Studies (CWS), white people often unwittingly perpetuate a system of values that reproduce white supremacy, which make them inadvertently complicit in the perpetuation of racism despite their good intentions. This perspective has popularized the notion of "white fragility," which, according to sociologist Robin DiAngelo, prevents white Americans from confronting racism. Unused to racial discomfort, white people allegedly lack the "racial stamina" to engage in difficult conversations about their racial missteps (both conscious and unconscious) and to acknowledge their participation in racist systems. White progressives, according to DiAngelo, "cause the most daily damage to people of color" because not only do they fail to understand their complicity but they take a self-serving approach to ongoing antiracism efforts.[21] DiAngelo's book became a best-seller during the Black Lives Matter protests. However, it was strongly criticized by Black scholars who suspect that white progressives (like DiAngelo) use antiracism as a mechanism to rehabilitate themselves, while nonetheless being unable to grasp the core meaning of racial prejudice. John McWhorter, professor at Columbia University, for example, argues that there is "no connection between DiAngelo's brand of re-education and vigorous, constructive activism in the real world on issues of import to the black community . . . Few books about race have more openly infantilized Black people than this supposedly authoritative tone."[22]

Therefore, the objective of the White Privilege Awareness (WPA) pedagogy is to dislodge whiteness from its position of dominance by making whites aware of their involvement in the resilience of racist practices, even when they believe that what they are doing is morally good.[23] This pedagogy encourages emotions such as shame and guilt as solvents for America's racial problem. Christopher Lebron, for example, argues in *The Color of Our Shame* that our collective response to racial inequality ought to be shame, in order to compel a higher level of racially relevant moral excellence from individuals and institutions.[24] Other scholars, such as Antoine Banks, advocate a similar perspective by assuming that "rather than blaming others, as in the case of anger, a person who experiences guilt blames oneself for moral transgression."[25]

The consequences of this approach contrast. There is evidence that heightening white Americans' awareness of their advantages, as opposed to disadvantages for African Americans, reduces racial discriminatory attitudes.[26] Prejudice reduction programs such as diversity training encourage whites to identify various forms of institutionalized racism, as well as insensitive practices related to "micro-aggressions" and "cultural appropriation." However, not all programs on WPA have proven successful. Some studies showed that racial prejudice decreases only among whites whose group identification with other whites is weak and whose prejudicial attitudes are already low.[27] Other studies simply found that participating in WPA programs does not improve the attitudes of whites toward other racial groups.[28] In fact, they can increase racial prejudice. As Nyla Branscombe and her colleagues note: "Encouraging whites to think about their privilege may evoke identity threat for doing so and places the ingroup's deservingness in question. Such implied benefits at the expense of another group could represent a threat to the moral value of the ingroup. Accordingly, when whites are confronted with racial inequality they benefit from, they may respond to this threat to their group's position with increased racism."[29] This sort of reaction fuels the current "whitelash," characterized as "the reactionary impulse of many white voters toward racial equality movements and societal shifts they perceive as excessive."[30]

Among those whites who find racism morally reprehensible and oppose racist practices, being nevertheless labeled as racist can fuel a "white fatigue syndrome." According to Joseph Flynn Jr, this fatigue occurs when whites—despite their understanding of the moral imperative of antiracist and anti-oppressive practices—are tired of discussing racism.[31] For Eric Kaufmann, antiracism can be perverted by "left-modernist offense archeologists" who reframe "the world as racist, sexist, homophobic, transphobic, ableist, and so on" without providing any clear definition of these terms. Instead, they "insist on the most suspicious interpretations of a person's motives when the subject matter is associated with their canonical totems of race, gender, sexuality." The result is "an atmosphere where interpersonal trust is as low as humanly possible while discursive power flows to the accuser."[32]

The lasting effect of distrust between and among ethnoracial groups is likely to remain significant because it fuels—and is fueled by—a more general fragmentation of American society. This declining trust raises concerns about the deleterious effect of an illiberalism promoted by radical liberals and the radical right. One is the preference for civil debate. In July 2020, for example, 150 renowned intellectuals, writers, journalists, and artists signed a letter on "Justice and Open Debate" to denounce "an intolerance of opposing views, a vogue for public shaming and ostracism, and the tendency to dissolve complex policy issues in a blinding moral certainty."[33] It is noteworthy that this letter was signed by both white and Black intellectuals, including experts on race studies and CWS, such as Nell Irvin Painter and Thomas Chatterton Williams. There is indeed a raging debate between antiradical and radical liberals that benefits the radical right. Among the antiradical liberals, Walter Benn Michaels argues that the "trouble with diversity" is that it has become "virtually a sacred concept in American life today" while losing its inclusive meaning. Furthermore, a "commitment to diversity is at best a distraction and at worst an essentially reactionary position that prevents us from putting equality at the center of the national agenda."[34] Meghan Daum also addresses the abuse of identity politics leading to "the myopia of tribalism"—characterized as the excesses of wokeness—and tensions among feminists about the #MeToo movement.[35]

These polemical analyses have generated a counterattack by radical liberals who denounce the anti-woke tropes popularized by Daum and others, urging instead a focus on the threat posed by right-wing thinkers and politicians.[36] As Laurent Dubreuil summarizes it, "identity politics has become a culture war cudgel, recklessly deployed by race baiters on the right as well as some activists on the social justice left."[37] This war is not confined to academic circles. It is amplified by social media and political rhetoric and takes place in a context characterized by increasing interpersonal distrust and democratic disenchantment.

Approaching 80 percent of Americans have "far too little" or "too little" confidence in each other today. Many believe the issue of declining interpersonal trust is a consequence of political polarization, especially when tied to tribalism (generated by a multitude of "special interest groups" created by race, religion, gender, and other cleavages) and to the decline of civil public debate.[38] Levels of trust in American institutions are extremely low (22 percent for the presidency, 18 percent for the Supreme Court, 10 percent for the criminal justice system, and 6 percent for Congress), as well in television news (9 percent) and unions (13 percent).[39] The trust in the government to handle domestic issues is actually at its lowest point since 1972, in the aftermath of President Nixon's resignation. The acceptance of the notion of a social contract, which turned subjects into citizens of a polity based on the consent to live in accord with some common principles, seems to be in decline. For much of its modern history, America has viewed itself as a model democracy, a "shining city upon the hill." There is little support for this hubris today: According to a study conducted by the University of Cambridge's Center for the Future of Democracy, more than 50 percent of Americans are dissatisfied with their system of government (compared to 25 percent who were disenchanted with US democracy in 2010).[40]

Promising Trends Toward Ethnoracial Peaceful Reconciliation

Discrepancies of interests, political skepticism, social distrust, ideological tensions, and polarized identities are likely to generate further societal conflict and intergroup tensions. There are, however, a few noticeable countervailing trends that may assuage intergroups relations by encouraging the depolarization and de-racialization of American society.

The Migrant Optimism

One trend, known as "migrant optimism," refers to the relatively high level of current satisfaction and optimism about the future among migrant minorities, especially members of the first generation. When they compare their life in the United States to their life in their country of origin, Hispanic immigrants are much more positive than American-born Hispanics (and American-born whites) about most political institutions, the education system, and job opportunities. About 68 percent of all Hispanics believe that their standard of living is better than their parents (a figure that increases to 71 percent among more recent arrivals). This sanguine view is inversely related to the length of time they or their families have been in the country. Forty-four percent of all Hispanics believe that their children will be better off than people are now—a spectrum varying between 50 percent among first-generation immigrants and 38 percent among their native-born children.[41] However, both foreign- and native-born Hispanics share a positive view of America, as illustrated by their optimism about the attainability of the American dream. They also express patriotic feelings at percentages equal to, or higher than, whites while maintaining strong ties with their country of origin.

Muslims immigrants, despite being targeted by security governance since 9/11, express similar optimistic beliefs and positive views of America. Studies show that they embrace American ideals more than other groups. Sixty-one percent report that they are "extremely happy" in the United States (compared with only 33 of other immigrants). Nearly 74 percent express faith in the American dream (compared with 62 percent of the US public overall), and 44 percent display the flag (up to 50 percent among those who are first generation).[42] Like other minorities, their life goals are having well-paying steady jobs, living in a safe neighborhood with high-quality schools for their children, enjoying basic freedoms, and being treated fairly and respectfully by others.

The fears and resentment generated by immigration and counterterrorism policies have not been translated into the rejection of American values, or a sense of enmity. A hostile environment hasn't undermined the opportunity for immigrants to maximize their sense of "Americanness," collectively mobilize for the principles they share, and thus achieve full social citizenship to protect their interests—without resorting to violence. Contrary to the assumption that immigrants and their descendants are a threat to traditional national norms, they are actual more likely than native whites to support and promote the key elements of the American creed. They endorse liberal principles and civic republicanism while trying to balance their integration with the maintenance of their cultural heritage. These behavioral inclinations may not erase the effects of ethnoracial distrust, but they are part of the complex definition of the content and meaning of American identity beyond its ethnoracial divides.

The Integration Paradox

Another trend that we need to take into account includes both the negative and positive aspects of the "integration paradox."[43] On the negative side, second and third generation immigrants are more integrated but feel more excluded than newcomers. Being born and socialized in America, they feel entitled to the same treatment as other citizens. They are also more sensitive to discrimination, and less inclined to tolerate social marginalization. As a result, they are more critical of the society at large, and less trustful of national institutions. This trend challenges some core components of the acculturation paradigm. For example, contrary to the assumption that new immigrants are more likely to be engaged in criminal activities, there is strong evidence that they are less likely to do so. But social and economic pressures, coupled with opportunities unavailable to many migrants, increase the propensity of their more assimilated children to engage in criminality.[44] According to Lorna Alvarez-Rivera et al., "acculturation is accompanied by greater access to tools that facilitate crime"—especially when young people are exposed to "a culture of violence" in high-crime inner-city neighborhoods.[45] As a result, paradoxically, the process of intergenerational Americanization and integration increases the likelihood of criminality.[46]

On the positive side, however, the integration paradox contributes to the de-ethnicization of minorities when it comes to democratic inclusion. According to the pluralist ethnic integration perspective, ethnic and racial groups select their political affiliation and try to make their way into positions of influence in political institutions on the basis of their ethnoracial identities. As a result, minorities tend to vote for parties and leaders defending their ethnoracial interests. In American politics, this trend is illustrated by the high degree of support for Democrats among minorities, and the subsequent effort of the Democratic party to adjust its platform by paying greater attention to diversity issues.

However, we should not dismiss the fact that Trump's popularity among some minorities increased between 2016 and 2020. Joe Biden did win the Hispanic vote nationally, but Trump consolidated his electorate support among Hispanics in some states. He won 45 percent of the Hispanic vote in Florida in 2016, for example, an 11-point improvement over his 2016 performance. Fragments of the Hispanic electorate, as I documented previously, have a record of backing Republicans, often supporting the GOP's messages about the economy and conservative social issues. The fact that some voted for the most anti-immigrant candidate in recent history puzzled many liberal commentators; yet this is an illustration of the complete assimilation of some minorities into the political mainstream.

The "integration paradox" involves two aspects that will have lasting effects on this de-ethnicization process. First, more than 60 percent of Hispanics today are native-born, and their opinions often mirror those of the general population on key issues. Hispanics may be a minority, but their status is no longer exclusively defined by their "immigrant experience." The assumptions that all Hispanics are immigrants and that most immigrants are Hispanic are increasingly misleading and fuel a deep misunderstanding of the management of diversity in America. Hispanics are assimilating in ways that echo how European immigrants were absorbed into the American mainstream a century ago, and, as they do so, they are diverging economically, socially, and politically. Second,

Hispanics increasingly identify first as "Americans" (up to 79 percent), with only 24 percent using a pan-ethnic label as their primary identity. For those who supported Trump, there is no contradiction. They express preferences that are less, if not at all, based on their ethnoracial identification. While we may assume a continuation of political polarization, we should also pay attention to the de-racialization of US politics—at least from the perspective of some minorities who reject the stereotypical "life script" commonly attributed to them.

The Multiracial Push

What may further facilitate the de-racialization of intergroup relations is the growing number of multiracial Americans. Evidence suggests a radical shift: the number of those reporting themselves as members of multiple races grew by 32 percent over the last decade, compared with those who identified with a single race, which grew by 9.2 percent. The number of multiracial Americans is expected to grow rapidly, as a result of both a multiracial baby boom and current immigration trends. And the former is significant: The proportion of multiracial babies among the baby population rose from 1 percent in 1970 to 10 percent by 2013. If these trends continue, the Census Bureau projects that the multiracial population will triple by 2060. This multiracialism will dismantle some racial boundaries but reinforce others. "There are limits to the porousness of racial identities," Lauren Davenport notes in his study of multiracial identity and attitudes in America. Hispanic-whites, for example, are less likely than Asian-whites and Black-whites to identity as multiracial. But in each of these subgroups, a high socioeconomic status increases the level of multiracial identification. These variations, Davenport adds, illustrate a "reformation of cultural attitudes toward race-mixing and what it means to belong to a racial group."[47] Multiracial Americans defy labels and react to discrimination against them by fighting for the recognition of their right to complexity and fluidity—among the key claims listed in the "Bill of Rights for Racially Mixed People," a widely popular manifesto among supporters of multiracialism.[48]

More to the point, multiracial Americans challenge policies based on traditional labels—such as affirmative action programs (notably college and university admissions)—as well as political positions and partisan affiliation. In sum, they convey a clear political progressivism and identify with causes such as equal opportunity and social justice. They may therefore contribute to the de-racialization of intergroup relations on the basis of their insider/outsider status and "middle-of-the road" political attitudes.[49] About 48 percent of them identify as independents (up from 46 percent in 2014), while 17 percent identify with the Democratic party (also up from 11 percent in 2014). Nearly 36 percent identify as political moderates.[50]

The legacy of the 1990s Multiracial Movement in favor of MOOM ("mark one or more") option remains vivid. Multiracial identity has reemerged as a topic of national debate since the late 2000s, encouraged by the election of President Obama and more recently the nomination of Kamala Harris as vice president. In California, home to the largest multiracial population in America, social movements increasingly advocate for the right multiracial people to self-identify as mixed—with long-term implications for how race is conceptualized and how intergroup relations are framed.[51] This multiracial activism helps engender the emergence of new cultural and social values, and thus make people "think in a different way." As Kim Williams argues, this encourages a movement beyond the "us" and "them" dichotomy, instead promoting "a community that straddles boundaries and validates mixture." Second-wave multiracial organizations such as the Mavin Foundation and Swirl today attest to the "potential for community building" by inching away from the black/white, one-race-only, divide.[52] The fluidity introduced by multiracialism does not mean that racism will disappear. The increased acceptance of interracial relationships will not dismantle a racial hierarchy. However, multiracialism has the potential to transform traditionally monoracial organizations and influence public policy, as well as cultural values, in America. For some scholars, we may soon be witnessing the emergence of a new social justice framework that incorporates multi-issue organizing and shared leadership that hastens the movement toward racial and social justice.[53]

The New Wave of Reactive Social Movements

More broadly, intergroup relations can be assuaged by the emergence of coalitions formed around a common purpose, one working on an inclusive agenda, thereby dismantling the traditional racial-political coalition model. Adversity provides opportunities for reacting against inequality and injustice, as illustrated by the historical overview of mobilization patterns. Previous episodes of contestation have shown that the probability that protest actions achieve their desired outcomes increases when coalitions fight for a larger, shared purpose. One major reason accounting for the success of the coalitions formed during the 1960s was the ability of various groups to frame racial issues both in terms of civil rights and general public welfare. The civil rights movement thus coalesced various ethnoracial groups around issues produced by institutional racism *as well as* other issues related to broader social and political changes. Collective grievances stemming from racial inequality and other structural strains (such as the negative effects of the Vietnam War on the War on Poverty) encouraged support for African American protests as well as other forms of activism (such as the early women's movement). In contrast, many examples of mobilization during the 1990s illustrated that coalitions tend to fail when the level of trust diminishes among their members and/or when there is competition between more isolated ethnoracial groups.

The current political and socioeconomic landscape creates favorable conditions for the emergence of reactive social movements for two reasons.[54] First, political polarization does not always preclude cooperation; it may also catalyze collective actions based on bargaining. In a context characterized by closely divided and competitive political situations, various groups have to secure their position by cooperating with political rivals and consolidate their electorate by attracting new voters. For example, several scholars in the field of social movements contend that the closely divided and highly competitive presidential elections in the early 1960s, coupled with small congressional majorities, opened the path to civil rights reform.[55] In his analysis of the social protests of the 1960s and early 1970s, Jenkins argues that "in the context of a series of closely contested presidential elections . . . two swing voting blocs (African Americans and the new middle class) became increasingly decisive in the electoral calculations of political elites."[56] Transposed to the current political situation, there are many voting blocs that both Republicans and Democrats need to focus on (ethnoracial minorities as well as gender minorities, LGBT groups, and young voters). We can anticipate, for example, that the GOP will have to abandon its hardline stance on key issues for these blocs to compensate for the demographic shrinking of its core electorate and, thus, will need to adjust to the increased normative acceptance of minority claims. Democrats may also be inspired in addressing these blocs' main concerns, based on their ethnoracial identities as well as in terms of demands for social justice for all. As a result, we may expect greater bipartisan support for issues that actually matter to all Americans, and which are quite independent from contentious identity politics, such as the state of the economy, the cost of health care, the management of pandemics, and the reform of the political system.

Second, racial-political coalitions no longer constitute the only effective medium for achieving significant reforms. This is not to say that they have lost their potential for successfully transforming American politics and framing societal debates, as BLM illustrates. However, this kind of mobilization remains fragile, susceptible to tensions between and among ethnoracial groups. When the crisis that initially brought the groups together has passed, ethnoracial coalitions either explode as the result of inner competition or decline as soon as public attention vanishes. Against this background, the multiplication of societal crises can inspire the mobilization of coalitional confederations—which are both larger and more flexible than traditional ethnoracial coalitions. This alternative approach requires identifying "common-interest problems, affecting a large broad-based constituency" and setting "specific interests and ideologies aside, thereby benefiting society as a whole."[57] In this network configuration, the identification of what may constitute a public good discourages competitive, opportunistic behavior from the various groups involved. Instead, it promotes the collective value of goodwill and allows for a flexible coordination of greater tangible value—where weak ties (associated with acquaintance rather than ethnoracial kinship) paradoxically help strengthen the social capital of the coalition.[58]

United around common values and principles, participants with very different backgrounds can combine their respective expertise and deploy resources in a variety of issue areas when they realize how their particular struggles are connected to other comparably connected struggles.[59] Moral Mondays, for example, is a grassroots coalition that groups together religious progressives with advocates for immigrant rights, LGBT rights, criminal justice rights, worker's rights, and environmental rights. It emerged in 2013 in North Carolina in reaction to the policies of Governor Pat McCrory, who implemented cutting social programs, restricting voting and abortion rights, and repealing the Racial Justice Act (which allows inmates facing the death penalty to challenge their sentences of the basis of racial discrimination). Invoking "A National Call for Moral Revival," the movement addresses the "five interlocking injustices of systemic racism, systemic poverty, ecological devastation, the war economy and militarism, and a distorted moral narrative of religious nationalism."[60]

The movement has spread to other states, including South Carolina, Georgia, Illinois, and New Mexico. It today has organizing committees in forty-three states. Since 2014, protests have been supported by the NAACP, teacher unions, environmental groups, religious associations such as the Poor People's Campaign, and many activist groups. In 2020, the Moral Monday movement organized caravans in twenty-four states, as well as a series of online protests, focusing on racism, inequality, and the mismanagement of the COVID-19 pandemic. On June 8th, two weeks after the killing of George Floyd, Moral Monday organized a National Moment of Silence (asking all participants to remain silent for 8 minutes and 46 seconds, the time Floyd "had the literal knee of the state on his neck").

The Industrial Areas Foundation (IAF) provides another example of how to create progressive pluralism out of polarized identity politics. Founded in 1940, it is now the nation's largest network of local faith and community-based organizations, with chapters in sixty-five cities across the United States (as well as in Canada, Australia, the United Kingdom, and Germany). The IAF partners with religious congregations, nonprofits, civic organizations and unions to develop a "new capacity in a community for leadership development, citizen-led action and relationships across the lines that often divide our communities." It sustains interracial cooperation by promoting community engagement, framing issues in a race-neutral manner while permitting its members to "also serve in other organizations that address race-and neighborhood-specific issues." As its mission statement notes, the IAF works on "imaginative responses to seemingly intractable problems, new relationships overcoming racial, religious and socio-economic divisions . . . that change communities for the better and inspire hope in the future."[61]

Many comparable coalitions have emerged during the last decade, notably in local urban settings.[62] This may prefigure the emergence of a new conception of civil society organized along mutual interests—a promising trend toward an effective reactive mobilization against the dramatic effects of the polarization of American society that, so far, has been detrimental to both racial justice and democratic inclusion. As many social movement theorists argue, collective action is more successful when activists can articulate a vast array of experiences so that they hang together in a unified fashion.[63] In the concluding chapter, I suggest policies that may make America more united while achieving racial justice and social equity for all. Before doing so, a detour via Europe, where ethnoracial groups are engaged in cycles of grievances comparable to the ones taking place in America, provides further insights about the future of intergroup tensions in Western democracies.

9

IS VIOLENT AMERICA EUROPE'S FUTURE?

The "American model of assimilation" has been debated in Europe since the 1990s. Some Europeans have praised the benefits of America's multiculturalism, the fluidity of its racial boundaries, the importance of its racially conscious policies (such as affirmative action programs), and the positive role played by minorities in changing US institutions. Others have rejected the main aspects of multicultural policies as "communitarianism" (or "communautarism" in European parlance)—criticizing its socio-ethnic separatism as leading to social fragmentation, exclusive cultural identity, and intergroup violence.

Controversies between these two camps now rage in Europe—with contending accusations of systemic racism and ethnoracial separatism. Supporters of identity-based activism celebrate the fact that the current mobilization of US minority groups has generated similar forms of contentious politics in Europe. Black Lives Matter protests, for example, spread to European countries in 2016 when people marched in London, Berlin, Paris, and Amsterdam in solidarity with their US counterparts. Another wave of protests took place in 2020, thousands again demonstrating in major European cities. According to the British writer and activist Rob Berkeley, BLM protests in the United States felt "like a call to action" to fight the "same disease" of institutional racism and oppose the disregard for Black lives. Black people in Europe, he explains, "wanted to express their support both for the struggle of the activists in the US with whom they identified, but also to make clear that Black Lives Matter in Britain, France, Germany, and the Netherlands."[1] This strong sense of solidarity has been shared by other groups employing a global analysis that links racial oppression in America to European issues: mass migrant deaths resulting from the perilous crossing of the Mediterranean, the escalation in the number of hate crimes, increased state-sanctioned Islamophobia because of antiterrorist policies, and growing discrimination against ethnoracial groups and other minorities fostered by greater nativism and populism. As a result, BLM has energized social movements in Europe—such as the "Migrant Lives Matter" coalition, Berlin's European Network of People of African Descent, and the Mouvement des Indigènes de la République in France.

Conversely, supporters of multiculturalism's current retreat in many European countries raise the specter of the fraying of societal unity—the product, they contend, of ethnic minority separatism and an American-style identity politics. They blame violence on the subsequent "failure of integration," from urban riots to the radicalization of some minorities. The multiplication of social movements inspired by feminist, LGBTQ, and postcolonial theories increases their concerns about a possible pernicious Americanization of identity politics. Bestselling conservative authors Douglas Murray and Lionel Shriver, for example, have railed against the British Black Lives Matter protests that they describe as "Britons marching for a problem that does not concern them." They define identity politics as "a single-minded obsession with viewing everything in life, in history, through the prism of rivalry and power relationships between groups," thus creating "an adversarial environment in a competition of who is more oppressed."[2] Kenan Malik comparably argues that, as in the United States, "personal and political grievances become refracted through the politics of identity to create a worldview shaped by noxious brew of visceral racism and conspiracy fantasies."[3] This allegedly provides a fertile ground for white violence against minorities (with racism rebranded as white identity politics), on the one hand, and aggressive contentious repertoires among some minorities damaging antiracist coalitions on the other.

To evaluate the scope, nature, and influence of American developments on intergroup relations in Europe is challenging. Ethnoracial relations in European countries are the product of very different national histories. Racial categorization, race relations, ethnoracial identification, and other key notions that frame intergroup relations in America have neither the same meaning nor content in Europe. Even in the United Kingdom, where the notion of "race relations" was first institutionalized in 1965 with the Race Relations Act, public conceptions of Blackness differ from American ones. In France, the very notion of race has been eradicated from the "French model of integration"—one based on equal rights for individuals irrespective of their ethnoracial identities, where group rights have been subsequently rejected. These critiques reinforce the assumption that there is indeed an unflattering American exceptionalism—one characterized by intense violence and the racial particularities of intergroup relations since the republic's founding. It is often used as an argument to dismiss similar minority issues on both sides of the Atlantic and/or to delegitimize European social movements inspired by their US counterparts.

I contend, however, that we should not overestimate the significance of American exceptionalism for at least three reasons. First, the experience of being racialized and discriminated against may be comparable. From the viewpoint of minorities, it does not matter how prejudice is conceptualized. Second, several issues that plagued American society are very topical in Europe such as police brutality, socioeconomic inequality, and racial injustice. Indeed, many European countries and the United States face similar problems, from migrant phobia to political populism. Third, just as in the United States, ethnoracial groups in Europe have an incentive to mobilize according to an identity-based strategy to integrate into the mainstream of politics and gain access to resources.

We may therefore wonder whether the pattern of ethnoracial mobilization in Europe is influenced by the "US style" combination of polarization and racialization or is the result of similar issues generating comparable responses—or both, one legitimizing the other. Posing this question requires us to put American exceptionalism in perspective. Events on the two continents are related. They reflect distinct but analogous trends, such as an increased political polarization and democratic disenchantment. As in America, contentious repertoires are spreading across Europe and simultaneously generating centripetal and centrifugal forces—simultaneous incentives for ethnoracial coalitions and societal fragmentation.

Transatlantic Reverberations

The belief in American exceptionalism is widespread in Europe. Its elements include a widespread "gun culture" unrecognizable in any other democracy; the indelible residual features of the Jim Crow regime despite decades of institutional reforms; the magnitude of socio-inequalities and societal violence (from gang activities to the death penalty); and various expressions of an exaggerated and possibly inauthentic or misplaced sense of patriotic "Americanism" largely reserved in Europe for national sports teams.

Many European observers, for example, compare the US daily death toll with other Western democracies. In England, gun homicides are about as common as deaths from agricultural machinery accidents are in the United States. In Germany, being murdered with a gun is as uncommon as being killed by a falling object is in the United States.[4] Majorities of Europeans believe, for example, that

Americans are violent—for example, 63 percent of respondents in Greece and France as well as 57 percent in the United Kingdom share this belief.[5]

Most Europeans are convinced that American society is a violent one par excellence because of the systemic racism inherited from slavery. This perception has been reinforced in recent years by a series of violent incidents related to police brutality, racial riots, and mass shootings. In the aftermath of the killing of Trayvon Martin in 2012, European media coverage portrayed the incident as a dramatic illustration of the pervasive and enduring problem of racism in America.[6] In Germany, media coverage described the 2014 violent riots triggered by police brutality in Ferguson as "commonplace." According to Ines Pohl, in *Deutsche Welle News*, "violence is disturbingly normal in the U.S. . . . a routine has developed, in which the news of a shooting surfaces, protests and arrests follow, officials express condolences, and life continues as though nothing happened—until the next police shooting."[7] For the British commentator Piers Morgan, "there is still an undeniable endemic racism strewn through America's police force which shows no sign of abating. Too many cops see a young Black man and automatically think: 'criminal.'"[8] British scholar Jonathan Jackson argued in the aftermath of the killing of George Floyd in 2020 that "the history of policing is an indisputably violent one: Many American police departments have their origins in white supremacist violence—for example hunting down Black Americans who had freed themselves from enslavement and returning to their captors."[9]

One objection to this view is that violence in America pales in comparison with centuries of wars, massacres, rebellions, violent revolutions (with a non-negligible number of leaders beheaded), ethnic cleansings, and social protest in Europe. From this perspective, it is not surprising that Sidney Tarrow and Charles Tilly conceptualized their analysis of contentious politics by studying European historical cases.[10] Furthermore, European countries like France and Great Britain were involved in the Atlantic slave trade and repressed slave-led revolutions in their overseas territories as part of their colonial domination. Furthermore, as I will discuss, European societies were never immune from racism, anti-Semitism, and xenophobia. Although eugenics policies were first implemented in America in the early 1900s, they culminated in Europe in the 1930s and paved the way for the Holocaust. As David Theo Goldberg points out, "death and violence have marked the European romance with race from its earliest moments. From fears of blood contamination through the necrophilia of scientific skull measurements to the death camps."[11]

Mass shootings are more common in America than in Europe, where access to guns is heavily regulated. However, violence linked to racial prejudice remains common in Europe. It dates back to the Middle Ages, characterized the colonial period and war of decolonization, and still afflicts European societies today. Notable historical examples include pogroms, mass killings in the colonies, exactions committed against minorities in Europe before and after World War II, and numerous forms of institutional brutality motivated by racism. The issue of police brutality, for example, was illustrated in Britain by the killing of Stephen Lawrence in 1993. A 1998 public inquiry concluded that the Metropolitan Police Service was institutionally racist. More recent cases involved Jimmy Mubenga in 2010, Sarah Reed in 2012, Rashan Charles and Edson Da Costa in 2017, and Simeon Francis in 2020. According to Kojo Koram, a professor at the University of London, "those who argue that Black Lives Matter protesters are jumping on an American bandwagon willfully miss the point." He concedes that "there are certain force multipliers in the United States that increase the scale of its problems: we do not have prisons the size of small towns or police officers walking around with AR-15s in Britain." Nevertheless, institutional racism "exists at every level of our criminal, justice system."[12] Nearly a quarter of a century after the Stephen Lawrence inquiry, the report's findings remain true: Black people account for 8 percent of recorded deaths in police custody in the United Kingdom, despite constituting only 3 percent of the total population.

Systemic racism and police brutality are also French problems. Examples include police abuse of immigrants (spanning from the demonstrators for Algerian independence who were shot and thrown into the Seine by the Police Nationale in 1961 to the violent evacuation of the migrant camp in the Place de la République in Paris in 2020) and the killing of Adama Traoré in 2016. Although investigations into his death remained inconclusive, it seems that Traoré was, like Floyd, asphyxiated by the police. In 2020, American protests of racism and police violence inspired similar demonstrations in France, with notably more than twenty thousand people attending one in Paris in June. There is no comparison in terms of the scale of police violence: the police in France kill fifteen to twenty people per year in a population of 70 million; the US police kill more than a thousand people per year in a population of 320 million. However, other comparisons are legitimate. In both countries, police brutality targets minorities: young men of Arab and Black African background are twenty times more likely to be stopped randomly by the police in France than the rest of the population. There are also similar concerns about racial profiling, stop-and-frisk policies, and other discriminatory practices.[13]

As in Great Britain, expressions of solidarity with BLM are either praised or ridiculed. For some commentators, protests for racial justice in America and France echo each other. Others, however, object on the grounds that American-style identity politics undermines the republican ideal of color-blind equality.

Even the activist Assa Traoré, sister of Adama and a key figure in the fight against racism, told an interviewer that she was reluctant to use the word "racism" for a long time because the vocabularies and realities of the French and American movements diverge. Yet, she added, it is time for the French to confront the question of Black rights in France and the problem of French racism more generally.[14]

Beyond national context, concerns about the evolution of intergroup relations are inter-related on both sides of the Atlantic. Synchronization with US identity-based movements generates distinct repertoires. Yet, the fact that there are differences in style does not mean that the actual concerns energizing the mobilization of various groups in Europe are lost in translation. There is an organic relationship between the two.

The Transatlantic Circulation of Ideas

Expressions of racism in American and in Europe significantly differ. However, we should remember that racist theories emerged in Europe before being popularized in America. Racism as an ideology was founded in the Enlightenment and during the European colonization of other parts of the globe.[15] French diplomat Arthur de Gobineau, the author of *An Essay on the Inequality of the Human Races* (1855), and other European contributors to pseudoscientific racial theories provided a mass of material for white supremacist, proslavery and anti-Semitic US thinkers. European Eugenics movements inspired US eugenicists such as Madison Grant, author of *The Passing of the Great Race* (1916). The European conception of Aryanism was, and remains, the core ideological component of US white supremacism.

At the other end of the ideological spectrum, Black Studies in the United States were strongly influenced by European intellectuals—notably French sociologists and philosophers such as Jacques Derrida, Michel Foucault, and Pierre Bourdieu. Racial studies benefited from the contribution of European theorists such as Michael Banton, John Rex, Robert Mills, Stuart Hall, and the work of the Race and Politics Group of the Center for Contemporary Cultural Studies (CCCS) at the University of Birmingham. Analyses of Nazi racism by the philosophers of Germany's Frankfurt School crossed the Atlantic through the work of Hannah Arendt and Herbert Marcuse. Angela Davis, Marcuse's student, earned her doctorate in Berlin. Today, core readings for racial activists in Europe include several American writers, spanning from Angela Davis to Ta-Nehisi-Coates, Cornel West, Stokely Carmichael, and James Baldwin. Conversely, American intersectional analyses of racism inspire European scholars using intersectional frameworks in their approaches to race and identity.[16] Numerous feminist scholars in Europe, inspired by Kimberlé Crenshaw, now work on intersectional discrimination.[17]

Ideologies and events in Europe and in America are often connected. In the past, a racial backlash in many European countries was inspired by US conservative assaults against the civil rights movement and subsequent affirmative action initiatives. Enoch Powell's "rivers of blood" speech for example, echoed the rhetoric of George Wallace, while US criticism of multiculturalism inspired some European scholars and policymakers. "Political developments regarding multiculturalism in the UK . . . and on the European mainland," Roger Hewitt notes, "were directly and indirectly influenced by developments in the USA."[18] He adds that there is "a striking synchronicity in the unfolding of backlash politics and white working-class resentments" in the United States and Europe.[19] American and European conservatives still have a lot in common, from the support of restrictive immigration policies to suspicions about identity-based policies.

Leftist US social protest movements have long influenced similar movements in Europe. Protests of the Vietnam War took place in Europe, notably in France in 1967 where they led to the "revolution" of May 1968. The US civil rights struggle also framed the mobilization of various ethnoracial groups in Europe. This struggle inspired, for example, civil protest in the United Kingdom, such as the Bristol bus boycott of 1963 that paved the way for the 1965 Race Relations Act. Martin Luther King's visit to London resulted in the creation in 1968 of Runnymede Trust, one of the United Kingdom's more influential racial justice think-tanks. A group of British activists created the British Black Panther Party after Malcolm X's visits to the United Kingdom in 1964 and 1965.

Symbolic politics and rites of protest have often crossed the Atlantic. US sprinters Tommie Smith and John Carlos famously raised their fists in protest of racial discrimination during the gold medal ceremony at the 1968 Olympics. Raising a fist in salute subsequently became a ritual. In reference to the former San Francisco quarterback Colin Kaepernick—who protested racial injustice in 2016 by kneeling during the American national anthem—Liverpool players took a knee in June 2020 in a message of support for Floyd. Every English team and official subsequently did the same for the entire season that followed. Demonstrators in Paris took a knee, paying tribute to both Floyd and Traoré. Popular sportsmen and celebrities across Europe now add their voices to worldwide protests of racism by using the same repertoire as their American counterparts. Comparable examples include debates about monuments linked to colonialism and slavery and controversial historical figures. In the United Kingdom, activists dumped a statue of slave trader Edward Colston into Bristol harbor in June 2020. Statues of Jean-Baptiste Colbert (controller general of finances under King Louis XVI) who drafted the Black Code organizing slavery in French colonies, were likewise damaged by protesters. Comparisons therefore abound.

Current Contextual Convergences

Europeans commonly express concerns about US white supremacist groups, the intensity of antimigrant rhetoric, and the expansion of discriminatory minority policies. They were appalled by the violent effects of polarization on American politics during the Trump administration and in the aftermath of the 2020 presidential election. Many leaders condemned the riots in the Capitol building in January 2021, describing what happened as "horrifying" and an "attack on democracy."[20] European countries, however, are not immune from various cycles of ethnoracial backlash, prejudice, xenophobia and antimigrant sentiments, and political polarization fueled by populism that leads to political violence.

Populism, both in its rightist and leftist formulations, has been widespread in Europe for decades. American movements have influenced European ones, and vice versa. Similar symptoms of a deeper societal crisis have generated a political convergence in the last two decades on both sides of the Atlantic. The first one is a wide democratic disenchantment, which like in the United States consists of several elements: a strong decline in institutional trust, a decrease in political participation, the rejection of the mainstream political establishment, and the toxic impacts of ideological polarization.[21] The number of people who consider it "essential" to live in a democracy has sharply declined, today constituting 32 percent of those born after 1980 according to the *World Values Survey*.[22] Not surprisingly, electoral support for European populist, authoritarian parliamentary parties has increased by an average of 50 percent since 2000. For European commentators, there were "echoes of Trumpism in the nationalist parties of Britain, Denmark, the Netherlands, Greece as well as France." Common to them is "a dissatisfaction with the status quo, the sense that middle-class and working class have been neglected by the existing political establishment, a feeling that politicians aren't honest with voters."[23] Trump himself was often compared to authoritarian leaders (such as Putin and Erdogan) and populist activists like Geert Wilder in the Netherlands, Marine Le Pen in France, and Frauke Petry in Germany. Nigel Farage, the UK Independence Party (UKIP) leader who strongly supported the exit from the European Union (EU), celebrated Trump's victory as a "win double" and later lobbied for Trump to receive the Nobel Peace Prize. President Trump, reciprocally, made Farage "a close but unofficial adviser" in the immediate aftermath of his inauguration.

The second dimension of the societal crises relates to economic inequality as a consequence of globalization of postindustrial economies. These crises include four elements: the decline of the manufacturing industry, the erosion of organized labor, increasing competition over scarce social resources (such as welfare benefits and educational opportunities), and the dramatic socioeconomic inequalities enhanced by neoliberal austerity policies.[24] According to Eurostat, in most EU states—and on average across the EU—the gap between the rich and the poor has been consistently widening: "the poor become poorer and the number of poor is increasing" as the number of people living in poverty has increased by about 9 percent since 2005.[25] These trends collectively fuel resentment among the so-called "losers of globalization." They have become susceptible to exploitative, anti-establishment, nativist, and xenophobic scare-mongering by populists who blame "Them" for stripping prosperity, employment, and public services from "Us."[26] Like in America, this narrative has taken two forms: Concerns about the "dark sides" of globalization have catalyzed support for far-right-wing Eurosceptic parties (such as the UKIP in Great Britain, the Freedom Party in Austria, and Golden Dawn in Greece) and left-wing populist groups (such as PODEMOS in Spain and Syriza in Greece).

The third dimension results from a *cultural backlash*. As Ronald Ingelhart and Pippa Norris argue, "the shift toward post-materialist values, such as cosmopolitanism and multiculturalism" triggers a "counter-revolutionary retro backlash, especially among the older generation, white men, and less educated sectors, who sense decline and actively reject the rising tide of progressive values."[27] Active participants in this process include various groups contesting key components of "identity liberalism"—such as gender and racial equality, and equal rights for the LGBT community. In addition, populist movements in Europe exploit a sense of cultural insecurity by raising the specter of the Islamization of the continent, denounce the decline of national identity, and reject progressive reforms (such as the legalization of same-sex marriage).

Against this background, most Europeans express antimigrant feelings. European opinion poll surveys show that 48 percent of Europeans feel there are too many immigrants in their country (up to 82 percent in Greece and 72 percent in Hungary). As in the United States, negative perceptions are based on the assumption that immigrants take jobs from natives, put pressure on denuded public services, abuse limited social benefits, and pose a threat to national identity. Most countries demonstrate strong preferences in terms of immigrants' country of origin, religion, and ethnicity. The least preferred immigrants are nonwhites, non-Europeans, and those from Muslim countries.[28] Antimigrant sentiments have been exacerbated by the dramatic surge of asylum seekers and economic migrants in 2015–2016, and by the coronavirus crisis. Furthermore, the increase in terrorist attacks in various countries has fueled the perception of Muslim immigrants and refugees as posing a threat. Indeed, most respondents in Poland, Greece, Hungary, Italy, and the United Kingdom believe that Muslim immigrants posed a major security threat. Although there is little substantive evidence linking refugees to recent terror attacks—most of these attacks being committed by "home-grown" radicalized individuals—large majorities also believe that refugees fleeing the Syrian crisis increase the likelihood of terrorism (up to 76 percent in Hungary, 71 percent in Poland, and 61 percent in Germany).[29]

Finally, European countries are plagued by discrimination against minorities. Data provided by the EU's Agency for Fundamental Rights (FRA), show that race-related violence, discriminatory profiling, and job discrimination against people of African descent is widespread, and further entrenches prejudice and exclusion. On average, about 30 percent of people of African descent said they experience everyday racism (albeit ranging widely from 63 percent in Finland to 21 percent in the United Kingdom). About 31 percent of immigrants with North African origins, for example, felt discriminated against in 2019, especially in employment and access to public or private services.[30] Seventeen percent of Muslim and 21 percent of Jewish respondents felt discriminated against on the basis of religion. Muslims, especially Muslim women, are targeted in Islamophobic attacks. In France, for example, women were the victims of 69 percent of Islamophobic acts in 2018.[31] Other minorities expressed serious concerns. For example, 47 percent of LGBT persons felt discriminated against or harassed on the grounds of sexual orientation in 2019 (up from 37 percent in 2012). Most respondents (58 percent) experienced harassment over the prior five years in the form of offensive or threatening situations at work, on the street, or on public transportation.[32]

Xenophobia and discrimination against minorities provide a fertile ground for anti-migrant political groups such as Alternative for Germany (AfD), which became the biggest opposition party in the Bundestag in 2017, Vox in Spain, the Greek Solution, and the Northern League in Italy. Their anti-immigrant rhetoric, based on an ethno-nationalist ideology, describes immigrants and migrant communities as a threat to national identity. Sharing an exclusionist and nativist notion of citizenship, these parties advocate that states should be inhabited exclusively by members of the native group, and that nonnative elements threaten homogenous nation-states. These "others" are portrayed as not sharing—or not being willing to share—the core values of the nation quite independently from their legal and socioeconomic status. As a result of this "inassimilability thesis," nativist groups ascribe an ethnic identity to migrant minorities based on the assumption that cultural differences are absolute and irreconcilable. These groups therefore combine traditional racial prejudice (such as anti-Black sentiments) with a cultural differential racism that stigmatizes the mixing of cultures. They use the racialist overlapping of biological and cultural arguments to legitimize violence against minorities as predicated by the imperative of protecting the purity of national identity.

Contentious Identity Politics in Europe

Concerns about the ethnic diversification of European societies have generated attacks against multiculturalism, as well as controversial debates around religious symbols and practices. The notion of integration in Europe predominantly carries the implicit ideal of cultural homogeneity, in contrast to the American conception of assimilation, which tolerates some degree of diversity. Fears that tolerance toward cultural and religious diversity leads to "disintegration" fuel a dominant restrictive trend in Europe designed to prevent "societal disunity allegedly associated with ethnic minority separatism in general, and Muslim alienation and estrangement in particular."[33] This trend has been illustrated in the past two decades by new "integration requirements" justified by the claim that they enhance cultural integrity and national security. The assumption that citizenship needs to be protected from "politically alien or culturally unadaptable outsiders"[34] has justified the implementation of pre-entry requirements (such as language and civic tests for immigration and family reunion), integration courses and examinations for new arrivals, and integration contracts for minorities already settled in Europe.[35] Furthermore, several countries have introduced laws banning religious clothing or symbols at work or in many public spaces. Although these laws are intended to signal that religious beliefs should remain in the private domain, they disproportionally affect Muslim women wearing clothing that covers their hair, face, or body.[36]

Supported by mainstream parties, these laws are approved by a majority of Europeans. In Denmark in 2017, for example, 62 percent of respondents said that they supported a full ban on wearing the burqa and niqab in public.[37] Seventy-three percent agreed with the adoption of a 2019 Ban on Face-Covering Clothing Act in the Netherlands.[38] Europeans in favor of these laws broadly share the assumption that "visible differences" such as "ostentatious symbols" are a proof of insufficient integration. In France, where headscarves were banned in public schools in 2004 before the burqa and niqab were outlawed from all public spaces in 2010, the key argument used by public authorities is that concealing one's face violates the fundamental values of the republic. It also threatens public safety and represents a rejection of equal citizenship. According to a parliamentary report, "the concealment of the face in public has the effect of breaking social ties, it manifests the refusal of living together."[39] Similar arguments are used by advocates in other countries (such as the Netherlands and the United Kingdom) where the current rush to legislate against cultural and religious differences illustrates the ongoing backlash against multiculturalism and a propensity to call for the criminalization of ethnic alterity—where difference becomes politically or culturally symbolic.

Opponents to these laws, by contrast, emphasize the discriminatory effects on Muslim minorities. They also notice the ambivalence of the distinction between illicit ostentatious symbols and licit non-ostentatious symbols—especially in European countries where laws imposing wearing a mask in public were adopted during the coronavirus pandemic. In France, for example, a Muslim woman covering her face will have to pay a fine and attend a citizenship education class, while all citizens have to wear a mask as a sign of civic duty. At the core of this paradox is the assumption that visible Muslim identities are inversely correlated to their civic and political loyalties.

Reactive Identifications

Adversity based on racial prejudice and cultural racism, in turn, generates forms of reactive identification among groups targeted by institutional violence, intolerance, and anti-multicultural sentiments and policies.

Muslim communities, for example, are extremely heterogeneous in terms of national origin, race, ethnicity, religious affiliation, and legal status.[40] The three features they generally have in common are a relatively low socioeconomic status; being discriminated against on the grounds of race and religion; and being targeted by security measures as potential terrorists, especially after 9/11 and subsequent terrorist attacks in European cities. Consequentially, Muslims are portrayed as permanent outsiders to the national community, and as a social threat because of the widespread association of Islam with crime, intolerance, and terrorist radicalization. Findings from European surveys show that Muslims in many European countries feel they are discriminated against—a feeling that tends to increase their collective identification and group consciousness.[41]

It is worth noting that an increased sense of Muslim identity includes religious and nonreligious markers. Muslims for whom religion is not a primary source of identity define themselves as "cultural Muslims" because they are born into a Muslim family and/or are proud of their ethno-cultural heritage without actively following Islamic principles. Their "Muslimness" is a sign of communal identity, mostly based on a common discrimination experience, mixed with other social markers.[42] Their cultural demands have focused since the late 1980s on being able to maintain their homeland-based identity, to ensure intergenerational continuity, and to counter assimilationist pressures by transmitting their culture and language.

Other Muslims react to discrimination by expressing a high level of religiosity. For example, 64 percent of Muslims in Great Britain and 52 percent in France declare that religion is "very important in their lives."[43] This religious identification contrasts with a widespread secularism in most European countries where most of the general populations do not identify with any religion (up to 53 percent in France and 52 percent in Great Britain). However, other religious groups express similar levels of religiosity: more than 50 percent of Jews and Sikhs in Great Britain say their religion is important to their self-identification; about 53 percent of French Jews describe themselves as practicing Judaism very intensely.[44] What matters is less the level of religiosity itself and more the meaning of this Islamic revival, especially among Muslim youth. Having grown up in European societies, they do not share their parents' diffidence, and they are more politically aware of domestic and international issues affecting the perception of Muslims in the West (from the continuing Arab-Israeli conflict to the Danish cartoons affair in 2005 and the Charlie Hebdo controversy in 2015). They tend to define themselves in exclusively religious terms—not as Turks or Moroccan Muslims (as their parents did). As Bhikhu Parekh notes, "as the wider society refer to them as Muslims and to associate negative ideas with the term, Muslim youth (in the spirit of 'black is beautiful') assert their Islamic identity with pride."[45] They introduce religion in social life—making demands based on religion (such as wearing the hijab), and reason about political matters in religious terms—independently from their actual knowledge of the Qur'an.

Black communities in Europe, comprising about 12 million Europeans of Sub-Saharan African or Afro-Caribbean descent, are divided along national, ethnic, racial, and religious lines.[46] Similar issues related to racial prejudice have led to the emergence of a pan-European Black identity in several countries. This group identification has been primarily framed using a cultural lens, through the contribution in the postcolonial era of African intellectuals who asserted the positive values linked to the "essence of being Black"—captured by the notion of *négritude* popularized by Aimé Césaire, Léopold Senghor, and Frantz Fanon.[47] This notion, based on the celebration of African history, practices, and values, has been instrumentalized in African countries as a social, political, and cultural response to imposed European values and beliefs. In European countries, it has been used by African diasporas as a tool to establish a common African identity—one imbued with pride and resilience—as well as celebrating the intellectual contributions of people of African descent to European history and culture.[48]

A more politicized conception of Black identity slowly emerged in Europe in the 1970s and 1980s. It fueled the political activism undertaken by African immigrant communities, from rent strikes to political protests, and the creation of formal organizations such as the Union Générale des Travailleurs Sénégalais en France (General Union of Senegalese Workers, UGTSF).[49] The British civil rights movement coalesced various groups that organized demonstrations against a color bar excluding nonwhite workers from the transport industry, and launched the Campaign against Racial Discrimination (CARD) to challenge racism in employment and housing. The "race riots" that took place in Great Britain during the 1980s (such as in Brixton and Liverpool in 1981, and in Birmingham in 1986) further incentivized black British activists to mobilize against police discrimination and institutional racism.

During the 1990s, African activism and other forms of antiracist mobilizations merged. Blackness emphasized the commonalities of various groups embattled by racist violence and engaged in the fight against racial violence, police brutality, and state complicity. In turn, antiracist organizations broadened the scope of their actions, including not only minorities of color but also all minority groups suffering from discrimination. Building upon the legacy of the British Black Power Movement, activists focused on eradicating racial discrimination and called for government action—notably during the Stephen Lawrence inquiry. Like the Anti-Nazi League that developed in the 1970s as a response to the emergence of the National Front, Unite Against Fascism grouped together various ethnoracial groups against the growing influence of the British National Party in the 1990s. In France, the emergence of the Front National stimulated an antiracist movement. Traditional antiracist organizations, mostly involved in the defense of color-blind-defined human rights, were superseded by new social movements that emphasized solidarity between ethnoracial groups and tolerance for diversity. These movements included SOS Racism (which grouped together North African immigrant groups), Jewish and Black activists, and members of the Socialist Party—the guiding principle of the association being "Touche pas à mon pote" (symbolized by a yellow hand meaning "Hands off my pal"). Another example of mobilization was provided by the "Black, Blanc, Beur" (Black, White, Arab) movement whose symbolism culminated in its popularity when an ethnically diverse French football team won the World Cup for the first time in 1998.

A more recent generation of activists have tended to prioritize specific claims over a symbolic "rainbow coalition" approach. Black activists, for example, have begun questioning prejudicial Black stereotypes inherited from the colonial period and call for reparations. In 2011, artists and human rights groups organized a campaign against Zwarte Piet (Black Pete)—the Afro-looking servant of Santa Claus popular in Belgium and the Netherlands. In Germany, activists put pressure on the government to acknowledge the mass atrocities committed before World War I in present-day Namibia. The Initiative for Black People in Germany now campaigns to change street names that celebrate colonizers. Dekoloniale, an organization created in 2020, seeks to bring colonial history into the mainstream high school curriculum.[50] The Representative Council of France's Black Association (Conseil Représentatif des Associations Noires de France,

CRAN) focuses on the issue of reparations and promotes the return of artwork collections to African countries. The better networked activists, like the British Black Curriculum, use social media to support the introduction of Black history workshops for college students.

These initiatives are part of a global trend fueled by the multiplication of identity-based groups who promote a differential conception of multiculturalism, and thus favor a more radical contentious identity politics. From the perspective of various minorities engaged in this process, their main goal is to secure their ethnocultural recognition, as well as specific rights based on their differences—instead of an equality of rights beyond ethnoracial and religious/cultural differences. They share a politicized collective identity that operates as a strong motor of conflictual political involvement, in addition to (and sometimes largely independent of) other classic determinants of collective action related to access to material resources. Their politicized collective identity fuels grievances and a power struggle for social change.[51]

The French Mouvement des Indigènes de la République (the Movement of the Indigenous of the Republic, MIR) provides a relevant illustration of this ethnoracial mobilization based on the emergence of a new essentialist strategy.[52] The movement was created in 2005 as a response to the vote of a law recognizing the positive role of the French colonial presence in North Africa. Its main concerns then were to denounce the confluence of racism and anti-Muslim policies, and to fight for a "truly egalitarian and universal democracy." Its original manifesto in 2005 referred to a "WE" made up of the descendants of the victims of slavery, the colonized and immigrants, as well as "French and non-French living in France, activists engaged in struggles against oppression and discrimination produced by the post-colonial Republic."[53] The movement morphed into a political party (PIR) in 2010, while turning toward the racial essentialization of social and political identities. Today, the PIR supports a more communitarian strategy focused on attacks against postcolonialism, white dominance and Islamophobia—to the detriment of a more inclusive approach.[54] Statements from some leaders and members of the PIR suggest a further shift from communitarianism to separatism—including expressing reservations about mixed-race marriages, criticism of mainstream "nativist" feminist organizations suspected of being complicit with white privilege, and the rejection of many minorities (including LGBT and religious minorities other than Muslim) suspected of perpetuating the colonial structure of French society.[55] These views have generated deep controversies with traditional antiracist organizations, as well as condemnation from former supporters who prefer to engage in a struggle for equality that rejects criticizing those "others" now ostracized by the PIR.

Issues Raised by the Polarization of Identity Politics and the Racialization of Intergroup Relations

The persistence of racial and religious prejudice, and significant socioeconomic inequalities, together explain the adoption of an identitarian strategy by minorities. This is reinforced by their political underrepresentation in most countries, as well as their disappointment with mainstream parties and traditional antiracist organizations that, they believe, do not properly address their concerns. Frustration fueled by the reluctance of most majority groups to engage in debates about racial prejudice has led to an increased sense of alienation, which radicalizes contentious repertoires.

There are at least three consequences of this strategy. First, minority groups are increasingly fragmented into subgroups who are more often engaged in conflictual relations than involved in multicultural and/or multiracial mobilizations. Among Muslim communities, for example, a "sense of Muslimness" does not erase political tensions between various subgroups. The multiplicity of Islamic organizations and their fragmentary interconnectedness has led some European governments to inaugurate unified institutional structures. The German Islam Conference (DIK), for example, has encouraged the largest umbrella Islamic organizations to cooperate within the umbrella Coordinating Committee of Muslims in Germany (KRM). The emergence of a "German Islam" is, however, undermined by the challenge of representing a heterogeneity of interests and objectives of a diverse set of participants. In a similar fashion, French governmental efforts to manage Islam domestically by creating organizations representative of "Islam of France" have consistently failed. Organizations affiliated with the state, such as the French Council of the Muslim Faith (Conseil Français du Culte Musulman, CFCM) created in 2003, do not reflect diverse Muslim communities. Tensions persist between the CFCM, suspected of disproportionally representing entities tied to Algeria, Morocco, and Saudi Arabia, and other organizations more aligned with the Muslim Brotherhood. These kinds of divisions among Muslims undermine their capacity for political representation and the effectiveness of their demands for cultural and religious accommodation in European societies.

Other examples of fragmentation involve feminist organizations. Inspired by their American counterparts, some Black feminist organizations characterize "white feminism" as part of the colonial and postcolonial structure of domination. According to Akwugo Emejulu and Francesca Sobande, "because white women benefit from white supremacy, they can be, at best, unreliable actors for liberation and at worst, active and willing agents for Black women's oppression."[56]

Other organizations criticize the import of American race politics to Europe, a trend perceived as an expression of American "soft power" and reflective of the domination of the English language—and thus detrimental to the recognition of the long history of anti-imperialist and anticolonial struggles in Europe. These movements focus instead on Afro-feminism as a more relevant perspective on the experiences of Black women in "the particular and specific histories of colonialism, racial formation and gender hierarchy of the various European nation-states."[57] Another subgroup, inspired by Black queer activism, questions the limits of the notion of Blackness when subsumed under the category of "people of color." As Fatima El-Tayeb argues, "black lesbians and trans people in particular do not only deal with structural racism, sexism, queer—and transphobia in society, but also within activist communities. The solidarity that they are asked to provide to feminist, LGBT, Black, Muslim communities is often not granted in return, because those identities remain deviant even in these communities."[58] When commenting on this fragmentation of feminism itself, some scholars complain about the "whitening of intersectionality achieved in part by excluding those who have multiple minority identities and are marginalized social actors—women of color and queers of color."[59] Others, conversely, express concerns about the effects of competition over "collective victimhood recognition" on group relations.[60] Nonetheless, increasing splintering has become endemic.

The second and related consequence of the current spillover of contentious repertoires links to the expressions of prejudice among majority and minority groups in Europe. Traditional forms of white backlash, noticeable since the 1980s, have been reconstituted in recent years as "reverse racism" or "antiwhite racism." Claims of white victimization are becoming increasingly popular among right-wing populist movements. These claims, based on the assumption that there is comparability between white vulnerability and minority marginalization, are used to legitimize attacks against minorities who are accused of exploiting antiracism to achieve a privileged status of victimhood. Muslims, immigrants, refugees, supporters of multiculturalism, feminist, and intersectional activists are among the main targets—all suspected of marginalizing white Europeans and destroying the "traditional honorable masculinity" foundational to Western civilization.[61]

On the minority side of the antiracist spectrum, discrimination faced by ethnoracial and religious groups sometimes leads to discursive and physical violence against other marginalized groups. In many European countries, for example, some non-Muslim communities express Islamophobic feelings, and some Muslims express prejudice toward other groups, notably in the form of antisemitic violence.[62] East European migrants, who suffer from racism, claim whiteness as their vantage point for racializing Black migrants and improving their precarious position in the labor market.[63] In all cases, the subverted meaning of antiracism undermines the efforts of antiracist organizations, divided politically and along identity-based repertoires.[64]

The third consequence of the polarization and racialization of contentious repertoires relates to an "identity panic" currently spreading in Europe. Attacks against multiculturalism have morphed into fears of separatism, especially the newly coined "Islamo-leftism."[65] This phenomenon involves Islamic movements, supported by small far-left groups, wanting to impose their own religious and cultural beliefs in Europe. In their fight against Islamophobia, for example, they oppose the secular conception of freedom of expression by demanding that books or cartoons they consider blasphemous to Muslims be banned. Furthermore, defining women's rights in their own religious terms, they claim that the wearing of the hijab is nonnegotiable, as well as the respect of a strict separation between men and women in various public spaces. These claims, as well as controversial statements about Jews, Zionism, and complacency with extremist ideologies operating in the name of Islam, fuel concerns about a blurring distinction between Islamic and Islamist agendas.

Attacks against "Islamo-leftism"—albeit still vaguely defined—group together (for varied and often conflictual reasons) far-right movements, mainstream rightist and leftist parties, and liberal and conservative intellectuals.[66] In France, some politicians denounce the "nefarious influence" of "Islamo-gauchisme" in universities as the result of the improper importation of US "cancel culture" and "wokeness."[67] Those targeted by these attacks respond by denouncing "state racism" and the violation of free speech.[68] In other countries, these controversies extend to the so-called "Sharia Zones" or "No Go Zones" excluding non-Muslims in large urban areas, from London in the United Kingdom to Malmö in Sweden. Partisans describe neighborhoods where Muslims are concentrated as a form of "Jihadist irredentism."[69] Politicians and scholars of Islam in Europe provide evidence that such zones do not exist; yet 32 percent of British people still believe that cities with large Muslim populations are turning into Islamist enclaves.[70]

All these controversies are extremely polarized, excluding the possibility of a constructive debate about the integration of minorities and accommodation of cultural and religious differences. Concerns about separatism provide further opportunities for European governments to enact antiseparatist laws designed to prevent the development of "parallel societies" and curtailing the avenues that may actually result in Islamist radicalization. Regulations commonly adopted in several European countries include a strict accounting of foreign funds to religious organizations; a ban on "virginity certificates;" measures enhancing a greater respect for the equality of men and women; and severe limits on homeschooling. These regulations complement existing security-driven legislation designed to fight Islamist radicalization and prevent terrorist attacks. Europeans have strong reasons to be traumatized by Islamist terrorist violence, as the result of attacks in recent years in Manchester, Paris, Brussels, Vienna, and Berlin. Yet, the efficacy of anti-separatism laws on preventing radicalization among young Muslims (and an increasing numbers of converts) remain to be seen. Furthermore, many completed, failed and foiled terrorist attacks are committed by right-wing, left-wing, and ethnonationalist groups or individuals.[71]

Against this background, what does it portend about the future of Europe? Europeans express legitimate concerns about various types of societal violence—against immigrants and various ethnoracial and religious groups (as a result of conflicts between state actors and minorities); between majority groups and minority groups (including conflicts between natives and non-natives); and among identitarian groups (as illustrated by intra-group tensions fueled by the radicalization of claims). The situation is clearly more complicated than it is assumed by most actors involved in sterile debates about Islamic/Islamist separatism, and the failure of multiculturalism.

I don't deny that some forms of separatism pose a threat to European societies. There were "Muslim patrols" in London a few years ago, led by the Sharia Project. However, participants were arrested and condemned by local Muslim leaders. There are current examples of violence committed by fringe fanatics in European suburbs trying to impose Islamic dress codes, for example, or preaching intolerance—sometimes to the point of encouraging allegiance to ISIS or Al Qaeda. The majority of Muslims, however, disapprove of these practices and support the deportation of extremist foreign Imams. Some Muslim groups ignore the normal rules of civility, spread anti-Western feelings, and dismiss democracy as a form of polytheism. Most Muslims, however, take a different view by expressing a strong sense of national belonging—coupled with their Muslimness, loyalty, and trust in the institutions of the countries they reside.[72] Fears of being victim of hate crimes are tangible among Jewish communities, as the numbers of anti-Semitic incidents has significantly increased in recent years;[73] and yet, for all the grim statistics, the fight against anti-Semitism has also intensified with countless initiatives launched and supported by European institutions, national governments, local activists, religious leaders (imams included), and teachers.

There is evidence of a disconnect between political and academic debates generated by the "identity panic" and realities on the ground—notably in interethnic neighborhoods where various groups peacefully coexist.[74] Ethnic minority and national identification are not mutually exclusive for the vast majority of ethnoracial and cultural-religious groups—a compatibility that contradicts the assumption that multiculturalism has failed.[75] Furthermore, the fight against racism is achieving some goals. A 2021 report from the Commission on Race and

Ethnic Disparities, for example, concluded that the United Kingdom "no longer has a system rigged against people from ethnic minorities." The report pointed out that children from ethnic communities did as well or better than white pupils in compulsory education; that the pay gap between minorities and the while majority population had shrunk to 2.3 percent overall; and that factors "such as geography, family influence, socio-economic background had more significant impact on life chances than the existence of racism." The report concluded that the "UK is not yet a post-racial country" but its success in fighting racial disparities "should be regarded as a model for other white-majority countries."[76] Antiracist activists objected that the authors of the report "missed the point" by downplaying institutional racism in the United Kingdom. Dr. Tony Sewell, in charge of the report, replied by emphasizing the difference between the acknowledgment of partial progress toward racial equity and the denial of the existence of racism. "No one is saying that racism doesn't exist," he said, which was the reason why the report listed recommendations aiming at building trust between ethnoracial groups, promoting fairness, and achieving inclusivity.[77]

While both progress of antiracism and limitations to racial equity are heavily debated in other European countries, two trends deserve attention. First, the number of multiracial Europeans is growing fast. In the United Kingdom, for example, those adults declaring themselves as having a mixed-ethnic background almost doubled between the census of 2001 and 2011, to about 1.2 million. When children are added to this number, mixed-race people constitute a larger portion of the population than any single minority ethnic group.[78] In Spain, the number of children of mixed unions rose from three percent of the total number of births in 1997 to 11 percent in 2017.[79] This trend questions the conventional understanding of minority status and encourages a move away from analyzing intergroup relations in a binary fashion. Second, as in the United States, positive and negative trends also simultaneously frame intergroup relations. US style controversies about identity politics inspire debates in Europe for the better—by providing opportunities to revisit the sources, contents, and effects of racial prejudice, and for the worse—by inciting incendiary polemics about competing separatist and anti-separatist claims. Both racist and antiracist intolerance poison intergroup relations. The stigmatization of minorities encourages the radicalization of contentious repertoires which, in turn fuels a nationalist backlash.

Pointedly, these polemics generate public policies that do not address the root causes of physical and discursive violence. The securitization of integration does not prevent the risk of societal fragmentation. Rather, it fuels alienation among targeted minorities. Anti-multicultural policies do not address the complex issues raised by the accommodation of cultural and religious diversity; they divert instead from salient concerns such as socioeconomic inequalities and democratic disenchantment. Political and academic controversies about identity politics do not provide useful insights on how to prevent the dual process of polarization and racialization; they rather spread discursive violence.

None of these issues will disappear soon and it is time to envision alternative conceptions of identity politics and policies in order to move from ethnoracial division and competing grievances to inclusivity and common values transcending group divides. What should be the principles of intergroup relations that may achieve both social justice and racial equity? I address this final question in the concluding chapter.

Conclusion

LESSONS FOR THE FUTURE

I have demonstrated that ethnoracial identities, racial prejudice, and violence have always been organically related in America in some surprising ways. Key dimensions of this relationship include violence fueled by racial prejudice committed by the state or individual actors against minorities; the emergence and consolidation of ethnoracial identities both through the use of violence and as a response to violence; and the subsequent involvement of all ethnoracial groups in cycles of contention, both as perpetrators and victims of physical and discursive violence, the former with the goal of consolidating their position in the mainstream of American society.

As I demonstrated in analyzing violence as part of an identity strategy, the story of inclusion and exclusion in America, as well as confrontation and cooperation between and among ethnoracial groups, is more complex than commonly assumed. Both majority and minority groups have engaged in proactive empowerment strategies based on a dynamic relationship between actual and perceived adversity, reactive identification, and contentious repertoires. Evidence presented in part one of this book shows that their strategies have evolved over time. In the 1990s, increasingly aggressive forms of the politics of recognition began breeding politicized collective identities. This trend shifted identity politics from a dynamic of inclusion to one of division. A growing multiracialism was expected to generate a greater solidarity. But in the last two decades, as analyzed in part two, the challenges of multiracialism have subsequently generated a series of ethnoracial identity crises that provided a fertile ground for the generation, polarization, and racialization of contentious repertoires. Racial divides widened during the Obama presidency, despite his efforts to neutralize their impact, and culminated during the Trump administration. By the time Joe Biden was elected, concerns about group position, and access to material and symbolic resources among all ethnoracial groups, had fueled grievances in the most politically racialized environment in modern times.

The Paradox of Identity Politics

My point is neither to advocate nor to deplore the effects of ethnoracial contentious politics on intergroup relations. A strong collective identification can provide resources in the pursuit of social justice, equal rights, the promotion of tolerance, and an inclusive recognition of "different differences." Identity politics increases a sense of group efficacy that, in turn, makes the fight against institutional racism and other forms of discrimination more effective. It has been used by various minority groups to obtain recognition and civil rights, and to be incorporated into the political mainstream. But today's problematic situation results from the combined effects of the racialization and polarization of group relations. They have led to escalating cycles of grievances that increasingly lack definable parameters. Right-wing populists use it to rebrand their ethnoracial prejudice and legitimize exclusionary practices by framing the question of identity in terms of "us" versus "them." Liberals, however, are not immune from perverting the meaning of identity politics, notably by promoting their conception of interest politics to the detriment of a more inclusive politics of solidarity. In its most dogmatic iterations, identity politics can demonize opponents—dividing us into smaller and smaller slivers of society or trapping individuals into an ascribed identity.[1] Neither is a recipe for solidarity.

Furthermore, controversies about identity politics can divert energy and resources away from combatting major social issues—from economic inequality and political exclusion to the fight against racism and various forms of discrimination. Mobilizations inspired by BLM led to some reforms that were long overdue, such as suppressing the names of slave owners from public and educational buildings. Names like President Woodrow Wilson were removed from campuses across the country as the result of an increased awareness among Americans of the "interiorization" of inherited racist ideas.[2] Revisiting history has allowed Americans to question what an inclusive national identity entails, as defined by the selection of symbolic figures that deserve to be honored. Yet, renaming buildings—although of symbolic value—falls short of the significant reforms needed to address the underlying resilience of institutional racism. In the case of universities, for example, this involves fighting ethnoracial inequalities in the educational system beyond paying lip service to diversity. In the case of local municipalities, painting BLM letters on the road reflects a commendable sentiment. But it should ideally inspire genuine efforts to deal with the issues of school segregation, disparities in housing, gang violence, and the improvement of public facilities (and enhanced access to them) in disadvantaged neighborhoods. Evaluating progress toward dismantling systemic racism in Richmond (Virginia), scholars and activists engaged in a series of debates organized by VPM and NPR in October 2021 noted that the removal of Confederate statues was a main step; yet, they noted it should not be a substitute for improving reforms in education, wealth, and housing.[3] It is also worth noting that America's fifty biggest companies and their foundations committed at least $49.5 billion after Floyd's murder to address racial inequality. In August 2021, however, only 37 companies confirmed disbursing about $1.7 billion. Of that, just a tiny fraction (about $70 million) went to organizations focused specifically on criminal justice reform.[4]

Another source of concern relates to the fact that identity politics today is becoming increasingly disconnected from class-based injustice. There are strong arguments—based on the evidence I have presented—for focusing on the effects of racially motivated socioeconomic discrimination with its disproportionate impact on African Americans and Hispanics. Since the 1990s, the disappearance of secure blue-collar jobs for minimally educated workers has had a deleterious effect on the job prospects for Black workers in urban centers. Yet, as Lawrence Blum notes, "if we view this development only in relation to its racial impact, we overlook its effect on all low-skilled poorly educated workers of any race."[5] Social-welfare policies that serve all poor and working-class people have weakened. Inequalities in several critical dimensions—starting with wealth and income but consequently extending to access to health care, good education, and housing—have increased. Blum therefore counsels, "the moral importance of these injustices against people of all races should not get lost in a focus on their disproportionate impact on blacks and Latinos, a development encouraged by the more familiar use of institutional racism."[6] The disconnect between racial and social injustice has two obvious negative consequences. First, it fuels grievances among poor whites, a core element of the white backlash that has reinforced the populist polarization of American politics. Second, it continues to damage the efficacy of the fight for both racial and social justice—to the detriment of a possible commonality of interests among the most vulnerable segments of American society.

The complexity of the circumstances in which contentious identity politics play out, and the multiple factors that affect ethnoracial relations, preclude simplistic prescriptions. Ambivalence abounds. Diversity, for example, fuels both tolerance and intolerance. Intergroup contact can lead simultaneously to cooperation and conflict. Various ethnoracial groups facing similar adversary challenges react differently, some groups using varied forms of violence more than others. These variations, as illustrated in this book, can be partly explained by contextual factors linked to our racial and social hierarchy. Clearly, distrust between and among groups is at a premium and needs to be rebuilt so that minorities can take greater control of the decisions that impact their lives, and for increasing social and cultural capital as a source of enrichment for all.

But, diagnostically, the most disturbing issues that need to be addressed include socioeconomic inequalities, infringements on civil liberties, and efforts to suppress voting rights. More tangibly, this includes addressing racial and any other forms of discrimination in several domains, extending from access to education and the labor market to protection against police brutality and judicial injustice. As these issues are related, they have to be addressed simultaneously. Democratic exclusion, for example, is fueled by socioeconomic inequalities and therefore will not be adequately addressed without a significant redistribution of wealth. Poor or low-income Americans—numbering approximately 140 million, over 40 percent of the total population—are less likely to vote in national elections: only 46 percent of potential voters with family income less than twice the federal poverty line voted in the 2016 presidential election, compared with 68 percent of those with family incomes above twice the poverty line. The pattern was repeated in the 2020 election where, according to some estimates, about 40 percent of Americans with lower incomes did not vote.[7] Protecting the basic principles of American democracy thus requires not only fighting against the abuse of gerrymandering and attempts to curtail voting rights but also significant socioeconomic reforms.

Access to education can be part of a solution to social inequality, but college graduation does not protect against discrimination in the labor market or guarantee a stable job, especially for minorities. Between 2007 and 2013, the unemployment rate for recent Black college graduates nearly tripled (up to 7.8 percent, compared to 5.6 percent among all college graduates).[8] In 2019, about 3.5 percent of Black college graduates were unemployed (compared to 2.2 percent of white college graduates). Young Black workers with a college degree tend to suffer less than their less-educated counterparts.[9] However, for those focused on educational reform, these data should be part of a global discussion about social justice. The willingness to promote a more inclusive curriculum is praiseworthy, efforts to increase diversity among student and faculty bodies are laudable, and debates about academic freedom are important. Yet, access to higher education should be conceived as an instrument for justice, not its end—and certainly requires other means that can secure a path to greater equality in the fields of employment and professional training.

Tackling these problems is a daunting but required task in order to turn a divisive contentious politics into a more inclusive "politics of difference."[10] This pluralistic form of democratic management of diversity requires an admission that claims being made by minority groups are responses to long-standing forms of stigmatization based on both racial and nonracial prejudice. Yet, recognizing the legitimacy of these claims also involves addressing the dangers of essentialism and a subsequent heightened, aggressive competition among groups—between majority and minority groups, but also among minority groups. The objective of the politics of difference should be twofold: first, to halt the spillover effect of grievances—by offering both majority and minority groups more opportunities to participate in a truly egalitarian deliberative democracy; second, to encourage the expression of diverse perspectives (even at the risk of being criticized as illegitimate) by respecting the democratic values of disagreement, contestation, and even (nonviolent) conflict. This should apply as much to political deliberation among elected representatives as it does to debates involving members of civil society engaged in the promotion of social solidarity, racial justice, and civic freedom.

From Antagonism to Agonism

This raises the question of how we can move from antagonism to agonism—defined as a positive means of discussing controversies in the arena of politics—where the discourse is predicated on respect, rather than the use of violence. Agonism is a form of democratic engagement that rejects the appeal of authoritative fixed identities, alternatively promoting democratic contestation based on a positive ethos of engagement.[11] This agonistic perspective has natural affinities with the "politics of reconciliation" that initially emerged in transitional countries moving from civil war and dictatorial regimes to civil discourse and democracy in Asia, Africa, and Latin America. According to Bashir Bashir and Will Kymlicka, elements of this approach "has migrated to the established Western democracies, and has become an influential framework for thinking about the claims of historically oppressed groups within these countries."[12] Examples include reparation programs for Japanese Americans, in redressing their wartime internment, and the Greensboro Truth and Reconciliation created in North Carolina in 2004 to address the legacy of slavery that led to the killing of antiracist protesters in 1979 by members of the KKK and the American Nazi Party.[13] More recently, Evanston, Illinois, became the first US city to issue slavery reparations by giving housing grants to Black residents and their descendants who suffered from historically discriminatory housing policies between 1919 and 1969. The contribution of this type of politics of reconciliation in the fight against racial oppression has been praised by many commentators. Andrew Valls, for example, argues that "we have much to learn from other societies that have undergone political transformations from regimes that systematically abuse human rights to regimes that respect, or at least purport to respect, human rights."[14]

It may now be time to expand the politics of reconciliation to every group engaged in the polarized fragmentation of American society in order to generate, perhaps paradoxically, a more inclusive "politics of difference" and prevent further violence. It is worth noting that calls for a National Truth and Reconciliation Commission were amplified in the aftermath of the attack on the US Capitol to address concerns of growing civil conflict and find common ground.[15] Critics objected to this idea, portraying it as a fearful "new McCarthyism," and expressed concerns about an abuse of power by the Biden administration.[16] Ironically, these objections were partisan in nature—in conflict with the intended goal of overcoming political polarization and radicalization. What matters is to clarify the intent of such activities—the pursuit of varied forms of justice and concurrence on the underlying values that will inspire the pacification of intergroup conflict. The goal is not to achieve some mythical neutrality or abstract moral consensus but is more instrumental: to identify commonalities that transcend racial boundaries and move beyond the current counterproductive ethnoracial polarization. Solidarity is a constitutive element of democracy.[17] In its absence, intergroup conflicts will persist as long as America cannot prioritize common interests over competing grievances.

Options for the Future

So, having diagnosed the problems, how do we move ahead? There are a few options, each entailing costs and benefits. One is to avoid what Robert Miles calls "the conceptual inflation" of racism.[18] A second is to consider other forms of categorizations than the ones exclusively focused on ethnoracial identity. Finally, the third entails a deracialization process involving the promotion of pragmatic, more interest-based than identity-based, ethnoracial coalitions.

The Deflation of Racism

The conceptual inflation of racism is encouraged today by commentators who, like Ibram Kendi, quizzically suggest that anything that is not antiracist is—perforce—racist, including policies trying to address racial gaps and studies of these gaps.[19] Yet, if institutional racism is so pervasive, structurally resistant to all actions aiming at achieving racial justice, it becomes difficult to recognize the accomplishments of antiracist movements over time and impossible to overcome racial barriers through changes in attitudes or policy reform. Furthermore, if racism is the source of all ills, other forms of discrimination are ignored—including those targeting African Americans in addition to race-based prejudice.

We should instead remember that the original raison d'être of intersectionality was to pay attention to the multiple overlapping forms of discrimination (such as gender, religion, culture, and sexual orientation). It thus effectively subsumed racism into a broader category of discrimination. But at this point, we may have to clarify again the relationship between racism and intersectionality: racism may be one form of prejudice, but other forms of prejudice are not racially motivated. This implies that we need a "more nuanced moral vocabulary" for talking about the meaning and scope of racism.[20] Otherwise, the conceptual inflation of racism may contribute to a process of diluting racial "wrongs" in a large pool of other "wrongs," effectively obscuring the distinction between—and the understanding of—the racial and nonracial sources of behavior and policies.

One potential objection is that a more nuanced approach leads to a color-blind one. Color-blindness has been used by conservatives to dismiss the continuation of racially inspired social inequality and oppression. In its worst form, color-blindness justifies racial injustice as the product of a group's attributes based on cultural differences or is used to explain an individual's failure to achieve the American dream. A soft liberal version assumes that racism is an artifact of the past because of the dismantlement of the Jim Crow regime and the effect of affirmative action programs. Proponents of post-racialism, therefore, equate color-blindness with a utopian egalitarian social order in which racial identities no longer substantially influence basic life chances.[21] I have provided evidence that the idea of post-racialism remains largely an ideal.

Yet, there is a more balanced alternative approach to color-blindness—one that distinguishes between a cognizant race/color consciousness and mobilizes against racial injustice in the name of race equity and neutrality. Fighting against the excesses of racialization is not tantamount to denying racism's existence or remaining blind to racial discrimination and injustice. It is actually the opposite: a truly inclusive politics of difference requires us to be aware of all forms of prejudice and to act by promoting a nondivisive, nonconfrontational conception of racial identity.

From this perspective, race consciousness extends to the identification of racial prejudice beyond the traditional white/black dichotomy and the recognition that, unfortunately, prejudice exists among all ethnoracial groups. The pursuit of justice and race equity cannot be applied selectively. We cannot use different standards for different groups, and the moral principles that inspire the support for BLM should be applied to other groups that are discriminated against. Anti-Asian hate crimes in 2020, for example, increased almost 150 percent over the previous year. In the aftermath of the killing of Asian women in the Atlanta area in March 2021, Asian activists and officials rightly asked: Who will march for us? Color blindness when applied here means that racial equity should prevail when it comes to protecting any group's right to justice and dignity—while recognizing and respecting the unique experience of each group.

Conceptual deflation should therefore apply to racism and antiracism. Imprecision in defining racism can be counterproductive, and antiracism can be weaponized when it is pushed to its limits into contestable terrain: when it makes it harder for people from diverse backgrounds to work and live together. All forms of racism are morally wrong, but not all antiracist practices are good, notably when they help actual racists legitimize their prejudice as illustrated by the ambivalent concepts of antiwhite racism and anti-antiracism. Understanding and solving social problems, almost all of which involve race, is difficult and often contentious. This requires more argumentation and less controversy.

Racial Eliminativism

A second option that might address conflictual intergroup relations is to stop evaluating these relations through an exclusively racial lens. Some scholars, for example, advocate eliminating racial categories on the decennial census and in public policies.[22] Proponents of "racial eliminativism" push the argument further by calling for the development of a raceless human commonality based on what Kwame Anthony Appiah defines as "the moral unity of humanity."[23] The main purpose—the ontological freedom of deciding who we are—is praiseworthy. Normative racial typologies may indeed impose "collective scripts" that constrain both groups and individuals, and pressure them to conform to racial patterns of behavior.[24] As I contend, when diversity is confined to a rigidly defined collection of ethnoracial groups, identity politics may imprison individuals in ascriptive collectivities, promote the unethical glorification of the ingroup, foster a suspicion of outsiders, and fuel violence.

In the real world, however, it remains questionable whether the suppression of racial categorizations would eradicate racial prejudice. Racism exists independently from these categorizations. It even exists without race—when the explicit racial component is replaced by religious, ethnic, or cultural characteristics. As I illustrated previously, official categorizations in most European countries are not explicitly based on race. Racial origin understood as skin color is notably absent. Data collection, instead, is based on proxies such as immigrant status, nationality, language, and certain religious practices. In some countries, like

France, the collection of data on ethnic origin and religion is prohibited except for a few exceptions (such as scientific studies using names and geographical origin under the supervision of the national statistical agencies).[25] As a result, the exact number of individuals belonging to or perceived as members of racial and ethnic minority groups in Europe is not known, although discrimination based on their ethnoracial identity is widespread.[26]

Conversely, racial categorizations do help to measure discrimination, allocate public funds, and fight racial injustice. These categorizations do not therefore always lead to exclusive racialized identities: they can encourage solidarity within one group and between various groups. Racial and ethnic data collection is a complex issue. Some argue that this data collection essentializes ethnic groups and thus contributes to racial discrimination. Others are concerned that the lack of relevant data undermines the fight against discrimination based on racial and ethnic origin. What really matters is the distinction between the useful contribution of data on ethnoracial inequality and the rigid census-style categorization used to justify "claims of inherency"—that racial identity is inescapable and defines not only someone's identity but also their fate and personal value.

The Deracialization Process

The ultimate challenge is therefore to envisage and implement a more modest but effective deracialization strategy. American society has been historically structured in such a way that it is almost impossible to escape from the labyrinth of racial categorizations. Rather than asking whether identity politics should be post- or a-racial, it is therefore more pragmatic to ask how intergroup relations can be less racialized and less conflictual than they are today.

Some noticeable trends provide part of the answer. The relationship between racial categorizations and ethnoracial identification, for example, is now more complex than ever among a growing number of Americans. Multiraciality, for example, defies conventional understandings of phenotype-based identity. Some multiracial people still position themselves in relation to existing racial groups. Others contest racially defined group boundaries and call for "connections across communities into a community of humanity."[27] The impact of multiraciality depends on how the second generation of multiracial children define themselves. Multiraciality will not automatically erase racial barriers. But being mixed is increasingly "ordinary," and such a broadening ordinariness may increase tolerance beyond multiraciality.

Another potential contribution to the process of deracialization is provided by immigrants and their children. There is plentiful evidence that members of the third generation are more likely to identify themselves in relation to their minority heritage than their second-generation counterparts.[28] Yet, they are also emancipated from the normative "collective scripts" that have determined the behavior of prior generations of immigrants. We have already witnessed significant changes among their predecessors. Over time, group members become more socially and economically heterogeneous, and they move away from a focus on ethnic politics as they deepen the process of integration. Part of this Americanization process is the de-ethnicization of political participation: Donald Trump lost the 2020 election, but he was supported by more minority voters in 2020 than in 2016. Democrats are benefiting from the support of a majority of minorities but cannot take this support for granted. Hispanics and other minorities of immigrant background actually share many of the social concerns, economic views, and political expectations of the general population. The political effectiveness of a purely ethnic appeal is thus declining because their political attitudes and loyalties become a function of broader concerns. Political labels and affiliation are increasingly open to redefinition and renegotiation—an adaptive trend that will force both Republicans and Democrats to rethink their electoral use of ethnoracial identity politics.

Do these trends provide new opportunities for the emergence of a more inclusive politics of difference? Pessimistically, many outcomes of depolarization and deracialization are contingent on reestablishing a basic consensus about what unites Americans. The 117th Congress is the most racially and ethnically diverse in history, with 23 percent of voting members comprising racial or ethnic minorities. Yet, if white and nonwhite—as well as Republican and Democrat—lawmakers on Capitol Hill cannot agree on what the primary threats are to American democracy, diversity will continue to fuel intolerance and intergroup violence. In the same vein, intergroup relations will remain conflictual if activists, thinkers, scholars, and other social actors involved in current controversies continue to prioritize their respective proprietary claims over specific rights and resources.

Optimistically, the dissociation of political affiliation from racial identification may help restore democratic pluralism. This requires admitting, for example, that all whites are not de facto racist or racist-blind and that all ethnoracial minorities have the right not to be progressive. "I am proud to be both a Black man and a Republican," writes US Senator Tim Scott when complaining that he is attacked because his "ideology does not match" what it is expected from him, based on his "complexion."[29] Hope for a less racialized polity is already fueled by the growing number of minorities who claim to be nonpartisan. Instead of being blindly loyal to one party based on their ethnoracial identity, their political allegiance shifts according to the attraction of partisan programs. This trend may prefigure a de-emphasis on race and a move toward the deracialization of politics. It may also presage the development of pragmatic, more interest-based than identity-based ethnoracial coalitions.

Some political issues will remain influenced by an ethnoracial disparity in preferences for governmental actions, such as affirmative action and immigration policies. Yet, there is potential for compromise—as illustrated by bipartisan agreement in other policy areas. Large majorities of Americans believe—beyond racial divide and political affiliation—that major corporations have too much power and make too much profit. A similar consensus is emerging about the unfair burdens of the federal tax system, particularly the need to increase corporate taxes.[30] American voters complain that the tone and nature of political debate has become negative (85 percent), less respectful (85 percent), and less fact-based (76 percent). Yet, they remain optimistic: Fully 84 percent think that trust in government can be improved, and 86 percent believe it is possible to improve trust in each other.[31] Public trust in many institutions remains low, but Americans express higher levels of confidence in the medical system and public schools, two institutions they believe have managed the pandemic very well.[32] More to the point, there is evidence that intergroup relations significantly improve under specific circumstances, built on a foundation of common goals, empathy, and cooperation. Building trust has beneficial outcomes for all parties involved. Ensuring that these conditions exist has become crucial to assuaging intergroup anxiety and outgroup intolerance.[33]

The collective pursuit of recognition and respect thus requires less ethnos and more ethos—defined as common basic principles of how to treat others respectfully and equitably, regardless of their identities, while paying attention to the needs of individual groups. This implies a move away from a narrow focus on competing rights. A fully inclusive tolerance involves a balance between obligations and entitlements, including a duty to respect the inherent worth of others. Key cognitive mechanisms that motivate improved intergroup attitudes include empathy rather than shame, and mutual respect instead of blame, in the ongoing struggle to redress the "evil past" and redefine the "demos" in a way that allows meaningful patterns of inclusion.

Notes

INTRODUCTION

1. Roger Daniels, *Coming to America: A History of Immigration and Ethnicity in American Life* (New York: Harper Collins), 104.
2. Speech in Washington, DC, July 27, 1967, https://americanarchive.org/catalog/cpb-aacip_80-74qjqrq1.
3. Jennifer Cobbina, *Hands Up, Don't Shoot: Why the Protests in Ferguson and Baltimore Matter, and How They Changed America* (New York University Press, 2019), 5.
4. Donald Horowitz, *Ethnic Groups in Conflict* (Berkeley: University of California Press, 1985).
5. Clifford Geertz, *The Interpretations of Culture* (New York: Basic Books, 1973).
6. The categorization of (and data on) white, Black, and Hispanic groups are based on the US Census. Depending on the scholars quoted in this book, the terms "Hispanic" and "Latino" are used interchangeably. "Latinx" is a more recent concept, and I mention it only when it is part of a quote. I acknowledge the recent debate about the capitalization of the word black—which has been adopted in 2020 by a growing number of scholars and news organizations (such as the Associated Press). I did not, however, introduce this capitalization in the quotations. Conversely, I kept it when scholars used it. See John Eligon, "A Debate Over Identity and Race Asks, Are African Americans Black or black?" *The New York Times*, June 26, 2020, https://www.nytimes.com/2020/06/26/us/black-african-american-style-debate.html?campaign_id=2&emc=edit_th_20200627&instance_id=19814&nl=todaysheadlines&regi_id=65105157&segment_id=32012&user_id=e8a5b8386cd6065948b1c4a36c8b059d.
7. Matthew Frye Jacobson, *Whiteness of a Different Color: European Immigrants and the Alchemy of Race* (Cambridge, MA: Harvard University Press, 1998); Theodore, Allen, *The Invention of the White Race: Racial Oppression and Social Control* (London: Verso, 1994); Mary Waters, *Ethnic Options: Choosing Identities in America* (Berkeley: University of California Press, 1990).
8. Noel Ignatiev, *How the Irish Became White* (New York: Routledge, 1995), 14.
9. See Sumi K. Cho, "Korean Americans v. African Americans: Conflicts and Reconstruction," in *Reading Rodney King/Reading Urban Uprising*, ed. Robert Gooding-Williams (New York: Routledge, 1993), 205–232; Talmadge Anderson, "Comparative Experience Factors among Black, Asian, and Hispanic Americans," *Journal of Black Studies* 23 (1992): 27–38; Edward Taehan Chang, "Korean-Black Conflict in Los Angeles: Perceptions and Realities," in *Dreams and Realities*, ed. Kwang Chung Kim and E. H. Lee (Seoul: Institute of Korea, 1990), 76–101.
10. Eric Yamamoto, *Interracial Justice: Conflict and Reconciliation in Post-Civil Rights America* (New York University Press, 1999), 16.
11. Eric Yamamoto, *Interracial Justice*, 29.
12. James Jones, *Prejudice and Racism*, 2nd ed. (New York: McGraw Hill, 1997), 115.
13. Nick Peterson and Geoff Ward, "The Transmission of Historical Racial Violence: Lynching, Civil Rights-Era Terror, and Contemporary Interracial Homicides," *Race and Justice* 5, no. 2 (2015): 114–143; Robert Defina and Lance Hannon, "The Legacy of Black Lynching and Contemporary Segregation in the South," *The Review of Black Political*

Economy 38 (2011): 165–181; Jeremy R. Porter, "Plantation Economics, Violence, and Social Well-Being: The Lingering Effects of Racialized Group Oppression on Contemporary Human Development in the American South," *Journal of Human Development and Capabilities* 12 (2011): 339–366.

14. Stewart E. Tolnay and E. M. Beck, *A Festival of Violence: An Analysis of Southern Lynchings, 1882–1930* (Champaign: University of Illinois Press, 1995).

15. See for example Jennifer Lee and Frank Bean, *The Diversity Paradox: Immigration and the Color Line in Twenty-First Century* (New York: Russell Sage Foundation, 2010). I present these various arguments in detail in the coming chapters.

16. Michael Omi and Howard Winant, *Racial Formation in the United States from the 1960's to the 1990s*, 2nd ed. (New York: Routledge, 1994), 154.

17. James M. Jasper, *The Emotions of Protest* (Chicago: University of Chicago Press, 2018); James M. Jasper, "The Emotions of Protest: Affective and Reactive Emotions in and around Social Movements," *Sociological Forum* 13, no. 3 (1998): 397–424; Jeff Goodwin, James M. Jasper, and Francesca Polleta, eds., *Passionate Politics: Emotions and Social Movements* (Chicago: University of Chicago Press, 2001).

18. Anthony Giddens, *Central Problems in Social Theory: Action, Structure, and Contradiction in Social Analysis* (Los Angeles: University of California Press, 1996); Talcott Parsons, *The Structure of Social Action* (New York: Free Press, 1937).

19. Karim Murji and John Solomos, eds., *Theories of Race and Ethnicity: Contemporary Debates and Perspectives* (Cambridge: Cambridge University Press, 2015), 10.

20. The Deacons for Justice and Justice, an armed African American self-defense group created in 1964 as a response to the violence perpetuated by the KKK, provided a relevant example of the coexistence of defensive strategies and a sense of agency based on a clear political and civic agenda. See Lance Hill, *The Deacons for Defense: Armed Resistance and the Civil Rights Movements* (Chapel Hill: University of North Carolina Press, 2004).

21. Michael Omi and Howard Winant, *Racial Formation in the United States,* 154.

22. Michael Omi and Howard Winant, *Racial Formation*, 154, 81.

23. Michael Omi, and Howard Winant, *Racial Formation*, 82.

24. Sidney Tarrow, *Power in Movement: Social Movements and Contentious Politics* (Cambridge: Cambridge University Press, 2011); Charles Tilly and Sidney Tarrow, *Contentious Politics* (Oxford, NY: Oxford University Press, 2007); Charles Tilly, *The Politics of Collective Violence* (Cambridge: Cambridge University Press, 2003); Doug McAdam, *Political Process and the Development of Black Insurgency 1930–1970* (Chicago: University of Chicago Press, 1999).

25. See for example Tom Tyler, Robert J. Boeckman, Heather J. Smith, and Yuen J. Huo, *Social Justice in a Diverse Society* (Boulder: Westview, 1997).

26. On the relationship between grievances and mobilization, see Bert Klandermans, Marle Roefs, and Johan Olivier, "Grievances Formation in a Country in Transition: South Africa, 1994–1998," in *Reading on Social Movements*, ed. Doug McAdam and David Snow (Oxford: Oxford University Press, 2010), 397–410; Bert Klandermans, *The Social Psychology of Protest* (Cambridge: Blackwell, 1997).

27. George Fredrickson, *Racism: A Short History* (Princeton, NJ: Princeton University Press, 2002), 131.

28. On the evolution of anti-Black racism after the civil rights era, see David O. Sears, "Symbolic Racism," in *Eliminating Racism: Profiles in Controversy*, ed. Phyllis A. Katz and Dalamas A. Taylor (New York: Plenum, 1988), 53–84.

29. I provide a detailed presentation of these concepts in chapter 1.

30. See, for example, Charles Gallagher, *Racism in Post-Race America: New Theories, New Directions* (Social Forces, 2008); Paul Gilroy, *Against Race: Imagining Political Culture beyond the Color Line* (Cambridge, MA: Belknap Press, 2000).

31. Jennifer Lee and Frank Bean, *The Diversity Paradox*; Jennifer Lee, "A Post-Racial America? Multiracial Identification and the Color Line in the 21st Century," *Nanzan Review of American Studies* 30 (2008): 13–31; Joel Perlmann and Mary Waters, "Intermarriage Then and Now: Race, Generation, and the Changing Meaning of Marriage," in *Not Just Black and White: Historical and Contemporary Perspectives on Immigration, Race, and Ethnicity in the United States*, ed. Nancy Foner and George Fredrickson (New York: Russell Sage Foundation, 2004).

32. Barry Glassner, *The Culture of Fear: Why Americans Are Afraid of the Wrong Things* (New York: Basic Books, 2010), 8. See also Frank Furedi, *The Culture of Fear: Risk-Taking and the Morality of Low Expectation* (London, Washington: Cassell, 1997).

33. Among the studies analyzing these trends, see Desmond King and Rogers M. Smith, *Still a House Divided: Race and Politics in Obama's America* (Princeton, NJ: Princeton University Press, 2012); John Sides, Michael Tesler, and Lynn Vavreck, *Identity Crisis: The 2016 Presidential Campaign and the Battle for the Meaning of America* (Princeton University Press, 2018); Michael Tessler, *Post-Racial or Most Racial? Race and Politics in the Obama Era* (Chicago: University of Chicago Press, 2016); Donald Kinder and Cindy Kam, *Us against Them: Ethnocentric Foundations of American Opinion* (Chicago: University of Chicago Press, 2009); Donald Kinder and Allison Dale-Riddle, *The End of Race? Obama, 2008, and the Racial Politics in America* (New Haven, CT: Yale University Press, 2012).

PART 1. LESSONS FROM THE PAST

1. Richard Hofstadter, "Reflections on Violence" in *American Violence: A Documentary History*, ed. Richard Hofstadter and Michel Wallace (New York: Alfred A. Knopf, 1970), 2.

2. Donald Horowitz, *The Deadly Ethnic Riot* (Berkeley: University of California Press, 2001), xiii.

3. The National Memorial for Peace and Justice, inaugurated in April 2018 in Montgomery (Alabama) documents racial terror lynching across the South. About 4,400 cases have been cataloged so far.

4. O. A. Rogers Jr., "The Elaine Riots of 1919," *The Arkansas Historical Quarterly* 19, no. 2 (1960): 148.

5. Harvard Sitkoff, "Racial Militancy and Interracial Violence in the Second World War," *The Journal of American History* 58, no. 2 (1971): 661–681.

6. Middle East tensions in the 1970s and 1980s, as well as the Persian Gulf War of 1991, generated a long series of violent crimes against Arabs and Muslims. Examples included the killing of the regional director of the American-Arab Anti-Discrimination Committee (ADC) Southern California Office in October 1985, the bombing of mosques in Houston (Texas) and Potomac (Maryland) in 1986, and the torching of businesses across the country in the early 1990s.

7. Gaston Espinosa, Virgilio Elizondo, and Jesse Miranda, *Latino Religions and Civic Activism in the United States* (Oxford: Oxford University Press, 2005).

8. In 1857, the Supreme Court declared in the Dred Scott v. Sandford decision that people of African descent born in the United States—whether free or enslaved—could not be considered citizens. This decision was nullified in 1868 by the Citizenship Clause of the Fourteenth Amendment. Black people attempted during the Reconstruction (1863–1877) to gain greater civic participation in public institutions, political parties, and local government agencies. Yet the US Supreme Court validated a series of infringements of civic rights supposedly guaranteed by the Fourteenth Amendment after the end of the Reconstruction. Notably, the Supreme Court ruled the 1875 Civil Rights Act unconstitutional in 1883. Moreover, the landmark Plessy v. Ferguson decision of 1896

introduced the infamous "separate but equal" system. As a result, Black people lost their hard-won voting rights and endured segregation in many public spaces (such as schools, transportation, public accommodations, and libraries) in Southern states where Redeemers' plan was to re-establish a complete white supremacy. The process of reinterpretation of the Fourteenth Amendment (originally drafted to establish Black men's citizenship) involved three main decisions: Mills v. Green (1895), Williams v. Mississippi (1898), and Giles v. Harris (1903). These decisions allowed states to racially disenfranchise African Americans legally (as well as poor whites). See Nell Irvin Painter, *Creating Black Americans: African American History and Its Meanings, 1619 to the Present* (New York: Oxford University Press, 2007); Henry Louis Gates, Jr., "The Lost Cause that Built Jim Crow," *The New York Times*, November 8, 2019, https://www.nytimes.com/2019/11/08/opinion/sunday/jim-crow-laws.html.

9. Linda Faye Williams, *The Constraints of Race: Legacies of White Skin Privilege in America* (University Park: Penn State University Press, 2003), 12.

10. See Graham Otis, *Unguarded Gates: A History of America's Immigration Crisis* (Lanham, MD: Rowman & Littlefield, 2004); Ellis Cose, *A Nation of Strangers: Prejudice, Politics, and the Populating of America* (New York: Morrow, 1992); David Bennett, *The Party of Fear: From Nativist Movements to the New Right in American History* (Chapel Hill: University of North Carolina Press, 1988).

11. Stuart Carroll, *Cultures of Violence* (London: Macmillan, 2007); Elijah Anderson, *The Code of the Street: Violence, Decency and the Moral Life in the Inner City* (New York: W.W. Norton, 1999); *The Culture of Violence*, ed. Kuman Rupesinghe and Martial Rubio (New York: United Nations University, 1994); W. Eugene Hollon, *Frontier Violence: Another Look* (New York: Oxford University Press, 1974).

12. Daniel Hopkins, "Politicized Places: Explaining Where and When Immigrants Provoke Local Opposition," *American Political Sciences Review* 104, no. 1 (2010): 40–60; John Mollenkopf and Jennifer Hochschild, "Setting the Context" in *Bringing Outsiders In: Transatlantic Perspective on Immigrant Political Incorporation*, ed. Jennifer Hochschild and John Mollenkopf (Ithaca, NY: Cornell University Press, 2009), 3–14; Kristi Andersen and Elizabeth F. Cohen, "Political Institutions and Incorporation of Immigrants," in *The Politics of Democratic Inclusion*, ed. Christina M. Wolbrecht and Rodney E. Hero, (Philadelphia: Temple University Press, 2005), 186–205; Ruud Koopmans and Paul Staham, "Migration and Ethnic Relations as a Field of Political Contention: An Opportunity Structure Approach," in *Challenging Immigration and Ethnic Relations: Comparative European Perspectives*, ed. Ruud Koopmans and Paul Staham (Oxford: Oxford University Press, 2000), 13–56; Heather Ann Thompson, "Understanding Rioting in Postwar Urban America," *Journal of Urban History* 26, no. 3 (2000): 391–402; Mary Brinton and Victor Nee, eds., *The New Institutionalism in Sociology* (New York: Russell Sage Foundation, 1998); Benjamin Bowling, *Violent Racism: Victimization, Policing and Social Context* (Oxford University Press, 1998); Daniel Myers, "Racial Riots in the 1960s: An Event History Analysis of Local Conditions," *American Sociological Review* 62, no. 1 (1997): 94–112; Thomas J. Sugrue, *The Origins of the Urban Crisis: Race and Inequality in Postwar Detroit* (Princeton, NJ: Princeton University Press, 1996); Patrick Ireland, *The Policy Change of Ethnic Diversity* (Cambridge, MA: Harvard University Press, 1994); John Benyon and John Solomos (eds.), *The Roots of Urban Unrests* (Oxford: Pergamon Press, 1987); Peter Eisinger, "The Conditions of Protest Behavior in American Cities," *American Political Sciences Review* 67 (1973): 1–12.

13. Susan Olzack and Suzanne Shanahan, "Deprivation and Race Riots: An Extension of Spilerman's Analysis," *Social Force* 74, no. 3 (1996): 931–961; Will H. Moore, "Deprivation, Mobilization and the States: A Synthetic Model of Rebellion," *Journal of Developing Societies*, 6 (1990): 17–36; David Snyder, "Collective Violence: A Research Agenda and Some Strategic Considerations," *Journal of Conflict Resolution* 23, no. 3 (1987): 499–534;

Seymour Spilerman. "Structural Characteristics of the Cities and the Severity of Social Disorders," *American Sociological Review* 41, no. 5 (1976): 771–793; Edna Bonacih, "A Theory of Ethnic Antagonism: The Split Labor Market," *American Sociological Review* 37 (1972): 547–559.

14. For example: Donald Horowitz, *The Deadly Ethnic Riots* (Berkeley: University of California Press, 2001); Susan Olzack, *The Dynamics of Ethnic Competition and Conflict* (Stanford, CA: Stanford University Press, 1992); Donald Horowitz, *Ethnic Groups in Conflict* (Berkeley: University of California Press, 1985); Graeme Newman, *Understanding Violence* (New York: J. B. Lippincott, 1979).

15. A relevant example is provided by Monica Blumenthal, Letha B. Chadiha, Gerald A. Cole, and Toby E. Jayaratne, *Justifying Violence: Attitudes of American Men* (Ann Harbor: University of Michigan Press, 1972).

16. John Herbers, "Introduction to Violence in America," in *Violence in America: Historical and Comparative Perspectives*, ed. Hugh Davis Graham and Ted Robert Gurr (New York: NYT Books, 1969): xiii.

17. Joe B. Frantz, "The Frontier Tradition: An Invitation to Violence," in *Violence in America*, ed. Hugh Davis Graham and Ted Robert Gurr: 51.

18. Henry Giroux, "America's Addiction to Violence," *Counterpunch*, December 25, 2015, http://www.counterpunch.org/2015/12/25/americas-addiction-to-violence-2/.

19. Since the killing of a dozen students and teachers at Columbine High (Colorado) in April 1999, several mass rampages (in which ten or more people were killed) took place around the country. They included, for example, twelve dead in a movie theater in Aurora (Colorado) in July 2012; the killing in December 2012 of twenty first graders and adults at the Sandy Hook Elementary School in Newton (Connecticut); the killing of fourteen in San Bernardino (California) in December 2015; and 549 killed in an Orlando nightclub (Florida) in June 2016. Between December 2012 (Sandy Hook) and February 2018 (Marjory Stoneman Douglas High School in Parkland, Florida), about 400 people were shot (138 of whom were killed) in more than 200 school shootings.

20. Editorial Board, "The Worst Kind of American Exceptionalism," *Washington Post*, October 2, 2017, https://www.washingtonpost.com/opinions/time-to-end-american-exceptionalism-on-guns/2017/10/02/0db40072-a7a9-11e7-b3aa-c0e2e1d41e38_story.html.

21. A mass killing is defined by the Justice Department as three or more killings in a single episode. The FBI collects data on "active shooter incidents," which it defines as "as one or more individuals actively engaged in killing or attempting to kill people in a populated area." Using the FBI's definition, 85 people—excluding the shooters—died in such incidents in 2018. The Gun Violence Archive, an online database of gun violence incidents in the United States, defines mass shootings as incidents in which four or more people—excluding the shooter—are shot or killed. Using this definition, 373 people died in these incidents in 2018 and 294 between January and August 2019. See https://www.gunviolencearchive.org/.

22. See, for example, John Kozy, "Violence: The American Way of Life," *Global Research*, January 27, 2018, https://www.globalresearch.ca/violence-the-american-way-of-life/5318698; Eric Schnurer, "Change Our Violent Culture," *US News*, October 16, 2017, https://www.usnews.com/opinion/thomas-jefferson-street/articles/2017-10-16/after-las-vegas-try-to-change-americas-violent-culture-not-gun-laws; Nicholas Thompson, "America's Culture of Violence," *The New Yorker*, December 15, 2012, https://www.newyorker.com/news/news-desk/americas-culture-of-violence.

23. Robert Park, *Race and Culture* (New York: Free Press, 1949); Gunnar Myrdal, *The Negro Problem and Modern Democracy* (New York: Harper & Row, 1944); Chicago Commission on Race Relations, *The Negro in Chicago: A Study of Race Relations and a Race Riot* (Chicago: The University of Chicago Press, 1922).

24. Fred Harris, "The 1967 Riots and the Kerner Commission Report," in *Quiet Riots: Race and poverty in the United States*, ed. Fred Harris and Roger Wilkins (New York: Pantheon, 1988), 5–15; Joseph Boskin, *Urban Racial Violence in the Twentieth Century* (Beverly Hills, CA: Glencoe Press, 1976); William Morgan and Terry Clark, "The Causes of Racial Disorders: A Grievance Level Explanation," *American Sociological Review* 38 (1973): 611–624; Robert Blauner, *Racial Oppression in America* (New York: Harper & Row, 1971); Bryan Downes, "Social and Political Characteristics of Riot Cities: A Comparative Study," in *Blacks in the United States*, ed. Norval Glenn and Charles Bonjean (San Francisco: Chandler, 1969), 427–443.

25. Allen Grimshaw, *Racial Violence in the United States* (Chicago: Aldine Publishing Company, 1969). According to Grimshaw, the Harlem riots were the first manifestation of a "modern form of rioting" characterized by three criteria: 1) violence directed almost entirely against property, 2) no major clashes between racial groups, and 3) conflict between the African American lower class and police forces.

26. Hugh Davis Graham and Ted Robert Gurr (eds.), *Violence in America: Historical and Comparative Perspective* (New York: NYT Book, 1970), 398.

27. Allen Grimshaw, "Urban Racial Violence in the United States: Changing Ecological Considerations," *American Journal of Sociology* 66 (1960): 109–119.

28. Susan Olzack and Suzanne Shanahan, "Deprivation and Race Riots: An Extension of Spilerman's Analysis," *Social Forces* 74, no. 3 (1996): 931–961; Will H. Moore, "Deprivation, Mobilization and the States: A Synthetic Model of Rebellion," *Journal of Developing Societies* 6 (1990): 17–36; David Snyder, "Collective Violence: A Research Agenda and Some Strategic Considerations," *Journal of Conflict Resolution* 23, no. 3 (1987): 499–534; Seymour Spilerman, "Structural Characteristics of the Cities and the Severity of Social Disorders," *American Sociological Review* 41, no. 5 (1976): 771–793.

29. Susan Olzack and Johan Olivier, "The Dynamics of Ethnic Collective Action in South Africa and the United States" (paper presented at the annual meeting of the International Sociological Association, Bielefeld, Germany, 1994); Peter Eisinger, "The Conditions of Protest Behavior in American Cities," *American Political Science Review* 67 (1973): 11–28; Ted Robert Gurr, "The Calculus of Civil Conflict," *The Journal of Social Issues* 66 (1972): 109–119; Stanley Lieberson and Arnold Silverman, "The Precipitants and Underlying Conditions of Race Riots," *American Sociological Review* 30, no. 6 (1965): 887–898.

30. Daniel Myers, "Racial Rioting in the 1960s: An Event History Analysis of Local Conditions," *American Sociological Review* 62, no. 1 (1997): 95. See also Leonard Berkowitz, "The Study of Urban Violence: Some Implications of Laboratory Studies of Frustration and Aggression," *American Behavioral Scientist* 2 (1968): 14–17.

31. Daniel Myers, "Racial Rioting in the 1960s," (1997): 95. See also Bryan Downes, "Social and Political Characteristics of Riot Cities: A Comparative Study," *Social Science Quarterly*, 49 (1968): 504–520.

32. Seymour Spilerman. "The Causes of Racial Disturbances: A Comparison of Alternative Explanations," *American Sociological Review* 35, no. 4 (1970): 628.

33. James Comer, "The Dynamics of Black and White Power," in *Violence in America*, ed. Hugh Davis Graham and Ted Robert, 448.

34. Robert Fogelson, "Violence and Grievances: Reflections on the 1960s Riots," *Journal of Social Issues* 26, no. 1(1970): 155.

35. Susan Olzak, Suzanne Shanahan, and Elizabeth McEneaney, "Poverty, Segregation and Race Riots," *American Sociological Review* 61, no. 4 (1996): 591. See also Doug McAdam, *Political Process and the Development of Black Insurgency* (Chicago: University of Chicago Press, 1982).

36. Craig Jenkins, "Resource Mobilization Theory and the Study of Social Movements," *Annual Review of Sociology* 9 (1983): 527–553.

37. Steven Krasner, "Approaches to the State: Alternative Conceptions and Historical Dynamics," *Comparative Politics* 16, no. 2 (1984): 234.

38. The controversy in Charlottesville was nominally focused on a statue honoring General Robert E. Lee. Approximately 700 monuments have raised similar concerns. Most of them were erected in the 1950s–1960s as a revanchist response by segregationists to the civil rights movement. In 2020, the destruction of statues and other racist symbols became one of the major claims of Black Lives Matter.

39. See http://www.minutemanhq.com/pdf_files/minutemanbrochure.pdf. This movement was dissolved in June 2016 after his founder, Chris Simcox, was found guilty of child molestation and sentenced to serve 19.5 years in an Arizona prison.

40. See https://www.oathkeepers.org/declaration-of-orders-we-will-not-obey/.

41. Michael Omi and Howard Winant, *Racial Formation in the United States from the 1960s to the 1990* (New York: Routledge, 1994), 1.

42. Harvard Sitkoff, "Racial Militancy and Interracial Violence in the Second World War," *The Journal of American History* 58, no. 3 (1971): 669–670.

43. From 1955 to 1967, 530 incidents took place in the region, including bombings, burnings, beatings, and killings. Each advance toward racial equality drew white backlash violence, such as the bombing in 1963 of a Baptist church (killing four girls) committed by extremists as a response to the March on Washington.

44. Matthew Frye Jacobson, *Whiteness of a Different Color: European Immigrants and the Alchemy of Race* (Cambridge, MA: Harvard University Press, 1998), 247.

45. Robert Fogelson, *Violence as Protest: Study of Riots and Ghettos* (Garden City, NY: Doubleday, 1971), 158.

46. Early attempts include, for example Robert Fogelson, "Violence and Grievances: Reflections on the 1960s Riots," *Journal of Social Issues* 26 (1970): 141–163; Allen D. Grimshaw, *Racial Violence in the United States* (Chicago: Aldine, 1969); H. L. Nieburgh, *Political Violence: The Behavioral Process* (New York: St Martin's Press, 1969); Johan Galtung, "Violence, Peace, and Peace Research," *Journal of Peace Research*, 6, no. 3 (1969): 167–191.

47. Hugh Davis Graham and Ted Robert Gurr, *Violence in America*, 396.

48. Joe Feagin and Harlan Hahn, *Ghetto Revolts: The Politics of Violence in American Cities* (New York: MacMillan, 1973); David Sears and John McConahay, *The Politics of Violence: The New Urban Blacks and the Watts Riots* (Boston, MA: Houghton Mifflin, 1973); Robert Fogelson, *Violence as Protest: Study of Riots and Ghettos* (Garden City, NY: Doubleday, 1971); Jerome Skolnick, *The Politics of Protest* (New York: Simon and Schuster, 1969).

49. Hugh Davis Graham and Ted Robert, *Violence in America*, xxvi.

50. August Mier and Elliott Mudwick, "Black Violence in the Twentieth Century," in *Violence in America*, ed. Hugh Davis Graham and Ted Robert, 401.

51. Edward Banfield, "Rioting Mainly for Fun and Profit," in *The Metropolitan Enigma: Inquiries into the Nature and Dimensions of America's "Urban Crisis,"* ed. James Wilson (Cambridge, MA: Harvard University Press, 1968), 283–308.

52. Alejandro Portes and Ruben Rumbaut, *Immigrant America: A Portrait*, 3rd ed. (Berkeley: University of California Press, 2006), 119.

53. Graeme Newman, *Understanding Violence* (New York: J. B. Lippincott Company, 1979), 120.

54. James Jennings, "Blacks and Latinos in the American City in the 1990s: Toward Political Alliances or Social Conflict," *National Political Science Review* 3 (1992): 158–63; Paula D. McClain, "Coalition and Competition: Patterns of Black-Latinos Relations in Urban Politics," in *From Polemics to Practice: Forging Political Coalition Among Racial and Ethnic Minorities*, ed. Wilbur C. Rich (New York: Praeger, 1996), 52–63; Kenneth J. Meier, Paula D. McClain, and Robert D. Wrinkle, "Divided or Together? Conflict

and Cooperation between African Americans and Latinos," *Political Research Quarterly* 57, no. 3 (2004): 399–409.

55. Edna Bonacich, "A Theory of Ethnic Antagonism: The Split Labor Market," *American Sociological Review* 37 (1972): 547–559; Hubert Blalock, *Toward a Theory of Minority-Group Relations* (Hoboken, NJ: Wiley, 1967).

56. Matthew Frye Jacobson, *Whiteness of a Different Color*, 5. See also Alexander Saxton, *The Rise and Fall of the White Republic: Class Politics and Mass Culture in the Nineteenth Century* (London: Verso, 1990); Theodore Allen, *The Invention of the White Race*, vol. 1, *Racial Oppression and Social Control* (London: Verso, 1994).

1. VIOLENCE AS A PROACTIVE RESPONSE TO ADVERSITY

1. Lawrence Blum, *I'm Not a Racist but . . . The Moral Quandary of Race* (Ithaca, NY: Cornell University Press, 2002), 2.

2. Lawrence Blum, *I'm Not a Racist but*, 223–224.

3. Ariane Chebel d'Appollonia, *Migrant Mobilization and Securitization in the US and Europe: How Does It Feel to Be a Threat?* (New York: Palgrave Macmillan, 2015).

4. Kathleen Blee, "Racial Violence in the United States," *Ethnic and Racial Studies*, 28, no. 4 (2005): 602. In this article, Blee provides an extremely relevant reconceptualization of racial violence. However, she only includes in her analytical frame violence against subordinate racial group members by dominant racial group members, therefore excluding violence between/among members of subordinate racial groups, as well as violence committed by minorities on dominant racial group members.

5. Nathan Eckstrand and Christopher Yates, *Philosophy and the Return of Violence: Studies from this Widening Gyre* (New York: Continuum International Publishing Group, 2011); Glenn Gray, *On Understanding Violence Philosophically* (New York: Harper and Row, 1970).

6. Donald Horowitz, *The Deadly Ethnic Riots* (Berkeley: University of California Press, 2001), 38.

7. Hannah Arendt, *On Violence* (New York: Harcourt Brace, 1970).

8. John Dodd, *Violence and Phenomenology* (New York: Routledge, 2009), 12.

9. René Girard, *Violence and the Sacred* (Baltimore, MD: Johns Hopkins University Press, 1979). 2. See also René Girard and Thomas Wieser, "Generative Violence and the Extension of Social Order," *Salmagundi* 63/64 (1984): 204–237. See also A. McKenna, *Violence and Difference: Girard, Derrida, and Deconstruction* (Urbana: University of Illinois Press, 1992).

10. Donatella Della Porta and Mario Diani, *Social Movements: An Introduction* (Oxford, UK: Blackwell Publishing, 2006), 20. They argue that such goals may be produced not only within social movements but also in many contexts that normally are not associated with social movements. Therefore, "when we analyze social movements, we deal with social processes that may also be of interest to researchers who do not define themselves at all as social movement analysts." (20). See also Robert D. Benford and David A. Snow, "Framing Processes and Social Movement: An Overview and Assessment," *Annual Review of Sociology* 26, no. 1 (2000): 611–639. Examples of studies analyzing ethnoracial mobilization or antiracist campaigns as forms of social movement include: Teun A. van Dijk, *Antiracist Discourse: Theory and History of a Macromovement* (Cambridge: Cambridge University Press, 2021); Alvin B. Tillery Jr., "What Kind of Movement Is Black Lives Matter?" *Journal of Race, Ethnicity, and Politics* 4, no. 2 (2019): 297–323; Doug McAdam, *Political Process and the Development of Black Insurgency* (Chicago: University of Chicago Press, 1982).

11. Mario Diani, "Networks and Social Movements: A Research Program," in *Social Movements and Networks: Relational Approaches to Collective Action*, ed. Mario Dani and Doug McAdam (Oxford: Oxford University Press, 2003), 301.

12. See Arnold H. Buss, *The Psychology of Aggression* (New York: Wiley, 1961); Seymour Feshbach, "The Function of Aggression and the Regulation of Aggressive Drive," *Psychological Review* 71 (1964): 257–272; Leonard Berkowitz, "Frustration-Aggression Hypothesis: Examination and Reformulation," *Psychological Bulletin* 106 (1989): 59–73.

13. Doug McAdam, *Political Process and the Development of Black Insurgency 1930–1970* (Chicago: University of Chicago Press, 1989). See also James Burton, *Black Violence: Political Impact of the 1960s Riots* (Princeton, NJ: Princeton University Press, 1978).

14. For a critic of the dichotomy between reactive and instrumental subtypes of violence, from the perspective of social interaction theory, see James T. Tedeschi and Richard B. Felson, *Violence, Aggression & Coercive Actions* (Washington, DC: American Psychological Association, 1994).

15. On the role of emotions in ethnic conflict, see Roger Petersen, *Understanding Ethnic Violence* (Cambridge: Cambridge University Press, 2002); David Franks and Viktor Gecas, *Social Perspectives on Emotions* (Greenwich, CT: JAI Press, 1992).

16. On the difficulty of balancing rational views and the role of nonrational factors (such as emotions and subjective perceptions), see Sidney Tarrow, *Power in Movement: Social Movements and Contentious Politics* (Cambridge: Cambridge University Press, 2011).

17. Seymour Spilerman, "The Causes of Racial Disturbances: A Comparison of Alternative Explanations," *American Sociological Review* 35, no. 4 (1970): 627–6.

18. Doug McAdam, "Beyond Structural Analysis: Toward a More Dynamic Understanding of Social Movements," in *Social Movements and Networks: Relational Approaches to Collective Action*, ed. Mario Dani and Doug McAdam (Oxford: Oxford University Press, 2003), 282.

19. Donatella Della Porta and Mario Diani, *Social Movements: An Introduction* (Oxford, UK: Blackwell Publishing, 2006), 15.

20. On the evolution of the mobilization agenda, see Davide Pero and John Solomos, "Migrant Politics and Mobilization: Exclusion, Engagement, Incorporation," *Ethnic and Racial Studies* 33, no. 1 (2010): 1–18.

21. On the collective action by high-status groups, see Martijn van Zomeren and Aaarti Iyer, "Introduction to the Social and Psychological Dynamics of Collective Action," *Journal of Social Issues* 65, no. 4 (2009): 645–660.

22. F. Polletta and J. M. Jasper, 2001, "Collective Identity and Social Movements," *Annual Review of Sociology* 27 (2001): 283–305.

23. Karl-Dieter Opp, "Collective Identity, Rationality and Collective Political Action," *Rationality and Society* 24, no. 1 (2012): 73–105; R. Brubaker and F. Cooper, "Beyond Identity," *Theory and Society* 29 (2000): 1–47; Alberto Melucci, "The Process of Collective Identity," in *Social Movements and Culture*, ed. Hank Johnston and Bert Klandermans (Minneapolis, MN: University of Minneapolis Press, 1995).

24. For a general discussion and critical evaluation of these various approaches, see James Fearon and David Laitin, "Violence and the Social Construction of Ethnic Identity," *International Organizations* 54, no. 4 (2000): 845–877.

25. Charles Tilly, *Social Movements* (Boulder, CO: Paradigm, 2004); Belinda Robnett, "External Political Events and Collective Identity," in *Social Movements: Identity, Culture and the State*, ed. David S. Meyer, Nancy Whittier, and Belinda Robnett (New York: Oxford University Press, 2002), 287–301.

26. On the distinction between primordialist and "optionalist" or "circumstantialist" conception of identity, see Philip Gleason, "Identifying Identity: A Semantic History," *The Journal of American History* 69, no. 4 (1983): 910–931; Nathan Glazer and Daniel Moynihan, *Ethnicity: Theory and Experience* (Cambridge: Cambridge University Press, 1975).

27. Jacquelien Van Stekelenburg, "The Political Psychology of Protest," *European Psychology* 18, no. 4 (2013): 224.

28. Lawrence Bobo and Hutchings Vincent Hutchings, "Perceptions of Racial Group Competition: Extending Blumer's Theory of Group Position to a Multiracial Social Context," *American Sociological Review* 61, no. 6 (1996): 951–72.

29. Gordon W. Allport, *The Nature of Prejudice* (Garden City, NJ: Doubleday, 1954); Thomas F. Pettigrew, "Prejudice," in *Dimensions of Ethnicity*, ed. Stephan Thernstrom, Ann Orlov, and Oscar Handlin (Cambridge, MA: Harvard University Press, 1982), 1–29; John Duckitt, *The Social Psychology of Prejudice* (New York: Praeger, 1992).

30. Herbert Blumer, "Race Prejudice as a Sense of Group Position," *Pacific Sociological Review* 1 (1958): 3–27.

31. Rupert Brown and Miles Hewstone, "An Integrative Theory of Intergroup Contact," *Advances in Experimental Social Psychology* 37 (2005): 255–343; Linda R. Tropp and Thomas F. Petigrew, "Relationships between Intergroup Contact and Prejudice among Minority and Majority Status Groups," *Psychological Science* 16, no. 12 (2005): 951–957); Lawrence Bobo, "Prejudice as a Sense of Group Position: Microfoundations of a Sociological Approach to Racism and Race Relations," *Journal of Social Issues* 55, no. 3 (1999): 445–472; Lincoln Quillian, "Group Threat and Regional Change in Attitudes toward African Americans," *American Journal of Sociology* 102, no. 3 (1996): 816–860; Lincoln Quillian, "Prejudice as a Response to Perceived Group Threat: Population, Composition and Anti-Immigrant and Racial Prejudice in Europe," *American Sociological Review* 60 (1995): 586–611; Hubert Blalock, *Toward a Theory of Minority Group Relations* (New York: John Willey, 1967).

32. Laura De Guissmé and Laurent Licata, "Competition over Collective Victimhood Recognition: When Perceived Lack of Recognition for Past Victimization is Associated with Negative Attitudes towards Another Victimized Group," *European Journal of Social Psychology* 47 (2017): 148–166.

33. Maureen A. Craig and Jennifer A. Richeson, "Stigma-Based Solidarity: Understanding the Psychological Foundations of Conflict and Coalition among Members of Different Stigmatized Groups," *Current Directions in Psychological Science* 25 (2016): 21–27.

34. Sidney Tarrow, *Power in Movement: Social Movements and Contentious Politics* (Cambridge: Cambridge University Press, 2011); Charles Tilly and Sidney Tarrow, *Contentious Politics* (Oxford, NY: Oxford University Press, 2007); Charles Tilly, *The Politics of Collective Violence* (Cambridge: Cambridge University Press, 2003); Doug McAdam, *Political Process and the Development of Black Insurgency 1930–1970* (Chicago: University of Chicago Press, 1999).

35. Chad Williams, *Torchbearers and Democracy* (Chapel Hill: University of North Carolina Press, 2010).

36. Lawrence Blum, *I'm Not a Racist but . . . The Moral Quandary of Race* (Ithaca, NY: Cornell University Press, 2002), 4.

37. Lawrence Blumer, *I'm Not a Racist but*, 5.

38. Nicole Tausch, Julia C. Becker, Russell Spears, Oliver Christ, Rim Saab, Purnima Singh, and Roomana N. Siddiqui, "Explaining Radical Group Behavior: Developing Emotion and Efficacy Routes to Normative and Nonnormative Collective Action," *Journal of Personality and Social Psychology* 101, no. 1 (2011): 129–148; Martijn van Zomeren, Russell Spears, Agneta H. Fisher, and Colin Wayne Leach, "Put Your Money where Your Mouth Is! Explaining Collective Action Tendencies through Group-Based Anger and Group Efficacy," *Journal of Personality and Social Psychology* 87, no. 5 (2004): 649–664.

39. Bert Klandermans, "Identity and Protest," in *Cooperation in Modern Society*, ed. Mark Van Vugt, Mark Snyder, Tom R. Tyler, and Anders Biel, (New York: Routledge,

2000), 163–183; Bern Simon, Michael I. Loewy, Stephen Stürmer, Ulrike Weber, Peter Freytag, Corinna Habig, and Peter Spahlinger, "Collective Identity and Social Movement Participation," *Journal of Personality and Social Psychology* 74 (1998): 646–658.

40. Emma Thomas, Craig McGarty, and Winnifred Louis, "Social Interaction and Psychological Pathways to Political Engagement and Extremism," *European Journal of Social Psychology* 44 (2014): 15–22; Jeremy Ginges and Scott Atran, "What Motivates Participation in Violent Political Action: Selective Incentives or Parochial Altruism?" *Annals of the New York Academy of Sciences* 1167 (2009): 115–123.

41. See James Jones, *Prejudice and Racism*, 2nd ed. (New York: McGraw Hill, 1997), chapter 1.

42. David Theo Goldberg, "The Semantics of Race," *Ethnic and Racial Studies* 15, no. 4 (1992): 543.

43. Martin Barker, *The New Racism* (London: Junction Books, 1981); Center for Contemporary Cultural Studies, *The Empire Strikes Back: Race and Racism in 70s Britain* (London: Hutchinson, 1982).

44. Michel Wieviorka, *Le racisme: Une introduction* (Paris: La Découverte, 2012); *The Arena of Racism* (Sage, 1996).

45. Lawrence Blum. *I'm Not a Racist, but*, 134.

46. On the evolution of racism from biology to culture, see Pierre-André Taguieff, *The Force of Prejudice; On Racism and Its Double* (Minneapolis: University of Minnesota Press, 2001); "The New Cultural Racism in France," *Telos* 83, no. 111 (1990): 123; Colette Guillaumin, *Racism Sexism, Power and Ideology* (London: Routledge, 1995).

47. Colette Guillaumin, *Racism, Sexism, Power and Ideology* (New York: Routledge, 1995), 133.

48. Gordon Allport, *The Nature of Prejudice* (Reading, MA: Addison-Wesley, 1954), 10.

49. Herbert Blumer, "Race Prejudice as a Sense of Group Position," *The Pacific Sociological Review* 1, no. 1 (1958): 3–7.

50. Charles Gallagher, "Color-Blind Egalitarianism as the New Racial Norm?" in *Theories of Race and Ethnicity*, ed. Karim Murji and John Solomos, 40–55; Eduardo Bonilla-Silva, *Racism without Racists: Color-Blind Racism and the Persistence of Racial Inequality in the United States* (New York: Rowman and Littlefield, 2003).

51. See the analysis of racial formation by Omi and Winant who analyzed how Blacks can be racist. See also Lawrence Blum, "Moral Asymmetries in Racism," in *Racism and Philosophy*, ed. Susan Babitt and Sue Campbell (Ithaca, NY: Cornell University Press, 1999), 69–73. As other minorities express racial prejudice toward whites, moral asymmetries are not limited to the white/black divide.

52. Michael Tesler, *Post-Racial or Most-Racial? Race and Politics in the Obama Era* (Chicago: The University of Chicago Press, 2016), 30.

53. Irene Taviss Thomson, *Culture Wars and Enduring American Dilemmas* (Ann Arbor: University of Michigan Press, 2010).

54. John Skrentny, *The Ironies of Affirmative Action* (Chicago: University of Chicago Press, 1996).

55. See for example Coleman Hughes, "Reflections on Intersectionality," *Quillette*, January 14, 2020, https://quillette.com/author/coleman-cruz-hughes/; Laurent Dubreuil, *La dictature des identités* (Paris: Gallimard, 2019); Walter Benn Michaels, *The Trouble with Diversity* (New York: Metropolitan, 2007); John McWhorter, *Losing the Race: Self-Sabotage in Black America* (New York: Free Press, 2000). Opposite arguments are expressed by Ryu Spaeth, "Between Thomas Chatterton Williams and Me," *The New Republic*, July 29, 2020, https://newrepublic.com/article/158644/thomas-chatterton-williams-identity-politics-debate; Robin DiAngelo, *White Fragility: Why It's So Hard for White People to Talk about Racism* (Beacon Press, 2018).

56. Discursive violence refers to hate speech, nativist propaganda, and antimigrant propaganda. It also includes more recent forms such as "microaggressions." It may be globally defined as harm committed in/by discourse. See Yasmin Jiwani, *Discourses of Denial: Mediations on Race, Gender, and Violence* (Vancouver, BC: UBC Press, 2006).

2. VIOLENCE AS A CAUSE OF ETHNORACIAL IDENTITIES

1. Nell Irvin Painter, *The History of White People* (New York: W.W. Norton, 2010), 12.
2. David R. Roediger, *Working toward Whiteness: How America's Immigrants Became White* (New York: Basic Books, 2005), 7.
3. David R. Roediger, *Working toward Whiteness*, 3.
4. Matthew Frye Jacobson, *Whiteness of a Different Color: European Immigrants and the Alchemy of Race* (Cambridge, MA: Harvard University Press, 1998), 3–4.
5. Nancy Foner and George Fredrickson, "Immigration, Race and Ethnicity in the United States: Social Constructions and Social Relations in Historical and Contemporary Perspective," in *Not Just Black and White: Historical and Contemporary Perspectives on Immigration, Race, and Ethnicity in the United States*, ed. Nancy Foner and George Fredrickson (New York: Russell Sage Foundation, 2005), 8
6. Nancy Foner and George Fredrickson, "Immigration, Race and Ethnicity," 106.
7. Stephen Steinberg, *The Ethnic Myth: Race, Ethnicity and Class in America* (Boston, MA: Beacon Press, 1981).
8. Michael Omi and Howard Winant, *Racial Formation in the United States from the 1960's to the 1990s* (New York: Routledge, 1994), 16.
9. Nancy Foner and George Fredrickson, "Immigration, Race and Ethnicity," 1.
10. On the mechanisms of assimilation, see Richard Alba and Victor Nee, *Remaking the American Mainstream: Assimilation and Contemporary Immigration* (Cambridge, MA: Harvard University Press, 2003).
11. Roger Daniels, *Coming to America: A History of Immigration and Ethnicity in American Life* (New York: HarperCollins, 2002), 145.
12. Matthew Frye Jacobson, *Whiteness of a Different Color*, 65.
13. Stefano Luconi, "The Venom of Racial Intolerance: Italian Americans and Jews in the United States in the Aftermath of Fascist Racial Laws," *Revue Française d'Etudes Américaines* 1, no. 107 (2006): 6.
14. Matthew Frye Jacobson, *Whiteness of a Different Color*, 95.
15. Nancy Carnevale, "Italian American and African American Encounters in the City and in the Suburb," *Journal of Urban History* 40, no. 3 (2014): 536. It is worth noting that the whitening strategy also helped Italians overcome their subnational divisions (as illustrated by tensions between northern and southern immigrants) and local parochialism.
16. Nancy Carnevale, "Italian American and African American Encounters," 542. See also Stefano Luconi, "Forging an Ethnic Identity: The case of Italian Americans," *Revue Française d'Etudes Américaines* 2, no. 96 (2003): 89–101.
17. Nancy Carnevale, "Italian American and African American Encounters," 537.
18. Joseph Harris, *African American Reactions to War in Ethiopia, 1936–1941* (Baton Rouge: Louisiana State University, 1994); John Digginns, *Mussolini and Fascism: The View from America* (Princeton, NJ: Princeton University Press, 1972).
19. Noel Ignatiev, *How the Irish Became White* (New York: Routledge, 1995), 41.
20. Noel Ignatiev, *How the Irish Became White*, 2.
21. Mischa Honeck. *We Are the Revolutionists: German-Speaking Immigrants and American Abolitionists After 1848* (University of Georgia Press, 2011), 186.
22. David R. Roediger, *Working toward Whiteness*, 124.
23. Quoted in Marc Schneier, *Shared Dreams: Martin Luther King Jr. and the Jewish Community* (Jewish Lights, 1999), 34.

24. Encyclopedia Judaica, "Black-Jewish Relations in the United States," 2008, http://www.jewishvirtuallibrary.org/black-jewish-relations-in-the-united-states.

25. Karen Brodkin, *How Jews Became White Folks and What That Says about Race in America* (New Brunswick, NJ: Rutgers University Press, 1999), 14.

26. Eric L. Goldstein, *The Price of Whiteness: Jews, Race, and American Identity* (Princeton, NJ: Princeton University Press, 2006), 51.

27. James Baldwin, "Negroes Are Anti-Semitic Because They're Anti-White," *New York Times Magazine*, April 9, 1967, 26.

28. Nell Irvin Painter, *The History of White People*, xv.

29. Michael Omi and Howard Winant, *Racial Formation in the United States*, 83.

30. Stephen Cornell and Douglas Hartmann, "Conceptual Confusions and Divides: Race, Ethnicity and the Study of Immigration," in *Not Just Black and White: Historical and Contemporary Perspectives on Immigration, Race, and Ethnicity in the United States*, ed. Nancy Foner and George Fredrickson (New York: Russell Sage Foundation, 2005), 23–41.

31. Nell Irvin Painter, *The History of White People*, 103.

32. Nell Irvin Painter, *The History of White People*, 104.

33. Alain Locke, ed., *The New Negro: An Interpretation* (New York: Albert and Charles Boni, 1925). See also Alain Locke, ed., *The New Negro: Voices of Harlem* (Touchstone, 1999).

34. W. E. B. Du Bois, "The Conservation of Races," in *Theories of Race*, ed. Les Back and John Solomos (New York: Routledge), 83–84.

35. Lawrence Blum, *I'm Not a Racist but*, 33.

36. Lawrence Blum, *I'm Not a Racist but*, 41.

37. Lawrence Blum, *I'm Not a Racist but*, 44.

38. Seymour Dresher, *Abolition: A History of Slavery and Anti-Slavery* (New York: Cambridge University Press, 2009).

39. Martin Luther King Jr., *A Testament of Hope: The Essential Writings and Speeches of Martin Luther King Jr.*, ed. James Washington (HarperCollins, 1990), 669.

40. Jeffrey Melnick, *A Right to Sing the Blues: African Americans, Jews, and American Popular Song* (Cambridge, MA: Harvard University Press, 2001), 196.

41. See for example Leonard Quart, "Jews and Blacks in Hollywood," *Dissent* (Fall, 1992).

42. Encyclopedia Judaica, "Black-Jewish Relations in the United States," 2008.

43. Loic Wacquant, "A Black City within the White: Revisiting America's Dark Ghetto," *Black Renaissance Noire* 2 (1998): 141–151.

44. See The Nation of Islam, *The Secret Relationship between Blacks and Jews*, 2nd ed., tome II: *How Jews Gained Control of the Black American Economy* (Nation of Islam, 2010), 25.

45. Encyclopedia Judaica, "Black-Jewish Relations in the United States," 2008. See also Seth Forman, "The Unbearable Whiteness of Being Jewish: Desegregation in the South and the Crisis of Jewish Liberalism," *American Jewish History* 85 (1997): 121–142; Waldo E. Martin, Jr., "'Nation Time!' Black Nationalism, the Third World, and Jews," in *Struggles in the Promised Land: Toward a History of Black-Jewish Relations in the United States*, ed. Jack Salzman and Cornel West (New York: Oxford University Press, 1997), 341–355.

46. See R. A. Holou, *The Most Influential Contemporary African Diaspora Leaders* (AuthorHouse, 2016), chapter 31; Michael Sherman, "The Leonard Jeffries Problem: Public University Professor/Administrators, Controversial Speech, and Constitutional Protection for Public Employees," *Loyola University Chicago Law Journal* 30, no. 4 (1999): 651–678, https://lawecommons.luc.edu/cgi/viewcontent.cgi?article=1396&context=luclj.

47. Chrystal A. George Mwangi, "Complicating Blackness: Black Immigrants & Racial Positioning in U.S. Higher Education," *Journal of Critical Thought and Praxis* 3, no. 2

(2014): 11. See also Mary C. Waters, Philip Kasinitz, and Asad L. Asad, "Immigrants and African Americans," *Annual Review of Sociology* 40 (2014): 369–90.

48. William Carrigan and Clive Webb, *Forgotten Dead: Mob Violence against Mexicans in the United States, 1848–1928* (Oxford: Oxford University Press, 2013).

49. The legal construction of a white racial identity revealed the inconsistency of the white/non-white divide and led to some major confusion. In Takao Ozawa v. United States (1922), for example, the Supreme Court relied on "scientific evidence" and "common knowledge" to exclude a Japanese applicant from citizenship, declaring he was neither Caucasian nor white. Yet in United States v. Bhagat Singh Thind (1923), the court stated than an Asian Indian immigrant was Caucasian only as a result of "scientific manipulation" and therefore not white. White skin by itself therefore did not guarantee membership in the "white race." *Re Najour*, a 1909 case in Georgia, concluded that Syrians were Caucasian and therefore white. Yet, in *Ex parte Shahid* (1913), the court decided that Syrians were not white—although they might be Caucasian—because they were not Europeans. According to Ian Haney Lopez, there were more than fifty court cases that challenged the narrowly defined provision regarding "white persons" in the Naturalization Act of 1790 before this racial prerequisite to citizenship was removed in 1952. These cases, including two that were argued before the US Supreme Court in the early 1920s, illustrated that the "white" category remained a "falsely homogenizing term" for more than a century and a half. See Ian Haney Lopez, *White by Law*, 2nd ed. (New York: New York University Press, 2006), xxi. See also Roy Martinez, ed., *On Race and Racism in America: Confessions in Philosophy* (University Park, PA: Penn State Press, 2010); James Barret and David Roediger, "Whiteness and the Inbetween Peoples of Europe," *Journal of American Ethnic History* 16, no. 3 (1997): 3–44.

50. See Joyce Kuo, "Excluded, Segregated and Forgotten: A Historical View of the Discrimination of Chinese Americans in Public Schools," *Asian American Law Journal* 5 (1998): 181–212.

51. Gordon K. Mantler, *Power to the Poor: Black-Brown Coalition and the Fight for Economic Justice* (Chapel Hill: The University of North Carolina Press, 2013).

52. Daryl Joji Maeda, *Rethinking the Asian American Movement* (New York: Routledge, 2012), 6.

53. Tanya K. Hernández, *Racial Subordination in Latin America. The Role of the State, Customary Law, and the New Civil Rights Response* (New York: Cambridge University Press, 2013). It is worth noticing that more than 90 percent of the approximately ten million enslaved Africans brought to the Americas were taken to Latin America and the Caribbean, whereas only 4.6 percent were brought to the United States. According to Hernández, immigrants from these regions arrived in the United States carrying the baggage of pervasive racism, especially anti-Black racism.

54. Tanya K. Hernández, *Racial Subordination in Latin America*, 9.

55. See Won Moo Hurth and Kwang-Chung Kim, "The 'Success' Image of Asian Americans: Its Validity, and Its Practical and Theoretical Implications," *Ethnic and Racial Studies* 12, no. 4 (1989): 512–523.

56. Trina Jones, "The Significance of Skin Color in Asian and Asian American Communities: Initial Reflections." *UC Irvine Law Review* 3 (2013): 1105.

57. Sumi K. Cho, "Korean Americans v. African Americans: Conflict and Construction," in *Reading Rodney King/Reading Urban Uprising*, ed. Robert Gooding-Williams (New York: Routledge, 1993), 205.

3. FROM PAST TO PRESENT ETHNORACIAL IDENTIFICATION STRATEGY

1. David R. Roediger, *Working toward Whiteness: How America's Immigrants Became White* (New York: Basic Books, 2005), 244.

2. Oscar Handlin, *The Uprooted: The Epic Story of the Great Migration that Made the American People* (Boston: Little Brown, 1951), 2.

3. Rupert Wilkinson, *The Pursuit of American Character* (Harper & Row, 1988).

4. Mary C. Waters, *Ethnic Options: Choosing Identities in America* (Berkeley: University of California Press, 1990), 150. See also the distinction between "minorities by will" and "minorities by force" made by J. A. Laponce, *The Protection of Minorities* (Berkeley: University of California Press, 1960).

5. N. Glazer and D. I. Moynihan, eds., *Ethnicity: Theory and Experience* (Cambridge, MA: Harvard University Press, 1975), 16.

6. Richard Alba, *Blurring the Color Line: The New Chance for a More Integrated America* (Cambridge, MA: Cambridge University Press, 2009); Philip Kasinitz, John H. Mollenkopf, Mary C. Waters, and Jennifer Holdaway, *Inheriting the City: The Children of Immigrants Come of Age* (Cambridge, MA: Harvard University Press and the Russell Sage Foundation, 2008); Andreas Wimmer, "Elementary Strategies of Ethnic Boundary Making," *Ethnic and Racial Studies* 31, no. 6 (2008): 1025–1055.

7. Jennifer Lee and Frank Bean, *The Diversity Paradox: Immigration and the Color Line in Twenty-First Century America* (New York: Russell Sage Foundation, 2010), 15.

8. David Hollinger, *Post-Ethnic America: Beyond Multiculturalism* (New York: Basic Books, 1995), 14.

9. Peter Salins, *Assimilation, American Style* (New York: Basic Books, 1997), 39.

10. Mary C. Waters, *Ethnic Options: Choosing Identities in America*, 18.

11. Ira Katznelson, *When Affirmative Action Was White: An Untold History of Racial Inequality in Twentieth-Century America* (New York: W.W. Norton, 2006).

12. Eric Lott, "White like Me: Racial Cross-Dressing and the Construction of American Whiteness," in *Cultures of United States Imperialism*, ed. A. Kaplan and D. E. Pease (Durham, NC: Duke University Press, 1993), 480.

13. James Johnson, Walter Farrell, and Chandra Guinn, "Immigration Reform and the Browning of America: Tensions, Conflicts and Community Instability in Metropolitan Los Angeles," *The International Migration Review* 31, no. 4 (1997): 1055–1095; Jack Citrin, Beth Reingold, and Donald Green, "American Identity and the Politics of Ethnic Change," *Journal of Politics* 52, no. 4 (1990): 1124–1154.

14. Richard Alba, "The Likely Persistence of a White Majority," *The American Prospect Magazine*, Winter issue, http://prospect.org/article/likely-persistence-white-majority-0.

15. George Borjas, *Heaven's Door* (Princeton, NJ: Princeton University Press, 1999); Peter Brimelow, *Alien Nation: Common Sense about America's Immigration Disaster* (New York: Random House, 1995).

16. P. Burns and J. G. Gimpel, "Economic Insecurity, Prejudicial Stereotypes, and Public Opinion on Immigration Policy," *Political Science Quarterly* 115, no. 2 (2000): 201–225; M. V. Hood and I. L. Morris, "Give Us Your Tired, Your Poor . . . But Make Sure They Have a Green Card: The Effects of Documented and Undocumented Migrant Context on Anglo-Saxon Opinion toward Immigration," *Political Behavior* 20, no. 1 (1998): 1–15; Jack Citrin, Donald P. Green, Christopher Muste, and Cara Wong, "Public Opinion toward Immigration: The Role of Economic Motivations," *The Journal of Politics* 59, no. 3 (1997): 858–881.

17. Pew Research Center, *America Immigration Quandary* (Washington, DC: Pew Research Center, 2006).

18. Marvin V. Hood, Irvin Morris, and Kurt Shirkey, "! Quedate o Vente! Uncovering the Determinants of Hispanics Public Opinion toward Immigration," *Political Research Quarterly* 50, no. 3 (1997): 627–647.

19. Nell Irvin Painter, *The History of White People*, (New York: W.W. Norton, 2010), xv.

20. Nell Irvin Painter, *The History of White People*, 317.

21. W. E. B. Du Bois, "The Conservation of Races," in *Theories of Race*, ed. Les Back and John Solomos (New York: Routledge), 83–84.

22. Nell Irvin Painter, *The History of White People*, 194. See also Nicole Philipps, *Patriotism Black and White: The Color of American Exceptionalism* (Waco, TX: Baylor University Press, 2018); Micah Johnson, "The Paradox of Black Patriotism: Double Consciousness," *Ethnic and Racial Studies* 41, no. 41 (2017): 1–19.

23. National Archives, "Vietnam War US Military Fatal Casualty Statistics," April 9, 2008, https://www.archives.gov/research/military/vietnam-war/casualty-statistics.

24. Juan Battle, Michael Bennett, and Anthony Lemelle Jr., *Free at Last? Black America in the Twenty-First Century* (New York: Routledge, 2017), 38.

25. Michael Omi and Howard Winant, *Racial Formation in the United States from the 1960's to the 1990s* (New York: Routledge, 1994), 16. See also Robert C. Smith, *Racism in the Post-Civil Rights Era: Now You See It, Now You Don't* (New York: State University of New York Press, 1995).

26. Quoted by John Eligon, "A Debate over Identity and Race Asks, Are African Americans 'Black' or 'black'?" *New York Times*, June 26, 2020, https://www.nytimes.com/2020/06/26/us/black-african-american-style-debate.html.

27. Nell Irvin Painter, *The History of White People*, 276.

28. Malcolm X broke with the NOI in 1963.

29. Stokely Carmichael (later know as Kwame Ture) and Charles V. Hamilton, *Black Power: The Politics of Liberation in America*, 2nd ed. (New York: Random House/Vintage Books, 1992), 39.

30. Stokely Carmichael and Charles V. Hamilton, *Black Power*, 44.

31. Ira Berlin, *The Making of African Americans* (New York: Viking, 2010), 78.

32. William Petersen, "Success Story, Japanese American Style," *New York Times Magazine*, January 9, 1996, 180

33. Gregg Lee Carter, "Hispanic Rioting during the Civil Rights Era," *Sociological Forum* 7, no. 2 (1992): 301.

34. Claire Jean Kim, "The Racial Triangulation of Asian Americans," *Politics & Society* 27, vol. 1 (1999): 105–138.

35. Eric Liu, *The Accidental Asian* (New York: Random House, 1998), 54.

36. Claire Jean Kim and Taeku Lee, "Interracial Politics: Asian Americans and Other Communities of Color," *PS, Political Science & Politics* 34, no. 53 (2001): 631–637; Angelo Ancheta, *Race, Rights, and the Asian American Experience* (New Brunswick, NJ: Rutgers University Press, 1998).

37. Gary Okihira, *Margins and Mainstreams: Asians in American History and Culture* (Seattle: University of Washington Press, 1994), 32.

38. Noel Ignatiev, "Treason to Whiteness is Loyalty to Humanity," in *Critical White Studies: Looking Behind the Mirror*, ed. Richard Delgado and Jean Stefancic (Temple, PA: Temple University Press, 1997).

39. In addition to the violent episodes I mentioned in chapter 1, it is worth remembering that in 1870 and 1872, the legislature modified the 1860 school code to prevent Chinese-American children from attending separate schools. In 1885, the California Supreme Court declared that Chinese students must be admitted into the public school system—effectively replacing legal exclusion with segregation in "separate but equal" facilities. Chinese, Japanese, and Korean children were subsequently sent to "oriental public schools." The Immigration Act of 1924 introduced a global racial hierarchy that excluded certain categories (mainly Asians) and criminalized others (mainly Hispanics). The process of racial exclusion targeted Mexican, Filipino, and Asian workers—labeled respectively as "illegal aliens," "colonial subjects," and "alien citizens." It provided the foundation

for the mass deportation of Filipinos during the 1930s, the internment of 120,000 Japanese during World War II, and the Denationalization Act of July 1944.

40. On the ACJ and other pan-Asian organizations created in the 1980s and early 1992, see Yen Lee Esperitu, *Asian American Panethnicity: Bridging Institutions and Identities* (Temple, PA: Temple University Press, 1992)

41. Daryl Joji Maeda, *Rethinking the Asian American Movement* (New York: Routledge, 2012).

42. France Winddance Twine and Charles A. Gallagher, "The Future of Whiteness: A Map of the Third Wave," in *Retheorizing Race and Whiteness in the 21st Century*, ed. Charles A. Gallagher and France Winddance Twine (New York: Routledge, 2012), 1–21.

43. See "Success Story of One Minority Group in the US," *U.S. News & World Report* (December 26, 1906), 73ff; Martin Kasindorf, "Asian-Americans: A Model Minority," *Newsweek* (December 6, 1982), 39ff; Davis Bell, "The Triumph of Asian Americans," *The New Republic* (July 1985); P. Wong, C. F. Lai, R. Nagasawa, and T. Lin, "Asian Americans as a Model Minority: Self Perceptions and Perceptions by Other Racial Groups," *Sociological Perspectives* 41, no. 1 (1998): 95–118.

44. Giselle Giselle, "The Model Minority Myth," *Independent School Magazine* (Winter 2011), https://www.nais.org/magazine/independent-school/winter-2011/the-model-minority-myth/

45. Ki-Taek Chun, "The Myth of Asian American Success and Its Educational Ramifications," in *The Asian American Educational Experience*, ed. Don Nakanishi and Tina Yamano Nishida (New York: Routledge, 1995).

46. Claire Jean Kim and Taeku Lee, "Interracial Politics" 634.

47. Richard Alba, Tomas Jimenez, and Helen Marrow, "Mexican Americans as a Paradigm for Contemporary Intra-Group Heterogeneity," *Ethnic and Racial Studies* 37, no. 3 (2014): 446–466; Tomas Jimenez, *Replenished Ethnicity: Mexican Americans, Immigration, and Identity* (Berkeley: University of California Press, 2010); Edward Telles and Vilma Ortiz, *Generations of Exclusion: Mexican Americans, Assimilation, and Race* (New York: Russell Sage, 2008).

48. Jessica Vasquez, "The Whitening Hypothesis Challenged: Biculturalism in Latino and Non-Hispanic White Intermarriage," *Sociological Forum* 29, vol. 2 (2014): 386–407; Jose Itzigsohn, "The Formation of Latino and Latina Panethnic Identities," in *Not Just Black and White: Historical and Contemporary Perspectives on Immigration, Race, and Ethnicity in the United States*, ed. Nancy Foner and George Fredrickson (New York: Russell Sage Foundation, 2004); Alcoff Linda, "Is Latina/o Identity a Racial Identity?" in *Hispanics/Latinos in the United States*, ed. Jorge J. E. Garcia and Pablo De Greiff (New York: Routledge, 2000); Clara Rodriguez, *Changing Race: Latinos, the Census, and the History of Ethnicity in the United States* (New York: New York University Press, 2000).

49. Carleen Basler, "White Dreams and Red Votes: Mexican Americans and the Lure of Inclusion in the Republican Party," in *Retheorizing Race and Whiteness in the 21st Century*, ed. Charles A. Gallagher and France Winddance Twine (New York: Routledge, 2012), 135.

50. Available at http://www.thearda.com/Archive/Files/Descriptions/LSASN.asp.

51. Alison Newby and Julie Dowling, "Black and Hispanic: The Racial Identification of Afro-Cuban Immigrants in the Southwest," *Sociological Perspectives* 50, no. 3 (2007): 343–366; Susan Greenbaum, *More than Black: Afro-Cubans in Tampa* (Gainesville: University Press of Florida, 2002); Mary Waters, *Black Identities: West Indian Immigrant Dreams and American Realities* (Cambridge, MA: Harvard University Press, 1999).

52. Yvette Alex, "Introduction," in *Blacks and Multiracial Politics in America*, ed. Yvette Alex and Lawrence Hanks (New York: New York University Press, 2000), 24.

53. Jennifer Hochschild, "Race Relations in a Diversifying Nation," 140.

54. Pei-te Lien, *The Political Participation of Asian Americans* (New York: Garland, 1997); Rodolfo De la Garza, "The Effect of Ethnicity on Political Culture," in *Classifying by Race*, ed. Paul Peterson (Princeton, NJ: Princeton University Press, 1995), 333–353; Rodolfo de la Garza, Louis DeSipio, Angelo Falcon, F. Chris Garcia, and John A. Garcia, *Latino Voices: Mexican, Puerto Rican, and Cuban Perspectives on American Politics* (Boulder, CO: Westview Press, 1992).

55. Zoltan Hajnal and Taeku Lee, "Out of Line: Immigration and Party Identification among Latinos and Asian Americans," in *Transforming Politics, Transforming America*, ed. Taeku Lee, S. Karthick Ramakrishnan, and Ricardo Ramirez (Charlottesville: University of Virginia Press, 2006), 129–150.

56. Anthony Wang, "Conservative: A Strange and New Political Animal?" *Asian Journal Law* 5 (1998): 215.

57. Pew Research Center, *Party Affiliation Among Voters: 1992–2016*, September 13, 2016, https://www.people-press.org/2016/09/13/the-parties-on-the-eve-of-the-2016-election-two-coalitions-moving-further-apart/.

58. Leah Wright Rigueur, *The Loneliness of the Black Republican* (Princeton, NJ: Princeton University Press, 2015); Angela Lewis, "Black Conservatism in America," *Journal of African Studies* 8, no. 4 (2005): 3–13; Lewis Randolph, "A Historical Analysis and Critique of Contemporary Black Conservatism," *Western Journal of Black Studies* 19 (1995): 149–163.

59. David Roediger, *The Wages of Whiteness: Race and the Making of the American Working Class* (New York: Verso, 1999).

60. David Jacobs and Daniel Tope, "The Politics of Resentment in the Post-Civil Rights Era: Minority Threat, Homicide, and Ideological Voting in Congress," *American Journal of Sociology* 112, no. 5 (2007): 1459.

61. Dominic Capeci Jr., "American Race Rioting in Historical Perspective," in *Encyclopedia of American Race Riots*, ed. Walter Rucker and James Nathaniel Upton, vol. 1 (Westport, CT: Greenwood Press, 2007), xxxiii.

4. THE DYNAMICS OF CONTENTION

1. Suzanne Shanahan and Olzak Olzak, "The Effects of Immigrant Diversity and Ethnic Competition on Collective Conflict in Urban America: An Assessment of Two Moments of Mass Migration, 1869–1924 and 1965–1993," *Journal of American Ethnic History*, Spring Issues 1999, 47.

2. Southern Poverty Law Center, "A Retrospective of Hate Incidents and Groups in the 1990s," March 15, 2000, https://www.splcenter.org/fighting-hate/intelligence-report/2000/retrospective-hate-incidents-and-groups-1900s.

3. Regina Branton and Bradford Jones, "Re-examining Racial Attitudes: The Conditional Relationship between Diversity and Socio-Economic Environment," *American Journal of Political Science* 49, no. 2 (2005): 359–372; Paula McClain and Steven Tauber, "Racial Minority Group Relations in a Multiracial Society," in *Governing American Cities*, ed. Michael Jones-Correa (New York: Russell Sage Foundation, 2001), 111–136.

4. Susan Olzak, *The Dynamics of Ethnic Competition and Conflict* (Stanford, CA: Stanford University Press, 1992).

5. See P. M. Blau and O. D. Duncan, *The American Occupational Structure* (New York: John Wiley and Sons, 1967); D. S. Massey and N. A. Denton, *American Apartheid: Segregation and the Making of the Underclass* (Cambridge, MA: Harvard University Press); William J. Wilson, *The Truly Disadvantaged: The Inner City, the Underclass, and Public Policy* (Chicago: University of Chicago Press, 1987).

6. Lawrence Bobo, "Racial Attitudes and Relations at the Close of the Twentieth Century," in *America Becoming: Racial Trends and their Consequences* volume 1, ed. Neil

Smelter, William Julius Wilson, and Faith Mitchell (Washington, DC: The National Academies, 2001), 264.

7. Jennifer Lee and Frank Bean, "America's Changing Color Lines: Immigration, Race/Ethnicity, and Multiracial Identification," *Annual Review of Sociology* 30 (2004): 228.

8. Kim Williams, *Mark One or More: Civil Rights in Multiracial America* (Ann Arbor: University of Michigan Press, 2008).

9. Richard Alba and Victor Nee, *Remaking the American Mainstream: Assimilation and Contemporary Immigration* (Cambridge, MA: Harvard University Press, 2003).

10. Thomas Byrne Edsall and Mary Edsall, *The Chain Reaction: The Impact of Race, Rights and Taxes on American Politics* (New York: W.W. Norton, 1991).

11. Pamela Paxton and Anthony Muhan, "What's to Fear from Immigrants? Creating an Assimilationists Scale," *Political Psychology* 27, no. 4 (2006): 549–568; Leo Chavez, *Covering Immigration: Population, Images and the Politics of the Nation* (Berkeley: University of California Press, 2001); Peter Burns and James Gimpel, "Economic Insecurity, Prejudicial Stereotype, and Public Opinion," *Political Science Quarterly* 115 (2000): 201–225; Jack Citrin, Donald P. Green, Christopher Muste, and Cara Wong, "Public Opinion toward Immigration: The Role of Economic Motivations," *Journal of Politics* 59 (1997): 858–881.

12. Michael Goldfield, *The Color of Politics: Race and the Mainspring of American Politics* (New York: New Press, 1997); Michael Giles and Kaenan Hertz, "Racial Threat and Partisan Identification," *American Political Science Review* 88 (1994): 317–326. At least fifteen restrictive immigration bills passed from 1965 to 2010. The Refugee Act of 1980, for example, abolished refugee preference and reduced the worldwide ceiling to 270,000. The Immigration Reform and Control Act of 1986 criminalized undocumented hiring and authorized the expansion of the US Border Patrol. Ten years later, the Anti-Terrorism and Effective Death Penalty Act of 1996 authorized expedited removal of noncitizens and deportation of aggravated felons. The Personal Responsibility and Work Opportunity Act declared immigrants (both legal and illegal) ineligible for certain entitlements.

13. Tanton also founded the Social Contract Press in 1990 to publish nativist publications, such as the French novel "The Camps of Saints" that inspired Steve Bannon. His associate, Roy Beck started NumbersUSA, which expressed populist claims (by faxes) to policymakers.

14. According to the Southern Poverty Law Center, leaders of the Minuteman Project also claimed that their volunteers were "White Martin Luther Kings" and compared their "fight to protect America" to the civil rights movement. See "Minutemen, Other Anti-Migrant Militia Groups Stake Out Arizona Border," *Intelligence Report* (Summer 2005), https://www.splcenter.org/fighting-hate/intelligence-report/2005/minutemen-other-anti-immigrant-militia-groups-stake-out-arizona-border.

15. Euna Oh, Chun-Chung Choi, Helen Neville, Carolyn Anderson, and Jocelyn Landrum-Brown, "Beliefs about Affirmative Action: A Test of the Group-Interest and Racism Beliefs Models," *Journal of Diversity in Higher Education* 3, no. 3 (2010): 163–176; Garriy Shteynberg, Lisa Leslie, Andrew Knight, and David Mayer, "But Affirmative Action Hurts Us! Race-Related Beliefs Shape Perceptions of White Disadvantage and Policy Unfairness," *Organizational Behavior and Human Decision Process* 115 (2011): 1–12; Paul Sniderman and Thomas Piazza, *The Scar of Race* (Cambridge, MA: Harvard University Press, 1993).

16. Jennifer Hochschild, "Race Relations in a Diversifying Nation," in *New Directions: African Americans in a Diversifying Nation*, ed. James Jackson (Washington: National Planning Association, 2000), 130.

17. Howard Schuman, Charlotte Steeh, Lawrence Bobo, and Maria Krysan, *Racial Attitudes in America: Trends and Interpretation* (Cambridge, MA: Harvard University

Press, 1997); Donald Kinder and Lynn Sanders, *Divided by Color: Racial Attitudes and Democratic Ideals* (Chicago: University of Chicago Press, 1996).

18. Gallup, "Black-White Relations in the United States," June 10, 1997, https://news.gallup.com/poll/9874/blackwhite-relations-united-states-1997.aspx.

19. Washington Post survey quoted by Jennifer Hochschild, "Race Relations in a Diversifying Nation," 123.

20. Jennifer Hochschild, "Race Relations in a Diversifying Nation," 127.

21. Jennifer Hochschild, "Race Relations in a Diversifying Nation," 1012.

22. Charles Hirschman, Richard Alba, and Reynolds Farley, "The Meaning and Measurement of Race in the US Census," *Demography* 37, no. 3 (2000): 382.

23. Kim Williams, *Mark One or More: Civil Rights in Multiracial America*, 5.

24. Quoted in Kim Williams, *Mark One or More: Civil Rights in Multiracial America*, 14.

25. Jennifer Lee and Frank Bean, *The Diversity Paradox: Immigration and the Color Line in Twenty-First Century* (New York: Russell Sage Foundation, 2010), 47.

26. Milton Gordon, *Assimilation in American Life: The Role of Race, Religion and National Origin* (Oxford: Oxford University Press, 1964). On the evolution of ethnic boundaries, see Aristide Zolberg and Long Litt Woon, "Why Islam Is Like Spanish: Cultural Incorporation in Europe and the United States," *Politics and Society* 27, no. 1 (1999): 5–38; Andreas Wimmer, "Elementary Strategies of Ethnic Boundary Making," *Ethnic and Racial Studies* 31, no. 6 (2008): 1025–1055.

27. George M. Fredrickson, *Racism: A Short History* (Princeton, NJ: Princeton University Press, 2002), 155.

28. George M. Fredrickson, *Racism: A Short History*, 141.

29. Kathleen Kemp, "Race, Ethnicity, Class and Urban Spatial Conflict: Chicago as a Crucial Test," *Urban Studies* 23 (1986): 199.

30. People of Haitian descend make up 20 percent of the Caribbean population in Flatbush. See Jeffrey Mays, "In Brooklyn, Push for a Special Haitian District Hits Resistance," *New York Times*, April 17, 2018, https://www.nytimes.com/2018/04/17/nyregion/brooklyn-little-haiti.html?emc=edit_th_180418&nl=todaysheadlines&nlid=651051570418.

31. Amy Chua, *Political Tribes: Group Instinct and the Fate of Nations* (New York: Penguin Random House, 2018), 34.

32. Todd Gitlin, "The Left, Lost in the Politics of Identity," *Harper's Magazine*, 1993, https://harpers.org/archive/1993/09/the-left-lost-in-the-politics-of-identity/.

33. Rebecca Walker, "Becoming the Third Wave," *Ms Magazine*, 1992, http://heathengrrl.blogspot.com/2007/02/becoming-third-wave-by-rebecca-walker.html. Walker wrote this manifest in support of Anita Hill's testimony against Clarence Thomas, who was nominated (and confirmed) to the US Supreme Court. See also Elizabeth Evans, "What Makes a (Third) Wave?" *Feminist Journal of Politics* 18, no. 3 (2016): 409–428; Jennifer Baumgardner and Amy Richards, *ManifestA: Young Women, Feminism, and the Future* (New York: Farrar, Straus and Giroux, 2000); Leslie Heywood and Jennifer Drake, eds., *Third-Wave Agenda: Being Feminist, Doing Feminism* (Minneapolis: University of Minnesota Press, 1997).

34. Kimberle Crenshaw, "Demarginalizing the Intersection of Race and Sex: A Black Feminist Critique of Antidiscrimination Doctrine, Feminist Theory and Antiracist Politics," *University of Chicago Legal Forum* 1, no. 8 (1989): 139–167.

35. Neil Smith, *The New Urban Frontier: Gentrification and the Revanchist City* (New York: Routledge, 1996), 42.

36. Jonathan Dean, "Who's Afraid of Third-Wave Feminism?" *International Feminist Journal of Politics* 11, no. 3 (2009): 334–352.

37. Peter Hopkins and Greg Noble, "Masculinities in Place: Situated Identities, Relations, and Intersectionality," *Social and Cultural Geography* 10, no. 8 (2009): 1470–1197.

38. Many mythopoetic groups referred to the work of Robert Bly, notably his book *Iron John: A Book about Men* (Reading, MA: Addison-Wesley) published in 1990. See also Thompson K. Thompson, ed., *To Be a Man: In Search of the Deep Masculine* (New York: Jeremy P. Tarcher/Perigee Book, 1991).

39. Alastair Bonnett, "The New Primitives: Identity, Landscape, and Cultural Appropriation in the Mythopoetic Men's Movement," *Antipodes* 28, no. 3 (1996): 277.

40. Katharyne Mitchell, "Geographies of Identity: Multiculturalism Unplugged," *Progress in Human Geography* 28, no. 5 (2004): 641–651; Richard Alba and Victor Nee, *Remaking the American Mainstream: Assimilation and Contemporary Immigration* (Cambridge, MA: Harvard University Press, 2003).

41. Rogers Brubaker, "The Return of Assimilation? Changing Perspectives on Immigration and Its Sequels in France, Germany and the United States," in *Toward Assimilation and Citizenship: Immigrants in Liberal Nation-States*, ed. Christian Joppke and Ewa Morawska (Basingstoke: Palgrave Macmillan, 2003), 51.

42. Samuel Huntington, *Who Are We: The Challenges to America's National Identity* (New York: Simon and Schuster, 2004); *The Clash of Civilization and the Remaking of the World Order* (New York: Simon and Schuster, 1996).

43. Alan Bloom, *The Closing of American Mind* (New York: Simon and Schuster, 1987). Other examples of anti-multicultural studies included: Richard Bernstein, *Dictatorship of Virtue: How the Battle over Multiculturalism Is Reshaping Our Schools* (New York: Vintage Books, 1994); E. D. Hirsh, *Cultural Literacy: What Every American Needs to Know* (Boston, MA: Houghton Mifflin, 1987).

44. David Savran, *Taking It Like a Man: White Masculinity, Masochism, and Contemporary American Culture* (Princeton, NJ: Princeton University Press, 1998), 4.

45. Charles Gallagher, "White Reconstruction in the University," *Socialist Review* 24, no. 1–2 (1995): 169.

46. Roberta Senechal de la Roche, "Collective Violence as Social Control," *Sociological Forum* 11, no. 1 (1996): 97–128; Floya Anthis and Nira Yuval-Davis, *Racialized Boundaries: Race, Nation, Gender, Colour and Class and the Anti-Racist Struggle* (London: Routledge, 1992); Donald Black, *The Behavior of Law* (New York: Academic Press, 1976).

47. Nancy Ehrenreich, "Subordination and Symbiosis: Mechanisms of Mutual Support between Subordinating Systems," *UMKC Law Review* 71 (2002), 251. See also Robert Change and Jerome Culp McCristal, "After Intersectionality," *UMKC Law Review* 71 (2002), 485.

48. This is illustrated, for example, by the work of Kyla Schuller, a white historian and feminist scholar, who analyzed the failure of white feminism in her book, *The Trouble With White Women: A Counterhistory of Feminism* (Bold Type Books, 2019).

49. Margaret Villanueva, "Ambivalent Sisterhood," *Discourse* 21, no. 3 (1999): 49–76; Maxine Baca Zim and Bonnie Thornton Dill, "Theorizing Difference from Multiracial Feminism," *Feminist Studies* 22 (1996): 321–333.

50. Marianne Debouzy, "Protest Marches in the United States in the Nineteenth and Twentieth Centuries," *Le Mouvement Social* 1, no. 202 (2003): 10.

51. Supported by the National Coalition of Blacks for Reparations in America (N'COBRA), HR 40 has never made it to the House floor.

52. Kevin Brown and Jeannine Bell, "Demise of the Talented Tenth: Affirmative Action and the Increasing Underrepresentation of Ascendant Blacks at Selective Higher Educational Institutions," *Ohio State Law Journal* 69 (2008): 1236.

53. Kevin Brown and Renee Turner, "Redefining the Black Face of Affirmative Action: The Impact on Ascendant Black Women," *Articles by Maurer Faculty* 48 (2012), https://www.repository.law.indiana.edu/facpub/1284/.

54. Michael Sherer and Amy Wang, "A Few Liberal Activists Challenged Kamala Harris's Black Authenticity," *Washington Post*, July 8, 2019, https://www.washingtonpost.com/politics/a-few-liberal-activists-challenged-kamala-harriss-black-authenticity-the-presidents-son-amplified-their-message/2019/07/07/f46c4b8a-9ccd-11e9-85d6-5211733f92c7_story.html.

55. Richard Collier, *Masculinity, Law and Family* (London: Routledge, 1995).

56. Alastair Bonnett, "Anti-Racism and the Critique of White Identity," *New Community* 22 (1996): 97–110.

57. Liam Stack, "Alt-Right, Alt Left, Antifa: A Glossary of Extremist Language," *New York Times*, August 15, 2017, https://www.nytimes.com/2017/08/15/us/politics/alt-left-alt-right-glossary.html.

58. Lawrence Bobo and Vincent L. Hutchings, "Perceptions of Racial Group Competition: Extending Blumer's Theory of Group Position to a Multiracial Social Context," *American Sociological Review* 61 (1996): 951–972.

59. David Meyer and Sidney Tarrow, eds., *The Social Movement Society: Contentious Politics for a New Century* (Lanham, MD: Rowman & Littlefield, 1998), 23.

60. Doug McAdam and Karina Kloos, *Deeply Divided: Racial Politics and Social Movements in Postwar America* (Oxford, NY: Oxford University Press, 2004).

61. Quoted by David Jacobs and Daniel Tope, "The Politics of Resentment in the Post–Civil Rights Era: Minority Threat, Homicide, and Ideological Voting in Congress," *American Journal of Sociology* 112, no. 5 (2007): 1460.

62. In 1992, non-Hispanic whites represented 84 percent of all registered voters. Only 10 percent were Blacks, and 5 percent were Hispanics. Furthermore, 93 percent of Republican voters were white—which explained the color-coded strategy followed by the GOP.

63. Doug Mc Adam and Karina Kloos, *Deeply Divided: Racial Politics and Social Movements in Postwar America*, 257.

64. In 2015, nine Black churchgoers were killed in Charleston, South Carolina, by an avowed white supremacist obsessed with Confederate symbology, sparking a public outcry to remove statues that celebrate the Confederacy. In total, at least eight statues were removed in 2015 and 2016, and thirty-six more were removed in 2017, the year a rally to protest the removal of a Robert E. Lee statue in Charlottesville, Virginia, turned violent. Already, at least another twenty-six have been taken down in 2020 in response to the police killing of George Floyd that led to protests worldwide.

65. ADL Center on Extremism, "New Hate and Old: The Changing Face of American White Supremacy" (2015), https://www.adl.org/new-hate-and-old.

66. Michael Dawson, *Not in Our Lifetimes: The Future of Black Politics* (Chicago: The University of Chicago Press, 2011), 153.

67. US Department of Justice, "Youth Gang Homicides in the 1990s," *OJJP Fact Sheet* 3 (2001): 3; Carolyn Rebecca Block, Antigone Christakos, Jacob Ayad, and Roger Przybylski, *Street Gang and Crime: Patterns and Trends in Chicago* (Chicago: Criminal Justice Information Authority, 1996); Malcom W. Klein, *The American Street Gang: Its Nature, Prevalence, and Control* (New York: Oxford University Press, 1995).

68. For a review of all the various theoretical explanations of gang violence, see S. E. Costanza and Ronald Helms, "Street Gangs and Aggregate Homicides: An Analysis of Effects During the 1990s Violent Crime Peak," *Homicide Studies* 16, no. 3 (2012): 280–307.

69. James C. Howell, Arlen Egley Jr., George E. Tita, and Elizabeth Griffiths, "U.S. Gang Problem Trends and Seriousness, 1996–2009," *National Gang Center Bulletin* 6 (US

Department of Justice, 2011), https://www.nationalgangcenter.gov/Content/Docume nts/Bulletin-6.PDF.

70. Ruben Rumbaut and Walter Ewing, "The Myth of Immigrant Criminality and the Paradox of Assimilation," *American Immigration Law Foundation* 1, no. 16 (2007); Ramiro Martinez and Matthew Lee, "On Immigration and Crime," *Criminal Justice* 1 (2007): 485–52.

71. Sam Torres, "Hate Crimes against Americans," *Journal of Contemporary Criminal Justice* 15, no. 1 (1999): 48–63.

72. Sam Torres, "Hate Crimes against Americans," 57.

73. Edward Dunbar, "Defending the Indefensible: A Critique and Analysis of Psycholegal Defense Arguments of Hate Crime Perpetuators," *Journal of Contemporary Criminal Justice* 15, no. 1 (1999): 67.

74. Carolyn Petrosino, "Connecting the Past to the Future: Hate Crime in America," *Journal of Contemporary Criminal Justice* 15, no. 1 (1999): 26.

75. Carolyn Petrosino, "Connecting the Past to the Future: Hate Crime in America," 38.

76. Caitlin Liu, "Beyond Black and White: Chinese Americans Challenge San Francisco's Desegregation Plan," *Asian Law Journal* 5 (1997): 350.

77. Bill Mullen and Fred Ho, *Afro-Asia: Revolutionary Political and Cultural Connections between African Americans and Asian Americans* (Durham and London: Duke University Press, 2008); Robin Kelley, "Black Like Mao," *Souls*, Fall Issue, 1999, 6–41.

78. Gordon Mantler, *Power to the Poor: Black-Brown Coalition and the Fight for Economic Justice* (Chapel Hill: The University of North Carolina Press, 2013).

79. Sylvia Zamora, "Black and Brown in Los Angeles: Beyond Conflict and Coalition," *Ethnic and Racial Studies* 38, no. 8 (2015): 1473–1475; David Barlow, "Black-Brown Solidarity: Racial Politics in the New Gulf South," *Ethnic and Racial Studies* 38, no. 8 (2015): 1429–1431; Frederick Douzet, *The Color of Power: Racial Coalitions and Political Power in Oakland* (Charlottesville: University of Virginia Press, 2012).

80. On other examples, see Rufus Browning, Dale R. Marshall, and David H. Tabb, *Protest Is Not Enough* (Berkeley: University of California Press, 1984); Bryan Jackson, Elizabeth R. Gerber, and Bruce E. Cain, "Coalition Prospects in a Multi-Racial Society: African American Attitudes toward Other Minority Groups," *Political Research Quarterly* 47, no. 2 (1994): 277–94; Ella Stewart, "Communication between African Americans and Korean Americans: Before and After the Los Angeles Riots," *Amerasia Journal* 19, no. 2 (1993): 23–53; Karen Kauffmann, "Cracks in the Rainbow: Group Commonality as a Basis for Latino and African-American Political Coalitions," *Political Research Quarterly* 56, no. 2 (2003): 199–210.

81. David Roediger, *The Wages of Whiteness: Race and the Making of the American Working Class* (New York: Verso Books, 1991), 204.

82. Kevin Wallsten and Tatishe Nteta, "Race, Partisanship, and Perceptions of Inter-Minority Commonality," *Politics, Groups, and Identities* 5, no. 2 (2017): 298–320; Leland Saito and Park Edward Park, "Multiracial Collaborations and Coalitions," in *The State of Asian Pacific America, Volume IV: Transforming Race Relations*, ed. Paul Ong (Los Angeles: UCLA Asian American Studies Center, 2000), 435–474; Walter L. Wallace, *The Future of Ethnicity, Race, and Nationality* (Westport, CT: Praeger, 1997); A. Melucci, "Getting Involved: Identity and Mobilization in Social Movements," in *From Structure to Action: Comparing Social Movement Research Across Cultures*, ed. Bert Klandermans, Kriesi Haspeter, and Sidney Tarrow (Greenwich, CT: JAI Press, 1988), 329–348; C. Enloe, "The Growth of the State and Ethnic Mobilization," *Ethnic and Racial Studies* 4 (1981): 123–136.

83. David Colburn and Jeffrey Adler, *African-American Mayors: Race, Politics, and the American City* (Chicago: University of Illinois Press, 2005).

84. Jason Rivera, DeMond Miller, and Deborah Wright, "The Future Effectiveness of Racial-Political Coalitions in American Politics," *Journal of Public Management & Social Policy* Spring Issue, 2008, 9.

85. Michael Jones-Correra, "Bringing Outsiders In: Questions of Immigrant Incorporation," in *The Politics of Democratic Inclusion*, ed. Christina Wolbrecht and Rodney E. Hero (Philadelphia, PA: Temple University Press, 2005), 86.

86. David Gutierrez, *Walls and Mirrors: Mexican Americans, Mexican Immigrants, and the Politics of Ethnicity* (Berkeley: University of California Press, 1995).

87. Christina Beltran, *The Trouble with Unity: Latino Politics and the Creation of Identity* (Oxford: Oxford University Press, 2010), 113.

88. Eric Yamamoto, *Interracial Justice: Conflicts and Reconciliation in Post-Civil Rights America* (New York: New York University Press, 1999); S. Dong, "Too Many Asians: The Challenge of Fighting Discrimination against Asian Americans and Preserving Affirmative Action," *Stanford Law Review* 47 (1995): 1027–1057.

89. Takeyuki Tsuda, "I'm American, Not Japanese! The Struggle for Racial Citizenship among Later-Generation Japanese Americans," *Ethnic and Racial Studies* 37, no. 3 (2014): 405–424.

90. Michael Flamm, *Law and Order: Street Crime, Civil Unrest, and the Crisis of Liberalism* (New York: Columbia University Press, 2005).

91. Wendy Brown, *States of Injury: Power and Freedom in Late Modernity* (Princeton, NJ: Princeton University Press, 1995), 32. See also Susan Bickford, "Anti-Anti-Identity Politics: Feminism, Democracy, and the Complexities of Democracy," *Hypathia* 12, no. 4 (1997): 111–131.

92. Todd Gitling, "The Left, Lost in the Politics of Identity," *Harper's Magazine*, September 1993, 18–19.

93. Jean Bethke Elshtain, *Democracy on Trial* (New York: Basic Books, 1995), 74.

PART 2. CURRENT TRAJECTORIES OF VIOLENCE IN POST-RACIAL AMERICA

1. From Operation Blockade in 1993 to Operation Copper Cactus in 2010, border escalation involved at least sixteen initiatives covering locations along the Mexico-United States border as well as within the United States. At least fifteen restrictive immigration bills were passed from 1965 to 2010. The Refugee Act of 1980, for example, abolished refugee preference and reduced the worldwide ceiling to 270,000. The Immigration Reform and Control Act of 1986 criminalized undocumented hiring and authorized the expansion of the Border Patrol. Ten years later, the Anti-Terrorism and Effective Death Penalty Act of 1996 authorized expedited removal of noncitizens and deportation of aggravated felons, and the Personal Responsibility and Work Opportunity Act declared immigrants (both legal and illegal) ineligible for certain entitlements.

2. Loïc Wacquant, *Punishing the Poor: The Neoliberal Government of Social Insecurity* (Durham, NC: Duke University Press, 2009).

3. The security requirements that proponents of this securitization process advocated subsequently discriminated against immigrants and their children (irrespective of their status), most pointedly Muslim nationals and foreigners. In November 2001, for example, John Ashcroft (then attorney general) initiated the interviewing of up to five thousand aliens from countries suspected of harboring terrorists. The State Department also slowed the process of granting visas for men aged sixteen to forty-five from specified Arab and Muslim countries. In March 2002, the Department of Justice announced that it was

conducting interviews with more than three thousand more Arabs and Muslim citizens and residents.

4. Matthew Hughey, "White Backlash in the Post-Racial United States," *Ethnic and Racial Studies* 37, no. 5 (2014): 726.

5. Alvin B. Tillery, "Barack Obama and American Race Relations," in *The Obama Legacy*, ed. Bert Rockman and Andrew Rudalevige (University of Kansas Press, 2019).

6. Jabari Assim, *What Obama Means: For Our Cultures, Our Politics, Our Future* (New York: William Morrow, 2009), 23.

7. Thomas L. Friedman, "Finishing Our Work," *New York Times*, November 4, 2008, https://www.nytimes.com/2008/11/05/opinion/05friedman.html.

8. Wilbur Rich, *The Post-Racial Society Is Here: Recognition, Critics and the Nation-State* (New York: Routledge), 108.

9. David Hollinger, "Obama, the Instability of Color Lines, and the Promise of a Post-Ethnic Future," *Callaloo* 31 (2008): 1033.

10. Richard Alba and Victor Nee, *Remaking the American Mainstream: Assimilation and Contemporary Immigration* (Cambridge, MA: Harvard University Press, 2005), 290.

11. Richard Alba and Victor Nee, *Remaking the American Mainstream*, 14.

12. Jennifer Lee and Frank Bean, *The Diversity Paradox: Immigration and the Color Line in Twenty-First Century* (New York: Russell Sage Foundation, 2010); Jennifer Lee, "A Post-Racial America? Multiracial Identification and the Color Line in the 21st Century," *Nanzan Review of American Studies* 30 (2008): 13–31; Joel Perlmann and Mary Waters, "Intermarriage Then and Now: Race, Generation, and the Changing Meaning of Marriage," in *Not Just Black and White: Historical and Contemporary Perspectives on Immigration, Race, and Ethnicity in the United States*, ed. Nancy Foner and George Fredrickson (New York: Russell Sage Foundation, 2004).

13. Eduardo Bonilla-Silva, *Racism without Racists: Color Blind Racism and the Persistence of Racial Inequality* (Boulder, CO: Rowman and Littlefield, 2013); "The 2008 Elections and the Future of Anti-Racism in 21st Century Amerika," *Humanity and Society* 34 (2010): 222–32.

14. Eduardo Bonilla-Silva, "We Are All Americans! The Latin Americanization of Racial Stratification in the USA," *Race and Society*, 2002, 5.

15. Alana Lentin, "What Does Race Do?" *Ethnic and Racial Studies* 38, no. 8 (2015): 1404.

16. Alana Lentin, "Post-Race, Post Politics: The Paradoxical Rise of Culture after Multiculturalism," *Ethnic and Racial Studies* 37, no. 8 (2014): 1270.

17. Thomas Sugrue, *Not Even Past: Barack Obama and the Burden of Race* (Princeton, NJ: Princeton University Press, 2010).

18. See, for example, Charles Gallagher, *Racism in Post-Race America: New Theories, New Directions* (Social Forces, 2008); Paul Gilroy, *Against Race: Imagining Political Culture beyond the Color Line* (Cambridge: Belknap Press, 2000).

19. David Hollinger, "The Concept of Post-Racial: How Its Easy Dismissal Obscures Important Questions," *Daedalus*, Winter Issue, 2011, 174.

20. Michael Tesler, *Post-Racial or More Racial? Race and Politics in the Obama Era* (Chicago: University of Chicago Press, 2016), 5.

21. Michael Tesler and John Sides, "How Political Science Helps Explain the Rise of Trump: The Role of White Identity and Grievances," *Washington Post*, March 3, 2016, https://www.washingtonpost.com/news/monkey-cage/wp/2016/03/03/how-political-science-helps-explain-the-rise-of-trump-the-role-of-white-identity-and-grievances.

22. American National Election Studies (ANES), Pilot Study, 2016, http://www.electionstudies.org/studypages/anes_pilot_2016/anes_pilot_2016.htm.

23. Christopher Parker and Matt Barreto, *Change They Can't Believe In: The Tea Party and Reactionary Politics in Contemporary America* (Princeton, NJ: Princeton University Press, 2013), 3.

24. John Sides, Michael Tesler, and Lynn Vavreck, *Identity Crisis: The 2006 Presidential Campaign and the Battle for the Meaning of America* (Princeton, NJ: Princeton University Press, 2008), 10.

25. Diana Mutz, "Status Threat, Not Economic Hardship Explains the 2016 Presidential Vote," *PNAS*, April 23, 2018, http://www.pnas.org/content/early/2018/04/18/1718155115.

26. Southern Poverty Law Center, "The Trump Effect," *Intelligence Report*, June 2017, https://www.splcenter.org/fighting-hate/intelligence-report/2017/trump-effect.

27. FBI Crime Statistics, 2018 Report, https://ucr.fbi.gov/hate-crime/2018/tables/table-2.xls.

28. Anti-Defamation League (ADL), "Anti-Semitic Incidents Surged Nearly 60% in 2017," 2018 Report, https://www.adl.org/news/press-releases/anti-semitic-incidents-surged-nearly-60-in-2017-according-to-new-adl-report.

29. Statistica, *Report on Anti-Semitism*, 2019, https://www.statista.com/statistics/816732/number-of-anti-semitic-incident-in-the-us/.

30. Human Rights Campaign, "New FBI Statistics Show Alarming Increase in Numbers of Reported Hate Crimes," November 13, 2018, https://www.hrc.org/blog/new-fbi-statistics-show-alarming-increase-in-number-of-reported-hate-crimes.

31. Charles Tilly, *From Mobilization to Revolution* (Reading, MA: Addison Wesley, 1978).

32. Nella Van Dyke and Sarah A. Soule, "Structural Social Change and the Mobilizing Effect of Threat," in *Readings on Social Movements: Origins, Dynamics, and Outcomes*, ed. Douglas McAdam and David A. Snow (Oxford: Oxford University Press, 2010), 39. See also David S. Meyer and Suzanne Staggenborg, "Movements, Countermovements and the Structure of Political Opportunity," *American Journal of Sociology* 101 (1996): 1628–1660; David S. Meyer and Douglas R. Imig, "Political Opportunity and the Rise and Decline of Interest Group Sectors," *Social Science Journal* 30 (1993): 253–70.

5. TWO TALES OF ONE NATION

1. Pew Research Center, *Views on Immigration's Impact on U.S. Society Mixed* (Washington, DC: Pew Research Center, 2015), https://www.pewresearch.org/wp-content/uploads/sites/5/2015/09/2015-09-28_modern-immigration-wave_REPORT.pdf.

2. Elizabeth Fussell, "Warmth the Welcome: Attitudes Towards Immigrants and Immigration Policy in the United States," *Annual Review of Sociology* 40 (2014): 479–98.

3. Pew Research Center, *Views on Immigrants' Willingness to Integrate Are Mixed* (March 12, 2019), https://www.pewresearch.org/global/2019/03/14/around-the-world-more-say-immigrants-are-a-strength-than-a-burden/pgmd_2019-03-14_global-migration-attitudes_0-05.

4. Deborah J. Schildkraut, *Americanism in the Twenty-First Century: Public Opinion in the Age of Immigration* (Cambridge: Cambridge University Press, 2011), 45.

5. Pew Research Center, *Multiracial in America: Proud, Diverse and Growing in Numbers* (Washington, DC: Pew Research Center, 2015).

6. David Masci, Anna Brown, and Jocelyn Kiley, *5 Facts about Same-Sex Marriage* (Washington, DC: 2019), https://www.pewresearch.org/fact-tank/2019/06/24/same-sex-marriage/.

7. Gallup, "Americans Slow to Back Interracial Marriage," *Gallup Vault*, June 1, 2017, http://news.gallup.com/vault/212717/gallup-vault-americans-slow-back-interracial-marriage.aspx.

8. Gretchen Livingston and Anna Brown, *Intermarriage in the U.S. 50 Years after Loving v. Virginia* (Washington, DC: Pew Research Center, 2017), https://www.pewsocialtrends.org/2017/05/18/acknowledgments-12.

9. Darrell Jackson and Michele Moses, "Understanding Public Perceptions of Affirmative Action," *The Kansas Journal of Law & Public Policy* 2 (2013), XXII: 205–234.

10. Pew Research Center, *The Partisan Divide on Political Values Grows Even Wider* (Washington, DC: Pew Research Center, 2017), http://assets.pewresearch.org/wp-content/uploads/sites/5/2017/10/05162647/10-05-2017-Political-landscape-release.pdf.

11. Pew Research Center, *Multiracial in America: Proud, Diverse and Growing in Numbers.* (Washington, DC: Pew Research Center, 2015).

12. J. Eric Oliver and Janelle Wong, "Intergroup Prejudice in Multiethnic Settings," *American Journal of Political Science* 47, no. 4 (2003): 567–582; Christopher G. Ellison, Heeju Shin, and David L. Leal, "The Contact Hypothesis and Attitudes toward Latinos in the United States," *Sociology Science Quarterly* 92, no. 4 (2011): 938–58.

13. Jennifer Lee and Frank Bean, *The Diversity Paradox: Immigration and the Color Line in Twenty-First Century America* (New York: Russell Sage Foundation, 2010).

14. Public Religion Research Institute (PRRI)/Governance Studies at Brookings, *What It Means to Be American: Attitudes in an Increasingly Diverse America Ten Years After 9/11* (Washington: PRRI and the Brookings Institution, 2011), https://www.brookings.edu/research/what-it-means-to-be-an-american-attitudes-in-an-increasingly-diverse-america-ten-years-after-911/

15. Hannah Hartig, *Most Americans View Openness to Foreigners as 'Essential to Who We Are as a Nation'* (Washington, DC: Pew Research Center, 2018), https://www.pewresearch.org/fact-tank/2018/10/09/most-americans-view-openness-to-foreigners-as-essential-to-who-we-are-as-a-nation/.

16. Monica Anderson, *For Black Americans, Experiences of Racial Discrimination Vary by Education Level, Gender* (Washington, DC: Pew Research Center, 2019), https://www.pewresearch.org/fact-tank/2019/05/02/for-black-americans-experiences-of-racial-discrimination-vary-by-education-level-gender/.

17. See Thomas Durant and Joyce Louden, "The Black Middle Class in America: Historical and Contemporary Perspectives," *Phylon* 47, no. 4 (1986): 253–263; Sarah Collins, "The Making of the Black Middle Class," *Social Problems* 30, no. 4 (1983): 369–382.

18. Black Demographics, "The African American Middle Class," *African American Population Report*, 2010, http://blackdemographics.com/households/middle-class.

19. U.S. Census Bureau, "Educational Attainment in the United States: 2015," *Current Population Reports*, 2016, https://www.census.gov/content/dam/Census/library/publications/2016/demo/p20-578.pdf.

20. U.S. Department of Health and Human Services, *Health, United States 2015.* (Washington, DC: National Center for Health Statistics, 2015), http://www.cdc.gov/nchs/data/hus/hus15.pdf#specialfeature.

21. Andrew Fenelon, *Causes of Death Contributions to Black and White Differences in Mortality, 1985–2013.* (Washington, DC: National Center for Health Statistics, 2015), http://www.cdc.gov/nchs/ppt/nchs2015/Fenelon_Tuesday_SalonD_AA1.pdf.

22. Tomás Jimenéz, *Immigrants in the United States: How Well Are They Integrating into Society* (Washington, DC: Migration Policy Institute, 2011).

23. Jens Manuel Krogstad, Renee Stepler, and Mark Hugo Lopez, *English Proficiency on The Rise Among Latinos* (Pew Research Center, 2015) http://www.pewhispanic.org/2015/05/12/english-proficiency-on-the-rise-among-latinos.

24. U.S. Bureau of Labor Statistics, *Labor Force Characteristics of Foreign-Born Workers,* 2018, https://www.bls.gov/news.release/forbrn.nr0.htm/Labor-Force-Characteristics-of-Foreign-Born-Workers-Summary.

25. Carnegie Corporation of New York, *A Place to Call Home: What Immigrants Say Now About Life in America* (Washington, DC: Public Agenda, 2010).

26. Alejandro Portes, Patricia Fernandez-Kelly, and William Haller, "The Adaptation of the Immigrant Second Generation in America: A Theoretical Overview and Recent Evidence," *Journal of Ethnic and Migration Studies* 35, no. 7 (2009): 1077–104; Alejandro Portes and Ruben Rumbaut, *Immigrant America: A Portrait* (Berkeley: University of California Press, 2006); Frank Bean and Gillian Stevens, *America's Newcomers: Immigrant Incorporation and the Dynamics of Diversity* (New York: Russell Sage Foundation, 2003).

27. Richard Alba, "The Likely Persistence of a White Majority," *The American Prospect Magazine*, Winter 2016, http://prospect.org/article/likely-persistence-white-majority-0.

28. Richard Alba and Guillermo Yriza Barbosa, "Room at the Top? Minority Mobility and the Transition to Demographic Diversity in the USA," *Ethnic and Racial Studies* 39, no. 6 (2016): 917–938.

29. Tomás Jiménez, *Immigrants in the United States: How Well Are They Integrating into Society* (Washington, DC: Migration Policy Institute, 2011), 5.

30. Pew Research Center, "English Proficiency on the Rise among Latinos."

31. Pew Research Center, *Second Generation Americans: A Portrait of the Adult Children of Immigrants* (Washington, DC: Pew Research Center, 2013).

32. See Elaine Howard Ecklung, Celina Davila, Michael O. Emerson, Samuel Kye, and Esther Chan, "Motivating Civic Engagement: In-Group Versus Out-Group Service Orientations among Mexicans in Religious and Nonreligious Organizations," *Sociology of Religion* 74, no. 3 (2013): 370–391; S. Karthick Ramakrishman and Celia Viramontes, "Civic Spaces: Mexican Hometown Associations and Immigrant Participation," *Journal of Social Issues* 66, no. 1 (2010): 155–173.

33. Pew Hispanic Center, *The 2004 National Survey of Latinos: Politics and Civic Participation* (Washington, DC: Pew Research Center, 2004).

34. Michael Tesler and David Sears, *Obama's Race: The 2008 Election and the Dream of a Post-Racial America* (Chicago: Chicago University Press, 2010).

35. Public Religion Research Institute (PRRI), *How Americans View Immigrants: Findings from the 2015 American Values Atlas*, 2016, https://www.prri.org/research/poll-immigration-reform-views-on-immigrants.

36. FBI, *Hate Crime Statistics*, Criminal Justice information, 2016, https://ucr.fbi.gov/hate-crime/2016/topic-pages/incidentsandoffenses.

37. Southern Poverty Law Center (SPLC), "2017: The Year in Hate and Extremism," *Intelligence Report*, February 11, 2018, https://www.splcenter.org/fighting-hate/intelligence-report/2018/2017-year-hate-and-extremism.

38. Pew Research Center, *How the U.S. General Public Views Muslims and Islam* (Washington, DC: Pew Research Center, 2017), http://www.pewforum.org/2017/07/26/how-the-u-s-general-public-views-muslims-and-islam.

39. Public Religion Research Institute (PRRI)/Governance Studies at Brookings, *What It Means to Be American: Attitudes in an Increasingly Diverse America Ten Years After 9/11* (Washington: PRRI and the Brookings Institution, 2011), https://www.brookings.edu/research/what-it-means-to-be-an-american-attitudes-in-an-increasingly-diverse-america-ten-years-after-911/.

40. Davis Masci, "Many Americans See Religious Discrimination in U.S.—Especially against Muslims," Pew Research Center, May 17, 2019, https://www.pewresearch.org/fact-tank/2019/05/17/many-americans-see-religious-discrimination-in-u-s-especially-against-muslims.

41. CNN/ORC, "Under Obama, 4 in 10 Say Race Relations Worsened," March 13, 2015, http://www.cnn.com/2015/03/06/politics/poll-obama-race-relations-worse.

42. Gallup, "Race Relations," 2015, http://www.gallup.com/poll/1687/race-relations.aspx.

43. Ryan Struyk, "Blacks and Whites See Racism in the United States Very Differently," CNN Politics, August 18, 2017, https://edition.cnn.com/2017/08/16/politics/blacks-white-racism-united-states-polls/index.html.

44. National Commission on Fair Housing and Equal Opportunity, *The Future of Fair Housing*, Civil Rights Publications, 2008, https://nationalfairhousing.org/wp-content/uploads/2017/04/Future_of_Fair_Housing_executive_summary.pdf; Douglas Massey, *Categorically Unequal* (New York: Russell Sage Foundation, 2007).

45. Heather Long and Andrew Van Dam, "The Black-White Economic Divide Is as Wide as It Was in 1968," *Washington Post*, June 4, 2020, https://www.washingtonpost.com/business/2020/06/04/economic-divide-black-households/?utm_campaign.

46. U.S. Census Bureau, "Income, Poverty, and Health Insurance: 2010," *Current Population Report* 22 (2011), https://dispatch.irp.wisc.edu/us-census-states-income-poverty-and-health-insurance-2010/.

47. Bureau of Labor Statistics, *TED: The Economics Daily*, 2018, https://www.bls.gov/opub/ted/2018/76-point-9-percent-of-hispanic-men-employed-january-2018.htm.

48. Reynolds Farley, "Fifty Years after the Kerner Report: What Has Changed, What Has Not, and Why?" *The Russell Sage Foundation Journal of the Social Sciences* 4, no. 6 (2018); Paul Attewell, David Lavin, Thurston, and Tania Levey, "The Black Middle Class: Progress, Prospects, and Puzzles," *Journal of African American Studies* 8, no. 1/2 (2004): 6–19.

49. US Census, "Current Population Survey, 1968 to 2019," *Annual Social and Economic Supplements*, 2019, https://www.census.gov/content/dam/Census/library/visualizations/2019/demo/p60-266/figure2.pdf.

50. Moritz Kuhn, Ulrike Steins, and Moritz Schularick, "Income and Wealth Inequality in America, 1949–2016" (Institute Working Paper 9, Federal Reserve Bank of Minneapolis, June, 2018), https://www.minneapolisfed.org/research/institute-working-papers/income-and-wealth-inequality-in-america-1949-2016.

51. Institute for Policy Studies, *The Ever-Growing Gap: Without Change, African-American and Latino Families Won't Match White Wealth for Centuries*, 2016, http://www.ips-dc.org/wp-content/uploads/2016/08/The-Ever-Growing-Gap-CFED_IPS-Final-2.pdf.

52. Richard V. Reeves and Nathan Joo, "White, Still: The American Upper Middle Class," *Social Mobility Memo*, October 4, 2017, https://www.brookings.edu/blog/social-mobility-memos/2017/10/04/white-still-the-american-upper-middle-class/.

53. Camille L. Ryan and Kurt Bauman, "Educational Attainment in the United States," *Current Population Reports*, March 2016, https://www.census.gov/content/dam/Census/library/publications/2016/demo/p20-578.pdf.

54. James Coleman, *Report on Equality of Educational Opportunity*, National Center for Educational Statistics, 1966, https://files.eric.ed.gov/fulltext/ED012275.pdf.

55. For aggregated data, see https://nces.ed.gov/programs/digest/d16/tables/dt16_104.20.asp.

56. U.S. Department of Education, *Trends in High School Dropout and Completion Rates in the United States: 1972–2012: Compendium Report*, 2013, https://nces.ed.gov/pubs2015/2015015.pdf.

57. U.S. Bureau of Labor Statistics, "Profile of the Labor Force by Educational Attainment," *Spotlight on Statistics*, 2017, https://www.bls.gov/spotlight/2017/educational-attainment-of-the-labor-force/home.htm.

58. U.S. Government Accountability Office, "K-12 Education: Better Use of Information Could Help Agencies Identify Disparities and Address Racial Discrimination," *Report to Congressional Requesters*, 2016, https://www.gao.gov/products/GAO-16-345.

59. Propublica, "Segregation Now," April 16, 2014, https://www.propublica.org/article/segregation-now-full-text.

60. Lincoln Quillian, Devah Pager, Arnfinn H. Midtboen, and Ole Hexel, "Hiring Discrimination against Blacks Hasn't Declined in 25 Years," *Harvard Business Review*, October 11, 2017, https://hbr.org/2017/10/hiring-discrimination-against-black-americans-hasnt-declined-in-25-years.

61. Matthew Desmond, "Unaffordable America: Poverty, Housing and Eviction," *Fast Focus* (Institute for Research on Poverty, University of Wisconsin-Madison, 2015), https://www.irp.wisc.edu/publications/fastfocus/pdfs/FF22-2015.pdf.

62. Matthew Durose, Erika Smith, and Patrick Langan, "Contacts between Police and the Public, 2005" *Bureau of Justice Statistics Special Report*, 2007, http://www.bjs.gov/content/pub/pdf/cpp05.pdf.

63. Pew Research Center, *From Police to Parole, Black and White Americans Differ Widely in Their Views of Criminal Justice System* (Washington, DC: Pew Research Center, 2019), https://www.pewresearch.org/fact-tank/2019/05/21/from-police-to-parole-black-and-white-americans-differ-widely-in-their-views-of-criminal-justice-system.

64. See for example Heather Mac Donald, *The War on Cops* (New York: Encounter Books, 2016).

65. Wesley Lowery, "Aren't More White People than Black People Killed by Police? Yes, but No," *Washington Post*, July 11, 2016, https://www.washingtonpost.com/news/post-nation/wp/2016/07/11/arent-more-white-people-than-black-people-killed-by-police-yes-but-no.

66. See Phillip Atiba Goff, Tracey Lloyd, Amanda Geller, Steven Raphael, and Jack Glaser, *The Science of Justice: Race, Arrest, and Police Use of Force* (New York: Center for Policing Equity, 2016), https://policingequity.org/images/pdfs-doc/CPE_SoJ_Race-Arrests-UoF_2016-07-08-1130.pdf; Cody Ross, "A Multilevel Baysesian Analysis of Racial Bias in Police Shootings at the Country-Level in the United States (2011–2014)," *PLOS ONE*, November 8, 2015, https://journals.plos.org/plosone/article?id=10.1371/journal.pone.0141854#sec005.

67. Wesley Lowery, "Aren't More White People than Black People Killed by Police?"

68. Philipp Stinson, *Criminology Explains Police Violence* (Oakland: University of California Press, 2020).

69. Amnesty International USA, *Threat and Humiliation: Racial Profiling, National Security, and Human Rights in the United States*, 2003–2004 Report, http://www.amnestyusa.org/pdfs/rp_report.pdf.

70. Sentencing Project, *Shadow Report to the United Nations on Racial Disparities in the United States Criminal Justice System*, 2013, http://www.sentencingproject.org/publications/shadow-report-to-the-united-nations-human-rights-committee-regarding-racial-disparities-in-the-united-states-criminal-justice-system.

71. Pew Research Center, *The Gap between the Number of Blacks and Whites in Prison Is Shrinking* (Washington, DC: Pew Research Center, 2019), https://www.pewresearch.org/fact-tank/2019/04/30/shrinking-gap-between-number-of-blacks-and-whites-in-prison/.

72. Marc Mauer, "Addressing Disparities in Incarceration," *The Prison Journal* supplement to 91, no. 3 (2011): 88.

73. Leadership Conference on Civil Rights (LCCR), *American Dream? American Reality! A Report on Race, Ethnicity and the Law in the United States* (Washington, DC: Leadership Conference on Civil Rights, 2008), 7. See also The Leadership Conference on Civil and Human Rights, *Confronting the New Faces of Hate: Hate Crime in America* (2009), http://www.protectcivilrights.org/pdf/reports/hatecrimes/lccref_hate_crimes_report.pdf.

74. K. J. Rosich, *Race, Ethnicity, and the Criminal Justice System* (Washington, DC: American Sociological Association Publications, 2007).

75. Judit Greene and Kevin Pranis, "Gang Wars: The Failure of Enforcement Tactics and the Need for Effective Public Safety Strategies," *Justice Policy Institute Report* (2007), http://www.justicepolicy.org/research/1961.

76. Sentencing Project, *Shadow Report to the United Nations on Racial Disparities in the United States Criminal Justice System* 8 (2013): 8.

77. Marc Mauer, "Addressing Disparities in Incarceration" 93.

78. Frank Baumgartner and Tim Lyman, "Louisiana Death Sentenced Cases and Their Reversals," *Journal of Race, Gender, and Poverty* 7 (2016): 74.

79. Lynda Dodd, "The Rights Revolution in the Age of Obama and Ferguson: Policing, the Rule of Law, and the Elusive Quest for Accountability," *Perspectives on Politics* 13, no. 3 (2005): 657.

80. Sentencing Project, "Felony Disenfranchisement Primer," Policy Brief, 2016, https://www.sentencingproject.org/publications/felony-disenfranchisement-a-primer/.

81. Denise Lieberman, "Barriers to the Ballot Box New Restrictions Underscore the Need for Voting Laws Enforcement," *Human Rights Magazine* 39 (2012): 39, https://www.americanbar.org/publications/human_rights_magazine_home/2012_vol_39_/winter_2012_-_vote/barriers_to_the_ballotboxnewrestrictionsunderscoretheneedforvoti.html.

82. The Leadership Conference Education Fund, *The Great Poll Closure* (2016), http://civilrightsdocs.info/pdf/reports/2016/poll-closure-report-web.pdf.

83. These laws included AL H.B. 285, AL H.B. 538, AR H.B. 1112, AR H.B. 1244, AR H.B. 1715, AR S.B. 643, AZ S.B. 1003, AZ S.B. 1485, AZ S.B. 1819, FL S.B. 90, GA S.B. 202, IA S.F. 413, IA S.F. 568, ID H.B. 290, IN S.B. 398, KS H.B. 2183, KS H.B. 2332, KY H.B. 574, LA H.B. 167, MT H.B. 176, MT H.B. 530, MT S.B. 169, MT S.B. 196, NH H.B. 523, NV S.B. 84, OK H.B. 2663, TX H.B. 3920, TX S.B. 1111, UT H.B. 12, WY H.B. 75. See Brennan Center for Justice, "Voting Laws Roundup: July 2021," July 22, 2021, https://www.brennancenter.org/our-work/research-reports/voting-laws-roundup-july-2021.

84. Pew Hispanic Center, *An Awakened Giant: The Hispanic Electorate is Likely to Double by 2030* (Washington, DC: Pew Hispanic Center, 2012).

85. Pew Research Center, "Blacks Have Made Gains in US Political Leadership, but Gaps Remain," *Factank*, January 18, 2019, https://www.pewresearch.org/fact-tank/2019/01/18/blacks-have-made-gains-in-u-s-political-leadership-but-gaps-remain.

6. FROM IDENTITY POLITICS TO ETHNORACIAL IDENTITY CRISIS

1. Robert Gooding-Williams and Charles W. Mills, "Race in a 'Postracial' Epoch," *Du Bois Review: Social Science Research on Race* 11, no. 1 (2014): 7.

2. For an analysis of the discrimination continuum, see Ariane Chebel d'Appollonia, *Migrant Mobilization and Securitization in the US and Europe: How Does it Feel to Be a Threat?* (New York: Palgrave Macmillan, 2015).

3. Richard Alba and Jan Willem Duyvendak, "What about the Mainstream? Assimilation in Super-Diverse Times," *Ethnic and Racial Studies* 42, no. 10 (2019): 109.

4. Fran Meissner and Steven Vertovec, "Comparing Super-Diversity," *Ethnic and Racial Studies* 38 (2015): 541–555; Steven Vertovec, "Super-Diversity and Its Implications," *Ethnic and Racial Studies* 30 (2007): 1024–1054.

5. Richard Alba and Victor Nee, *Remaking the American Mainstream* (Cambridge, MA: Harvard University Press, 2003), 289.

6. Richard Alba and Victor Nee, *Remaking the American Mainstream*, 291.

7. Richard Alba and Victor Nee, *Remaking the American Mainstream*, 290.

8. Joe Feagin and José Cobas, *Latinos Facing Resistance: Discrimination, Resistance, and Endurance* (Boulder, CO: Paradigm Publishers, 2014).

9. Wornie Reed and Louis Bertin, "No More Excuses: Problematic Responses to Barack Obama's Election," *Journal of African American Studies* 13 (2009): 101.

10. Richard Alba and Jan Willem Duyvendak, "What about the Mainstream?," 108.

11. Pew Research Center, "Growing Share of Republicans Say U.S. Risks Losing Its Identity If it is Too Open to Foreigners," *Factank*, July 17, 2019, https://www.pewresearch.org/fact-tank/2019/07/17/growing-share-of-republicans-say-u-s-risks-losing-its-identity-if-it-is-too-open-to-foreigners.

12. Pew Research Center, "Americans See Advantages and Challenges in Country's Growing Racial and Ethnic Diversity," *Social and Demographic Trends*, May 8, 2019, https://www.pewsocialtrends.org/2019/05/08/americans-see-advantages-and-challenges-in-countrys-growing-racial-and-ethnic-diversity/.

13. Richard Brookhiser, "Taming the Tribes of America," *National Review*, November 5, 1990: 65.

14. Charles Krauthammer, "Identity Politics Isn't Working," *Record Searchlight*, November 24, 2016, https://www.redding.com/story/opinion/columnists/charles-krauthammer/2016/11/24/charles-krauthammer-identity-politics-isnt-working/94413250/.

15. Mark Lila, *The Once and Future Liberal: After Identity Politics* (New York: Harper, 2017), 9–10.

16. Amy Chua, *Political Tribes: Group Instinct and the Fate of Nations* (New York: Penguin/Random House, 2018).

17. John Sides, Michael Tesler, and Lynn Vavreck, *Identity Crisis: The 2016 Presidential Campaign and the Battle for the Meaning of America* (Princeton, NJ: Princeton University Press, 2018), 4.

18. Thomas Jiménez, *The Other Side of Assimilation: How Immigrants Are Changing American Life* (Oakland: University of California Press, 2017).

19. Ashley Jardina, *White Identity Politics* (Cambridge, MA: Cambridge University Press), 56.

20. Pew Research Center, "Growing Partisan Differences in View of Discrimination," *US Politics & Policy*, April 15, 2019, https://www.pewresearch.org/politics/2019/04/15/sharp-rise-in-the-share-of-americans-saying-jews-face-discrimination/.

21. Pew Research Center. 2019. "Growing Partisan Differences in View of Discrimination."

22. Daniel Cox, Rachel Lienesh, and Robert P. Jones, "Beyond Economics: Fears of Cultural Displacement Pushed the White Working Class to Trump," *PPRI/The Atlantic* (2017), https://www.prri.org/research/white-working-class-attitudes-economy-trade-immigration-election-donald-trump/.

23. John Sides et al., *Identity Crisis*, 89.

24. Daniel Hopkins and Samantha Washington, "The Rise of Trump, the Fall of Prejudice? Tracking White Americans' Racial Attitudes 2008–2018," *SSRN* (2019), https://papers.ssrn.com/sol3/papers.cfm?abstract_id=3378076.

25. Lawrence Bobo, "Racism in Trump's America: Reflections on Culture, Sociology, and the 2016 US Presidential Election," *The British Journal of Sociology* 68, no. 1 (2017): 95.

26. Nancy Isenberg, *White Trash: The 400-Year Untold History of Class in America* (New York: Viking, 2016), 4.

27. Exit polls conducted during the presidential primaries estimated the median household income of Trump supporters to be about $72,000. But even this lower number is almost double the median household income of African Americans and $15,000 above the American median.

28. Nate Silver, "The Mythology of Trump's 'Working Class' Support," *Politics* (2016), https://fivethirtyeight.com/features/the-mythology-of-trumps-working-class-support/.

29. Michael Tesler, *Post-Racial or Most-Racial? Race and Politics in the Obama Era* (Chicago: Chicago University Press, 2016). See also "Economic Anxiety Isn't Driving Racial Resentment. Racial Resentment Is Driving Economic Anxiety," *Washington Post*, August 22, 2016, https://www.washingtonpost.com/news/monkey-cage/wp/2016/08/22/economic-anxiety-isnt-driving-racial-resentment-racial-resentment-is-driving-economic-anxiety.

30. Michael Tesler and John Sides, "How Political Science Helps Explain the Rise of Trump: The Role of White Identity and Grievances," *Washington Post*, March 3, 2016, https://www.washingtonpost.com/news/monkey-cage/wp/2016/03/03/how-political-science-helps-explain-the-rise-of-trump-the-role-of-white-identity-and-grievances.

31. John Sides et al., *Identity Crisis*, 9.

32. Pew Research Center, "Race in America 2019," *Social & Demographic Trends*, April 9, 2019, https://www.pewsocialtrends.org/2019/04/09/race-in-america-2019/.

33. Pew Research Center, "On Views of Race and Inequality, Blacks and Whites Are Worlds Apart," *Social and Demographic Trends*, June 17, 2016, https://www.pewsocialtrends.org/2016/06/27/2-views-of-race-relations/#most-say-obama-at-least-tried-to-improve-race-relations.

34. Pew Research Center, "Race in America 2019."

35. Pew Research Center, "Race in America 2019."

36. Jonathan Capehart, "Ben Carson and Cornel West Actually Agree: Obama's 'Not Black Enough,'" *Washington Post*, Feb 23, 2016, https://www.washingtonpost.com/blogs/post-partisan/wp/2016/02/23/ben-carson-and-cornel-west-actually-agree-obamas-not-black-enough/.

37. Joe Feagin, *White Party, White Government: Race, Class and U.S. Politics* (New York: Routledge, 2012); Wendy Moore and Joyce Bell, "Embodying the White Racial Frame: The (In) Significance of Barack Obama," *Journal of Race and Policy* 6, no. 1 (2010): 123–138. A journalist at the *Los Angeles Times*, David Ehrenstein, argues that Obama was a "Magic Negro"—a term from films studies that refers to Black characters in movies whose main purpose is to help whites solve their issues. For "most white Americans, the desire for a noble, healing Negro hasn't faded. That's where Obama comes in: as (Sidney) Poitier's 'real' fake son" (2007). Other commentators noted the "browning" of Obama by people who questioned his patriotism, name, religion, and citizenship. This browning process placed him into a "sort of social quarantine," held up for public scrutiny because he was allegedly posing a "terrorist threat against the United States" (Carmen Lugo-Lugo and Mary Bloodsworth-Lugo, "Black as Brown: The 2008 Obama Primary Campaign and the U.S. Browning of Terror," *Journal of African American Studies* 13 (2009): 110–120.

38. For an analysis of this debate, see Jamelle Bouie, "Black Like Kamala," *The Washington Post*, August 14, 2020, https://www.nytimes.com/2020/08/14/opinion/kamala-harris-black-identity.html.

39. John McConahay, "Symbolic Racism," *Journal of Social Issues* 32, no. 2 (1976): 23–24. See also D. O. Sears and J. B. McConahay, *The Politics of Violence: The New Urban Blacks and the Watts Riots* (Boston, MA: Houghton Mifflin, 1973).

40. Eduardo Bonilla-Silva and David Dietrich, "The Sweet Enchantment of Color-Blind Racism in Obamerica," *The Annals of the American Academy of Political and Social Science* 643 (2011): 202. See also Eduardo Bonilla-Silva, *Racism without Racists: Color-Blind Racism and Inequality in the United States* (Lanham, MD: Rowman & Littlefield, 2003).

41. Lawrence Blum, "White Privilege: A Mild Critique," *Theory and Research in Education* 6, no. 3 (2008): 311. See also L. Gordon, "Critical Reflections on Three Popular Tropes in the Study of Whiteness," in *What White Looks Like: African-American Philosophers on the Whiteness Question*, ed. George Yancy (New York: Routledge, 2004); Zeus Leonardo, "The Color of Supremacy: Beyond the Discourse of 'White Privilege,'" *Educational Philosophy*

and Theory 36, no. 2 (2004): 137–152; Peggy McIntosh, "Unpacking the Invisible Knapsack: White Privilege and Male Privilege," in *Race, Class, and Gender: An Anthology*, ed. Margaret Andersen and Patricia Hill Collins (Belmont, CA: Wadsworth, 1998).

42. During the summer of 2020, almost all the top best-selling books on Amazon (seven out of ten), at Barnes & Noble (nine out of ten), and on the *New York Times* list of best-sellers related to WPA, racism, and anti-racism—including *How to Be an Antiracist* by Ibram X. Kendi, *White Fragility* by Robin DiAngelo, *So You Want to Talk About Race* by Ijeoma Oluo, *Stamped: Racism, Antiracism and You* by Jason Reynolds and Ibram X. Kendi, and *The New Jim Crow* by Michelle Alexander.

43. Black Lives Matter (BLM) is how the movement is commonly referenced. Actually, it is part of the Black Lives Matter Global Network (BLMGN) which is part of a larger constellation of groups included in the Movement for Black Lives (M4BL).

44. Fred Harris, "The Next Civil Rights Movement," *Dissent* 62, no. 3 (2015): 34–40.

45. Dewey Clayton, "Black Lives Matter and the Civil Rights Movement: A Comparative Analysis of Two Social Movements in the United States," *Journal of Black Studies* 49, no. 5 (2018): 448–480.

46. This intersectional approach reflects the works of Black women radicals and feminists such as Sojourner Truth, Angela Davis, Audre Lorde, Barbara Smith, Kimberlé Crenshaw, Cathy Cohen, and Beverly Guy-Sheftal. See Barbara Ransby, "The Class Politics of Black Lives Matter," *Dissent* 62, no. 4 (2015): 31–34.

47. Alicia Garza, "A Herstory of the #BlackLivesMatter Movement," *The Feminist Wire*, October 7, 2014, https://thefeministwire.com/2014/10/blacklivesmatter-2/.

48. Jenna Wortham, "How a New Wave of Black Activists Changed the Conversation," *New York Times Magazine*, August 25, 2020, https://www.nytimes.com/2020/08/25/magazine/black-visions-collective.html.

49. Quoted by Jenna Wortham, "How a New Wave of Black Activists Changed the Conversation."

50. Quoted by Jenna Wortham, "How a New Wave of Black Activists Changed the Conversation."

51. Barbara Ransby, *Making All Black Lives Matter* (Oakland: University of California Press, 2018), 18.

52. Richard Alba and Tariqui Islam, "The Case of Disappearing Mexican Americans: An Ethnic Identity Mystery," *Population Research and Policy Review* 28, no. 2 (2009): 111.

53. Pew Research Center, "Race in America 2019."

54. Richard Alba and Tariqui Islam, "The Case of Disappearing Mexican Americans," 112.

55. Pew Research Center, "Hispanic Identity Fades across Generations as Immigrant Connections Fall Away," *Hispanic Trends*, December 20, 2017, https://www.pewresearch.org/hispanic/2017/12/20/hispanic-identity-fades-across-generations-as-immigrant-connections-fall-away/.

56. Nicholas Vargas, "Latina/o Whitening? Which Latina/o Self-Classify as White and Report Being Perceived as White by Other Americans?" *Du Bois Review: Social Science Research on Race* 12, no. 1 (2015): 119–136.

57. Pew Research Center, "Hispanics with Darker Skin Are More Likely to Experience Discrimination Than Those with Lighter Skin," *Facttank*, July 2, 2019, https://www.pewresearch.org/fact-tank/2019/07/02/hispanics-with-darker-skin-are-more-likely-to-experience-discrimination-than-those-with-lighter-skin/.

58. Ed Morales, *Latinx: The New Force in American Politics and Culture* (London: Verso, 2018), 30.

59. Quoted by Haya El Nasser, "Police Killings of Latinos Spark Less Outrage than when Victims Are Black," *Aljazeera America*, August 13, 2015, http://america.aljazeera.com/multimedia/2015/8/police-killings-of-latinos-spark-less-outrage.html.

60. See for example, Frances Negron-Muntaner, Chelsea Abbas, Luis Figueroa, and Samuel Robson, *The Latino Media Gap: A Report on the State of Latinos in US Media* (Columbia University/Center for the Study of Ethnicity and Race, 2012), accessed September 6, 2020, https://media-alliance.org/wp-content/uploads/2016/05/Latino_Media_Gap_Report.pdf.

61. Haya El Nasser, "Police Killings of Latinos Spark Less Outrage."

62. Pew Research Center, "Key Facts about Asian Americans," *Facttank*, September 8, 2017, https://www.pewresearch.org/fact-tank/2017/09/08/key-facts-about-asian-americans/.

63. David Yi, "As an Asian American, I Am Invisible in This Country," *Huffpost*, November 14, 2016, https://www.huffpost.com/entry/as-an-asian-american-i-am-invisible-in-this-country_b_582a019be4b02b1f5257a6f8. See also Wei Sun, "Perceptions of Minority Invisibility among Asian American Professionals," *Howard Journal of Communication* 17, no. 2 (2006): 119–142.

64. US Census, "The Asian Population," *2010 Census Briefs*, March 2012, https://www.census.gov/content/dam/Census/library/publications/2012/dec/c2010br-11.pdf.

65. Qin Zhang, "Asian Americans beyond the Model Minority Stereotype: The Nerdy and the Left Out," *Journal of International and Intercultural Communication* 3, no. 1 (2010): 24.

66. Quoted by Alex Wagner, "Why Are Asian Americans Politically Invisible?," *The Atlantic*, September 12, 2016, https://www.theatlantic.com/politics/archive/2016/09/why-dont-asians-count/498893/.

67. Quoted by Caroline Kitchener, "Kamal Harris' Asian American Identity Is Left Out of the Story," *The Lily*, August 12, 2020, https://www.thelily.com/kamala-harriss-asian-american-identity-is-left-out-of-the-story-that-stings-many-women-say/.

68. Namratha Kandula and Nilay Shah, "Asian Americans Invisible in COVID-19 Data and in Public Health Response," *The Chicago Reporter*, June 16, 2020, https://www.chicagoreporter.com/asian-americans-invisible-in-covid-19-data-and-in-public-health-response/.

69. Helier Cheung, Zhaoyin Feng, and Boer Deng, "Coronavirus: What Attacks on Asians Reveal about American Identity," *BBC News*, May 27, 2020, https://www.bbc.com/news/world-us-canada-52714804. According to Stop AAPI Hate, a grass-roots group based in California, approximately 6,603 hate incidents against Asian people took place between March 2020 and March 2021, https://stopaapihate.org/national-report-through-march-2021/.

70. Andrew Yang, "We Asian Americans Are Not the Virus, but We Can Be Part of the Cure," *The Washington Post*, April 1, 2020, https://www.washingtonpost.com/opinions/2020/04/01/andrew-yang-coronavirus-discrimination/.

71. Quoted by Stacy Chen, "Andrew Yang Faces Backlash from the Asian American Community over Op-ed," *ABC News*, April 15, 2020, https://abcnews.go.com/US/andrew-yang-faces-backlash-asian-american-community-op/story?id=69961672.

7. CENTRIFUGAL DYNAMICS OF ETHNORACIAL FRAGMENTATION

1. Pew Research Center, "Americans Say the Nation's Political Debate Has Grown More Toxic and Heated Rhetoric Could Lead to Violence," *Facttank*, July 18, 2019, https://www.pewresearch.org/fact-tank/2019/07/18/americans-say-the-nations-political-debate-has-grown-more-toxic-and-heated-rhetoric-could-lead-to-violence/.

2. Zoltan Hajnal, *Dangerously Divided: How Race and Class Shape Winning and Losing in American Politics* (Cambridge: Cambridge University Press, 2020); Antoine J. Banks, *Anger and Racial Politics: The Emotional Foundation of Racial Attitudes in America* (Cambridge: Cambridge University Press, 2014).

3. Pew Research Center, *Trends in American Values (1987–2012)*, 2012, https://www.pewresearch.org/wp-content/uploads/sites/4/legacy-pdf/06-04-12-Values-Release.pdf.

4. Doug McAdam and Karina Kloos, *Deeply Divided: Racial Politics and Social Movements in Postwar America* (Oxford, NY: Oxford University Press, 2014), 253.

5. Riley Dunlap, Aaron McCright, and Jerrod Yarosh, "The Political Divide on Climate Change: Partisan Polarization Widens in the US," *Environment: Science and Policy for Sustainable Development* 58, no. 5 (2016): 4–23.

6. Matthew Baum, "Red State, Blue State, Flu State: Media Self-Selection and Partisan Gaps in Swine Flu Vaccination," *Journal of Health Politics, Policy and Law* 36, no. 6 (2011): 1021–1049.

7. Pew Research Center, "The People and Their Government: Distrust, Discontent, Anger and Partisan Rancor," News Release, April 18, 2010, https://www.pewresearch.org/wp-content/uploads/sites/4/legacy-pdf/606.pdf.

8. Donald Kinder and Wendy Kam, *Us Against Them: Ethnocentric Foundations of American Opinion* (Chicago: University of Chicago Press, 2012); Nicholas Valentino, Ted Brader, and Ashley Jardina, "The Antecedents of Immigration Opinion among US Whites: General Ethnocentrism or Media Priming of Latino Attitudes?" *Political Psychology* 34, no. 2 (2013): 149–166.

9. John Sides, Michael Tesler, and Lynn Vavreck, *Identity Crisis: The 2016 Presidential Campaign and the Battle for the Meaning of America* (Princeton University Press, 2018), 10–11.

10. Alan Abramowitz, *The Great Alignment: Race, Party Transformation, and the Rise of Donald Trump* (New Haven, CT: Yale University Press, 2018); Stephen Morgan and Jiwon Lee, "The White Working Class and Voter Turnout in US Presidential Elections," *Sociological Science* 4 (2017): 656–685.

11. Alan Abramowitz and Jennifer McCoy, "United States: Racial Resentment, Negative Partisanship, and Polarization in Trump's America," *The Annals of the American Academy* 68, no. 1 (2019): 137–156.

12. Michael Tessler, *Post-Racial or Most Racial? Race and Politics in the Obama Era* (Chicago: University of Chicago Press, 2016), 8.

13. Matthew Yglesias, "The Great Awokening," *Vox*, April 1, 2019, https://www.vox.com/2019/3/22/18259865/great-awokening-white-liberals-race-polling-trump-2020.

14. Pew Research Center, "Voters' Attitudes About Race and Gender Are Even More Divided Than in 2016," *US Politics and Policy*, September 10, 2020, https://www.pewresearch.org/politics/2020/09/10/voters-attitudes-about-race-and-gender-are-even-more-divided-than-in-2016.

15. Public Religion Research Institute (PRRI), "Dueling Realities: Amid Multiple Crises, Trump and Biden Supporters See Different Priorities and Futures for the Nation," *State of the Union*, October 19, 2020, https://www.prri.org/research/amid-multiple-crises-trump-and-biden-supporters-see-different-realities-and-futures-for-the-nation.

16. Daniel Hopkins and Samantha Washington, "The Rise of Trump, The Fall of Prejudice: Tracking White Americans' Racial Attitudes 2008–2018," *SSRN Papers* (2019): 1–28.

17. ANES 2018 Pilot Survey quoted by Yglesias, "The Great Awokening."

18. Stephen Hawkins, Daniel Yudkin, Miriam Juan-Torres, and Tim Dixon, *Hidden Tribes: A Study of American Polarized Landscape* (New York: More in Common, 2018).

19. Mike Males, "White People Should Be More Afraid of Other Whites Than They Are of People of Color," *Los Angeles Times*, August 3, 2017, https://www.latimes.com/opinion/op-ed/la-oe-males-white-americans-violence-sanctuary-cities-20170803-story.html.

20. R. E. Morgan, *Race and Hispanic Origin of Victims and Offenders, 2012–15*, Bureau of Justice Statistics (BJS), US Dept of Justice, Office of Justice Programs, & United States of America, 2017, 15.

21. Pew Research Center, "America's Complex Relationship with Guns," *Social & Demographic Trends*, June 22, 2017, https://www.pewsocialtrends.org/2017/06/22/the-demographics-of-gun-ownership.

22. Steven Windish, Peter Simi, Kathleen Blee, and Matthew DeMichele, "Understanding the Micro-Situational Dynamics of White Supremacist Violence in the United States," *Perspectives on Terrorism* 12, no. 6 (2018): 23–27.

23. Chip Berlet and Stanilav Vysotsky, "Overview of U.S. White Supremacists," *Journal of Political and Military Sociology* 34, no. 1 (2006): 11–48.

24. Michael Tessler, "Views about Race Mattered More in Electing Trump than in Electing Obama," *Washington Post*, September 22, 2016, https://www.washingtonpost.com/news/monkey-cage/wp/2016/11/22/peoples-views-about-race-mattered-more-in-electing-trump-than-in-electing-obama.

25. Terry Smith, *Whitelash: Unmasking White Grievance at the Ballot Box* (Cambridge: Cambridge University Press, 2020), 33. See also Antoine Banks, *Anger and Racial Politics: The Emotional Foundation of Racial Attitudes in America* (Cambridge: Cambridge University Press, 2014).

26. Davin Phoenix, *The Anger Gap: How Race Shapes Emotion in Politics* (Cambridge: Cambridge University Press, 2020).

27. Shana Bernstein, *Bridges of Reforms: Interracial Civil Rights Activism in Twentieth-Century Los Angeles* (New York: Oxford University Press, 2011).

28. Pew Research Center, "Support for BLM Has Decreased Since June but Remains Strong among Black Americans," *Factank*, September 16, 2020, https://www.pewresearch.org/fact-tank/2020/09/16/support-for-black-lives-matter-has-decreased-since-june-but-remains-strong-among-black-americans.

29. The Muslim ban refers to the Executive Order 13769 titled Protecting the Nation from Foreign Terrorist Entry into the United States, which was in effect from January to March 2017. It was superseded by Executive Order 1370.

30. Pew Research Center, "More Latinos Have Serious Concerns about Their Place in America Under Trump," *Hispanic Trends*, October 25, 2018, https://www.pewresearch.org/hispanic/2018/10/25/more-latinos-have-serious-concerns-about-their-place-in-america-under-trump.

31. Associated Press, "Police Killings of Latinos Lack Attention, Say Activists," *NEWS*, August 18, 2020, https://www.nbcnews.com/news/latino/police-killings-latinos-lack-attention-say-activists-n1237172.

32. ADL, "Reports of Anti-Asian Assaults, Harassment and Hate Crimes Rise as Coronavirus Spreads," *News*, June 18, 2020, https://www.adl.org/blog/reports-of-anti-asian-assaults-harassment-and-hate-crimes-rise-as-coronavirus-spreads.

33. Pew Research Center, "Many Black and Asian Americans Say They Have Experienced Discrimination amid the COVID-19 Outbreak," *Social Trends*, July 1, 2020, https://www.pewsocialtrends.org/2020/07/01/many-black-and-asian-americans-say-they-have-experienced-discrimination-amid-the-covid-19-outbreak.

34. Federal Reserve Bank of Chicago, "The COVID-19 Pandemic and Asian American Employment," *Working Paper*, no. 2020-19 (2020), https://www.chicagofed.org/publications/working-papers/2020/2020-19.

35. Pew Research Center, "US Muslims Concerned about their Place in Society, But Continue to Believe in the American Dream," *Report: Findings from Pew Research Center's 2017 Survey of US Muslims* (2017), https://www.pewforum.org/2017/07/26/demographic-portrait-of-muslim-americans.

36. Southern Poverty Law Center (SPLC), *Anti-Muslim*, accessed November 30, 2020, https://www.splcenter.org/fighting-hate/extremist-files/ideology/anti-muslim.

37. Geraldo Cavada, *The Hispanic Republican: The Shaping of an Identity from Nixon to Trump* (New York: HarperCollins, 2021); Isvett Verde, "Some Latinos Voted for Trump. Get Over It," *New York Times*, November 5, 2020, https://www.nytimes.com/2020/11/05/opinion/sunday/trump-latino-vote.html; Paulina Villegas, "Despite Trump's Actions Against Immigrants, These Latino Voters Want Four More Years," *Washington Post*, September 24, 2020, https://www.washingtonpost.com/politics/2020/09/24/arizona-latino-trump-supporters.

38. Pew Research Center, "Path to Legal Status for the Unauthorized Is Top Immigration Policy Goal for Hispanics in the US," *FACTANK*, February 11, 2020, https://www.pewresearch.org/fact-tank/2020/02/11/path-to-legal-status-for-the-unauthorized-is-top-immigration-policy-goal-for-hispanics-in-u-s.

39. Pew Research Center, "Support for Black Lives Matter Has Decreased Since June but Remains Strong among Black Americans," *Facttank*, September 16, 2020, https://www.pewresearch.org/fact-tank/2020/09/16/support-for-black-lives-matter-has-decreased-since-june-but-remains-strong-among-black-americans.

40. Quoted by Haya El Nasser, "Police Killings of Latinos Spark Less Outrage than When Victims Are Black," *Al Jazeera America*, August 13, 2015.

41. Haya El Nasser. "Police Killings of Latinos Spark Less Outrage."

42. Pew Research Center, "Do Blacks and Hispanics Get Along?" *Social & Demographics Trends*, January 31, 2018, https://www.pewsocialtrends.org/2008/01/31/do-blacks-and-hispanics-get-along.

43. See Stephanie Valencia and Denise Collazo, "Latinos Must Acknowledge Our Own Racism Then We Must Pledge to Fight It," *Miami Herald*, June 8, 2020, https://www.miamiherald.com/opinion/op-ed/article243375201.html.

44. Pew Research Center, "Afro-Latino: A Deeply Rooted Identity Among US Hispanics," *Facttank*, March 1, 2016, https://www.pewresearch.org/fact-tank/2016/03/01/afro-latino-a-deeply-rooted-identity-among-u-s-hispanics.

45. Kimmy Yam, "Asian Americans voted for Biden 63% to 31% But the Reality Is More Complex," *NBC News*, November 9, 2020, https://www.nbcnews.com/news/asian-america/asian-americans-voted-biden-63-31-reality-more-complex-n1247171. See also Asian and Pacific Islander American (APIA) Vote, "2020 Asian American Voter Survey," September 15, 2020, https://www.apiavote.org/research/2020-asian-american-voter-survey.

46. Dhrumil Mehta, "How Asian Americans Are Thinking About the 2020 Election," *FiveThirtyEight*, September 18, 2020, https://fivethirtyeight.com/features/how-asian-americans-are-thinking-about-the-2020-election.

47. See for example, Eda Yu, "3 Ways Asian Americans Can Fight Anti-Black Racism," *KQED*, June 25, 2020, https://www.kqed.org/arts/13882499/3-ways-asian-americans-can-fight-anti-black-racism; Black Women Radicals, "Black and Asian-American Feminist Solidarities: A reading List," April 30, 2020, https://www.blackwomenradicals.com/blog-feed/black-and-asian-feminist-solidarities-a-reading-list; # Asians4Blacklives, https://a4bl.wordpress.com/who-we-are.

48. Terry Nguyen, "Support for Trump Is Tearing Apart Vietnamese American Families," *VOX*, October 30, 2020, https://www.vox.com/first-person/2020/10/30/21540263/vietnamese-american-support-trump-2020.

49. According to the National Museum of African American History and Culture, about 10 percent of slaves brought from West Africa were Muslims. See Amir Hussain, "Muslim Americans Assert Solidarity with Black Lives Matter, Finding Unity within a Diverse Faith Group," *The Conversation*, June 30, 2020, https://theconversation.com/muslim-americans-assert-solidarity-with-black-lives-matter-finding-unity-within-a-diverse-faith-group-141344.

50. Curtis Evans, *The Burden of Black Religion* (Oxford: Oxford University Press, 2008); Sherman Jackson, *Islam and the Blackamerican: Looking Toward the Third Resurrection* (Oxford: Oxford University Press, 2005).

51. Pew Research Center, "Muslims in America: Immigrants and Those Born in US See Life Differently in Many Ways," *Religion & Public Life*, April 17, 2018, https://www.pewforum.org/essay/muslims-in-america-immigrants-and-those-born-in-u-s-see-life-differently-in-many-ways.

52. Pew Research Center, "US Muslims Concerned About their Place in Society."

53. Pew Research Center, "Black Muslims Account for a Fifth of All US Muslims," *Facttank*, January 17, 2019, https://www.pewresearch.org/fact-tank/2019/01/17/black-muslims-account-for-a-fifth-of-all-u-s-muslims-and-about-half-are-converts-to-islam.

54. See for example Husain Lateef and Osman Umarji, "Being Black and Muslim in America: A Study on Identity and Well-Being," *Yaqeen Institute Report* (August 6, 2020), https://yaqeeninstitute.org/osman-umarji/being-black-and-muslim-in-america.

55. Joint Statement Against Anti-Black Police Violence, "Black Lives Matter, An American Muslim Community Statement Against Police Violence," published by Muslim Advocates, 2020, https://muslimadvocates.org/joint-statement-against-anti-black-police-violence.

56. Maha Elgenaidi, "Does the Muslim American Community Have a Problem with Intra-Muslim Racism?" *ING Website*, 2020, https://ing.org/muslim-american-community-problem-intra-muslim-racism.

57. Abu Laith Luqman Ahmad, "As America Talks About Racism, Is Muslim America Ready to Talk about Its Own Racism?" *The Lotus Tree Blog*, 2002, https://imamluqman.wordpress.com/2020/06/05/as-america-talks-about-racism-is-muslim-america-ready-to-talk-about-its-own-racism-imam-abu-laith-luqman-ahmad.

58. Institute for Social Policy and Understanding (ISPU), "Research on Racism and the Experiences and Responses of American Muslims," 2020, https://www.ispu.org/research-on-racism-and-the-experiences-and-responses-of-american-muslims.

59. MuslimARC (Anti-Racism Collaborative), *Study of Intra-Muslim Ethnic Relations*, 2015, https://www.yumpu.com/en/document/read/42250948/muslimarc-interethnic-study-2015.

60. ABC News, "Super Tuesday Republican Exit Poll Analysis," March 1, 2016, https://abcnews.go.com/Politics/live-super-tuesday-republican-exit-poll-analysis/story?id=37309493.

61. Chancellor Williams, *The Destruction of Black Civilization: Great Issues of a Race from 4500 B.C. to 2000 A.D.* (Chicago: Third World, 1974).

62. Molefi Kete Asante, *An Afrocentric Manifesto: Toward an African Renaissance* (Boston, MA: Polity, 2007); *Egypt Vs Greece and the American Academy: The Debate over the Birth of Civilization* (Chicago: AA Images, 2002).

63. Miranda Lovett, "Reflecting on the Rise of the Hoteps," *SAPIENS*, July 21, 2020, https://www.sapiens.org/culture/hotep; Ann-Derrick Gaillot, "The Rise of Hotep," *The Outline*, April 19, 2017, https://theoutline.com/post/1412/what-hotep-means?zd=1&zi=ql3qpiyr.

64. Black Lives Matter (BLM) is how the movement is commonly referenced. Actually, it is part of the Black Lives Matter Global Network (BLMGN) which is part of a larger

constellation of groups included into the Movement for Black Lives (M4BL). See https://m4bl.org/black-power-rising/.

65. Alicia Garza, "A Herstory of the #BlackLivesMatter Movement," *The Feminist Wire*, October 7, 2014.

66. CIVIQS, Opinion Poll on "Black Lives Matter." 2020, https://civiqs.com/results/black_lives_matter?uncertainty=true&annotations=true&zoomIn=true.

67. Gallup Poll, July 28, 2020, https://news.gallup.com/poll/316106/two-three-americans-support-racial-justice-protests.aspx.

68. Washington Post-Schar Poll, "Big Majorities Support Protests Over Floyd Killings," June 9, 2020, https://www.washingtonpost.com/context/june-2-7-2020-washington-post-schar-poll/6b811cdf-8f99-4e28-b8f1-c76df335c16a/?itid=lk_inline_manual_2.

69. Pew Research Center, "Many Black and Asian Americans Say They Have Experienced Discrimination amid the COVID-19 Outbreak."

70. Centers for Disease Control and Prevention (CDC), "COVID-19 Hospitalization and Death by Race and Ethnicity," *Case, Data & Surveillance*, August 18, 2020, https://www.cdc.gov/coronavirus/2019-ncov/covid-data/investigations-discovery/hospitalization-death-by-race-ethnicity.html.

71. Quoted by Dewey Clayton, "Black Lives Matter and the Civil Rights Movement: A Comparative Analysis of Two Social Movements in the United States," *Journal of Black Studies* 49, no. 5 (2018): 457.

72. Glenn Loury, "The Political Inefficacy of Saying 'Black Lives Matter,'" *The Brown Daily Herald*, November 6, 2015, https://www.browndailyherald.com/2015/11/06/loury-the-political-inefficacy-of-saying-black-lives-matter.

73. Quoted by Madeleine Carlisle, "Two Black Trans Women Were Killed in the Past Week as Trump Revokes Discrimination Protections for Trans People," *Time*, June 13, 2020, https://time.com/5853325/black-trans-women-killed-riah-milton-dominique-remmie-fells-trump.

74. Quoted by Sony Salzman, "From the Start, Black Lives Matter Has Been about LGBTQ Lives," *ABC News*, June 21, 2020, https://abcnews.go.com/US/start-black-lives-matter-lgbtq-lives/story?id=71320450.

75. Kelsey Smoot, "White people Say They Want to Be an Ally to Black People. But Are They Ready for Sacrifice?" *The Guardian*, June 29, 2020, https://www.theguardian.com/commentisfree/2020/jun/29/white-people-ally-black-people-sacrifice. See also John Blake, "How 'Good White People' Derail Racial Progress," *CNN*, August 2, 2020, https://www.cnn.com/2020/08/01/us/white-liberals-hypocrisy-race-blake/index.html.

76. Elwood Watson, "Dear White Liberal Allies: The Ball of Political, Social, Economic and Cultural Progress Is Now in Your Court!" *Medium*, June 10, 2020, https://medium.com/the-polis/dear-white-liberal-allies-the-ball-of-political-social-economic-and-cultural-progress-is-now-in-c9c764a6847c.

77. Blue Lives Matter, 2020, https://www.facebook.com/bluematters.

78. On the racist connotations, see Maurice Chammah and Cary Aspinwall, "The Short, Fraught History of the 'Thin Blue Line' American Flag," *Politico*, September 6, 2020, https://www.politico.com/news/magazine/2020/06/09/the-short-fraught-history-of-the-thin-blue-line-american-flag-309767.

79. Quoted by Laura Schulte, "Thin Blue Line Flag Has Taken a Prominent Place at Trump rallies," *USA TODAY*, October 28, 2020, https://www.usatoday.com/story/news/factcheck/2020/10/28/fact-check-thin-blue-line-flag-prominent-trump-rallies/6058924002.

80. Deanna Pan and Dasia Moore, "A New Survey Says White Support for Black Lives Matter Has Slipped. Some Historians Say They're Not Surprised," *Boston Globe*, Septem-

ber 24, 2020, https://www.bostonglobe.com/2020/09/24/metro/new-survey-says-white-support-black-lives-matter-has-slipped-some-historians-say-theyre-not-surprised.

81. Deanna Pan and Dasia Moore, "A New Survey Says White Support for Black Lives Matter."

82. Alvin B. Tillery Jr., "What Kind of Movement Is Black Lives Matter? The View from Twitter," *Journal of Race, Ethnicity, and Politics* 4, no. 2 (2019): 305. See also Keeanga-Yamahtta Taylor, *From #BlackLivesMatter to Black Liberation* (Chicago: Haymarket Books, 2016).

83. Tomiko Brown-Nagin, "Want to See What Protests Can Be? Look at What They Have Been," *Vox*, March 3, 2017, https://www.vox.com/polyarchy/2017/3/3/14808532/what-protests-can-be.

PART 3. CURRENT LESSONS FROM AMERICA

1. For a long-term analysis, see Kevin Kruse and Julian Zelizer, *Fault Lines: A History of the United States Since 1974* (New York: W.W. Norton, 2019).

2. Michael Grunwald, "How Everything Became the Culture War," *Politico Magazine*, November/December 2018, https://www.politico.com/magazine/story/2018/11/02/culture-war-liberals-conservatives-trump-2018-222095.

3. Quoted by Tim Craig, "US Political Divide Becomes Increasingly Violent, Rattling Activists and Police," *The Washington Post*, August 27, 2020, https://www.washingtonpost.com/national/protests-violence/2020/08/27/3f232e66-e578-11ea-970a-64c73a1c2392_story.html.

4. Thomas Carothers, "Postelection Forecast: More Polarization Ahead," *Commentary*, November 9, 2020, https://carnegieendowment.org/2020/11/09/postelection-forecast-more-polarization-ahead-pub-83156.

8. IS A VIOLENT SOCIETY AMERICA'S ONLY POSSIBLE FUTURE?

1. Kaiser Family Foundation (KFF), "Public Opinion on Single-Payer, National Health Plans, and Expanding Access to Medicare Coverage," October 16, 2020, https://www.kff.org/slideshow/public-opinion-on-single-payer-national-health-plans-and-expanding-access-to-medicare-coverage.

2. See John Sides, Michael Tesler, and Lynn Vavreck, *Identity Crisis: The 2016 Presidential Campaign and the Battle for the Meaning of America* (Princeton, NJ: Princeton University Press, 2018), Chapter 9 in particular; and Daniel Hopkins and Samantha Washington, "The Rise of Trump, the Fall of Prejudice? Tracking White Americans' Racial Attitudes 2008–2018," *SSRN Papers* (October 2019), https://papers.ssrn.com/sol3/papers.cfm?abstract_id=3378076.

3. Pew Research Center, "Hispanic Voters Say Economy, Health Care and COVID-19 Are Top Issues in 2020 Presidential Election," *FactTank*, September 1, 2020, https://www.pewresearch.org/fact-tank/2020/09/11/hispanic-voters-say-economy-health-care-and-covid-19-are-top-issues-in-2020-presidential-election.

4. Pew Research Center, "Path to Legal Status for the Unauthorized Is Top Immigration Policy Goal for Hispanics in the U.S," *Facttank*, February 11, 2020, https://www.pewresearch.org/fact-tank/2020/02/11/path-to-legal-status-for-the-unauthorized-is-top-immigration-policy-goal-for-hispanics-in-u-s.

5. Amy Stringer, "Crossing the Border: Latino Attitudes toward Immigration Policy," *Journal of International Migration and Integration* 19 (2018): 701–715.

6. Third Way, "A Nuanced Picture of What Black Americans Want in 2020," December 30, 2019, Available at https://www.thirdway.org/memo/a-nuanced-picture-of-what-black-americans-want-in-2020.

7. NAACP, "2020 American Election Polls," November 25, 2020, https://naacp.org/latest/2020-american-election-eve-poll-finds-coronavirus-pandemic-and-racial-justice-among-most-important-issues-for-african-american-voters.

8. Emmanuel Saez, "Striking it Richer: The Evolution of Top Incomes in the United States," *Pathway Magazine*, 2020, https://eml.berkeley.edu/~saez/saez-UStopincomes-2018.pdf.

9. Andre Perry and Carl Romer, "The Black Middle Class Needs Political Attention, Too," *Brookings Report*, February 27, 2020, https://www.brookings.edu/research/the-black-middle-class-needs-political-attention-too.

10. Traci Parker, *Department Stores and the Black Freedom Movement: Workers, Consumers, and Civil Rights From the 1930s to the 1980s* (Chapel Hill: University of North Carolina Press, 2019).

11. Candice Jenkins, *Black Bourgeois: Class and Sex in the Flesh* (Minneapolis: University of Minnesota Press, 2019).

12. Daniel Lichter, "Integration or Fragmentation? Racial Diversity and the American Future," *Demography*, 50, no. 2 (2013): 359–391.

13. Carol Graham, *Happiness for All? Unequal Hopes and Lives in Pursuit of the American Dream* (Princeton, NJ: Princeton University Press, 2017), 28.

14. Carol Graham and Leo Pasvolsky, "Why Are Black Poor Americans More Optimistic than White Ones?" *BBC News*, January 29, 2018, https://www.bbc.com/news/world-us-canada-42718303.

15. United States Census Bureau, "Inequalities Persist Despite Decline in Poverty for All Major Race and Hispanic Origin Groups," *Brief on Income and Poverty*, September 15, 2020, https://www.census.gov/library/stories/2020/09/poverty-rates-for-blacks-and-hispanics-reached-historic-lows-in-2019.html.

16. Stacy Patton, "Why Blacks Aren't Embracing Occupy Wall Street," *The Washington Post*, November 25, 2011, https://www.washingtonpost.com/opinions/why-blacks-arent-embracing-occupy-wall-street/2011/11/16/gIQAwc3FwN_story.html.

17. Astra Taylor, "Occupy Wall Street's Legacy Runs Deeper Than You Think," *Economic Hardship Reporting Project*, December 17, 2019, https://economichardship.org/2019/12/occupy-wall-streets-legacy-runs-deeper-than-you-think/.

18. Davin Phoenix, *The Anger Gap* (Cambridge: Cambridge University Press, 2020), 20.

19. Chris Lebron, *The Color of Our Shame* (Oxford: Oxford University Press, 2013).

20. Mary-Frances Winters, *Black Fatigue: How Racism Erodes the Mind, Body, and Spirit* (Oakland: Berrett-Koehler Publishers, 2020), 4.

21. Robin DiAngelo, *White Fragility: Why It's So Hard for White People to Talk About Racism* (Boston: Beacon Press, 2018), 33; See also Ibram X. Kendi, *How to Be an Antiracist* (London: Bodley Head, 2019).

22. John McWhorter, "The Dehumanizing Condescension of White Fragility," *The Atlantic*, July 15, 2020, https://www.theatlantic.com/ideas/archive/2020/07/dehumanizing-condescension-white-fragility/614146/.

23. Barbara Applebaum, "Critical Whiteness Studies," *Oxford Research Encyclopedia*, 2020, https://oxfordre.com/education/view/10.1093/acrefore/9780190264093.001.0001/acrefore-9780190264093-e-5?print=pdf.

24. Christopher Lebron, *The Color of Our Shame: Race and Justice in Our Time* (Oxford: Oxford University Press, 2013).

25. Antoine Banks, *Anger and Racial Politics*, 168.

26. Tracie Stewart, Iona M. Latu, Nyla R. Branscombe, Nia Phillips, and H. Ted Denney, "White Privilege Awareness and Efficacy to Reduce Racial Inequality Improve White Americans' Attitudes Toward African Americans," *Journal of Social Issues*, 68, no. 1 (2012):

11–27; Adam Powell, Nyla R. Branscombe, and Michael T. Schmitt, "Inequality as Ingroup Privilege or Outgroup Disadvantage: The Impact of Group Focus on Collective Guilt and Interracial Attitudes," *Personality and Social Psychology Bulletin* 31 (2005): 508–521.

27. Nyla R. Branscombe, "A Social Psychological Process Perspective on Collective Guilt," in *Collective Guilt: International Perspectives*, ed. Nyla R. Branscombe and Bertjan Doosje, (New York: Cambridge University Press, 2004), 320–334.

28. Kim A. Case, "Raising White Privilege Awareness and Reducing Racial Prejudice: Assessing Diversity Course Effectiveness," *Teaching of Psychology* 34 (2007): 231–235.

29. Nyla R. Branscombe, Michael Schmitt, and Kristin Schiffhauer, "Racial Attitudes in Response to Thoughts of White Privilege," *European Journal of Psychology* 37 (2007): 205.

30. Terry Smith, *Whitelash*, 3. See also Carol Anderson, *White Rage: The Unspoken Truth of Our Racial Divide* (New York, London: Bloomsbury Publishing, 2016).

31. Joseph, Jr. Flynn, *White Fatigue: Rethinking Resistance for Social Justice* (New York: Peter Lang, 2018).

32. Eric Kaufmann, "The Great Awokening and the Second American Revolution," *Quillette*, June 22, 2020, https://quillette.com/2020/06/22/toward-a-new-cultural-nationalism.

33. "A letter on Justice and Open Debate," *Harper's Magazine*, July 7, 2020, https://harpers.org/a-letter-on-justice-and-open-debate.

34. Walter Benn Michaels, *The Trouble with Diversity: How We Learned to Love Identity and Ignore Inequality* (Holt McDougal, 2007), 12.

35. Meghan Daum, *The Problem with Everything: My Journey Through the New Culture Wars* (Gallery Books, 2019). See also Wesley Yang, *The Souls of Yellow Folk* (W.W. Norton, 2018) and Bret Easton Ellis, *White* (New York: Knopf, 2019).

36. See for example, Ryu Spaeth, "The Strange Liberal Backlash to Woke Culture," *The New Republic*, November 25, 2019, https://newrepublic.com/article/155681/strange-liberal-backlash-woke-culture; Scott Indrisek, "The Problem With Meghan Daum's 'The Problem With Everything,'" *Observer*, October 22, 2019, https://observer.com/2019/10/meghan-daum-book-the-problem-with-everything-culture-wars-review/.

37. Laurent Dubreuil, *La Dictature des Identités* (Paris: Gallimard, 2019). See "Nonconforming: Against the Erosion of Academic Freedom by Identity Politics," *Harper's Magazine*, September 2020, https://harpers.org/archive/2020/09/nonconforming.

38. Pew Research Center, *Report on Trust and Distrust in America*, 2019, https://www.pewresearch.org/politics/2019/07/22/the-state-of-personal-trust/.

39. Gallup, "Confidence in Institutions," 2020, https://news.gallup.com/poll/1597/confidence-institutions.aspx.

40. See Yascha Mounk and Roberto Stefan Foa, "This Is How Democracy Dies," *The Atlantic*, January 29, 2020, https://www.theatlantic.com/ideas/archive/2020/01/confidence-democracy-lowest-point-record/605686/.

41. Pew Research Center, "The Optimistic Immigrant," 2006, https://www.pewresearch.org/2006/05/30/the-optimistic-immigrant; See also Antje Röder and Peter Mühlau, "Low Expectations or Different Evaluations? What Explains Immigrants' High Level of Trust in Host Country Institutions?" *Journal of Ethnic and Migration Studies* 38, no. 5 (2012): 777–792.

42. Pew Research Center, "Muslim Americans: No Sign of Growth in Alienation," 2011. For analysis of these trends, see Ariane Chebel d'Appollonia, *Migrant Mobilization and Securitization in the US and Europe* (New York: Palgrave MacMillan, 2015).

43. Rahsaan Maxwell, "Assimilation and Political Attitudes Trade-Offs," in *Outsiders No More? Models of Immigrant Political Incorporation*, ed. Jennifer Hochschild, Jacqueline Chattopadhyay, Claudine Gay, and Michael Jones-Correa (Oxford: Oxford University Press, 2013), 270–287; Emily Estrada, Yung-Mei Tsai, and Charles Chandler,

"Assimilation and Discriminatory Perceptions and Experiences: The Case of Hispanics in the United States," *Social Science Journal* 45, no. 4 (2008): 673–681.

44. Deanna M. Pérez, Wesley G. Jennings, and Angela R. Gover, "Specifying General Strain Theory: An Ethnically Relevant Approach", *Deviant Behavior* 29 (2008): 544–578; Ruben Rumbaut and Walter Ewing, "The Myth of Immigrant Criminality and the Paradox of Assimilation," Report, Immigration Policy Center, American Immigration Law Foundation (2007): 1–16; Ramiro Martinez and Matthew Lee, "On Immigration and Crime," *Criminal Justice*, vol. 1 (2000): 485–524.

45. Lorna Alvarez-Rivera, Matt Nobles, and Kim Lersh, "Latino Immigrant Acculturation and Crime," *American Journal of Criminal Justice* 39 (2014): 321.

46. Victor M. Rios, "The Consequences of the Criminal Justice Pipeline on Black and Latino Masculinity," *Annals of the American Academy of Political and Social Science* 623 (2009): 150–162.

47. Lauren Davenport, *Politics Beyond Black and White: Biracial Identity and Attitudes in America* (Cambridge: Cambridge University Press, 2018), 164.

48. Maria Root, *Racially Mixed People in America* (Sage Publications, 1992).

49. Jennifer Hochschild, Vesla Weaver, and Traci Burch, *Creating a New Racial Order: How Immigration, Multiracialism, Genomics, and the Young Can Remake Race in America* (Princeton, NJ: Princeton University Press, 2012)

50. Oyindamola Bola, "Who Are the Multiracial Americans?" *PRRI Spotlight Analysis*, February 21, 2020, https://www.prri.org/spotlight/who-are-multiracial-americans.

51. See for example the Multiracial Americans of Southern California (MASC) on Linkedin, https://www.linkedin.com/company/multiracial-americans-of-southern-california/about.

52. Kim Williams, "Multiracial Movement and the End of American Racial Categories," *Studies in American Political Development* 31, no. 1 (2017): 101.

53. Kathleen Odell Korgen, ed., *Race Policy and Multiracial Americans* (Chicago: Policy Press, 2016)—in particular the final chapter by Andrew Jolivette.

54. On the notion of reactive social movement, see Charles Tilly, *From Mobilization to Revolution* (Reading, MA: Addison-Wesley, 1978).

55. Doug McAdam, *Political Process and the Development of Black Insurgency* (Chicago: University of Chicago Press, 1999); Richard Valley, "Party, Coercion and Inclusion: The Two Reconstructions of the South's Electoral Politics," *Politics and Society* 21 (1993): 37–68.

56. Craig Jenkins, *The Politics of Insurgency* (New York: Columbia University Press, 1987), 218. See also Craig Jenkins, David Jacobs, and Jon Agnone, "Political Opportunities and African American Protest, 1948–1997," in Doug McAdam and David Snow, *Readings on Social Movements: Origins, Dynamics, and Outcomes* (New York: Oxford University Press, 2010): 57–70.

57. Jason Rivera et al, "The Future Effectiveness of Racial-Political Coalitions in American Politics": 14.

58. Mark Granovetter, "The Strength of Weak Ties: A Network Theory Revisited," *Sociological Theory* 1 (1983): 201–233; James Coleman, "Social Capital in the Creation of Human Capital," *The American Journal of Sociology* 94 (1988): 95–120.

59. Walter Nichols, "The Urban Question Revisited: The Importance of Cities for Social Movements," *International Journal of Urban and Regional Research*, 1 (2008): 841–859.

60. Repairers of the Breach, "Moral Monday Caravans in 24 states Mourn COVID Deaths," 2020, https://www.breachrepairers.org/press-releases/moral-monday-caravans-in-24-states-mourn-covid-deathsnbspnbsp.

61. Industrial Areas Foundation website, https://www.industrialareasfoundation.org.

62. Many coalitional confederations are located in the California Bay area, such as the San Francisco Foundation and Thrive civic engagement alliance.

63. See David A. Snow and Robert D. Benford, "Master Frames and Cycles of Protest," in *Frontiers in Social Movement Theory*, ed. Aldon Morris and Carol McClurg (New Haven: Yale University Press, 1992), 135–155; David A. Snow and Robert D. Benford, "Ideology, Frame, Resonance, and Participant Mobilization," *International Social Movement Research* 1, no. 1 (1988): 197–217.

9. IS VIOLENT AMERICA EUROPE'S FUTURE?

1. Rob Berkeley, "The Missing Link? Building Solidarity among Black Europeans," in *Do I Belong? Reflections from Europe*, ed. Anthony Lerman (London: Pluto Press, 2017), 44.

2. The Spectator, "Identity Politics: Lionel Shriver & Douglas Murray," 2019, https://www.reddit.com/r/samharris/comments/dq1gy4/identity_politics_lionel_shriver_douglas_murray/; See also Douglas Murray, *The Strange Death of Europe* (London: Bloomsbury Continuum, 2017).

3. Kenan Malik, "Beware the Politics of Identity. They Help Legitimize the Toxic Far Right," *The Guardian*, Feb 23, 2020, https://www.theguardian.com/commentisfree/2020/feb/23/beware-politics-of-identity-they-help-legitimise-toxic-far-right.

4. Politifact, "More Killed by Guns Since '68 than in All US Wars," January 18, 2013, http://www.politifact.com/truth-o-meter/statements/2013/jan/18/mark-shields/pbs-commentator-mark-shields-says-more-killed-guns/.

5. Pew Research Center, "America's International Image." 2016, http://www.pewglobal.org/2016/06/28/americas-international-image/.

6. Heather Horn, "Europe Sees History of American Racism in Trayvon Martin Killing," *The Atlantic*, April 2, 2012, https://www.theatlantic.com/international/archive/2012/04/europe-sees-history-of-american-racism-in-trayvon-martin-killing/255362/.

7. Ines Pohl, "Police Violence Is Disturbingly Normal in the U.S.," *Deutsche Welle News*, July 7, 2016, http://www.dw.com/en/opinion-police-violence-is-disturbingly-normal-in-us/a-19387135.

8. Piers Morgan. "If America Wasn't Awash with Guns, It Wouldn't Have to Be Bloodbath," *The Daily Mail*, July 9, 2016, http://www.dailymail.co.uk/news/article-3680941/PIERS-MORGAN-cops-racist-cops-make-mistakes-people-hate-America-wasn-t-awash-guns-wouldn-t-bloodbath.html.

9. Jonathan Jackson, Tasseli McKay, Leonidas Cheliotis, Adam Fine, Rick Trinkner, and Ben Bradford, "Racist Policing Is Making Black and White Americans Question Police Authority," *LSE US Center* (2020), https://blogs.lse.ac.uk/usappblog/2020/07/14/racist-policing-is-making-black-and-white-americans-question-police-authority/.

10. See for example Charles Tilly, *The Vendée* (Cambridge, MA: Harvard University Press, 1964); and *The Contentious French* (Cambridge, MA: Harvard University Press, 1986); Sidney Tarrow, *Democracy and Disorder: Protest and Politics in Italy, 1965–1974* (New York: Oxford University Press, 1989).

11. David Theo Goldberg, "Racial Europeanization," *Ethnic and Racial Studies* 29, no. 2 (2006): 362.

12. Kojo Koram, "Systemic Racism and Police Brutality Are British Problems Too," *The Guardian*, June 4, 2020, https://www.theguardian.com/commentisfree/2020/jun/04/systemic-racism-police-brutality-british-problems-black-lives-matter.

13. Sebastien Roché, "Les policiers ciblent particulièrement les minorités en France et aux Etats-Unis,"*20 Minutes*, June 6, 2020, https://www.20minutes.fr/faits_divers/2791107-20200602-mort-george-floyd-policiers-ciblent-particulierement-minorites-france-comme-etats-unis. See also Mathieu Rigouste, *La Domination Policière* (Paris: La Fabrique, 2012).

14. Lauren Collins, "Assa Traoré and the French Fight for Black Lives in France," *The New Yorker*, June 18, 2020, https://www.newyorker.com/news/letter-from-europe/assa-traore-and-the-fight-for-black-lives-in-france.

15. George Mosse, *Toward the Final Solution: A History of European Racism* (Madison: University of Madison Press, 1985).

16. See for example, Bob Carter and Satnam Virdee, "Racism and the Sociological Imagination," *British Journal of Sociology* 59, no. 4 (2008): 661–679.

17. See Emilia Roig, "Intersectionality in Europe: A Depoliticized Concept," *Völkerrechtsblog*, 6, 2018. https://voelkerrechtsblog.org/de/intersectionality-in-europe-a-depoliticized-concept/. Andrea Krizsan, Violetta Zentai, Tamas Dombos, and Erika Kispeter, *Report Analyzing Intersectionality in Gender Equality Policies for Hungary and the EU* (Budapest: Central European University, 2008); Johanna Kantola, *Gender and the European Union* (London: Palgrave, 2016). See also Stefanie Boulila, *Race in Post-Racial Europe: An Intersectional Analysis* (London: Rowman & Littlefield Publishers, 2019).

18. Roger Hewitt, *White Backlash and the Politics of Multiculturalism* (New York: Cambridge University Press, 2005), 4.

19. Roger Hewitt, *White Backlash*: 25.

20. *BBC News*, "US Capitol Riots: World Leaders React to 'Horrifying' Scenes in Washington," January 8, 2021, https://www.bbc.com/news/world-us-canada-55568613.

21. Gerry Stoker, "Explaining Political Disenchantment: Finding Pathways to Democratic Renewal," *The Political Quarterly* 77, no. 2 (2016): 184–194; Christopher Parker and Matt Barreto, *Change They Can't Believe in: The Tea Party and Reactionary Politics in Contemporary America* (Princeton, NJ: Princeton University Press, 2013).

22. Roberto Stefan Foa and Yascha Mounk, "The Democratic Disconnect," *Journal of Democracy* 27, no. 3 (2016): 6–18.

23. Ketty Kay, "Europe Hates Trump. Does it Matter?" *BBC*, March 4, 2016, http://www.bbc.com/news/magazine-35702584.

24. Thomas Piketty, *Capital* (Cambridge, MA: Belknap Press, 2014); Jacob Hacker, *The Great Risk Shift: The New Economic Insecurity and the Decline of the American Dream* (New York: Oxford University Press, 2006).

25. Eurostat, *Sustainable Development in the European Union* (Luxembourg: Publications Office, 2019), 186.

26. Ronald Inglehart and Pippa Norris, "Trump, Brexit, and the Rise of Populism: Economic Have-Nots and Cultural Backlash," *Faculty Research Working Paper* (Cambridge, MA: Kennedy School, 2016).

27. Ronald Inglehart and Pippa Norris, "Trump, Brexit," 3.

28. Helen Dempster, Amy Leach, and Karen Hargrave, *Public Attitudes towards Immigration and Immigrants* (London: Overseas Development Institute, 2020).

29. Osiewicz Przemyslaw, "Europe's Islamophobia and the Refugee Crisis," MEI@75, September 19, 2017, https://www.mei.edu/publications/europes-islamophobia-and-refugee-crisis.

30. FRA (European Union Agency for Fundamental Rights), *Fundamental Rights Report 2020* (Luxembourg: FRA, 2020), 20.

31. FRA (European Union Agency for Fundamental Rights), *Fundamental Rights*, 92.

32. FRA (European Union Agency for Fundamental Rights), *EU-LGBTI II Report* (Luxembourg: FRA, 2020).

33. Anna Triandafyllidou, Tariq Modood, and Nasar Meer, eds., *European Multiculturalism: Cultural, Religious and Ethnic Challenges* (Edinburgh: Edinburgh University Press, 2012), 3.

34. Per Mouritsen, "Beyond Post-National Citizenship: Access, Consequence, Conditionality," in *European Multiculturalism: Cultural, Religious and Ethnic Challenges*, ed.

Anna Triandafyllidou, Tariq Modood, and Nasar Meer (Edinburgh: Edinburgh University Press, 2012), 95.

35. Examples include the Dutch Nationality Act of 2003 and the New Integration Act of 2007; the Nationality, Immigration, and Asylum Act of 2002 and the Borders, Citizenship, and Immigration Act of 2009 in the United Kingdom; and the introduction of integration contracts in France in 2003 (with further restrictive requirements added in 2006 and 2007).

36. France was the first country to ban in 2010 the full-face Islamic veil in public places. Similar laws were passed in Belgium (2012), the Netherlands (2016), in the Lombardy region of Italy (2016), Austria (2017), and Denmark (2018). In other countries, such as the United Kingdom, the decision to ban religious clothing is decided at the local levels.

37. "Majority of Danes Want to Ban Burqa," *The Local dk*, 2017, https://www.thelocal.dk/20170929/majority-of-danes-want-to-ban-burqa-survey.

38. Statistica, "Do You Agree or Disagree with the Introduction of the Burqa Ban?" 2019, https://www.statista.com/statistics/1039096/opinions-on-the-burqa-ban-in-the-netherlands/.

39. Quoted by James Mcauley, "France Mandates Face Masks, While Continuing to Ban the Burqa," *The Seattle Times*, May 10, 2020, https://www.seattletimes.com/nation-world/france-mandates-face-masks-while-continuing-to-ban-the-burqa/.

40. Muslims are currently estimated to constitute about 5 percent of the EU's 425 million inhabitants (before Brexit). There are about 4.5 Muslims in France (mostly from former colonies in North Africa), followed by 3 million in Germany (mostly Turks), 1.6 million in the United Kingdom (mostly of South Asian descent) and 0.5 million in Italy and the Netherlands. The largest ethnic group is Arab (about 45 percent of European Muslims). Most European Muslims are immigrants or have an immigrant background. Not all those born in Europe have automatic access to citizenship because of the restrictions to jus soli. Most Muslims are Sunnis, although there is also a small Shiite minority. There are significant variations among Sunnis along ethnic lines, as there are several schools of law within Sunni Islam. Furthermore, some Muslims originate from Sub-Saharan African countries—for example, about 10 percent of the Nigerians living in the United Kingdom.

41. For a review of these European surveys, see Ariane Chebel d'Appollonia, *Migrant Mobilization and Securitization in the US and Europe: How Does It Feel to Be a Threat?* (New York: Palgrave Macmillan, 2015); Jocelyne Cesari, *Why the West Fears Islam?* (New York: Palgrave Macmillan, 2013).

42. Sharam Akbarzadeh and Joshue M. Roose, "Muslims, Multiculturalism and the Question of the Silent Majority," *Journal of Muslim Minority Affairs* 31, no. 3 (2011): 310.

43. Pew Research Center, "How Religious Commitment Varies by Country," *Demographic Study*, June 13, 2018, https://www.pewforum.org/2018/06/13/how-religious-commitment-varies-by-country-among-people-of-all-ages/.

44. Rapporteur Général de l'Observatoire de la Laïcité, *Synthèse de étude sur l'expression et la visibilité religieuses dans l'espace public aujourd'hui en France* (Paris: Observatoire de la Laïcité, 2019).

45. Bhikhu Parekh, "Feeling at Home: Some Reflections on Muslims in Europe," *Harvard Middle Eastern and Islamic Review* 8 (2009): 53.

46. It is difficult to quantify the overall Black population in Europe because many European countries do not collect racial data. According to data based on the country of origin, the largest Black communities are located in France (5 million), the United Kingdom (2.5 million), Italy (0.7 million), Spain (0.6 million), and Germany (0.53 million). In some countries—like France, the United Kingdom, Belgium, Spain, and Portugal—large numbers of Black people arrived in the 1950–1970s. In other countries—like Italy, Sweden, and Norway—African communities arrived in the 1990s and are less culturally assimilated.

Newcomers (about 1.1 million since 2010) are mostly refugees from sub-Saharan countries.

47. Léopold Senghor, *Foundations of Africanité, Négritude and Arabité* (Paris: Présence Africaine, 1967). See also Paul Gilroy, *Postcolonial Melancholia* (New York: Columbia University Press, 2005).

48. Felix Germain, *Decolonizing the Republic* (East Lansing: Michigan State University Press, 2016); Thomas Earle and Kate J. P. Lowe, eds., *Black Africans and Renaissance Europe* (Cambridge: Cambridge University Press, 2005).

49. Gillian Glaes, *Activism in Postcolonial France: State Surveillance and Social Welfare* (London: Routledge, 2019); Pap Ndiaye, *La condition noire: Essai sur une minorité Française* (Paris: Calmann-Levy, 2008); Heike Raphael-Hernandez, *Blackening Europe: The Afro-American Presence* (London: Routledge, 2004); Brent Hayes Edwards, *The Practice of Diaspora: Literature, Translation, and the Rise of Black Internationalism* (Cambridge, MA: Harvard University Press, 2003).

50. Valeriya Safronova, "Black Germans Say It's Time to Look Inward," *The New York Times*, Oct 5, 2020, https://www.nytimes.com/2020/10/04/style/black-germans-say-its-time-to-look-inward.html.

51. Bernd Simon and Olga Grabow, "The Politicization of Migrants: Further Evidence that Politicized Collective Identity Is a Dual Identity," *Political Psychology* 31, no. 5 (2010): 717–738; Bert Klandermans and Van Stekelenburg. "Embeddedness and Identity: How Immigrants Turn Grievances into Action," *American Sociological Review* 73 (2008): 992–1012.

52. Itay Lotem, "Beyond Memory Wars: The Indigènes de la République's Grass Roots Anti-Racism Between the Memory of Colonialism and Antisemitism," *French History* 32, no. 4 (2018): 573–593; Clemens Zobel, "The Indigènes de la République and Political Mobilization Strategies in Postcolonial France," *e-Cedernos CES* 7 (2010): 52–67.

53. Mouvement des Indigènes de la République, "We Are the Indigenous of the French Republique," 2005, http://www.decolonialtranslation.com/english/AppelEng.php.

54. Houria Bouteldja, *Whites, Jews and Us*, trans. Rachel Valinsky (Cambridge: MIT Press, 2017); Houria Bouteldja and Sadri Khiari, *Nous Sommes les Indigènes de la République* (Editions Amsterdam, 2012)

55. See for example Houria Bouteldja, "Féministe ou pas? Penser la possibilité d'un féminisme décolonial," PIR Archives, 2014, http://indigenes-republique.fr/feministes-ou-pas-penser-la-possibilite-dun-feminisme-decolonial-avec-james-baldwin-et-audre-lorde/.

56. Akwugo Emejulu and Francesca Sobande, eds., *To Exist Is to Resist: Afrofeminism and Black Feminism in Europe* (London: Pluto Press, 2019), 5.

57. Akwugo Emejulu and Francesca Sobande, eds., *To Exist Is to Resist*, 9.

58. Fatima El-Tayeb, "Beyond the Black Paradigm? Queer Afro-Diasporic Strategies," *Black Perspectives*, October 22, 2018, https://www.aaihs.org/beyond-the-black-paradigm-queer-afro-diasporic-strategies.

59. Sirma Bilge, "Intersectionality Undone: Saving Intersectionality from Feminist Intersectionality Studies," *Du Bois Review*, 10, no. 2 (2013): 412. See also Barbara Tomlinson, "Colonizing Intersectionality: Replicating Racial Hierarchy in Feminist Academic Arguments," *Social Identities: Journal for the Study of Race, Nation and Culture*, 19, no. 2 (2013): 254–272; Gail Lewis, "Celebrating Intersectionality? Debates on a Multi-Faceted Concept in Gender Studies," *European Journal of Women's Studies*, 16 (2009): 203–210.

60. See, for example, Laura De Guissmé and Laurent Licata, "Competition over Collective Victimhood Recognition: When Perceived Recognition for Past Victimization Is Associated with Negative Attitudes toward Another Victimized Group," *European Journal of Psychology* 47 (2017): 148–166.

61. Miri Song, "Challenging a Culture of Racial Equivalence," *The British Journal of Sociology*, 65 (2014): 107–129; Gérard Noiriel and Stéphane Beaud, "Racisme anti-blancs, non à une imposture," *Le Monde*, November 14, 2012.

62. Pierre-André Taguieff, *Judéophobie, la dernière vague (2000–2017)* (Paris: Fayard, 2018); Günther Jikeli, *European Muslim Antisemitism: Why Young Urban Males Say They Don't Like Jews* (Bloomington: Indiana University Press, 2015); Paul Iganski and Barry Kosmin, eds., *The New Antisemitism? Debating Judeophobia in the 21st Century* (London: Profile Book, 2003).

63. Jon Fox, "The Uses of Racism: Whitewashing New Europeans in the UK," *Ethnic and Racial Studies* 36, no. 11 (2013): 1871–1889.

64. Alana Lentin, "Racism in Public or Public Racism: Doing Anti-Racism in Post-Racial Times," *Ethnic and Racial* Studies, 39, no. 1 (2015): 33–48; Alana Lentin and Titley Gavan, *The Crisis of Multiculturalism: Racism in a Neoliberal Age* (London: Zed, 2011).

65. Valentine Faure, "Islamo-gauchisme: Histoire tortueuse d'une expression devenue une invective," *Le Monde*, December 11, 2020, https://www.lemonde.fr/idees/article/2020/12/11/islamo-gauchisme-histoire-tortueuse-d-une-expression-devenue-une-invective_6063006_3232.html.

66. The most virulent controversy takes place in France, where movements suspected of "Islamo-gauchisme" separatism (like the Collectif contre l'Islamophobie en France, CCIF, and some supporters of the PIR) are criticized by intellectuals and political leaders. A manifesto signed by one hundred intellectuals was published by *Le Monde* in November 2020, expressing concerns about the negative effect of "Islamist, indigenist, racialist, and post-colonial" ideologies on French universities. The trigger event was the killing of a schoolteacher, beheaded by a young Islamist fanatic, after he attempted to teach principles of free speech by showing a cartoon of Prophet Muhammad (cartoon previously published by the satirical magazine *Charlie Hebdo*, which incentivized Islamist fanatics to organize a terrorist attack killing twelve people in January 2015). The CCIF was dissolved in December 2020, and in February 2021, a law against Islamist separatism (Law Consolidating Respect for the Principles of the Republic) was adopted.

67. Norimitsu Onishi, "Will American Ideas Tear France Apart? Some of Its Leaders Think So," *The New York Times*, February 9, 2021, https://www.nytimes.com/2021/02/09/world/europe/france-threat-american-universities.html. For a response to this *New York Times* article by the scholars who signed the "100 Manifesto," see http://decolonialisme.fr/?p=2405.

68. See Houria Boutledja, "French Intelligentsia and Little Tom Thumb: The Questionable Ethics of the '100' French Academics," *Open Democracy*, December 9, 2020, https://www.opendemocracy.net/en/can-europe-make-it/french-intelligentsia-and-little-tom-thumb-the-questionable-ethics-of-the-100-french-academics. Also see Rokhaya Diallo, "France's Ideological Wars Have Found a New Battleground: Universities," *The Washington Post*, December 29, 2020, https://www.washingtonpost.com/opinions/2020/12/29/france-academic-freedom-universities-backlash. For an analysis of the debate, see Michel Wieviorka, *Racisme, antisémitisme, antiracisme: Apologie pour la recherche* (Paris: Les Editions La Boîte à Pandore, 2021).

69. See for example, Raheem Kassam, *No Go Zones: How Sharia Is Coming to a Neighborhood Near You* (London: Regnery Publishing, 2017), with a foreword by Nigel Farage.

70. Bridge Team Initiative, "No-Go Zone Conspiracy Theory," *Bridge* (Georgetown University), May 22, 2020, https://bridge.georgetown.edu/research/factsheet-no-go-zone-conspiracy-theory.

71. Europol, *European Union Terrorism Situation and Trend Report* (Brussels: European Union Agency for Law Enforcement Cooperation, 2020).

72. Bhikhu Parekh, "Feeling at Home: Some Reflections on Muslims in Europe," *Harvard Middle Eastern and Islamic Review* 8 (2009): 51–85.

73. Eva Cossé, "The Alarming Rise of Anti-Semitism in Europe," *Human Rights Watch*, June 4, 2019, https://www.hrw.org/news/2019/06/04/alarming-rise-anti-semitism-europe#.

74. Nonna Mayer and Vincent Tiberj, *Enquête sur les relations interculturelles: Le cas de Sarcelles* (Paris: Presses de Sciences Po, forthcoming).

75. Christel Kesler and Luisa Schwartzman, "From Multiracial Subjects to Multicultural Citizens: Social Stratification and Ethnic and Racial Classification among Children of Immigrants in the United Kingdom," *International Migration* Review 49, no. 3 (2015): 790–836; Jaspal Rusi and Marco Cinnirella, "The Construction of British National Identity Among British South Asians," *National Identities* 15, no. 2 (2013): 157–167; John Berry and Colette Sabatier, "Acculturation, Discrimination, and Adaptation Among Second Generation Immigrant Youth in Montreal and Paris," *International Journal of Intercultural Relations* 34 (2010): 191–207; Frank Bechhofer and David McCrone, "Changing Claims in Context: National Identity Revisited," *Ethnic and Racial Studies* 37, no. 8 (2012): 1–21.

76. Commission on Race and Ethnic Disparities, *The Report*, 2021, https://assets.publishing.service.gov.uk/government/uploads/system/uploads/attachment_data/file/974507/20210331_-_CRED_Report_-_FINAL_-_Web_Accessible.pdf.

77. See https://www.bbc.co.uk/newsround/56591022.

78. Alita Nandi and Lucinda Platt, "Patterns of Minority and Majority Identification in a Multicultural Society," *Ethnic and Racial Issues* 38, no. 15 (2015): 2615–2634.

79. Sayaka Osanami Törngren and Nahikari Irastorza, "Understanding Multiethnic and Multiracial Experiences Globally: Towards a Conceptual Framework of Mixedness," *Journal of Ethnic and Migration Studies*, 47, no. 4 (2021): 763–781.

CONCLUSION

1. See Carlos Lozada, "Show Me Your Identification: Identity Politics May Divide Us. But Ultimately We Can't Unite without It," *Washington Post*, October 18, 2020, https://www.washingtonpost.com/news/book-party/wp/2018/10/18/feature/identity-politics-may-divide-us-but-ultimately-we-cant-unite-without-it.

2. Etienne Balibar and Immanuel Wallerstein, *Race, Nation, Class: Ambiguous Identities* (London: Verso, 1991).

3. See VPM Series, *Racism: Challenging Perceptions*, October 2021, https://vpm.org/articles/15334/challenging-perceptions-discussion-series-on-systemic-racism#section-7916483. See also Hamilton Lombard, "Inside the Income Gap for Some Black Virginians," Report for the University of Virginia, July 2020, http://statchatva.org/2020/07/31/inside-the-income-gap-for-some-black-virginians.

4. Tracy Jan, Jena McGregor, and Meghan Hoyer, "Corporate America's $50 Billion Promise," *Washington Post*, August 20, 2021, https://www.washingtonpost.com/business/interactive/2021/george-floyd-corporate-america-racial-justice.

5. Lawrence Blum, *I'm Not a Racist but . . . The Moral Quandary of Race* (Ithaca, NY: Cornell University Press, 2002), 26.

6. Lawrence Blum, *I'm Not a Racist but*, 28.

7. Robert Paul Hartley, *Unleashing the Power of Poor and Low-Income Americans* (Poor People's Campaign), 2020, https://www.poorpeoplescampaign.org/wp-content/uploads/2020/08/PPC-Voter-Research-Brief-18.pdf. Poor and low-income people today include 65.6 million white (non-Hispanic), 38 million Hispanics, 23.7 percent Black (non-Hispanic), 8 million Asian, and 2 million Native-Indigenous people.

8. Janelle Jones and John Schmitt, "A College Degree Is No Guarantee," *Research Brief*, Center for Economic and Policy Research, 2014, https://cepr.net/documents/black-coll-grads-2014-05.pdf.

9. Unemployment rates among Black workers were 15.4 percent for those with less than high school education, 8.2 percent for those with high school degrees, and 5.6 percent for those with some college (compared to 8.4, 3.8, and 3 percent respectively among white workers). See Jhacova Williams and Valerie Wilson, "Black Workers Endure Persistent Racial Disparities in Employment Outcomes," *Labor Day 2019* (Economic Policy Institute, 2019), https://www.epi.org/publication/labor-day-2019-racial-disparities-in-employment.

10. See Kwame Anthony Appiah, *The Ethics of Diversity* (Princeton, NJ: Princeton University Press, 2004); Jeff Spinner, *Surviving Diversity* (Baltimore, MD: Johns Hopkins University, 2000); Seyla Benhabib, *Democracy and Difference: Contesting the Boundaries of Political* (Princeton, NJ: Princeton University Press, 1996); Will Kymlicka, *The Rights of Minority Culture* (Oxford: Oxford University Press, 1995); Michael Walzer, *Spheres of Justice: A Defense of Pluralism and Equality* (New York: Basic Books, 1983).

11. William Connelly, *Identity/Difference: Democratic Negotiations of Political Paradox* (Ithaca, NY: Cornell University Press, 1991). See also Mark Wenman, *Agonistic Democracy* (Cambridge: Cambridge University Press, 2013); Chantal Mouffe, "Deliberative Democracy or Agonistic Pluralism?" *Social Research*, 66, no. 3 (1999): 745–758.

12. Bashir Bashir and Will Kymlicka, eds., *The Politics of Reconciliation in Multicultural Societies* (Oxford: Oxford University Press, 2008), 4.

13. See https://greensborotrc.org/, accessed March 17, 2021.

14. Andrew Valls, "Racial Justice as Transitional Justice," *Polity*, 36, no. 1 (2003): 53. See also John Torpey, *Making Whole What Has Been Smashed: On Reparation Politics* (Cambridge: Cambridge University Press, 2006); Andrew Schaap, "Political Reconciliation as Struggles for Recognition?" *Social & Legal Studies* 13, no. 4 (2004): 523–540.

15. See for example Will Bunch, "Congress Needs to Create a Truth and Reconciliation Process," *Concord Monitor*, January 16, 2021, https://www.concordmonitor.com/Congress-must-expel-its-coup-plotters-38335514; Robert Gottlieb, "America Needs a Truth, Justice and Reconciliation Commission to Heal," *New York Law Journal*, March 12, 2021, https://www.law.com/newyorklawjournal/2021/03/12/america-needs-a-truth-justice-and-reconciliation-commission-to-heal/?slreturn=20210217130509; NPR, Podcast on "Healing US Divides Through Truth and Reconciliation Commissions," October 11, 2022, in *All Things Considered*, podcast, https://www.npr.org/2020/10/11/922849505/healing-u-s-divides-through-truth-and-reconciliation-commissions.

16. See for example Jill Lepore, "Let History, Not Partisans, Prosecute Trump," *Washington Post*, October 16, 2020, https://www.washingtonpost.com/outlook/truth-reconciliation-tribunal-trump-historians/2020/10/16/84026810-0e88-11eb-b1e8-16b59b92b36d_story.html; Henry Olsen, "Call the Proposed Probe of Trump and His Enablers What It Really Is: McCarthyism," *Washington Post*, October 2020, https://www.washingtonpost.com/outlook/truth-reconciliation-tribunal-trump-historians/2020/10/16/84026810-0e88-11eb-b1e8-16b59b92b36d_story.html.

17. Sara Song, "The Boundary Problem in Democratic Theory: Why the Demos Should Be Bounded by the State," *International Theory* 4, no. 1 (2012): 39–68.

18. Robert Miles, *The Unity of Racism: A Critique of Conceptual Inflation* (London: Routledge, 1989).

19. Ibram X. Kendi, *How to Be an Antiracist* (London: Bodley Head, 2019).

20. Lawrence Blum, *I'm Not a Racist but*, 2.

21. For a critical evaluation of this perspective, see Charles Gallagher, "Color-Blind Egalitarianism as The New Social Norm," in *Theories of Race and Ethnicity*, ed. Karim Murji and John Solomos (Cambridge: Cambridge University Press, 2015), 40–56.

22. Melissa Nobles, *Shades of Citizenship: Race and the Census in Modern Politics* (Stanford, CA: Stanford University Press, 2000).

23. Kwame Anthony Appiah, "Race, Culture, Identity: Misunderstood Connections," in *Colour Conscious: The Political Morality of Race*, ed. Appiah Kwame Appiah and Amy Gutman (Princeton, NJ: Princeton University Press, 1996), 30–105.

24. Jason Hill, *Becoming a Cosmopolitan: What It Means to Be a Human Being in the New Millennium* (Lanham, MD: Rowman and Littlefield, 2000). For a critical evaluation of racial eliminativism, see Brett Louis, "Can Race Be Eradicated?" in *Theories of Race and Ethnicity*, ed. Karim Murji and John Solomos (Cambridge: Cambridge University Press, 2015), 114–137.

25. One example is the *Trajectories and Origins (TeO)* survey that focused on immigrants, descendants of immigrants, persons from the French overseas territories and their descendants. It was conducted in 2015 by researchers at the National Institute for Demographic Studies and the National Institute for Statistics and Economic Studies, and it was closely supervised by the official bodies that oversee the collection and use of public statistics.

26. Lilla Farkas, *Data Collection in the Field of Ethnicity: Analysis and Comparative Review of Equality Data Collection Practices in the European Union* (Brussels: European Commission, 2017).

27. Cynthia Nakashima, "Voices from the Movement: Approaches to Multiraciality," in *The Multiracial Experience: Racial Borders as the New Frontier*, ed. Maria Root (Thousand Oaks, 1996), 81. See also Miri Song, *Multiracial Parents: Mixed Families, Generational Change and the Future of Race* (New York: New York University Press, 2017); Cathy Tashiro, *Standing on Both Feet* (New York: Routledge, 2016).

28. Tomàs Jimenez, Julie Park, and Juan Pedroza, "The New Third Generation: Post 1965 Immigration and the Next Chapter in the Long Story of Assimilation," *International Migration Review*, 52, no. 5 (2018): 1040–1079; Tomàs Jimenez, "Affiliative Ethnic Identity," *Ethnic and Racial Studies*, 33, no. 10 (2010): 1756–1775.

29. Tim Scott, "Let's Set the Record Straight on 'Woke Supremacy' and Racism," *Washington Post*, March 23, 2021, https://www.washingtonpost.com/opinions/2021/03/23/tim-scott-woke-supremacy-intolerance.

30. Pew Research Center, "In a Politically Polarized Era, Sharp Divides in Both Partisan Coalitions," *US Politics & Policy*, 2019, https://www.pewresearch.org/politics/2019/12/17/in-a-politically-polarized-era-sharp-divides-in-both-partisan-coalitions.

31. Pew Research Center, "How Americans View Trust, Facts, and Democracy Today," *Trust Magazine*, February 19, 2020, https://www.pewtrusts.org/en/trust/archive/winter-2020/how-americans-view-trust-facts-and-democracy-today.

32. In two years, confidence in the medical system has increased by 15 percent (up to 51 percent in 2020), and by 12 percent in the public school system (up to 41 percent in 2020). See Brenan Megan Brenan, "Amid Pandemic, Confidence in Key US Institutions Surges," *Gallup*, 2020, https://news.gallup.com/poll/317135/amid-pandemic-confidence-key-institutions-surges.aspx.

33. Magdalena Wojcieszak and Benjamin Warner, "Can Interparty Contact Reduce Affective Polarization? A Systematic Test of Different Forms of Intergroup Contact," *Political Communication* 37 no. 6 (2020): 789–811; Birte Gundelach, "In Diversity We Trust: The Positive Effect of Ethnic Diversity on Outgroup Trust," *Political Behavior* 36 (2014): 125–142; Thomas Pettigrew, Linda R. Tropp, Ulrich Wagner, and Oliver Christ, "Recent Advances in Intergroup Contact Theory," *International Journal of Intercultural Relations* 35, no. 3 (2011): 271–280.

Index

Figures, notes, and tables are indicated by f, n, and t following the page number.

Abramowitz, Alan, 139
Acevedo, Joel, 145
ACRI (American Civil Rights Institute), 85
ADOS (American Descendants of Slavery), 80
adversity. *See* contextual adversity
affirmative action
   Asian Americans and, 85, 134
   Black identity formation and, 65, 70–71, 103
   competition theory and, 9, 12, 26
   deracialization process and, 204
   group position and, 74–75
   Hispanics and, 131
   identity politics and, 41–42, 80, 85, 122–123
   legal challenges to, 85, 93
   multiracialism and, 168
   white identity formation and, 61, 122–123
Affordable Care Act of 2010, 157
African Americans, use of term, 64, 66. *See also* Blacks and Blackness
Agency for Fundamental Rights (EU), 181
Ahmad, Abu Laith Luqman, 149
Alba, Richard, 62, 94, 107, 121, 123, 131
Alex, Yvette, 69
Alien and Sedition Acts of 1798, 21
Alien Registration Act of 1940, 21
Allport, Gordon, 40
Alternative for Germany (political party), 182
Alvarez-Rivera, Lorna, 167
AMEA (Association of Multiethnic Americans), 74–75, 108
American Asian Movement, 58
American Bar Association, 117
American Citizens for Justice, 67
American Civil Rights Institute (ACRI), 85
American Defense Society, 47
American Descendants of Slavery (ADOS), 80
American exceptionalism, 17, 23, 32, 174–175
American Jewish Committee, 50
American Jewish Congress, 50–51
American National Election Study, 126, 139
American Protective Association, 20
Amnesty International USA, 115
Anti-Nazi League, 186

antiracism, 43, 63, 158, 164, 186–188, 190, 192, 201
anti-Semitic violence, 6, 20, 47–48, 55, 97, 108
Anti-Terrorism and Effective Death Penalty Act of 1996, 91–92, 223n12, 228n1
A Place for Us (APFU), 74, 108
Appiah, Kwame Anthony, 201
Arendt, Hannah, 33, 178
Aronson, Arnold, 50
Aryanism, 178
Asante, Molefi Kete, 150
Ashcroft, John, 228n3
Asians
   cultural racism and, 40
   demographic trends, 130
   educational attainment and, 113
   ethnoracial coalitions and, 85–86
   ethnoracial identity formation and, 56–58, 127
   ethnoracial violence against, 4, 49, 83
   gang violence and, 83
   group position and, 73–75
   identification strategy, legacy of, 66–69
   identity politics and, 69–70, 127, 130–135
   immigration policy and, 56, 62
   institutional racism and, 21
   invisibility of, 130–135
   migrant optimism among, 107
   as model minority, 85
   nonviolent contentious politics and, 85
   racial polarization and, 143, 148
   socioeconomic discrimination and, 111–114, 111*t*
Asim, Jabari, 94
assimilation and integration
   adversity as vector for, 32
   Black/white paradigm of, 5, 98
   ethnoracial identity formation and, 46, 60–61, 64, 68
   in Europe, 183
   identity politics and, 120–122
   immigration policy and, 5, 26, 30, 40, 166–168

257

assimilation and integration (*continued*)
  intermarriage and, 104
  multiracialism and, 61
  nativism and, 30
  relational, 124
Association of Multiethnic Americans (AMEA), 74–75, 108
Aurora, Colorado mass shooting (2012), 209n19
Austria, race relations in, 251n36

Baldwin, James, 130, 178
Bannon, Steve, 223n13
Banton, Michael, 178
Barreto, Matt, 96
Bashir, Bashir, 198
Battle, Juan, 64
Battle of Liberty Place (1874), 19
Bean, Frank, 61, 76, 104
Beck, Roy, 223n13
Belgium
  Blacks in, 261n46
  race relations in, 251n36
  social protest movements in, 186
Bell, Joyce, 127
Berkeley, Rob, 173
Berlin, Ira, 65–66
Biden, Joe
  election of, 155
  Hispanics voting for, 167
  voter demographics and attitudes, 140, 144, 147
Black History Month, 64
Black Lives Matter (BLM)
  Asians and, 147–148
  Black identity and, 129–130
  ethnoracial fragmentation and, 150–154
  in Europe, 173–174, 177
  founding of, 129, 150
  goals of, 7, 150–151
  Hispanics and, 146–147
  identity politics and, 125, 195
  protests, 14–15, 27, 97, 142, 146–147, 149, 151, 173
  racial polarization and, 142
  whites and, 161
Black Muslims, 65, 80, 87, 148–149. *See also* Nation of Islam
Black Panther Party, 57, 65
Black Power Movement, 51, 57, 65, 186
Blacks and Blackness. *See also* Black Lives Matter
  affirmative action programs and, 65, 70–71, 103

  civic participation and, 117–119, 226n62
  cultural racism and, 40
  diversity and tolerance experience of, 104–106
  educational attainment and, 105–106, 112–113
  ethnoracial coalitions and, 85–89
  ethnoracial identity formation and, 52–55, 63–66
  in Europe, 261n46
  Great Migration and, 24, 50, 54
  identity politics and, 126–130
  immigration policy and, 65
  institutional racism and, 20–21
  law enforcement disparities and, 7–8, 114–117
  middle class, 71, 104, 160
  racial polarization and, 143–150
  as reactive identity, 52–53
  segregation and, 5, 9, 20, 25, 27–28, 39, 52, 54, 113–114, 128, 196, 208n8, 220n39
  socioeconomic discrimination and, 110–114, 111*t*, 159–162, 196
  unemployment rate, 111, 255n9
  use of term, 205n6
Blee, Kathleen, 32, 212n4
BLM. *See* Black Lives Matter
Bloom, Alan, 79
Blue Lives Matter, 153
Blum, Lawrence, 31–32, 39, 53, 196
Blumer, Herbert, 36, 38, 40
Bly, Robert: *Iron John: A Book about Men*, 225n38
Bobo, Lawrence, 36, 73, 81, 125
Bonilla-Silva, Eduardo, 94, 128
Bonnett, Alastair, 78
Borders, Citizenship, and Immigration Act of 2009 (UK), 251n35
Bourdieu, Pierre, 178
Branscombe, Nyla, 163
Brodkin, Karen, 51
Brown, Gregory, 146
Brown, Jerry, 86
Brown, Kevin, 80
Brown, Michael, 1, 7, 27, 95, 110, 129, 137, 151
Brown, Rap, 1
Brown, Wendy, 88
Brown v. Board of Education (1954), 28, 113, 142
Brown Berets, 57
Brubaker, Rogers, 78
Buchanan, Pat, 93, 123
Bureau of Justice Statistics, 114

INDEX

Bush, George H. W., 70
Bush, George W., 70–71, 137–138, 144

Cafe Con Leche Republicans, 70
Cain, Herman, 149
California. *See also specific cities*
   anti-immigrant legislation in, 68
   Black identity formation in, 105
   ethnoracial coalitions in, 85–86, 87
   ethnoracial violence in, 18
   gang violence in, 83
   Governor's Commission on Los Angeles riots, 21
   intergroup relations in, 58
   multiracialism in, 169
   school segregation in, 56, 220n39
   white identity formation in, 4, 48–49
Caminetti, Anthony, 48
Campaign Against Racial Discrimination (CARD), 186
CAPAC (Congressional Asian Pacific American Caucus), 133
Capeci, Dominic, Jr., 71
Carlos, John, 179
Carmichael, Stokely, 65, 178
Carnevale, Nancy, 48
Carothers, Thomas, 156
Carson, Ben, 127, 149
Carter, Gregg Lee, 66
Catholics, 19–20
CCCS (Center for Contemporary Cultural Studies), 178
CCIF (Collectif contre l'Islamophobie en France), 253n66
Center for Contemporary Cultural Studies (CCCS), 178
Center for Immigration Studies (CIS), 74, 93
Center for the Future of Democracy, 165
Center on Juvenile and Criminal Justice, 7
Césaire, Aimé, 185
Chaney, James, 51
Charles, Rashan, 177
Charleston, South Carolina church shooting (2015), 23, 82, 226n64
Chase, Jonovia, 152
Chauvin, Derek, 115
Chicago
   Commission on Race Relations, 21, 24, 25
   gang violence in, 83
   Police Accountability Task Force, 27
Chicago Freedom Movement, 57
Chicano Moratorium (1970), 57
Chicano Movement, 38, 57, 68

Chin, Vincent, 67
Chinese Exclusion Act of 1882, 21
Cho, Sumi, 58
Choi, Tony, 134
Chow, Giselle, 67
Chua, Amy, 77, 123
CIS (Center for Immigration Studies), 74, 93
civic exclusion, 117–119, 207–208n8
Civil Liberties Act of 1988, 85
Civil Rights Act of 1875, 207n8
Civil Rights Act of 1964, 26, 64
Clinton, Bill, 88
Clinton, Hillary, 141, 144, 147
Coalition Against Anti-Asian Violence, 86
Coates, Ta-Nehisi, 178
Cobas, José, 121
Cobbina, Jennifer, 1
Cohen, Cathy, 238n46
Colbert, Jean-Baptiste, 179
Coleman Report (1966), 112
Collectif contre l'Islamophobie en France (CCIF), 253n66
collective action
   ethnoracial coalitions and, 86
   identity politics and, 38, 187
   political polarization and, 170
   reactive identity formation and, 35
Colston, Edward, 179
Columbine mass shooting (1999), 209n19
Comer, James, 26
Commission on Race and Ethnic Disparities, 191–192
Commission to Study Reparation Proposals for African Americans, 80
competition theory, 24, 26–27, 30, 36–37, 40
conceptual definitions, 39–43
   prejudice, 40–41
   racialization, 41–42
   racism, 39–40
Confederate statues, removal of, 27, 82, 196, 226n64
Congressional Asian Pacific American Caucus (CAPAC), 133
Congressional Hispanic Caucus, 70
Congress on Racial Equality, 25
Connerly, Ward, 85
Conseil Français du Culte Musulman (French Council of the Muslim Faith), 188
contextual adversity, 31–43
   analytical framework, 8–11, 9f
   identity politics and, 36–39
   identity strategy, violence as, 35–39

contextual adversity (*continued*)
  reactive identification and, 35–36
  utility of violence and, 32–35
Cooperative Campaign Analysis Project, 126
Coordinating Committee of Muslims in Germany, 188
Cornell University, 20
Correra, Michael Jones, 86
Coughlin, Charles E., 47–48
COVID-19 pandemic, 41, 110, 113, 134, 151–152
Coyle, James, 20
Craig, Maureen, 37
Crenshaw, Kimberlé, 77, 178, 238n46
Critical Whiteness Studies (CWS), 162
Cullors, Patrisse, 129, 150
"culture of violence," 22–23, 27, 141, 167
current trajectories of violence, 91–154
  analytical framework for, 97–99
  diversity and, 101–119. *See also* diversity
  from identity politics to ethnoracial identity crisis, 120–135
  post-racialism, ambivalence of, 93–96
  Trump effect, 96–97
  from "war on terror" to attacks on minorities, 91–93
CWS (Critical Whiteness Studies), 162

DACA (Deferred Action for Childhood Arrival) program, 143
Da Costa, Edson, 177
Daniels, Roger, 1
Daum, Meghan, 164
Davenport, Lauren, 168
David, Alphonso, 152
Davis, Angela, 178, 238n46
Deacons for Defense and Justice, 206n20
Debouzy, Marianne, 80
Debt Collective, 162
deflation of racism, 199–201
Dekoloniale (organization), 186
Della Porta, Donatella, 212n10
Democratic Party
  affirmative action programs and, 103
  Asian Americans and, 147
  deracialization process and, 203
  ethnoracial coalitions and, 88
  Hispanics and, 144
  identitarian strategies and, 69, 70
  identity politics and, 123, 125–126, 203
  immigration policy and, 159
  integration paradox and, 167
  patterns of mobilization and, 82
  political polarization and, 138–142
  race relations and, 109
  racial riots and, 19
  same-sex marriage and, 102–103
  social protest movements and, 170
Denmark
  identity politics in, 183
  nationalism in, 180
  race relations in, 251n36
Department of Health and Human Services (US), 106
Deportation Act of 1929, 56
deracialization process, 202–204
Derrida, Jacques, 178
Desmond, Matthew, 114
DiAngelo, Robin, 162–163
Diani, Mario, 33, 212n10
Diaz, Manuel Angel, 132, 145
Dietrich, David, 128
discrimination
  anti-Semitism, 6, 20, 47–48, 55, 97, 108
  as contextual adversity, 37, 40–42
  cycles of violence and, 28
  deflation of racism option and, 200–201
  employment, 113
  ethnoracial coalitions and, 86
  ethnoracial fragmentation and, 143–145, 147–149, 151
  ethnoracial identity formation and, 47, 60, 66, 84
  in Europe, 15, 182, 184, 186–187, 189
  housing, 20–21
  identity politics and, 125–126, 128, 132, 135, 195, 197
  integration paradox and, 166–167
  intergroup relations and, 104
  law enforcement and, 114–117
  multiracialism and, 168
  perceptions of, 2, 78, 98, 104, 120–121, 131, 148
  post-racialism and, 95
  race relations and, 109–110
  racial eliminativism option and, 202
  social movement protests against, 28
  socioeconomic, 110–114, 111*t*
  violence and, 28
discursive violence, defined, 2, 216n56. *See also* microaggressions
disenfranchisement, 117–119, 208n8. *See also* civic exclusion
distrust. *See* trust and distrust issues
diversity
  Black experience and, 104–106
  civic exclusion and, 117–119

current trajectories of violence and, 101–119
demographic trends, 62
identity challenges of, 121–124
intergroup relations and, 103–104
intolerance and, 13, 108–119
law enforcement disparities, 114–117
migrant optimism and, 106–108
migrant phobia and race relations, 108–110
socioeconomic discrimination, 110–114, 111t
tolerance and, 13, 101–108
Dodd, John, 33
DREAM Act of 2021, 145
Dred Scott v. Sandford (1857), 5, 207n8
Du Bois, W. E. B., 53, 63, 142
Dubreuil, Laurent, 164
Dunbar, Edward, 84
Dutch Nationality Act of 2003, 251n35
Duyvendak, Jan Willem, 121, 123
dynamics of contention, 72–89
ethnoracial coalitions and, 85–89
group position, effect of, 73–76
multiplication of contentious repertoires, 79–81
patterns of mobilization, 81–89. *See also* patterns of mobilization
spillover process of identity politics, 76–79

Ehrenreich, Nancy, 79
Ehrenstein, David, 237n37
elections
1960, 20
1982, 144
1992, 70, 88, 226n62
2004, 70, 144
2008, 91, 93–94, 122, 144, 169
2016, 91, 96–97, 110, 118, 125–126, 138, 144, 147, 167, 197, 203
2020, 127–128, 137, 140, 144, 147, 154, 158, 167, 197, 203
Elgenaidi, Maha, 149
El Nasser, Haya, 132
Elshtain, Jean Bethke, 88
El-Tayeb, Fatima, 189
Emejulu, Akwugo, 188
Enlightenment, 178
Equal Opportunity Act of 1972, 65
Equal Rights Amendment (ERA), 78
Erdogan, Recep Tayyip, 180
Espionage Act of 1917, 21
essentialism, 2, 57–58
ethnoracial coalitions, 85–89

ethnoracial identities
Asians, 55–58. *See also* Asians
Blacks, 52–55, 63–66. *See also* Blacks and Blackness
conflicted and conflictual identitarian strategies, 69–71
current trajectories of violence and, 120–135. *See also* current trajectories of violence
fragmentation of, 136–154. *See also* fragmentation of ethnoracial identities
Hispanics, 55–58. *See also* Hispanics
identification strategies, history of, 59–71
violence as cause of, 44–58
whites, 45–51, 60–63. *See also* whites and whiteness
ethnoracial violence
analytical framework for, 97–99
conventional views of, 22–27
"culture of violence" and, 22–23
current trajectories of, 91–154. *See also* current trajectories of violence
in Europe, 173–193. *See also* Europe
history of, 18–30. *See also* history of violence in America
institutionalist approaches, 25–27
integration paradox, 166–168
lessons for the future, 194–204. *See also* lessons for the future
multiracial demographics and, 168–169
physical vs. discursive, 2
reactive social movements and, 169–172
socioeconomic approaches, 24–25
eugenics, 178
Europe. *See also specific countries*
ethnoracial violence in, 14, 173–193
identity politics in, 183–193
ideological diffusion in, 14–15, 175–182
immigration to America from, 45–46, 50, 60–62, 83, 167
racialization of intergroup relations in, 188–193
reactive identification strategies in, 184–187
socioeconomic inequalities in, 180–181
European Network of People of African Descent, 174

FAIR (Federation for American Immigration Reform), 74
Fair Employment Practices Committee (FEPC), 25
Fair Labor Standards Act of 1938, 20
Falcon, Angelo, 132, 146

Fanon, Frantz, 185
Farage, Nigel, 180
Farrakhan, Louis, 54, 80
Feagin, Joe, 121, 127
Federal Housing Administration (FHA), 20–21, 60
Federation for American Immigration Reform (FAIR), 74, 93
Fells, Dominique "Rem'mie," 152
feminism, 77–79, 155, 188–189
FEPC (Fair Employment Practices Committee), 25
Finland, racism in, 182
Flatbush boycott (1990), 58, 76–77
Flatbush riots (2013), 137
Floyd, George, 27, 97, 115, 129, 137, 151
Flynn, Joseph, Jr., 164
Fogelson, Robert, 26, 29
Foner, Nancy, 44–45, 46
Foucault, Michel, 178
Fourteenth Amendment, 5, 56, 207–208n8
fragmentation of ethnoracial identities, 136–154
   Black Lives Matter and, 150–154
   contentious repertoires, racial polarization of, 137–150
   minority repertoires and, 143–150
   socioeconomic differentiation, 159–162
   white repertoires and, 139–142
France
   Blacks in, 261n46
   BLM protests in, 173, 177–178
   identity politics in, 183, 184, 190
   Muslims in, 251n40, 253n66
   nationalism in, 180
   police brutality in, 177
   race relations in, 174, 182, 251n36
   secularism in, 185
   social protest movements in, 179, 186–187
Frank, Leo, 20, 47
Frantz, Joe B., 22
Frazier, E. Franklin, 25
Fredrickson, George, 12, 44–45, 46, 76
French Council of the Muslim Faith (Conseil Français du Culte Musulman), 188
Friedman, Thomas L., 94

Gallagher, Charles, 79
Galleani, Luigi, 47
Gandhi, Mahatma, 52
gang violence, 46, 83, 196
GAO (Government Accountability Office), 113
Garner, Eric, 95, 137, 151

Garza, Alicia, 129, 150
General Union of Senegalese Workers (Union Générale des Travailleurs Sénégalais en France), 185
German Islam Conference, 188
Germany
   Blacks in, 261n46
   BLM protests in, 173
   Muslims immigrants in, 182, 251n40
   public opinion on violence in America, 176
   social protest movements in, 186
gerrymandering, 117
Giles v. Harris (1903), 208n8
Gingrich, Newt, 88
Girard, Rene, 33
Giroux, Henry, 22–23
Gitlin, Todd, 77, 88
Giuliani, Rudolph, 78
Glazer, Nathan, 60–61
Gobineau, Arthur de: *An Essay on the Inequality of the Human Races,* 178
Goldberg, David Theo, 39, 176
Goldstein, Eric, 51
Gooding-Williams, Robert, 120
Goodman, Andrew, 51
Government Accountability Office (GAO), 113
Graham, Carol, 160
Graham, Hugh Davis, 24, 29
Grant, Madison, 21
   The Passing of the Great Race, 178
Gratz v. Bollinger (2003), 93
Gray, Freddie, 1, 95, 109, 137
Great Migration, 24, 50, 54
Greece
   Muslim immigrants in, 181
   nationalism in, 180
grievance theories, 9–10, 25
Grimshaw, Allen, 24, 210n25
group position, effect of, 10, 40, 73–76
Grunwald, Michael, 155
Grutter v. Bollinger (2003), 93
gun violence, 23, 141, 175–176, 209n19
Gurr, Ted Robert, 24, 29
Guy-Sheftal, Beverly, 238n46

Hall, Stuart, 178
Hamilton, Charles V., 65
Handlin, Oscar, 60
Harlem Renaissance, 53
Harris, Kamala, 127–128, 134, 169
Hart-Cellar Act of 1965, 55, 62
Harvard Business Review, 113
Harvard University, 20

Hate Crimes Prevention Act of 1999, 72
Hawkins, Yusef, 48–49
Herbers, John, 22
Hernandez, Juano, 57
Hernández, Tanya K., 218n53
Hernandez v. Texas (1954), 56
Heschel, Abraham Joshua, 51
Hewitt, Roger, 179
Heyer, Heather, 137
Higher Education Act of 1965, 26
Hill, Anita, 224n33
Hirschman, Charles, 75
Hispanics
    affirmative action programs and, 103
    civic participation and, 18, 117–119, 167, 226n62
    cultural racism and, 40
    demographic trends, 130
    deracialization process option and, 203
    educational attainment and, 107, 112–113
    election of 2020 and, 158–159
    ethnoracial coalitions and, 85–87
    ethnoracial fragmentation and, 140–141
    ethnoracial identity formation and, 56–58
    gang violence and, 83
    group position and, 73–75
    identification strategy, legacy of, 66–69
    identity politics and, 42, 69–70, 121–122, 127, 130–135
    immigration policy and, 35, 93
    integration paradox and, 167–168
    intergroup relations and, 103–104
    invisibility of, 130–135
    law enforcement disparities and, 7–8, 114–116
    migrant optimism among, 106–107, 165–166
    patterns of mobilization and, 81
    race relations and, 107–108
    racial polarization and, 143–148
    segregation and, 56–57, 66, 68
    socioeconomic discrimination and, 110–113, 111*t*, 159–162, 196
    unemployment rate, 111
    use of term, 205n6
    white identity formation and, 62–63
history of violence in America
    cycles of violence, 18–22
    ethnoracial violence, 22–27. *See also* ethnoracial violence
    institutional racism, cycles of, 20–22
    lessons from, 27–30
    nativism, cycles of, 20–22
    racial riots and violence, cycles of, 18–19
    religious violence, cycles of, 19–20
Ho v. San Francisco Unified School District (1997), 85
Hochschild, Jennifer, 69
Hofstadter, Richard, 22
    Reflections on Violence in the United States, 17
Hollinger, David, 61, 94, 95
Honeck, Mischa, 50
Hooks, Mary, 130
Horowitz, Donald, 2, 17, 33
housing discrimination, 20–21, 113–114
Hungary, Muslim immigrants in, 181
Huntington, Samuel, 79
Hutchings, Vincent, 36, 81

Ice Cube (rap artist), 58
identity politics. *See also* ethnoracial identities
    analytical framework, 8–11, 9*f*
    Asians and, 130–135
    Blacks and, 126–130
    contentious identity politics, 37–39
    current trajectories of violence and, 120–135
    dynamics of contention and, 76–79
    in Europe, 183–193
    Hispanics and, 130–135
    minority repertoires, 143–150
    multiplication of, 79–81
    paradox of, 195–198
    racial polarization of, 137–150
    spillover process of, 76–79
    violence as response to adversity and, 36–39
    white repertoires, 139–142
Ignatiev, Noel, 3
immigrants and immigration policy. *See also* assimilation and integration; *specific immigrant groups*
    assimilation and, 5, 26, 30, 40, 166–168
    Black identity formation and, 65
    civic exclusion and, 118
    deracialization process option and, 202–203
    ethnoracial coalitions and, 87
    ethnoracial fragmentation and, 138–140, 145, 147
    ethnoracial identity formation and, 11, 29, 56, 58, 60–63, 66–68
    in Europe, 177, 181–182, 187, 189, 191
    group position, effect of, 73–75
    identity politics and, 76, 79, 120, 125, 130–131
    illegal immigration, 58, 92–93, 145, 159

immigrants and immigration policy (*continued*)
  integration paradox and, 166–168
  law enforcement disparities and, 115–116
  migrant optimism, 106–108, 165–166
  nativism and, 9, 20–22
  post-racialism and, 94
  public opinion on, 101–102
  race relations and, 106–110
  Trump and, 96
  "war on terror" and, 91–93
  white identity formation and, 6, 44–51
Immigrant Workers Freedom Rides (IWFR), 145
Immigration Act of 1917, 21
Immigration Act of 1924, 220n39
Immigration Act of 1965, 26
Immigration and Nationality Act of 2001, 92
Immigration Reform and Control Act of 1986, 223n12, 228n1
income inequalities, 159–162
Industrial Areas Foundation (IAF), 171–172
inferiorization, 39–40
Ingelhart, Ronald, 181
Institute for Policy Studies, 112
Institute for Research on Poverty, 114
Institute for Social Policy and Understanding, 149
institutionalist approaches, 25–27
integration paradox, 166–168. *See also* assimilation and integration
intergroup relations. *See also* specific ethnoracial groups
  diversity and, 103–104
  in Europe, 188–193
  group position, effect of, 10, 40, 73–76
  multiracialism and, 2
  racialization of, 188–193
intermarriage, 73–74, 103
intersectionality, 42, 77, 129, 152, 178, 189, 200, 238n46
intragroup relations, 3, 11, 13, 36, 59, 71, 97–99
Irish Americans
  assimilation and integration of, 61
  religious violence and, 19–20
  white identity formation and, 2–4, 30, 46, 49
Isenberg, Nancy, 125
Islam, Tariqui, 131
Islamic Networks Group (ING), 149
Islamic Society of North America (ISNA), 88
Italian Americans, 2–3, 6, 216n15
Italy
  Blacks in, 261n46
  Muslim immigrants in, 181
  Muslims in, 251n40
  race relations in, 251n36
IWFR (Immigrant Workers Freedom Rides), 145

Jackson, Jesse L., 64, 80
Jackson, Jonathan, 176
Jacob, Andrew, 153
Jacobson, Matthew Frye, 30, 44, 48
Japanese Exclusion League of California, 49
Jeffries, Leonard, 55
Jenkins, Craig, 27, 170
Jews
  anti-Semitic violence against, 6, 20, 47–48, 55, 97, 108
  Blacks and, 53–55
  ethnoracial identity formation and, 50–51
  as model minority, 51
Jim Crow laws, 5, 20, 28, 54
Jiménez, Tomás, 106, 124
Jolson, Al, 54
Jones, James, 4
Juneteenth, 64
Justice Policy Institute, 116

Kaepernick, Colin, 179
Kaufmann, Eric, 164
Kemp, Kathleen, 76
Kendi, Ibram, 199
Kennedy, John F., 20
Kerner Commission, 21, 25–26, 27
Keyes, Alan, 70
Kim, Claire Jean, 68
Kim, Seung Min, 134
King, Martin Luther, Jr., 19, 50–51, 52, 54, 57, 63, 179
King, Rodney, 72–73
KKK, 6, 18, 20, 28, 47, 51
Kloos, Karina, 82, 138
Know-Nothing Party, 19
Koram, Kojo, 177
Krauthammer, Charles, 123
Krugler, David, 153
Kymlicka, Will, 198

Labor Council for Latin American Advancement (LCLAA), 108
LaGuardia, Fiorello, 25
Lamar, Anthony, 137
Latino community. *See* Hispanics
Latino National Political Survey (1992), 87
Latino Victory Project, 145–146

law enforcement. *See also* police brutality
    as contextual adversity, 9
    racial disparities in, 1, 5, 7–8, 114–117
    racial profiling by, 7, 114
Lawrence, Stephen, 177, 186
LCLAA (Labor Council for Latin American Advancement), 108
Leadership Conference on Civil Rights, 50
League for White Supremacy, 28
League of United Latin American Citizens (LULAC), 108, 144
Lebron, Christopher: *The Color of Our Shame*, 163
Lee, Jennifer, 61, 76, 104
Lee, Robert E., 211n38, 226n64
Lee, Taeku, 68
Lentin, Alana, 95
Le Pen, Marine, 180
lessons for the future, 194–204
    deflation of racism option, 199–201
    deracialization process option, 202–204
    moving from antagonism to agonism, 198–199
    paradox of identity politics, 195–198
    racial eliminativism option, 201–202
Lewis, John, 161
LGBTQ social movements, 42, 77–78
Lichter, Daniel T., 160
Lieberman, Denise, 117
Lila, Mark, 123
Lilly Survey of American Attitudes and Friendships (1999), 68
Liu, Caitlin, 85
Liu, Eric: *The Accidental Asian*, 66
Liu, Simu, 135
Locke, Alain, 53
Lopez, Ian Haney, 218n49
Lorde, Audre, 238n46
Los Angeles
    gang violence in, 83
    Hispanic activism in, 57–58
    history of ethnoracial violence in, 18
    intergroup relations in, 81
    law enforcement disparities in, 116
    racial polarization of white repertoires in, 140, 142
    riots (1992), 4, 72–73, 110
    social movement protests in, 145
Lott, Eric, 61–62
Louis, Bertin, Jr., 122
Loury, Glen, 152
Loving v. Commonwealth of Virginia (1967), 73
Lowery, Wesley, 114–115

Luconi, Stefano, 47
LULAC (League of United Latin American Citizens), 108, 144

Malcolm X, 65, 148, 179
Males, Mile, 140
Malik, Kenan, 174
Marcuse, Herbert, 178
Martin, Trayvon, 95, 129, 150, 176
mass shootings, 23, 209n19, 209n21. *See also* gun violence
Mauer, Marc, 115, 116–117
Mavin Foundation, 169
McAdam, Doug, 34, 82, 138
McCain, John, 144
McCarran-Walter Act of 1952, 26
McConahay, John, 128
McCone Commission, 21
McCoy, Jennifer, 139
McCrory, Pat, 171
McEneaney, Elizabeth, 26
McWhorter, John, 163
Medicare, 157
Melnick, Jeffrey, 54
#MeToo movement, 164
Metropolitan Police Service (UK), 177
Mexican American Defense and Educational Fund, 144
Mexican American Legal Defense Fund, 76
Mexican Americans. *See also* Hispanics
    assimilation and integration of, 68
    ethnoracial coalitions and, 85–87
    ethnoracial identity formation and, 56–58, 66, 68
    history of ethnoracial violence against, 18
    immigration policy and, 159
Mexican United Farm Workers, 57
Meyer, David, 81
Mfume, Kweisi, 75–76
Michaels, Walter Benn, 164
microaggressions, 2, 35, 163, 216n56
middle class, 105, 112
Mier, August, 29
Mi Familia Vota, 145–146
Migrant Lives Matter coalition, 174
migrants. *See* immigrants and immigration policy
Miles, Robert, 199
Million Man March (1995), 80
Million Women March (1997), 79
Mills, Charles, 120
Mills, Robert, 178
Mills v. Green (1895), 208n8

Milton, Riah, 152
Minuteman Civil Defense Corps, 27–28, 211n39, 223n14
MIR (Mouvement des Indigènes de la République), 174, 187
mobilization patterns. *See* patterns of mobilization
Mohamed, Yassin, 144
Montgomery Improvement Association, 52
Moore, Antonio, 80
Moore, Wendy, 127
Moral Monday movement, 14, 171
Morgan, Piers, 176
Mouvement des Indigènes de la République (MIR), 174, 187
Movimiento Hispano, 108
Moynihan, Daniel Patrick, 60–61
Mubenga, Jimmy, 177
Muhammad, Elijah, 54
Muhammad, Khalid Abdul, 54
multiracialism
  assimilation and, 61
  demographic trends, 13, 98, 168–169
  ethnoracial identity formation and, 70, 194
  in Europe, 192
  group position and, 73–74
  identity politics and, 121–124
  intergroup relations and, 2, 5
  intermarriage and, 73–74, 103
  post-racialism and, 93–94
  race relations and, 108
Murji, Karim, 7
Murray, Douglas, 174
Muslims. *See also* Black Muslims
  discrimination against, 6
  ethnoracial fragmentation and, 148–150
  ethnoracial violence and, 8, 207n6
  in Europe, 181–182, 184–185, 187–191, 251n40
  identity politics and, 77
  immigration policy and, 20, 143, 148–149, 166, 181–182, 241n49
  intergroup relations and, 104
  law enforcement disparities and, 92, 115
  migrant optimism and, 166
  race relations and, 109
  racial polarization of minority repertoires and, 143–144, 148–150
  slavery and, 150, 243n49
  travel ban, 143, 149, 241n29
  Trump and, 96, 158
  "war on terror" and, 92–93, 228n3
Mussolini, Benito, 47

Mutz, Diana, 96
Mwangi, Chrystal A. George, 55
Myers, Daniel, 25

NAACP, 50, 142, 171
Najour, In re (1909), 218n49
National Advisory Commission on Civil Disorders (Kerner Commission), 21
National Assessment for Education Progress, 112
National Commission on the Causes and Prevention of Violence, 21–22
National Council of American Indians, 76
National Council of La Raza, 76, 144
National Day Laborer Organizing Network (NDLON), 145
National Front, 186
National Health Survey (2000), 67
Nationality, Immigration, and Asylum Act of 2002 (UK), 251n35
Nationality Act of 1790, 4–5
National Memorial for Peace, 207n3
National Museum of African American History and Culture, 243n49
National Rifle Association (NRA), 22
Nation of Islam (NOI), 54–55, 64–65, 148
nativism, 9, 20–22
Naturalization Act of 1790, 45, 218n49
Naturalization Act of 1870, 45, 56
NDLON (National Day Laborer Organizing Network), 145
Nee, Victor, 94, 121
Netherlands
  BLM protests in, 173
  Dutch Nationality Act of 2003, 251n35
  identity politics in, 183
  Muslims in, 251n40
  nationalism in, 180
  New Integration Act of 2007, 251n35
  race relations in, 251n36
  social protest movements in, 186
New Integration Act of 2007 (Netherlands), 251n35
Newman, Graeme, 30
New Orleans, 18–19, 47
New York City
  Commission on Conditions in Harlem, 25
  ethnoracial coalitions in, 86
  gang violence in, 83
  intergroup relations in, 58
  NYPD Muslim Surveillance Program, 92
  social movement protests in, 58, 76–77, 136–137

Nguyen, Terry, 147–148
Nixon, Richard, 82
nonviolent contentious politics, 25, 52, 84–85
Norris, Pippa, 181
Northern League (Italy), 182
NRA (National Rifle Association), 22
NumbersUSA, 223n13

Oath Keepers, 28
Obama, Barack
    election of, 28, 93–94, 122
    ethnoracial fragmentation and, 13
    post-racialism and, 12–13, 93–94
    race relations and, 109–110, 127, 237n37
Obergefell v. Hodges (2015), 102
Occupy Wall Street Movement, 136, 142, 161, 162
Office of National Drug Control Policy, 116
Okihiro, Gary, 67
Olivier, Johan, 24
Olzak, Susan, 24, 26, 72
Omi, Michael, 6, 8, 28, 45, 64
Orbán, Viktor, 14
Order of Caucasians, 49
Orlando nightclub mass shooting (2016), 209n19
Ozawa v. United States (1922), 56, 218n49

Page Act of 1875, 56
Painter, Nell Irvin, 52, 63, 164
    History of White People, 44
Parekh, Bhikhu, 185
Parker, Christopher, 96
Parks, Rosa, 80
Patriot Act of 2001, 92
Patriot movement, 27
patterns of mobilization
    analytical framework, 8–11, 9*f*
    defined, 7–8
    dynamics of contention and, 81–89
    ethnoracial coalitions, 85–89
    nonviolent contentious politics, 84–85
    violent confrontations, 82–84
Patton, Stacy, 161
Payne, Donald, 80
pendulum effect, 26, 28
Personal Responsibility and Work Opportunity Reconciliation Act of 1996, 92, 223n12, 228n1
Petersen, William, 66
Petrosino, Carolyn, 84
Petry, Frauke, 180
Pew Research Center, 96, 102

Phelan, James D., 49
Philipps, Kevin, 82
Phoenix, David, 142, 162
physical vs. discursive violence, 2
PIR (political party, France), 187
Pitcavage, Mark, 156
Plessy v. Ferguson (1896), 207–208n8
Pohl, Ines, 176
Poland, Muslim immigrants in, 181–182
police brutality. *See also* law enforcement
    Black identity formation and, 126–127, 186
    as contextual adversity, 9
    ethnoracial coalitions and, 86
    ethnoracial identity formation and, 143–144
    in Europe, 175, 177, 186
    Hispanic identity formation and, 132, 143, 146
    identity politics and, 197
    institutionalist approaches and, 25–26
    persistence of, 4
    social movement protests and, 7, 25, 38, 137, 151–152
political opportunity structures (POS), 22
Politifact, 23
Poor People's Movement, 57, 171
populism, 180
Portes, Alejandro, 30
post-racialism, ambivalence of, 93–96
poverty. *See* socioeconomic discrimination
Powell, Colin, 71
Powell, Enoch, 14, 179
Prager, Robert, 47
prejudice, defined, 40–41
Project Race, 108
"prosperity gospel," 160
Protect America Act of 2007, 92
Protestants, 19–20
PRRI (Public Religion Research Institute), 104, 109, 125
Public Works Administration, 60
Puerto Ricans
    ethnoracial coalitions and, 87
    ethnoracial identity formation and, 57, 66, 69
Putin, Vladimir, 180

Race Relations Act of 1965 (UK), 174, 179
racial eliminativism, 201–202
racialization, defined, 41–42
racial profiling, 7, 9
racial riots, historical cycles of, 18–19, 28

racism
- as contextual adversity, 9
- cultural conceptions of race and, 39–40
- defined, 39–40
- ethnoracial coalitions and, 86
- evolution of, 12
- inferiorization and, 39–40
- institutional racism, cycles of, 20–22
- reactive, 53
- symbolic, 128
- systemic, 7, 12, 27, 128, 133, 171, 173, 176, 196

Ransby, Barbara: *Making All Black Lives Matter,* 130
Raster, Hermann, 49–50
reactive identification
- analytical framework, 8–11, 9f
- Black identity formation and, 52–53
- in Europe, 184–187
- as response to violence, 2, 35–36

Reagan, Ronald, 78, 82, 144
Real ID Act of 2005, 92
redlining, 21
Reed, Sarah, 177
Reed, Wornie, 122
Refugee Act of 1980, 223n12, 228n1
Reid, Harry, 23
relational assimilation, 124
religious violence, historical cycles of, 19–20
rent controls, 25
reparations, 80, 151, 186–187, 198–199
Representative Council of France's Black Association (Conseil Représentatif des Associations Noires de France), 186–187
Republican Party
- affirmative action programs and, 103
- Asian Americans and, 147
- deracialization process option and, 203
- Hispanics and, 144
- identitarian strategies and, 69, 70
- identity politics and, 125
- immigration policy and, 159
- Muslim immigrants and, 149
- patterns of mobilization and, 82
- political polarization and, 138–139, 141
- race relations and, 108–109
- same-sex marriage and, 102–103
- social protest movements and, 170

resource mobilization theories, 10, 27
revanchism, 13, 78–79, 88, 91, 136
Rex, John, 178
Reynolds, Barbara, 129

Rhodes, Thomas L. "Dusty," 85
Ricardo, Ricky, 57
Rice, Condoleezza, 71
Rich, Wilbur, 94
Richardson, Jennifer, 37
Rittenhouse, Kyle, 137
Rivera, Jason, 86
Robeson, Paul, 63
Roediger, David, 44, 71, 86
Romero, Jesse, 145
Roosevelt, Franklin D., 25
Rudwick, Elliott, 29
Rumbaut, Ruben G., 30

Salins, Peter, 61
Salvini, Matteo, 14
same-sex marriage, 102–103
Sanders, Bernie, 162
San Francisco Foundation, 249n62
Savran, David, 79
school segregation, 56–57, 113
Schuller, Kyla, 225n48
Schwerner, Michael, 51
SCLC (Southern Christian Leadership Conference), 52, 57
Scott, Keith Lamont, 137
Scott, Tim, 203
Sears, D. O., 128
Secure Fence Act of 2006, 92–93
Sedition Act of 1918, 21
segregation
- Asian identity formation and, 56, 58, 85
- Black identity formation and, 52, 128
- as contextual adversity, 9
- Hispanics identity formation and, 56–57, 66, 68
- institutional racism and, 20, 25, 27, 39
- Jim Crow laws, 5, 20, 28, 54
- residential, 113–114
- of schools, 196, 208n8, 220n39
- white identity formation and, 48

Senghor, Léopold, 185
Sentencing Project, 115, 117
Sewell, Tony, 192
Shahid, Ex parte (1913), 218n49
Shanahan, Suzanne, 26, 72
Sharia Project, 191
Shelby County v. Holder (2013), 117
Shelley v. Kraemer (1948), 142
Shriver, Lionel, 174
Sides, John, 96, 123–124, 126, 138
Silent Protest Parade (1917), 38
Simcox, Chris, 211n39

slavery
   Jews and, 53–54, 55
   in Latin America, 218n53
   Muslims and, 148, 150, 243n49
   psychological residues of, 29
   reparations for, 80, 198
   structural racism and, 4, 6, 39, 176
   white European immigrants and, 49–50
Smith, Barbara, 238n46
Smith, John, 26
Smith, Tommie, 179
Social Contract Press, 223n13
social disorganization thesis, 25
social movement theory, 8, 9–10, 212n10
socioeconomic discrimination, 24–25, 110–114, 111t, 159–162, 180–181
Solomos, John, 7
Somos Republicans, 70
SOS Racism, 186
Southern Christian Leadership Conference (SCLC), 52, 57
Southern Poverty Law Center (SPLC), 97, 109, 223n14
Sowell, Thomas, 70
Spain
   Blacks in, 261n46
   multiracialism in, 192
special interest groups, 165
Spencer, Richard B., 81
Spilerman, Seymour, 26
Stekelenburg, Jaquelien van, 36
Student Nonviolent Coordinating Committee (SNCC), 52, 129
Sugrue, Thomas: *Not Even Past: Barack Obama and the Burden of Race*, 95
Swain, Carol, 152
Sweden
   Blacks in, 261n46
   identity politics in, 190
Swirl (organization), 169
symbolic racism, 128

Tancredo, Tom: *In Mortal Danger: The Battle for America's Borders and Security*, 93
Tanton, John, 74, 223n13
Tarrow, Sidney, 81, 176
Taylor, Breonna, 137
Tea Party, 109, 136, 138, 142
terrorism, 91–92, 181–182, 184, 191. *See also* "war on terror"
Tesler, Michael, 41, 96, 126, 139
Thind, United States v. (1923), 56, 218n49
Thirteenth Amendment, 20

Thomas, Clarence, 70, 224n33
Thomas, Timothy, 137
Thrive (civic engagement alliance), 249n62
Tillery, Alvin B., Jr., 153
Tilly, Charles, 98, 176
Tometi, Opal, 129, 150
Torres, Christopher, 145
Torres, Sam, 84
Traoré, Adama, 177, 179
Traoré, Assa, 178
Truman, Harry S., 64
Trump, Donald
   current trajectories of violence and, 96–97
   election of, 125–126, 236n27
   ethnoracial fragmentation and, 13–14, 140, 144, 147, 167
   minority voters and, 203
   poor whites and, 160
   race relations and, 110, 127, 157–158
   racialized political violence and, 155
   revanchism and, 78
   voter demographics and attitudes, 140, 144, 147, 167
trust and distrust issues
   deracialization process option and, 204
   ethnoracial coalitions and, 86, 170
   ethnoracial identity formation and, 60
   intergroup relations and, 197
   political polarization and, 138
   race relations and, 162–165
   socioeconomic differentiation and, 160
Truth, Sojourner, 238n46
Tulsa race massacre (1921), 18

Union Générale des Travailleurs Sénégalais en France (General Union of Senegalese Workers), 185
Unite Against Fascism, 186
United Kingdom
   Blacks in, 261n46
   BLM protests in, 173–174, 177
   Borders, Citizenship, and Immigration Act of 2009, 251n35
   identity politics in, 183, 184, 190, 192
   multiracialism in, 192
   Muslim immigrants in, 181, 251n40
   nationalism in, 180
   Nationality, Immigration, and Asylum Act of 2002, 251n35
   police brutality in, 177
   race relations in, 174, 179, 182, 251n36
   secularism in, 185
   social protest movements in, 179, 186, 187

United States Conference of Catholic Bishops, 145
Universal Negro Improvement Association, 38
University of Birmingham, 178
University of Cambridge, 165
University of Virginia, 27
USA Patriot Act of 2001, 92
utility of violence, 32–35

Valenzuela, Antonio, 146
Valls, Andrew, 199
Vertovec, Steven, 121
Veterans Administration, 20–21
Vietnam War, 63–64
violence. *See also* ethnoracial violence; history of violence in America
  collective, 17, 24
  culture of, 22–23, 27, 141
  as identity strategy, 35–39
  utility of, 32–35
Violent Crime Control and Law Enforcement Act of 1994, 91
voluntaristic theory of action, 7
voting rights, 117–119, 207–208n8
Voting Rights Act of 1965, 26, 41, 64, 117

Wacquant, Loïc, 92
Walker, Rebecca, 77, 224n33
Wallace, George, 14, 179
Wang, Anthony, 70
"war on terror," 91–93, 228n3
Washington March for Lesbian, Gay and Bi Equal Rights and Liberation (1993), 77–78
Waters, Mary C., 60, 61
Watson, Elwood, 152
West, Cornel, 127, 161, 178
West, Kanye, 161
White, Walter, 50
White Privilege Analysis (WPA) perspective, 128–129, 163
whites and whiteness
  affirmative action programs and, 103
  civic exclusion and, 118
  crisis of white identity, 124–126
  deracialization process option and, 203
  diversity and, 105–106
  ethnoracial coalitions and, 85
  ethnoracial identity formation and, 4–7, 12, 36, 40–41, 45–58, 60–69
  group position, effect of, 73–75
  history of ethnoracial violence and, 18–20, 28–30
  identity politics and, 121–122, 124, 126–128, 130–131, 133
  intergroup relations and, 103–104
  intermarriage and, 103
  legal construction of, 56, 218n49
  middle class whites, 160
  migrant optimism and, 166
  multiplication of contentious repertoires and, 79–81
  patterns of mobilization and, 81–83
  post-racialism and, 95–96
  race relations and, 108, 109–110
  racial polarization of white repertoires, 139–142
  socioeconomic discrimination and, 24, 110–116, 111t, 159–161
  unemployment rate and, 105, 143
  voting patterns, 226n62
  "whitelash" responses, 163–164
white supremacists, 6, 28, 39, 82, 109, 141, 147, 162, 178, 188
white trash, 61, 125, 134
Wilder, Geert, 180
Wilkinson, Rupert, 60
Williams, Chancellor, 150
Williams, Kim, 75, 169
Williams, Thomas Chatterton, 164
Williams v. Mississippi (1898), 208n8
Wilson, Darren, 27
Wilson, Pete, 85
Wilson, William, 71
Wilson, Woodrow, 192
Winant, Howard, 6, 8, 28, 45, 64
Windisch, Steven, 141
Winters, Mary-Frances, 162
WPA (White Privilege Analysis) perspective, 128–129, 163

Yamamoto, Eric, 4
Yang, Andrew, 134–135
Yglesias, Matthew, 139
Yi, David, 133
Young Chicanos for Community Action (YCCA), 57
Yriza Barbosa, Guillermo, 107

Zambrano-Montes, Antonio, 7–8
Zhang, Qin, 133
Zimmerman, George, 129, 150

Lightning Source UK Ltd.
Milton Keynes UK
UKHW041812130123
415256UK00003B/88